Revolution and the People in R

This book is a unique comparative account of the roots of Communist revolution in Russia and China. Steve Smith examines the changing social identities of peasants who settled in St Petersburg from the 1880s to 1917, and in Shanghai from the 1900s to the 1940s. Russia and China, though very different societies, were both dynastic empires with backward agrarian economies that suddenly experienced the impact of capitalist modernity. This book argues that far more happened to these migrants than simply being transformed from peasants into workers. It explores the migrants' identification with their native homes; how they acquired new understandings of themselves as individuals and new gender and national identities. It asks how these identity transformations fed into the wider political, social and cultural processes that culminated in the revolutionary crises in Russia and China, and how the Communist regimes that emerged viewed these transformations in the working classes they claimed to represent.

S. A. SMITH is Professor of History in the Department of History, University of Essex. His previous publications include *Like Cattle and Horses: Nationalism and Labor in Shanghai, 1895–1927* (2002), *A Road is Made: Communism in Shanghai, 1920–27* (2000) and *Red Petrograd: Revolution in the Factories, 1917–18* (1983).

To Julia

With warm regards

Steve

Revolution and the People in Russia and China

A Comparative History

S. A. Smith

The Wiles Lectures

CAMBRIDGE
UNIVERSITY PRESS

CAMBRIDGE UNIVERSITY PRESS
Cambridge, New York, Melbourne, Madrid, Cape Town, Singapore,
São Paulo, Delhi

Cambridge University Press
The Edinburgh Building, Cambridge CB2 8RU, UK

Published in the United States of America by Cambridge University Press,
New York

www.cambridge.org
Information on this title: www.cambridge.org/9780521713962

First published 2008

Printed in the United Kingdom at the University Press, Cambridge

A catalogue record for this publication is available from the British Library

Library of Congress Cataloguing in Publication Data

Smith, S. A.
   Revolution and the people in Russia and China : a comparative history /
S. A. Smith.
      p.   cm.
   ISBN 978-0-521-88637-6 (hardback : alk. paper) – ISBN 978-0-521-71396-2
(pbk.)
   1.   Communism–Russia–History. 2.   Communism–China–History.
I.   Title.
   HX311.5.S63 2008
   947′.210841–dc22
   2007051669

ISBN 978-0-521-88637-6 hardback
ISBN 978-0-521-71396-2 paperback

Contents

Acknowledgments

This book originated in an invitation by the School of History at Queen's University, Belfast, to deliver the Wiles Lectures in 1998. These lectures, founded by Mrs Austen Boyd in 1953 in memory of her father, Thomas S. Wiles, with the encouragement of Sir Herbert Butterfield, set the lecturer the daunting task of relating his or her historical research 'to the general history of civilization' or to 'reflection on the wider implications of more detailed historical studies'. I cannot claim that the four lectures that constitute the central chapters of this book go anywhere near to meeting the challenge set by the Wiles Trustees. However, the invitation provided me with an opportunity to think afresh about the roots of revolution in Russia and China and to try out a somewhat unusual style of comparative history. The Wiles Lectures are a wonderful institution that allow the lecturer to present ambitious ideas to an informed audience, consisting of members of Queen's University, members of the wider community in Belfast, and half a dozen invited scholars of his or her choosing. I would thus like to thank the Trustees and the School of History for the invitation to give the lectures, and my audience for their thoughtful and critical responses to my rudimentary efforts to sketch out my ideas. I would also like to thank the School of History for its magnificent hospitality, especially Professor David Hempton, then Director of the School, now of the School of Theology at Boston University, and the late Professor Peter Judd, who organized some memorable trips for myself and my guests, including tours to the Northern Ireland Assembly at Stormont and the Ulster Folk Museum. For their patience and critical engagement, I would like to thank my guests, who included Gregor Benton, Delia Davin, Henrietta Harrison, Catriona Kelly, Diane Koenker, Rana Mitter, David Moon and Chris Ward, and Ian Kershaw and Terence Ranger, both then Wiles Trustees. Gregor Benton and Chris Ward deserve additional thanks for providing me with critical feedback on the manuscript of the book. Finally, my longstanding colleague,

John Walter, gave characteristically astute advice in the last stages of revision. The usual disclaimers appertain: all errors of fact and judgment are my own. Finally, I owe a debt of thanks to the Nuffield Foundation for the award of a Social Science Research Fellowship in 1997–8 which allowed me to undertake much of the research for the lectures. As presented in chapters 1 to 4 of the book, the lectures have been much revised and expanded, but I have tried to preserve something of their original spirit. They are intended as arguments about the past that will stimulate argument about the roots of revolution in the modern era. They cannot hope to make a contribution to 'the general history of civilization', but if they provoke debate on some big historical questions, I shall be happy.

Introduction: Capitalist Modernity and Communist Revolution

This book is an exploration of how the social identities of peasants who left their villages to work and settle in St Petersburg, from the 1880s to 1917, and in Shanghai, from the 1900s to the 1940s, were transformed under the impact of capitalist modernity. St Petersburg and Shanghai stood out as the exemplars of capitalist modernity in Russia and China, respectively, two societies that were very different in cultural terms yet which shared the condition of being overwhelmingly agrarian and politically enfeebled. The book explores how the experience of wage labour and city life challenged migrants' understandings of themselves, and asks how changes in their social identities contributed to the political, social and cultural ferment that eventuated in revolution. It is an attempt to explore the formation of a working class from a new angle, by focusing on transformations of social identity that did not relate directly to the growth of class consciousness or to the growth of revolutionary political sentiment, the aspects of class formation on which the historiography to date has tended to concentrate. Its central thesis is that the identities of peasants who became workers were transformed by a number of processes other than those directly related to wage labour and capitalist production and along a number of axes other than that of class, and that capitalist modernity provides a better optic than capitalist production through which to analyse identity formation.

In 2007, according to the United Nations, the earth's population for the first time tilted from being predominantly rural to predominantly urban.[1] The subjects of this book – those who left the countryside during the first wave of capitalist industrialization and urbanization – may be seen as harbingers of this most significant of twentieth-century developments. The focus of the book is on that subset of rural-to-urban migrants who chose to settle in the cities of St Petersburg and Shanghai. This group may have been outnumbered by seasonal migrants and

[1] Jonathan Watts, 'Invisible City', *Guardian*, 15 March 2006.

1

temporary sojourners, but it was they who evolved, however unevenly, into an industrial working class and it was among them that transformations in social identity were most marked.[2] The social identities with which the four central chapters deal are, respectively: native-place identity, i.e. the identification of these peasants-turned-workers with their place of birth; individuality, i.e. their new understandings of selfhood; gender identity, i.e. their changed conceptions of themselves as men and women; and, finally, their identifications with the nation state. Each chapter asks how far identities did change as a result of the move to the city and then analyses the implications of any such changes for how peasants-turned-workers conceived of their place in the larger social and political order.

The book contends that we can best appreciate why migrants responded to revolution – however short-lived that response may have been – by situating their experiences and self-understandings against a backdrop in which capitalist modernity irrupted into economically, socially and politically backward societies. It argues that the response of workers to revolution was shaped not only by the experience of capitalist exploitation, bleak though that was, but also by the crisis of an entire order that encompassed autocratic government, rural patriarchy, the constraints of the Confucian moral order, which was compounded by the upheavals wrought by war and foreign imperialism; more positively, it was shaped by exposure to the disorientation and speed of urban life, to the pleasures of consumer culture, to the intimacy of the nuclear family, and to the emancipating influence of literacy and mass entertainment. The argument is not that the challenges posed by capitalist modernity in a context of economic and political backwardness served seamlessly to render workers receptive to revolution. Workers experienced these challenges variably and their significance was always contested; indeed many of the new orientations fostered by modernity, such as interest in fashion, pulp fiction, or new forms of religious affiliation, were seen by revolutionaries as fundamentally antipathetic to the promotion of revolutionary consciousness. By widening the analytical focus in this way, however, the book hopes to show that the identity transformation undergone by migrants to St Petersburg and Shanghai went beyond the transformation of peasants into proletarians, and hopes to help answer the question posed by the late Reginald Zelnik, pioneering

---

[2] Daniel Brower reckons that in 1900 up to one-fifth of the population of Moscow and St Petersburg had either just arrived or would leave before the end of the year. Daniel Brower, 'Urban Revolution in the Late Russian Empire', in Michael F. Hamm (ed.), *The City in Late Imperial Russia* (Bloomington: Indiana University Press, 1986), p. 327.

historian of Russian labour, who asked with characteristic perspicacity: 'What further readings of workers' life experiences would help us to make sense of the revolution in their values that preceded the revolution in the streets?'[3]

In both Russia and China powerful working-class movements sprang up in societies where many of the prerequisites conventionally deemed crucial to working-class formation – such as significant levels of industrialization and urbanization, basic rights to organize, a relatively high level of popular education – were absent. In the revolutions of 1905 and 1917 in Russia and in the 'national revolution' of 1925–7 in China, a small industrial working class, comprising mainly if not exclusively former peasants, came to the fore of the revolutionary movement. This is not to claim that either revolution was 'proletarian' in any substantial sense. In Russia in 1905, the political leverage exercised by the general strike was critical in forcing Nicholas II to concede a constitutional monarchy; but for most of that year, the nascent labour movement operated in uneasy conjunction with the liberal and radical opposition groups in an 'all-nation struggle' against autocracy. Similarly, in 1917, workers proved to be the most organized and politically conscious of the mobilized masses, spearheading the formation of soviets, factory committees, trade unions and other organizations, yet the labour movement was only one of the forces – the others being a peasant war against the landowning gentry, a mutiny in the army and navy, and mobilization by non-Russian ethnicities – that undermined the Provisional Government.

In China the political potential of the tiny working class became evident in the May Thirtieth Movement of 1925, a broad-based anti-imperialist movement, triggered by the shooting of unarmed demonstrators in the British-controlled International Settlement in Shanghai, which spilled over into a sixteen-month-long strike-boycott in Guangzhou (Canton) and Hong Kong. During the Northern Expedition of 1926–7, when the Guomindang (GMD), or Nationalist Party, and its National Revolutionary Army led an armed campaign to suppress warlordism and reunify the country, conditions were created that were conducive to the formation of mass associations of workers, peasants, students, women and even merchants. Throughout this period of 'national revolution', mass politics took place within the framework of a 'united front' (1923–7) between the Chinese Communist Party (CCP) and the GMD. In spring 1927, workers led by the CCP briefly took power

---

[3] Reginald E. Zelnik, 'On the Eve: Histories and Identities of Some Revolutionary Workers, 1870–05', in Lewis H. Siegelbaum and Ronald Grigor Suny (eds.), *Making Workers Soviet: Power, Class and Identity* (Ithaca NY: Cornell University Press, 1994), p. 29.

in Shanghai, expelling northern warlord forces from the Chinese areas of the city in advance of the arrival of the National Revolutionary Army. This provoked Chiang Kai-shek into brutally suppressing his erstwhile Communist allies. Thereafter, it is often suggested, the CCP was forced out of the cities, with the result that the Chinese revolution became a 'peasant revolution'. Recent scholarship has questioned this characterization. Local studies of the CCP's activities in rural areas in the period of the Sino-Japanese war (1937–45) and the civil war (1946–9) suggest, above all, that the key to the CCP's success lay in its skill in building coalitions of diverse social constituencies, including teachers, students, intellectuals, 'enlightened gentry', merchants, nationalist army officers, former warlords, workers, religious groups and secret-society members. Certainly, peasants – usually middle rather than poor peasants – were mobilized by the CCP, but usually only after it had managed to establish a secure base by manipulating the aforementioned social coalitions.[4] In the words of Lucien Bianco, 'the fact that the revolution triumphed with the assistance of the peasantry does not make it a peasant revolution. The peasants participated in a revolution undertaken and directed by others, and this little by little modified their conceptions and behaviour.'[5] The working class, moreover, did not disappear as an agent of revolution after 1927, especially in Shanghai. Workers in that city made a major contribution to the national salvation movement of the 1930s, a substantial contribution to the creation of the Communist New Fourth Army after 1937, and a more modest contribution to the CCP's final victory in 1949. In broad terms, as Odoric Wou contends, 'the revolution was a circular movement that shifted from the cities to the countryside and then back to the cities'.[6]

In the former Soviet Union and in Maoist China, the official explanation of the political precocity of the working class rested heavily on a narrative of proletarianization. Peasants coming to the cities were deemed to have been proletarianized both objectively, i.e. separated from their means of production and made fully dependent on waged work, and subjectively, i.e. to have undergone a transformation of consciousness as they went from being a class 'in itself' to a class 'for itself'. According to the legitimating ideology, the acquisition of class

---

[4] Feng Chongyi and David S. G. Goodman (eds.), *North China at War: The Social Ecology of Revolution, 1937–45* (Lanham MD: Rowman and Littlefield, 2000); Odoric Y. K. Wou, *Mobilizing the Masses: Building Revolution in Henan* (Stanford: Stanford University Press, 1994).

[5] Lucien Bianco, *Jacqueries et révolution dans la China du XXe siècle* (Paris: Éditions de La Martinière, 2005), p. 454.

[6] Wou, *Mobilizing the Masses*, p. 12.

consciousness was made possible because of the political leadership provided by the Bolshevik party and the CCP. According to Mao Zedong, the Chinese revolution during its 'new-democratic' stage took the historically original form of 'New Democracy', a bloc comprising workers, peasants, the intelligentsia and sections of the petty bourgeoisie, yet it fell to the proletariat to lead the bloc onward towards socialism.[7] In the Soviet Union, where the state claimed to have been born out of a proletarian revolution, the narrative of proletarianization spawned a huge historiography that sought to demonstrate that a majority of workers in tsarist Russia had become proletarianized. Soviet historians invested great energy in analysing such issues as workers' ownership of land in the countryside; the extent to which they farmed it; the extent to which workers' families resided in the village; the extent to which workers sent money back to the village; the proportion of workers who were children of workers and/or who had been born in the city. While western historians were broadly sceptical of the claim that most Russian workers had cut their ties with the land and become fully dependent on wages, they nevertheless tended to cast their own researches within this peasant-to-proletarian paradigm. This book tries to bypass this now rather stale debate, by exploring how the experience of moving from village to the city set in train a multiplicity of transformations in social identity that cannot be captured by single-minded focus on class identity.

The book examines transformations in workers' social identities in the broad context of capitalist modernity rather than of capitalist industrialization narrowly understood.[8] It sees the different dimensions of modernity – technological innovation, industrialization, urbanization, demographic growth, the forging of nation states, and mass political movements – as ultimately embedded in what Marshall Berman calls the 'ever-expanding, drastically fluctuating' capitalist world market.[9] Towards the end of the twentieth century, it became increasingly clear that despite its western origins, capitalist modernity has developed in

[7] Mao Zedong, 'On New Democracy' (1940), *Selected Works of Mao Tse-tung*, vol. 2 (Peking: Foreign Languages Press, 1972), pp. 339–84.
[8] Within historiography in general there has been a revival of interest in 'modernity' as a result of the shift from social to cultural history. In the case of Russia, this has led to a lessening of emphasis on the traditionalism of Russian society, on the crisis of autocracy, the revolutionary movement and the growth of social classes and a new emphasis on the fragmentation of social groups and on the ways in which identities were constructed within different cultural fields. David Hoffman and Yanni Kotsonis (eds.), *Russian Modernity: Politics, Knowledge, Practices* (Basingstoke: Macmillan, 2000); David L. Hoffman, *Stalinist Values: The Cultural Norms of Soviet Modernity* (Ithaca NY: Cornell University Press, 2003).
[9] Marshall Berman, *All that is Solid Melts into Air: The Experience of Modernity* (London: Verso, 1983), p. 16.

geographically and historically variable forms. Modernities are 'multiple', insofar as the processes of structural differentiation of economy, society and polity common to modernization are powerfully shaped by factors such as the historical point at which a society is incorporated into the global capitalist system, its position within the international state system (in the Chinese case, a position that took the form of semi-colonialism), its domestic social structures and power relations and, not least, its cultural heritage.[10] The western version of capitalist modernity now appears as one variant among several, and may not be taken as a norm against which other modernities – whether capitalist or Communist – are judged to be more or less successful, more or less complete. As a study of the growth and development of a working class in two areas of the globe outside the 'West', the book contributes to the debate about multiple modernities by pointing up not only the striking similarities between transformations of the workers' identities in two vastly different countries but also the ways in which different social, political and cultural contexts inflected the process of working-class formation. In so doing, the book endorses the view of Goran Thernborn that modern development can no longer be 'encapsulated in "the West and the rest" formula'.[11]

Shmuel Eisenstadt suggests that modernity begins at the moment when the unquestioned legitimacy of a divinely ordained social order begins to be challenged, thereby enabling alternative social and political orders to be envisioned.[12] With modernity, self-consciousness comes into its own, allowing people to reflect on available social roles and possibilities and to gain a critical distance on tradition. Out of it emerges what Marshall Berman calls the 'amazing variety of visions and ideas that aim to make men and women the subjects as well as the objects of modernization, to give them the power to change the world that is changing them, to make their way through the maelstrom and make it their own'.[13] According to Douglas Kellner, in traditional societies, 'identity was a function of predefined social roles and a traditional system of myths that

---

[10] Although I use the term 'multiple modernities', I broadly agree with Volker Schmidt that it is preferable to speak of 'varieties of modernity', mainly because the 'multiple modernities' literature tends to explain variations in forms of modernity in terms of essentialized conceptions of 'civilizations'. Shmuel Eisenstadt exemplifies this tendency. See Shmuel N. Eisenstadt, 'Some Observations on Multiple Modernities', in Dominic Sachsenmaier and Jens Riedel (eds.), *Reflections on Multiple Modernities* (Leiden: Brill, 2002), pp. 27–41. Volker H. Schmidt, 'Multiple Modernities or Varieties of Modernity?' *Current Sociology* 54, 1 (2006), 77–97.

[11] Goran Thernborn, 'Routes to/through Modernity', in Mike Featherstone, Scott Lash and Roland Robertson (eds.), *Global Modernities* (London: Sage, 1995), p. 137.

[12] S. N. Eisenstadt, 'Multiple Modernities', *Daedalus*, 129 (2000), 4.

[13] Berman, *All that is Solid*, p. 16.

provided orientation and religious sanctions to one's place in the world, while rigorously circumscribing the realm of thought and behaviour'.[14] The onset of modernity undermined all-encompassing identity schemes, such as those based on kinship, and brought forth what Craig Calhoun describes as 'an increase in the multiplicity of identity schemes so substantial that it amounted to a qualitative break, albeit one unevenly distributed in time and space'.[15] Modernity faces people with choices, yet at the same time can make it more difficult for them to determine who they are and thus to sustain a unified identity in their own eyes and those of others. As Leopold Haimson, the first historian of Russian labour to engage with the 'growing confusion of social identities' in late-imperial Russia, observed, during this era of acute political and social crisis 'individuals and groups had to establish – indeed to decide – who they were in order to determine how they should feel and ultimately act'.[16]

The shift of focus away from the construction of class identity is not intended to deny that the experience of work under industrial capitalism, together with the poverty and suffering that typified the lives of those compelled to sell their labour-power, were the primary forces shaping worker identities.[17] Chapters 3, 4 and the first half of chapter 5 pay full attention to the workplace, and throughout the book is concerned to recognize that the particular types of social identity examined, though not reducible to class, nevertheless became overdetermined by a discourse of class or, in the Chinese case, by a discourse of what I have called 'class-inflected anti-imperialist nationalism'.[18] The point of the

---

[14] Douglas Kellner, 'Popular Culture and the Construction of Postmodern Identities', in Scott Lash and Jonathan Friedman (eds.), *Modernity and Identity* (Oxford: Blackwell, 1992), p. 141.

[15] Craig Calhoun, 'Social Theory and the Politics of Identity', in Craig Calhoun (ed.), *Social Theory and the Politics of Identity* (Oxford: Blackwell, 1994), p. 12.

[16] Leopold H. Haimson, 'The Problem of Social Identities in Early Twentieth Century Russia', *Slavic Review*, 47, 1 (1988), 3–4; and William G. Rosenberg, 'Identities, Power and Social Interaction in Revolutionary Russia', *Slavic Review*, 47,1 (1988), 21–28. In the historiography of republican China, Frederick Wakeman and Wen-hsin Yeh were among the first to use the concept of identity when discussing the cultural backgrounds and modes of belonging of Shanghai sojourners in the 1920s and 1930s. F. Wakeman and Wen-hsin Yeh, 'Introduction', in Frederic Wakeman and Wen-hsin Yeh (eds.), *Shanghai Sojourners* (Berkeley: Institute of East Asian Studies, 1992), pp. 11–12.

[17] For worker identities in the context of production see some of my earlier work: S. A. Smith, *Red Petrograd: Revolution in the Factories, 1917–18* (Cambridge: Cambridge University Press, 1983); 'Gender and Class: Women's Strikes in St Petersburg, 1895–1917, and Shanghai, 1895–1927', *Social History*, 19, 2 (1994), 141–68; 'Workers and Supervisors in St Petersburg, 1905–1917, and Shanghai, 1895–1927', *Past and Present*, 139 (1993), 131–77; 'Craft Consciousness, Class Consciousness: Petrograd 1917', *History Workshop*, 11 (1981), 33–56.

[18] S. A. Smith, *Like Cattle and Horses: Nationalism and Labor in Shanghai, 1895–1927* (Durham NC: Duke University Press, 2002), ch. 10.

book, however, is not to repeat what previous historians have done by reaffirming the salience of class identity, but to shift attention towards the less noticed and less well understood transformations of social identity that took place as migrants struggled to come to terms with the gamut of experiences engendered by capitalist modernity in the context of a multifaceted crisis of the old order.

The comparative study of revolutions has a distinguished pedigree. Most such work, however, has been done by historical sociologists rather than by historians and it has been primarily concerned either with building theories of revolution, or with constructing models of causal explanation, or with testing hypotheses about issues such as the origins and precipitating conditions of revolutions, the role of social classes and political parties, the dynamics of mass mobilization and mass demobilization, the typical stages of development of revolution and its typical outcomes. Much of this work is of great value, not least in forcing historians to think rigorously about the standard explanations and suppositions proffered within the historiographies of national revolutions. But such nomothetic endeavours are usually based on secondary historical works – i.e. they offer interpretations of other historians' interpretations – and often lack the detailed knowledge of sociopolitical and cultural context, historical conjuncture and historical timing that matter to the practising historian.[19] In these essays I try my hand at a style of comparative history that is designed to meet these latter desiderata: one that is less concerned with the 'big structures, large processes and huge comparisons' so fruitfully studied by Charles Tilly, and more with culture, human agency and the reconstruction of the micro-level contexts in which individuals acted upon and were shaped by those contexts.[20] My concern is not to build an overarching explanatory model of revolution but to illuminate similarities and differences between the two revolutions by building local arguments inductively out of close engagement with the primary sources. In choosing two radically different societies for comparison, my concern is, partly, to show how similar processes and practices played out differently in different cultural contexts: to demonstrate that culture matters. My methodology, however, is emphatically not a culturalist one. If modernity played out differently in different cultural contexts, its fundamental character was determined by its place within the global capitalist system and by the

---

[19] Raymond Grew, 'The Case for Comparing Histories' and 'On Rereading an Earlier Essay', in Aram A. Yengoyan (ed.), *Modes of Comparison: Theory and Practice* (Ann Arbor: University of Michigan Press, 2006), pp. 98–117, 118–136.

[20] Charles Tilly, *Big Structures, Large Processes, Huge Comparisons* (New York: Russell Sage Foundation, 1984).

competitive pressures of the international state system. Migrants were thrust into the modern world by these impersonal forces, yet they also made themselves modern by using the cultural resources at their disposal to confront and mould the impact of these forces on their lives.[21]

The book may be seen as an attempt to bring together the two 'analytics' which, according to Geoff Eley, continue to be polarized at the start of the twenty-first century: the 'older prioritizing of societal development and change', on the one hand, and the 'new preference for more modest and individualized sites of social and cultural investigation', on the other.[22] In breaking the unities of time and place, the hope is to stimulate the historical imagination, to open up a new perspective on labour history, to provoke new questions about the twentieth century's most important revolutions and to contribute a historical perspective to somewhat reified debates about 'multiple modernities'.

In addition to engaging with the contexts of capitalist industrialization and urbanization, the analysis offered in each of the first four chapters puts emphasis on three supplementary contexts that shaped the changing identities of migrants to the cities, contexts that may be seen as dimensions of capitalist modernity. First, and arguably the most important of these supplementary arenas of identity formation, was the crisis of the old order. This was a political crisis – centred on the inability of dynastic empires and autocratic polities to cope with the demands of modernization and the pressures of the international state system – but it was not merely a crisis of state: it extended to the entire traditional social order. In China a sense of national crisis – the fear that Chinese faced extinction at the hands of aggressive foreign powers – cast a shadow over the entire period from 1895 to 1945, and it is impossible to understand the production of social identity except in that context. I have argued elsewhere, in relation to Shanghai, that insofar as a working-class movement came into existence in that city, it did so as the by-product of the growth of nationalism, which was itself a response to the collapse of the imperial bureaucracy and to the encroachment on China's sovereignty by the foreign powers.[23] In Russia the political crisis took a different form, a growing perception that every level of the social order was characterized by arbitrariness and despotism, and that only the overthrow of tsarism and the establishment of a democratic polity (and/or some form of socialism) could bring about social progress and individual

---

[21] Dilip Parameshwar Gaonkar, 'On Alternative Modernities', in D. P. Gaonkar (ed.), *Alternative Modernities* (Durham NC: Duke University Press, 2001), p. 18.

[22] Geoff Eley, *A Crooked Line: from Cultural History to the History of Society* (Ann Arbor: University of Michigan Press, 2005), p. 193.

[23] Smith, *Like Cattle and Horses*.

freedom. In Russia, moreover, socialist revolution came about very much as a consequence of war between rapacious states not as a consequence of a crisis of the capitalist system per se. Each of the four chapters thus highlights different aspects of the political crisis that beset the traditional order and seeks to show how this influenced the process of identity formation among migrants to the city.

Second, the book explores the ways in which identities were shaped by transnational forces, whether economic, political or cultural in nature. For those who came to St Petersburg and Shanghai the experience of modernity was indistinguishable from exposure to western technology, commodities, institutions, practices and ideologies. For centuries, Russians had measured themselves against the West, either positively – by aspiring to its norms, lifestyle and prosperity – or negatively, by rejecting it as a bastion of materialism antithetical to the spirituality of the Russian people. St Petersburg, as is discussed below, was the major vector of westernization in Russian culture, even as it served as a symbolic site on which debate about the value of things western and Russian could be played out. In China, traditional culture was called into question far more dramatically than in Russia. The intrusion of foreign powers following the Opium War, the decline and ultimate collapse of the imperial bureaucracy, the attack on Confucianism by champions of 'science and democracy' all led to profound questioning as to what it might mean to be Chinese in the modern world. Paradoxically, the struggle to 'save' China encouraged intellectuals and nationalist politicians to turn to European, Japanese, American and Soviet models for inspiration. However, in neither Russia nor China did modernization equate with westernization: much as the experience of modernity was about exposure to things foreign, differences in Russian and Chinese modernities derived very much from the ways in which resources within the indigenous culture were used to cope with the practices and representations that flooded in from outside.

Third, emphasis is laid on the sphere of consumption – understood broadly to include everything from mass-produced subsistence items, to fashions in clothes or home furnishings, to newspapers and pulp fiction, to mass entertainment – as a site of identity construction. Gary Cross defines consumerism as 'the belief that goods give meaning to individuals and their role in society', and dubs it the 'ism that won' in the twentieth century.[24] Neither Russia nor China became 'consumer

[24] Gary S. Cross, *An All-Consuming Century: Why Commercialism Won in Modern America* (New York: Columbia University Press, 2000), p. 1; Robert Bocock, *Consumption* (London: Routledge, 1993), p. 50.

societies' in this sense. It was only in the 1890s in Russia and in the 1920s in China that the beginnings of a consumer society become visible, as basic goods were made cheaper by new forms of mass production. Poverty was no bar to increased desire for consumer goods, and in both St Petersburg and Shanghai very poor people, especially the young, fell under the influence of discourses that suggested that the path to individual and collective happiness lay through the acquisition of desirable goods and became aware that what you consume in part defines who you are.[25] It bears repeating that I do not minimize the wretched poverty, terrifying levels of overcrowding, chronic ill health, grinding deprivation, pervasive arbitrariness and sheer hopelessness of most working people's lives. But as people moved off the land, they began to consume more than they produced even if consumption was largely determined by what they could afford to buy in retail outlets such as the 8,600 local tobacco and paper stores (*yanzhidian*) that existed in Shanghai by 1949.[26]

New forms of leisure constituted another dimension of this consumer culture. As the *China Year Book* observed in 1927:

The worker in Shanghai lives, on the whole, in improved quarters far beyond anything he knew in the villages from which he came. He has a wider range of amusements: motion picture theatres, New Worlds, cheap theatres etc. On the roofs of the large department stores are roof gardens where there are a variety of amusements for the proletariat at cheap prices. He may learn to read in the various schools for the learning of a thousand characters.[27]

Writing of how commercialized forms of entertainment challenged the customary values of lower-class consumers in Russia, James von Geldern and Louise McReynolds observe:

To understand these works, or even to read or watch them, audiences had to have absorbed very new and very different notions of the human personality, of social decorum, and of cause and effect in the public sphere. Rude resistance to authority, the predatory sexuality of gold-diggers, even the sharpened ethnic consciousness of city folk were all new experiences that gave characters motives unknown in the past. Individual characters with their idiosyncrasies and desires peopled commercial culture and moved plots in unpredictable directions.[28]

---

[25] By the 1930s, the Shanghai press sometimes addressed its readers as 'consumers' (*xiaofeizhe*), a term introduced from Japan towards the end of the Qing dynasty. Weipin Tsai, 'Nationalism, Consumerism and the Image of the Individual in Shenbao Newspaper', University of Leeds, PhD, 2004, p. 140.

[26] Hanchao Lu, *Beyond the Neon Lights: Everyday Shanghai in the Early Twentieth Century* (Berkeley: University of California Press, 1999), p. 251.

[27] H. G. W. Woodhead (ed.), *China Year Book, 1926–27* (Tientsin: North China Daily News and Herald, 1927), p. 898.

[28] James von Geldern and Louise McReynolds (eds.), *Entertaining Tsarist Russia* (Bloomington: Indiana University Press, 1998), p. xx.

Consumption and commercialized mass culture thus constitute a third arena in which migrants to the city forged new identities.

The Concept of Identity

It has become a tedious cliché that identities are socially constructed rather than primordial, that they are multiple rather than unitary, that they are fluid rather than fixed. The present study tries to get beyond such truisms by asking how economic, political, social and cultural processes facilitated identity change, how inherited identity schemes were utilized to cope with change, how new identity schemes were put into circulation and how certain groups proved more or less responsive to such schemes. Certain forms of group affiliation proved stronger than others. In Russia, starting in the 1890s and persisting into the 1930s, class identity came to be hegemonic among workers. In China, by contrast, 'class-inflected' national identity became hegemonic among workers, albeit unevenly, between the mid-1920s and 1945. Other identities, however, intersected with these hegemonic identities, reinforcing or diluting them, and the book seeks to reveal these interactions. In separating out native-place, individualist, gender and national identities, it runs the risk of suggesting that these were discrete and clearly bounded identities, each rooted in specific sets of social relations. In reality, these identities were interwoven, the salience of each depending on the flux of events, and all became overdetermined by class or class-inflected nationalism as the Russian and Chinese polities slid into crisis.

The use of 'identity' as a category of analysis has recently come under fire from Frederick Cooper and Rogers Brubaker, who claim that it is 'riddled with ambiguity, riven with contradictory meanings and encumbered by reifying connotations'.[29] A key point in their critique is that 'identity is used to designate both strongly groupist, exclusive,

---

[29] Frederick Cooper and Rogers Brubaker, 'Identity', in Frederick Cooper, *Colonialism in Question: Theory, Knowledge, History* (Berkeley: University of Calfornia Press, 2005), p. 88. A further difficulty with the concept of 'identity' is that it was foreign to the two cultures with which I am dealing. No word in modern Russian or Chinese captures the double sense of the English word 'identity' as both 'sameness' and 'the condition of being a specified person'. In Russian the dual sense of the English term was carried by different words: *tozhdestvennost'* (sameness) and *lichnost'* (personal identity), as in *ustanovit' ch'iu-nibud' lichnost'* which means 'to establish someone's identity'. In recent times, *identichnost'* has been used to convey contemporary English usage. The situation is somewhat different in Chinese. The English term now tends to be translated as *shenfen*, which also means 'status' or 'dignity', as in *shenfenzheng*, 'identity card'; but it carries, too, the sense of identity as social role, whereas *gexing* or *texing* carry the sense of individuality. For a discussion of whether the concept of 'identity' is applicable to the pre-modern or non-western worlds, see Richard Handler, 'Is "Identity" a Useful

affectively charged self-understandings and much looser, more open self-understandings, involving some sense of affinity or affiliation, commonality or connectedness to particular others, but lacking a sense of overriding oneness vis-à-vis some constitutive "other" '.[30] This is a perceptive charge, the gravamen of which is relevant to the four identities under consideration in this book. First, there were indeed critical differences in the nature of identifications based on native place, autonomous individuality, gender, and nation. Loosely speaking, native-place, gender and national identities are categorical modes of identification, insofar as people identify with others on the basis of a perceived common attribute, whereas the sense of self patently is not.[31] Yet the nature of the groups that coalesced around these categorical understandings – the sense of commonality that fellow provincials, or women, or members of the nation felt with one another – varied greatly. Gender identity, for example, may be seen as a deep and abiding feature of the self, yet the extent to which it cements men or women together into bounded and sociopolitically consequential groups is limited. By contrast, national identity may be less constitutive of personhood yet it has the capacity to forge potent group affiliations to the point that people will lay down their lives for the sake of the nation.

Second, the degree of influence of these identities on historical developments also varied. Each chapter suggests how a particular identity transformation fed into the pre-revolutionary crisis, but does not argue that each had the same political influence. As already mentioned, the political significance of the identities depended, in part, on the extent to which they became hegemonized by discourses of class or class-inflected nationalism. However, so long as one is alert to differences in existential depth and permanency, as well as to the differences in political effectivity between these identities, it seems to me the category of 'social identity' can do useful analytical work. In what follows, I use the category along lines argued for by Ronald Suny, as 'a provisional stabilization of a sense of self or group that is formed in actual historical time and space, in evolving economies, polities, and cultures, as a continuous search for some solidity in a constantly shifting world – but without closure, without forever naturalizing or essentializing the provisional identities arrived at'.[32] Such a historicized approach, it seems, is flexible enough yet sufficiently focused to enable

Cross-Cultural Concept?', in John R. Gillis, *Commemorations: The Politics of National Identity* (Princeton: Princeton University Press, 1994), pp. 27–40.
[30] Cooper, 'Identity', p. 75.
[31] Cooper, 'Identity', p. 71.
[32] Ronald Gregor Suny, 'Constructing Primordialism: Old Histories for New Nations', *Journal of Modern History*, 73 (2001), 866.

useful differentiation of the axes along which the identities of peasants who became city-dwelling workers were transformed.

Cooper and Brubaker make another important point when they draw a distinction between categorical modes of identification, which they see as typical of modern societies, and relational modes of identification, which perceive the social world in terms of the degree and quality of connection among people rather than in terms of clearly bounded categories. In a relational mode of identification, one understands oneself in terms of a web of connections – such as those of kinship or patron–client networks – of differential proximity and intensity.[33] Such relational identifications were of paramount importance in China: indeed one of the striking features of Chinese modernity is that these were reconfigured and reutilized by workers and other groups struggling to come to terms with the new power relations and social practices brought into being through incorporation into global capitalism. Indeed the distinction made by Cooper and Brubaker is remarkably similar to one made by the eminent Chinese anthropologist Fei Xiaotong back in the 1930s, when he argued that social groups in the West represent an 'organizational mode of association', in that they are relatively bounded and members have defined rights and duties, whereas social groups in China represent a 'differential mode of association' in that they comprise discontinuous and overlapping networks, made up of personalistic ties that are often hierarchical in nature.[34] We shall see that migrants in China and, to a lesser extent, in Russia drew sustenance and solidarity from relational modes of identification, using networks based on native place, secret-society membership or sworn brotherhood or sisterhood, or clientelist ties to foremen and labour contractors to meet the challenges of the urban-industrial environment. Such relational modes of identification could powerfully inhibit the development of categorical modes of identification, such as class identity, since they were embodied in vertical and particularistic solidarities that blocked the emergence of horizontal and more inclusive forms of organization. Yet as we shall see in chapter 1, the political significance of relational solidarities was not fixed: when caught up in wider social and political movements, they could paradoxically facilitate collective action and endow workers with a sense of purpose that, in moments of crisis, could be reconfigured within more universalistic languages of nation or of class.

---

[33] Cooper, 'Identity', p. 74.
[34] Fei Xiaotong, *From the Soil: The Foundations of Chinese Society*. With an introduction and epilogue by Gary G. Hamilton and Wang Zheng (Berkeley: University of California Press, 1992), p. 20. Originally, *Xiangtu Zhongguo* (1947).

Identity formation is never the straightforward product of exposure to new social practices and power relations, since such exposure must always be made meaningful. As Dorinne Kondo explains, identities are the shifting outcome of 'culturally available meanings and the open-ended, power-laden enactments of those meanings in everyday situations'.[35] The concept 'discourse' has perhaps become so overextended that it is best abandoned; yet carefully defined, it can still do useful service. I use the concept not in the narrow sense of linguistic performance, but in a broader sense to denote a symbolically articulated field of social practice that construes and organizes experience in particular ways.[36] A discursive approach reminds us that identity construction is very much about power. The migrants to the cities struggled to create and sustain new identities by challenging the power relations that underpinned entrenched identities and this fed into the wider crisis of the *anciens régimes*. In the modern world it is the task of politics – of parties, ideologies, leaders, movements and grass-roots activists – to persuade people to understand themselves, their interests, and their predicaments in particular ways, i.e. to foreground certain identities and marginalize others, so that collective action can be built around them. The revolutions in Russia and China, therefore, were as much about conflict over identities as conflict over who got what, when and how.

St Petersburg and Shanghai: Contradictions of Modernity

St Petersburg and Shanghai were not only the largest commercial and industrial centres in their respective countries, but also the cities that exemplified capitalist modernity in its most advanced form. It goes

---

[35] Dorinne K. Kondo, *Crafting Selves: Power, Gender, and Discourses of Identity in a Japanese Workplace* (Chicago: University of Chicago Press, 1990), pp. 10, 24.

[36] Steven Best and Douglas Kellner, *Postmodern Theory: Critical Interrogations* (London: Macmillan, 1991), p. 26; Peter Schöttler, 'Historians and Discourse Analysis', *History Workshop Journal* 27 (1989), 37–65. See also William G. Rosenberg, 'Some Observations on the Question of "Hegemonic Discourse"', in Michael Melancon and Alice Pate (eds.), *New Labor History: Worker Identity and Experience in Russia, 1840–1918* (Bloomington: Slavica Publishers, 2002), pp. 177–206. Some readers may expect a book on social identities to draw upon Foucault's conception of governmentality. I agree with Peter Holquist that a form of governmentality began to emerge in Russia during the First World War, as forms of population surveillance and statistics developed, but the extent of state penetration of society in both late-tsarist Russia and republican China was limited, and state functions remained essentially extractive and coercive in nature (more so in China than in Russia). Peter Holquist, *Making War, Forging Revolution: Russia's Continuum of Crisis, 1914–21* (Cambridge MA: Harvard University Press, 2002); Graham Burchell, Colin Gordon and Peter Miller (eds.), *The Foucault Effect: Studies in Governmentality* (Chicago: University of Chicago Press, 1991).

without saying that they cannot be seen as proxies for Russia and China as a whole: it was precisely their atypicality within their respective countries – their functioning as symbols of modernity that the rest of the society was expected to emulate – that makes them comparable. Yet with their factories and waterfronts, their modern banks and offices, their department stores and hotels, their wide avenues, trams and motor cars, their electric lighting, piped water, cinemas, dance halls and public parks, their fashionably dressed inhabitants, they seemed to prefigure the future of the nation as a whole.[37] Each city encapsulated the speed of modern life, the increased density of social interaction, the proliferation of consumer desire, the challenges to once-hallowed values posed by the pursuit of money and pleasure. Yet each, too, epitomized the ambivalence at the heart of modernity, promising increased personal autonomy and social progress, on the one hand, but anomie, anxiety and instability, on the other. Moreover, if the cities served as emblems of modernity, for every expression of the modern there were countless more reminders of backwardness.

From the time Peter the Great ordered a new capital to be built on wooded, swampy ground along the Gulf of Finland, St Petersburg elicited sharply contrasting reactions from educated Russians. Some lauded this 'window on the West', seeing the city's magnificent baroque and neo-classical palaces as a triumph of human will over inhospitable nature. Others deplored the artificiality and theatricality of the capital's building and public spaces, as well as the forced labour that had brought them into being. Pushkin celebrated the imperial grandeur of the city in 'The Bronze Horseman', his ode to Falconet's monument to Peter, yet his poem also limned the suffering that the city was destined to undergo. It fell to Gogol, with his phantasmagoric vision of a city of 'fog, darkness, cold reflecting surfaces, and fear of vast open spaces', to inaugurate a negative tradition of literary representation.[38] This continued with Dostoevsky, who deplored the city's lack of national roots and the squalor that lay behind its splendid visage. His *Crime and Punishment* (1866), set amid the wretched tenements and factories of what had now become Russia's leading industrial city, depicted the brutalized existence of its lower-class inhabitants. Mark Steinberg beautifully captures the paradoxical image of the city as: 'a simultaneously vital and sinister

---

[37] For an outstanding history of Shanghai that concentrates on the daily life of ordinary people, see Hanchao Lu, *Beyond the Neon Lights* (Berkeley: University of California Press, 1999). For an equally outstanding study of St Petersburg, see James H. Bater, *St Petersburg: Industrialization and Change* (London: Edward Arnold, 1976).

[38] Solomon Volkov, *St Petersburg: A Cultural History* (London: Sinclair-Stevenson, 1996), p. 30.

place, a place of interwoven virtue and vice, of the fantastic and grotesque beside the orderly and the rational, of bright lights and furtive shadows, of artistic creativity and smug vulgarity'.[39]

Shanghai had none of the imperial pretensions of St Petersburg: as China's largest centre of industry and commerce, 'its idol was Mammon and its heart lay wholly in the marketplace'.[40] It had rather a long history as a centre of the cotton trade, but its prominence as a major international entrepôt was recent and it was perceived essentially as a young city whose denizens were not hidebound by tradition. For conservatives the city was a standing affront to Confucian values, a place where money talked and where it did not pay to be morally upstanding.[41] For the educated youth of the New Culture generation, the city symbolized emancipation from the crippling ties of the patriarchal family and the traditional social order. For migrant workers, Shanghai, with its sky-scrapers and double-decker buses, its good food and stylish clothes, symbolized undreamed of possibilities of self-advancement. In Wen-hsin Yeh's terse formula, 'Shanghai modernity connected an elitist project of enlightenment with a populist commodification and consumption of images of a westernised cosmopolitan style of life'.[42] As this suggests, far more than St Petersburg, the city represented a modernity that was deeply foreign.[43] The International Settlement and the French Concession, far more developed and prosperous than the Chinese-administered sectors, dominated the life of the city, and the number of foreign residents grew from 4,265 in 1890 to 73,273 in 1937.[44] Foreign businessmen, foreign goods, foreign missionaries, foreign schools all served as conduits of western influence. Shanghai thus became a symbolic site

---

[39] Mark D. Steinberg, *Proletarian Imagination: Self, Modernity and the Sacred in Russia, 1910–1925* (Ithaca NY: Cornell University Press, 2002), p. 148.

[40] Pan Ling, *In Search of Old Shanghai* (Hong Kong: Joint Publishing Company, 1982), p. 134. Cf. Xin Ping: 'The growth and maturation of a market economy created an economic personality, a commercial personality, a worldly personality that combined to produce astuteness as the principal feature (of the personality of the people of Shanghai).' Xin Ping, *Cong Shanghai faxian lishi: xiandaihua, jinchengzhong de Shanghai ren ji qi shehui shenghuo, 1927–37* [Discovering History from Shanghai: Modernization, Urban Shanghainese and their Social Life, 1927–37] (Shanghai: Shanghai renmin chubanshe, 1996), p. 243.

[41] Shen Bojing (ed.), *Shanghai shi zhinan* [Guidebook to Shanghai] (Shanghai: Zhonghua shudian, 1933), pp. 138–9.

[42] Wen-hsin Yeh, 'Introduction: Interpreting Chinese Modernity, 1900–1950', in Wen-hsin Yeh (ed.), *Becoming Chinese: Passages to Modernity and Beyond* (Berkeley: University of California Press, 2000), p. 5

[43] Leo Ou-fan Lee, *Shanghai Modern: The Flowering of New Urban Culture in China, 1930–1945* (Cambridge MA: Harvard University Press, 1999), ch. 1.

[44] Zou Yiren, *Jiu Shanghai renkou bianqian de yanjiu* [Research on Population Change in Old Shanghai] (Shanghai: Shanghai renmin chubanshe, 1980), p. 141.

on which intellectuals agonized as to how far modernization – a prerequisite for national liberation – must necessitate cultural westernization. At the same time, there was an irresistible irony in the fact that Shanghai, emblem of cosmopolitanism, became a key centre of nationalism; and the fact that Shanghai, emblem of individualism and liberalism, became the birthplace of the CCP. Shanghai thus served as a polyvalent symbol: an emblem of consumer affluence and of class exploitation, of foreign imperialism and patriotic resistance, of individualism and mass society.

It was precisely in the contradictoriness of the experience of modernity that the roots of revolution lay. In his *History of the Russian Revolution*, Trotsky noted how 'under the whip of external necessity', 'the development of historically backward nations leads necessarily to a peculiar combination of different stages of development in the historic process', to an 'amalgam of archaic with more contemporary forms.'[45] The compression of time and space – what Ernst Bloch called the 'synchronicity of the non-synchronous, the simultaneity of the non-contemporaneous' – was fully evident in our two cities and a phenomenon remarked on by contemporaries.[46] One of the future founders of the CCP, Li Dazhao, complained in 1918 that 'the gap in time between old and new is too big, that the spatial juxtaposition is too close'. Writing of Beijing, he explained:

I often walk along the thoroughfare that goes by Qianmen, which I feel is such a narrow stretch of road, yet which manages to contain phenomena of so many periods: there are saddled camels, carts with signs saying 'Brother, would you step out of the way', there are mule carts, horse-drawn carts, rickshaws, carriages and motor cars, all the things of the twentieth century alongside those from before the fifteenth are brought together in one place. Wheels and hooves move side by side, sirens hoot, there is the sound of cars and horses, of rickshaw pullers spitting and cursing one another. There is diversity and confusion, complexity to an extreme degree. ... The new resents the obstacles posed by the old. The old resents the dangers posed by the new.[47]

While seeking to capture the contradictoriness of migrant experience, this book puts a stronger accent on the changes that migrant identities underwent than do many historians of Russian and Chinese labour, who

[45] *Trotsky's History of the Russian Revolution*, vol. 1 (in three vols.) (London: Sphere, 1967), p. 23.
[46] Cited in Harry Harootunian, *Overcome by Modernity: History, Culture and Community in Interwar Japan* (Princeton: Princeton University Press, 2000), p. xvii.
[47] *Li Dazhao wenji* [Collected Writings of Li Dazhao], vol. 1 (2 vols.) (Beijing: Renmin chubanshe, 1984), p. 539.

tend to view migrants to the city as peasants in all major respects.[48]
Whereas investigators of Chinese labour in the 1930s and 1940s took it
for granted that proletarianization was taking place, labour historians of
the 1980s and 1990s were much more sceptical, arguing that workers,
holed up in shanties and slums, prey to poverty and disease, continued
to behave like peasants rather than proletarians. Wen-hsin Yeh sums up
this work when she writes: 'Few rural provincials ... were able to dis-
engage themselves from the norms and ties into which they had been
born.'[49] Similarly, historians of Russia have tended to insist that factory
workers remained largely peasants. Dave Pretty, writing about workers
in Ivanovo-Voznesensk, describes his aim as being to show that 'Russian
working-class culture was not genetically different from peasant culture'.[50] It is not my purpose to reject this claim *in toto*: indeed it is a
useful corrective to Communist accounts that plot a narrative of labour
history in terms of ever-increasing proletarianization and class consciousness. Migrants to Moscow, for example, did retain stronger ties
with the land than their counterparts in St Petersburg, and tended to
work in smaller enterprises, though these were still relatively large by the
standards of western Europe.[51]

Nevertheless, because I am dealing with the two cities where modernity was most developed and with migrants who settled in the city, the

---

[48] Hanchao Lu stresses the resilience of older patterns of life in Shanghai, whereas Xin
Ping stresses the rapidity with which the city's inhabitants were acculturated to city life.
Li Changli, writing of the late-Qing period, argues that while many aspects of the social
life of Shanghai's denizens were rapidly affected by contact with foreign ideas and
material culture, moral attitudes did not change so rapidly. Hanchao Lu, *Beyond the
Neon Lights*; Xin Ping, *Cong Shanghai faxian lishi*; Li Changli *Wan Qing Shanghai shehui
de bianqian: shenghuo yu lunli de jindaihua* [Social Change in Late Qing Shanghai: The
Modernization of Life and Ethics] (Tianjin: Renmin chubanshe, 2002).

[49] Wen-hsin Yeh, 'Shanghai Modernity: Commerce and Culture in a Republican City',
China Quarterly, 150 (1997), 380.

[50] Dave Pretty, 'Neither Peasant Nor Proletarian: The Workers of Ivanovo-Voznesensk',
Brown University, PhD, 1997, p. 44. McKean argues that the workforce of the capital
was 'still at the transitory stage between agriculture and industry'. Robert B. McKean,
St Petersburg: Between the Two Revolutions (New Haven: Yale University Press, 1990),
p. 29. An important exception is Evel Economakis who writes that St Petersburg's
industrial workers 'on the eve of the First World War were proletarians in the western-
European sense of the term'. Evel G. Economakis, *From Peasant to Petersburger*
(Basingstoke: Macmillan, 1998), p. 139.

[51] Robert E. Johnson, *Peasant and Proletarian: The Working Class of Moscow in the Late
Nineteenth Century* (Leicester: Leicester University Press, 1979), pp. 50, 24. In Russia
many factories were located in rural areas, and in the Central Industrial Region and the
Urals it was quite common for workers to continue to farm land. This phenomenon was
also found, albeit to a much lesser extent, in China, as at the Da Shang No. 1 cotton
mill in Tangjiazha village, north-east of Nantong. Elisabeth Köll, *From Cotton Mill to
Business Empire: The Emergence of Regional Enterprises in Modern China* (Cambridge MA:
Harvard University Press, 2003), pp. 105–7.

accent of my account will be on change. The longer migrants were exposed to urban-industrial life – and large numbers quickly discovered that any intention to return to the village was unachievable – the more their understanding of who they were changed.[52] This is, incidentally, a phenomenon noted by anthropologists of shanty town dwellers in the developing world today. Joan Nelson writes: 'Much of their lives, their aspirations, and their problems are shaped more by the pressures and the opportunities of the city than by their migrant status, and these pressures and opportunities are shared with urban natives of similar economic and educational backgrounds.'[53] Yet while I would insist that in the long term urban-industrial culture proved stronger than rural culture in shaping the identities of migrants to the city, to strike the balance between continuity and change – a balance that shifted over time – is not easy, and in chapter 1, especially, I take care to stress the persistence of 'tradition' among migrants to the two cities.

As the last sentence indicates, it is hard to forgo the shorthand use of the categories of 'tradition' and 'modernity', but they are far too abstract to provide the kind of analytical purchase on the highly differentiated and fast-changing developments that are the theme of the four main chapters. Migrants were formed by 'traditional' relations, practices, cultural norms and values and took these with them to the city. In the city they encountered new relations and practices which they resisted and assimilated in complex ways, using the cultural resources at their disposal. The move to the city could revitalize customary norms and orientations, putting them to new uses; or it could erode them, some-times remarkably quickly. The new could be vigorously rejected, or selectively appropriated; in moments of political and social crisis, it could be seized on with alacrity. Old and new cultural elements existed in a variety of relationships, ranging from the painless substitution of new for old, to peaceful coexistence of old and new, to painful antag-onism between old and new, to various forms of hybridity. The new could triumph comprehensively: more commonly, it could be adapted and synthesized with elements of the old. The old could persist unchanged; more commonly, it could be reconfigured and put to new

---

[52] The relatively greater opportunities for female employment in both St Petersburg and Shanghai may have been a key reason why migrants could make the permanent commitment to city life. Writing of Bombay, where an even larger proportion of the population were immigrants than in Shanghai, Raj Chandavarkar argues that for most the purpose of migration was the desire to enhance the family's resources in the village, but he suggests that this was due partly to the fact that there were so few employment opportunities for women in Bombay. Raj Chandavarkar, *Origins of Industrial Capitalism in India* (Cambridge: Cambridge University Press, 1992), ch. 4.

[53] Quoted in Charles Tilly, *Big Structures*, p. 55.

uses. Frank Dikötter has characterized Chinese modernity as a whole as a process of 'pick and mix' and his perspective can usefully be adapted to the migrant experience.[54] So although the accent in the following pages is on change, the book seeks to grapple with the relationship between old and new practices and representations, not least because if one does not give due weight to the resilience of 'tradition', it becomes difficult to explain the apparent resurgence of 'traditional' values and orientations during what Crane Brinton called the 'thermidorean' phases of revolution, i.e. high Stalinism in the Soviet Union and high Maoism in the People's Republic of China (PRC), which provides the subject of the second half of chapter 5.[55]

Peasants on the Move

In the modern era, movement not stasis has become the typical condition. For the anthropologist James Clifford, the very meaning of modernity is constituted by the experience of displacement and discontinuity. Challenging the assumption that 'roots always precede routes', he argues that a perspective of 'people in transit, variously empowered and compelled' reveals that 'practices of displacement emerge as constitutive of cultural meanings rather than their simple transfer or extension'.[56] To anyone looking at China today the force of this observation hits one in the face, for it is estimated that some 200 million people in 2006 were working away from their villages, making this apparently the largest migration in history.[57] In the early twentieth century, the scale of migration was much smaller, yet the idea of displacement and discontinuity as fundamental in forming new identities is at the heart of this study. We should, of course, be wary of exaggerating the expansion of human agency that geographical mobility brought about. An earlier generation of scholars was keenly aware of the constraints and uncertainties that displacement brings. Hannah Arendt spoke of the 'uprootedness and superfluousness which have been the curse of the modern masses since the beginning of the industrial revolution' and suggested that people uprooted are people rendered physically and

[54] Feng Ke (Frank Dikötter), 'Minguo shiqi de modeng wanyi, wenhua pincou yu richang shenghuo' [Modern things, cultural pick-and-mix and daily life in the republican era], in Li Xiaoti (ed.), *Zhongguo de chengshi shenghuo* [Urban Life in China] (Taipei: Lianjing chubanshe, 2005), pp. 477–95.
[55] Crane Brinton, *Anatomy of Revolution*, 2nd edn (London: Cape, 1953).
[56] James Clifford, *Routes: Travel and Translation in the Late Twentieth Century* (Cambridge MA: Harvard University Press, 1997), pp. 2, 5, 3.
[57] Zai Liang, 'The Age of Migration in China', *Population and Development Review* 27, 3 (2001), 499–524.

morally superfluous.[58] It serves to remind us that if many chose to leave their villages, others had no choice but to do so.

The emancipation of the serfs in 1861 – in combination with the debate about preserving the peasantry as a social estate that was sparked by the 'great reforms' of Alexander II – was the act that proved most consequential for the renegotiation of Russian peasant identities in the latter part of the nineteenth century. Significantly, the legislation did not give peasants the right to leave their villages, for the tsarist government was set on discouraging geographical mobility. Peasants who wished to leave the village had to get the permission of the commune, which was responsible for ensuring that households paid their share of the taxes and redemption payments owed on the land they received at emancipation. The elders of the commune, known as the *mir*, were ever fearful that those leaving the villages would renege on these obligations, even though they generally welcomed the income that migrants brought into the village. The government further discouraged outmigration by issuing passports for short periods only and by allowing commune elders to withdraw passports or confiscate the property of migrants who were in arrears with taxes.[59] Passports recorded tax liability and the amount of tax paid, and a law of 1899 obliged employers to deduct village taxes from the wages of workers in debt.[60] Commune elders might also require a young man to marry as a condition of receiving a passport, in order to encourage him to continue to farm his land. I. M. Golubev, son of a poor peasant family in Tver' province, worked as a youth in the leather factories of Torzhok, where his grandfather and father had worked before him. 'After long efforts and struggle within the family I was lucky enough to get out of Torzhok in 1896 and go to Petersburg, but to do that I had first to get married in order to leave a female worker in the household.'[61] From the end of the century, the tsarist government eased restrictions on outmigration. In 1894 peasants were given the right to five-year passports, irrespective of arrears in taxes or redemption payments, and in 1903 the joint responsibility of the commune for payment of redemption dues and taxes was rescinded. From 1907,

---

[58]   Hannah Arendt, *The Origins of Totalitarianism* (London: Allen and Unwin, 1966), p. 475.
[59]   Jeffrey Burds, 'The Social Control of Peasant Labor in Russia: the Responses of Village Communities to Labor Migration in the Central Industrial Region, 1861–1905', in Esther Kingston-Mann and Timothy R. Mixter (eds.), *Peasant Economy, Culture and Politics in European Russia, 1800–1921* (Princeton: Princeton University Press, 1991), pp. 52–100.
[60]   P. G. Ryndziunskii, *Krest'iane i gorod v kapitalisticheskoi Rossii vtoroi poloviny XIX veka* (Moscow: Nauka, 1983), pp. 102–3.
[61]   Quoted in U. A. Shuster, *Peterburgskie rabochie v 1905–07gg.* (Leningrad: Nauka, 1976), p. 23.

redemption payments were abolished completely, and peasants thus regained a right to move freely that they had lost more than 300 years previously. That right was further enhanced by the Stolypin reforms of 1906, which allowed households to leave the commune and to privatize their land holdings.[62]

None of the legal restrictions on migration prevented a huge outflow of peasants from their villages in the last decades of the nineteenth century. Between 1860 and 1914, the population of the Russian Empire grew from 74 million to 164 million, putting pressure on the land, especially in the fertile black-soil provinces of central Russia and the Volga region. Largely as a result of migration, the population of St Petersburg grew from 1.26 million in 1897 to 2.4 million in 1917, making it the fifth largest city in Europe and roughly the size of Shanghai in the early 1920s.[63] In 1900, 56% of migrants in the capital were drawn from nine provinces, which were, in declining order of importance: Tver', Iaroslavl', Novgorod, Petersburg, Pskov, Riazan', Vitebsk, Smolensk and Kostroma.[64] Among factory workers the biggest cohorts came from Tver', Vitebsk, Pskov, Novgorod and Smolensk.[65] These were provinces relatively distant from the capital, and this contrasted with Moscow where migrants tended to come from contiguous areas.[66]

Tver' and Iaroslavl', the two provinces that sent most migrants to St Petersburg, were situated in the Central Industrial Region close to Moscow, yet the two provinces were very different in character. Tver' was the least industrially developed and least fertile of the provinces in the region.[67] The rising level of emigration was caused by a decline in the ratio of land to population, a fall in employment on the Volga river as a result of the development of railways and steamships, a fall in rural wage levels, and a rise in arrears on redemption payments. In addition, the expansion of dairy farming and flax production in Tver' province led to growing social differentiation among the peasantry.[68] M. I. Kalinin, future president of the Soviet Union, was born in 1875 in Verkhniaia Troitsa, a village of 51 households, 17 of which owned neither a horse nor a cow. In half the poor households men worked as labourers for

[62] Ryndziunskii, *Krest'iane i gorod*, pp. 98–105; Jeffrey Burds, *Peasant Dreams and Market Politics: Labour Migration and the Russian Village, 1861–1905* (Pittsburgh: University of Pittsburgh Press, 1998), p. 57.

[63] Smith, *Red Petrograd*, p. 5.

[64] A. G. Rashin, *Formirovanie rabochego klassa Rossii* (Moscow: Izdatel'stvo sotsial'no-ekonomicheskoi literatury, 1958), p. 143.

[65] Evel G. Economakis, 'Patterns of Migration and Settlement in Prerevolutionary St Petersburg: Peasants from Iaroslavl and Tver' Provinces', *Russian Review*, 56 (1997), 24.

[66] Johnson, *Peasant and Proletarian*, p. 31.   [67] Economakis, 'Patterns', p. 12.

[68] Economakis, 'Patterns', pp. 16–18.

the local landowner or for well-off peasants, while the rest toiled in St Petersburg. Migration from Tver' province generally entailed the abandonment of farming, with most migrants opting to rent out their land.[69] In Iaroslavl', by contrast, social differentiation of the peasantry was much less advanced. Migrants set off in search of earnings in order to bolster their family farms which their wives stayed behind to tend.[70] If outmigrants from Tver' were often caught up in a process of proletarianization, those from Iaroslavl' may be seen as using off-farm earnings to bolster their family farms. In neither case should we assume that peasants were necessarily unwilling to leave their village. Certainly, many were driven out by poverty; but the best predictor of the level of outmigration in a province was not the ratio of population to land, a rough proxy for the level of poverty, but the level of literacy among its population. The greater the extent of literacy in a province, especially the extent of schooling, the more likely was it to export migrants.[71]

Men between the ages of 16 and 35 were the most likely group in the rural population to migrate to St Petersburg.[72] In 1897, there were 121 men for every 100 women in that city, although by 1910, this had fallen to 110.[73] In Shanghai, too, men greatly outnumbered women; so both cities were dissimilar from the major European cities, such as Berlin, Vienna or London, where women predominated in the urban population.[74] However, from the end of the nineteenth century, the number of female migrants to St Petersburg rose rapidly. These were mainly young single women, widows or women from impoverished households, since wives required the permission of husbands to migrate and were thus more constrained in their ability to move.[75] The majority of female migrants, unskilled and often illiterate, secured employment as servants, cooks and nursemaids. Only a minority found jobs in the city's factories where they earned about half the wages of men. Several thousands ended up as registered prostitutes, subjected to regular police medical inspections and surrendering their passports for an infamous 'yellow ticket'.[76]

[69] Economakis, 'Patterns', p. 17.
[70] Economakis, 'Patterns', pp. 20–21.
[71] Barbara A. Anderson, *Internal Migration During Modernization in Late Nineteenth-Century Russia* (Princeton: Princeton University Press, 1980), pp. 73, 88, 151–2.
[72] Shuster, *Peterburgskie rabochie*, p. 23.
[73] Joseph Bradley, *Muzhik and Muscovite: Urbanization in Late Imperial Russia* (Berkeley: University of California Press, 1985), p. 34; *Statisticheskie dannye Petrograda* (1916), p. 9.
[74] Economakis, *From Peasant*, pp. 181–2.
[75] Barbara Alpern Engel, *Between the Fields and the City: Women, Work and Family in Russia, 1861–1914* (Cambridge: Cambridge University Press, 1994), p. 99.
[76] Engel, *Between the Fields*, ch. 6.

Between 1900 and 1910, the proportion of women in the city's active population over the age of sixteen rose from 44.9% to 47.4%; and the proportion of women in the industrial workforce rose from 20.5% to 25.5% in the same decade.[77] This increase was associated with a tendency for whole families to settle in the city, a tendency that was particularly marked among industrial workers. The tsarist government still classified the population by social estate and the proportion of the peasant estate (to which most industrial workers belonged) that had been resident in St Petersburg for ten years or more grew from 31.6% to 35.5% between 1900 and 1910. In the same period the proportion of the inhabitants that had been born in the capital rose from 19.3% to 22.4%. In 1910, only 10% of those classed as peasants returned to the village for the summer months, and among factory workers the proportion was much lower, since employers required a permanent workforce.[78]

Between 1912 and 1933, China's population grew from 430 million to around 500 million. There were no formal restrictions on the right to leave one's birthplace in late-imperial China, but the imperial government tended to assume that people would have no desire to leave their native place unless forced to do so.[79] Historically, the modern term for migrants (*yimin*) carried the sense that people moved because the authorities had decided they must move for economic or defence reasons.[80] Those forced to leave their homes because of natural disaster, war or penury were referred to as *liumin*, a word which suggests they had been set adrift and forced to wander.[81] Despite the connotation of these terms, the reality was that many left their villages of their own accord. Until the last quarter of the nineteenth century, the bulk of migrants to Shanghai consisted of the more marginal and mobile elements of the rural population, such as boatmen, smugglers, pole carriers and day labourers. By the twentieth century, migrants came predominantly from farming families; but since many found only casual employment, contemporaries continued to see them as members of the 'floating population' (*youmin*) or as 'vagabonds' (*liumang*).[82] In 1895, Shanghai's population stood at between 800,000 and 900,000 and it grew to over

---

[77] Leopold Haimson and Eric Brian, 'Changements démographiques et grèves ouvrières à Saint-Petersbourg, 1905–14', *Annales ESC*, 40, 4 (1985), 792.

[78] Haimson and Brian, 'Changements démographiques', 791. In 1900–2, among textile workers only 5% went away for summer work.

[79] William T. Rowe, *Hankow: Commerce and Society in a Chinese City, 1796–1889* (Stanford: Stanford University Press, 1984), pp. 233–43.

[80] *Cihai*, vol. 3 (Shanghai: Shanghai cishu chubanshe, 1979), p. 4010.

[81] *Cihai*, vol. 2, p. 2178.

[82] Chen Baoliang, *Zhongguo liumang shi* [History of Chinese Vagrants] (Beijing: Shehui kexue chubanshe, 1993), pp. 31–4.

two million by 1915 and to 3,114,805 by 1930.[83] Growth came about overwhelmingly as a result of inmigration. Even by 1930, people born in Shanghai formed only 22% of the city's population (the same proportion, incidentally, as the city-born population of St Petersburg in 1910).[84] As in St Petersburg, the gross figures for population growth minimize the true scale of migration, since much of the latter was short-term or seasonal in nature. In the course of 1929, for example, 190,106 people arrived in Shanghai and 66,299 left.[85] The majority of migrants came from the two provinces closest to the city: from Jiangsu, the province in which the city itself was located, and from Zhejiang, south of the Yangtze river. In 1925, 42.7% of the Chinese population of the International Settlement was born in Jiangsu (including Shanghai natives) and 31.7% in Zhejiang.[86]

It is customary to distinguish between the area of Jiangsu province south of the Yangtze river, which was known as Jiangnan, a term that usually also included the Ningbo-Shaoxing region of Zhejiang province, and the area of Jiangsu north of the Yangtze and south of the old route of the Huai river (now the Huaibei irrigation canal), which was known as Jiangbei or Subei. The latter was generally an impoverished and declining region, although the salt trade along the Grand Canal and its tributaries had once lent cities like Yangzhou an air of sophistication.[87] Subei was itself divided between its southern area, which abutted the north bank of the Yangtze, and the northern and central areas, below and above the Huai river. In the latter areas, commerce – with the partial exception of salt – was underdeveloped; and although rates of tenancy and absentee landlordism were low, many peasants lived perilously close to subsistence. Droughts or floods could easily precipitate mass emigration, especially from areas around Yancheng and Funing. Gu Zhenghong, the worker whose death at the hands of a Japanese mill guard in 1925

[83] Zou Yiren, *Jiu Shanghai renkou*, pp. 90–1.   [84] Zou Yiren, *Jiu Shanghai renkou*, p. 112.
[85] Luo Zhiru (ed.), *Tongjibiao zhong zhi Shanghai* [Shanghai through Statistical Tables] (Nanjing: 1932), Table 56. This represents an 'efficiency of migration' of 48%. During the period 1930–6 this fell very low, to an average of 19%, though there were huge variations from year to year, a reflection of the serious unemployment in the city during the years of the Depression. See Mark Elvin, 'Introduction', Mark Elvin and G. William Skinner (eds.), *The Chinese City Between Two Worlds* (Stanford: Stanford University Press, 1974), p. 11.
[86] *North China Herald*, 12 December 1925, p. 490. In spite of the large proportion of migrants from Jiangsu and Zhejiang, the workforce of Shanghai was far more diverse in its regional origins than those of Canton, Beijing or Hunan. *Chinese Economic Journal*, 3, 5 (1928), 922.
[87] Antonia Finnane, 'Yangzhou: A Central Place in the Qing Empire', in Linda Cooke Johnson (ed.), *Cities of Jiangnan in Late Imperial China* (Albany: SUNY Press, 1993), pp. 124–5.

indirectly triggered the May Thirtieth Movement, was born in Funing county in 1905. His father owned about five *mu* of land and rented a further twenty *mu* of saline land on which he struggled to support Gu and his eight younger brothers and sisters.[88] In 1916, Gu set off for Shanghai to work as a coolie in an oil mill, and was joined by the rest of his family after the flood of 1921.

By contrast, the southern part of Subei was more commercially developed. From the turn of the twentieth century, rapid commercialization of cotton cultivation along the north bank of the Yangtze, centred on Nantong, benefited medium and small landlords and rich peasants, but the majority of peasants, with restricted access to land, became increasingly dependent on disguised forms of wage labour, such as labour rents, debt labour, sharecropping and female bondage. Outmigration from this area began on a substantial scale in the 1920s and 1930s. In 1940, Japanese investigators from the South Manchurian Railway Company who surveyed Touzongmiao, a village forty kilometres north of Nantong, were shocked by the indigence of the population. Forty per cent of farming families had one or more members hired out as agricultural labourers and 47.7% had one or more members working away from home seasonally or full-time. Outmigrants tended to come either from the wealthiest or the most impoverished families. Better-off families, mostly joint family households, opted to send males to work away in order to avoid dividing up land on inheritance, leaving women to handle farm work, whereas the poorest families did so in order to eliminate surplus labour and avoid land division. Most males from these poorer families settled in Shanghai where they worked as rickshaw pullers or porters. Few remitted money, unless they landed secure factory jobs, and many could not afford to return home at New Year.[89]

Jiangnan was altogether more prosperous, with wealthier landlords, a well-developed silk industry, a fertile agriculture and a reputation for civilized refinement. Tenancy rates were higher than in Subei, but rents were lower and security of tenure was greater. From the 1920s, however,

---

[88] Zhonggongdang shi renwu yanjiu hui (ed.), *Zhonggongdang shi renwu zhuan* [Biographies of Past Members of the Communist Party], vol. 9 (Xi'an: Shaanxi renmin chubanshe, 1983), p. 107. One mu equals 0.0667 of a hectare or about 0.165 of an acre.

[89] Kathy Le Mons Walker, *Chinese Modernity and the Peasant Path: Semicolonialism in the Northern Yangzi Delta* (Stanford: Stanford University Press 1999), pp. 216–19. The majority of rickshaw pullers in Shanghai, however, came from the northern parts of Subei. Zhu Bangxing, Hu Linge and Xu Sheng, *Shanghai chanye yu Shanghai zhigong* [Shanghai Labour and Shanghai Labour] (Shanghai: Shanghai renmin chubanshe, 1984; orig. 1939), p. 674.

conditions began to deteriorate.[90] In Wuxi county peasant households compensated for the small size of their landholdings by raising silkworms and engaging in other sideline occupations. Work became increasingly gendered, with women raising silkworms while men worked away for wages. Sericulture yielded slightly higher returns to land than rice or wheat cultivation, but much lower returns on labour. Peasants accepted the latter – along with the higher risks of sericulture – because the opportunity cost of female labour was very low. Even in this one county, however, there were significant differences between villages close to the urban core, which fared reasonably well, and those in remoter areas. A survey by the South Manchurian Railway Company in 1940 showed that in one village, 37 out of 80 households had one or more family members working permanently away from home. Most of these were male heads of household or eldest sons, and the largest number were employed in Shanghai. Most found work as skilled factory workers or as shop clerks, which suggests that the relatively high status of the area from which they came translated into better job opportunities in the city (a point discussed in chapter 1).[91]

The cultural pressure for migrants to maintain the link with their native place was intense. Most aspired to marry in, retire to and be buried in their native village. In 1926 the *China Year Book* commented: 'when the cost of living reaches a point where it does not pay a labourer to continue to work, he returns to his farm. Religious festivals, marriages, birthdays, funerals, illness of a parent, the desire to consult a local Chinese doctor or even a fortune-teller are still further causes for labourers leaving jobs.'[92] Nevertheless employers in Shanghai increasingly demanded a stable workforce, and in 1924 the Nanyang tobacco company discontinued the practice of allowing workers to take a month off each year to sweep their ancestors' graves.[93] In any case, it was not easy for very poor migrants to sustain economic ties with the village. In 1927–8, only 10% of 230 cotton-worker families in the Caojiadu district of the city sent money to rural relatives, although a survey of 100 worker families in Yangshupu district the following year showed that they sent

[90] Robert Ash, *Land Tenure in Pre-Revolutionary China: Kiangsu Province in the 1920s and 1930s* (London: Contemporary China Institute/SOAS, 1976), p. 40; David Faure, *The Rural Economy of Pre-Liberation China* (Hong Kong: Oxford University Press, 1989), pp. 168–72.

[91] Lynda S. Bell, *One Industry, Two Chinas: Silk Filatures and Peasant-Family Production in Wuxi County, 1865–1937* (Stanford: Stanford University Press, 1999), pp. 127–9.

[92] H. G. W. Woodhead (ed.) *China Year Book, 1926–27*, p. 912.

[93] Shanghai shehui kexueyuan jingji yanjiusuo (ed.), *Nanyang xiongdi yancao gongsi shiliao* [Historical Materials on Nanyang Bros. Tobacco Company] (Shanghai: Shanghai renmin chubanshe, 1958), p. 308.

an average of 4.7% of their income to parents in the countryside, a not inconsiderable sum.[94] The growing trend for wives to join their husbands in this city further weakened ties with the village. In 1927 thirty-four-year-old Shi Zhilin came from Yancheng in Subei to work as a rickshaw puller in Shanghai, leaving his wife to take care of the 13 mu of land which he and his four brothers had each inherited. In 1929 he explained: 'This year the famine in Jiangbei is extremely bad, so my wife has recently come with our [six] children to join me in Shanghai. Our land is farmed by my brothers to support my parents and to help with my brothers' expenses. I do not want the output of the land, but if my parents die I would take the land back.' His wife was fortunate enough to get a job at the Tongxing cotton mill where she earned $14 a month, his eldest son, aged fourteen, got a job as a cleaner in the mill, where he earned $10 a month, and his second son, aged twelve, got a job as a cleaner at the Yihe mill, where he earned $6 a month.[95] The tendency for migration to become permanent was reinforced by the onset of warlordism after 1916. In 1926, the *China Year Book* observed: 'Civil wars make returning to villages unattractive and dangerous. Increasingly, large numbers of workers are remaining in the cities more permanently and are coming more definitely under the influence of urbanization processes.'[96]

As in St Petersburg, it was young men who were the section of the rural population most likely to migrate. In 1925, there were 172 men for every 100 women in the Shanghai International Settlement.[97] The disparity was diminishing, however, and by 1930 women made up 41% of the city population.[98] Shanghai offered considerable employment opportunities to women in everything from prostitution, to domestic service, to work in the factory and retail sectors. It is impossible to estimate the number of prostitutes in the city, because so much of the trade was casual, but it may have reached as high as 100,000 by the 1930s, making it the largest source of female employment.[99] It was

---

[94] Simon Yang and L. K. Tao, *A Study of the Standard of Living of Working Families in Shanghai* (Peiping: Institute of Social Research, 1931), p. 77; Fang Fu-an, 'Shanghai Labour', part 1, *Chinese Economic Journal*, 7, 2 (1930), 883.

[95] Hanchao Lu, *Beyond the Neon Lights*, pp. 78–9, 84.

[96] H. G. W. Woodhead (ed.) *China Year Book, 1926–27*, p. 912.

[97] In the International Settlement the ratio of Chinese men to women (=100) was 226 in 1890, 175 in 1910, 160 in 1920, and 172 in 1925. In the French Concession the corresponding ratio was 197 in 1910, 173 in 1920, and 166 in 1925. Zou Yiren, *Jiu Shanghai renkou*, pp. 122–3.

[98] Zou Yiren, *Jiu Shanghai renkou*, p. 45.

[99] Gail Hershatter, 'The Hierarchy of Shanghai Prostitution, 1870–1949', *Modern China*, 15, 4 (1989), 463. The city directory in 1933 estimated the number of registered prostitutes at 50,000. *Shanghai shi zhinan*, 1933, pp. 150–1.

extremely difficult for a single woman to migrate by herself, so labour contractors played a bigger role in migration than in Russia, recruiting workers in villages where they had personal connections. In 1924, the Shanghai Child Labour Commission reported:

In some instances, contractors obtain young children from the country districts, paying the parents $2 a month for the services of each [girl] child. By employing such children in the mills and factories the contractor is able to make a profit of about $4 month in respect of each child. These children are frequently most miserably housed and fed. They receive no money and their conditions of life are practically those of slavery.[100]

This appears to be a description of the contract labour system in its full-blown form, known as *baoshenzhi*, which was limited at this stage to a number of Japanese cotton mills that were introducing a system pion-eered in Japan.[101] Under this system parents would sign a contract agreeing that their daughter's wages would go to the contractor for the duration of the contract, usually three years, in return for which they would be paid a sum of $30 to $40, and the contractor would undertake to provide housing, food and clothing for their daughter.[102] The system only became widespread in Shanghai from the late 1920s, mainly in cotton mills and silk filatures.[103] By 1932, it was reckoned there were 10,000 contract workers in Shanghai, a figure that had risen to 70,000 to 80,000 by 1937.[104]

The Growth of a Labour Movement

By 1917, the population of the Russian Empire had reached 182 million. Within European Russia, i.e. the empire west of the Urals, the urban population stood at 14.6% (17.5% if one adopts the definition of 'urban'

---

[100] H. G. W. Woodhead (ed.), *China Year Book, 1925* (Tientsin: North China Daily News, 1925), p. 548.

[101] Patricia Tsurumi, *Factory Girls: Women in the Thread Mills of Meiji Japan* (Princeton: Princeton University Press, 1990), p. 59.

[102] Deng Tai, *Shenghuo sumiao* [Sketches of Life] (Shanghai: Daxia shudian, 1937) p. 50; Sun Baoshan, 'Shanghai fangzhi chang zhong de baoshenzhi gongren' [Contract Workers in the Shanghai Textile Factories], *Huanian*, 1, 22 (1932), 431; Emily Honig, 'The Contract Labour System and Women Workers: Pre- Liberation Cotton Mills in Shanghai', *Modern China*, 9, 4 (1983), 421–54.

[103] E. O. Hauser, *Shanghai: City for Sale* (New York: Harcourt Brace, 1940), p. 138; D. K. Lieu, *Silk Industry of China* (Shanghai: Kelly and Walsh, 1941), p. 224.

[104] Sun Baoshan, 'Shanghai fangzhi chang', p. 431. Honig explains the expansion of the system as a lucrative racket of the Green Gang. See Emily Honig, *Sisters and Strangers, Women in the Shanghai Cotton Mill, 1919–49* (Stanford: Stanford University Press, 1986), p. 126.

used in the 1926 census). The waged workforce in the empire as a whole was close to 20 million, but of these only 3.5 million worked in factories and mines.[105] By 1917, well over a third of the workforce under the Factory Inspectorate, which had jurisdiction over two-thirds of enterprises, were women. In St Petersburg the waged workforce was diverse, including factory workers, workers in transportation, construction, the retail and service sectors and those in artisanal enterprises. Victoria Bonnell has calculated that at the turn of the century, 48% of the 312,633 workers in manufacturing in the city were artisans rather than factory workers.[106] These different types of worker did not necessarily share much in common in terms of working conditions and work experience. Those who spearheaded the creation of the labour movement in the period after 1906, when the government allowed limited rights to form trade unions, as in virtually all western labour movements, were skilled, relatively well-paid, literate males. Metalworkers, especially, who formed the largest sector of the factory workforce of the capital, were in the van of the strike movement and the labour movement. Yet if the propensity of different types of worker to participate in the labour and revolutionary movements was loosely determined by sociological criteria such as skill, literacy and gender, it proved possible for activists in 1917 to constitute the exploitation, poverty and hardship suffered by most workers into a discourse of class that brought workers of different backgrounds and experiences into a common struggle against the war, the employers and the Provisional Government.

From the 1870s, the Populists (*Narodniki*) sought to mobilize industrial workers – and not solely peasants – in the struggle to overthrow the tsarist government.[107] By the 1890s, 'circles' (*kruzhki*) of Social Democrats and Populists had put into circulation a discourse of socialism that was characterized by strident hostility to autocracy and 'arbitrariness' (*proizvol*), burning hatred of class exploitation, a passionate commitment to equality and social justice, and a utopian vision of a new society. Deborah Pearl has shown the richness of the forms of revolutionary propaganda utilized, which included pamphlets, brochures, legal and illegal literary fiction, fairy tales (*skazki*), poetry, songs, woodcuts and cartoons. During the 1905 Revolution, a significant layer

[105] Rashin, *Formirovanie*, p. 172.
[106] Victoria E. Bonnell, *Roots of Rebellion: Workers' Politics and Organizations in St. Petersburg and Moscow, 1900–1914* (Berkeley: University of California Press, 1983), p. 23.
[107] Johnson, *Peasant and Proletarian*, pp. 99–110; R. E. Zelnik, 'Populists and Workers: The First Encounter between Populist Students and Industrial Workers in St Petersburg, 1971–74', *Soviet Studies*, 24, 2 (1972), 251–69.

of workers came into contact with socialist ideas for the first time, and working-class consciousness began to develop.[108] Loyalty to the tsar eroded rapidly among the majority of workers, although a minority swung behind the reactionary Black Hundreds, whose influence, however, was waning by 1914.[109]

There was nothing intrinsically revolutionary about the Russian working class: it was the political context – the absence of civil and political rights and the perception that a despotic government was in cahoots with unscrupulous employers – that served to politicize economic discontent. Nevertheless this was sufficient to fuel a level of militancy that had few parallels in the working classes of other European countries. During the years 1905–6 and 1912–14, the peak periods of strike activity in Russia, the average annual proportion of strikers approached three-quarters of the entire factory labour force, a proportion unparalleled in western Europe or the USA. Many strikes, moreover, were classed by the authorities as 'political'. In 1912, in response to the massacre of workers in the Lena goldfields in Siberia, 63.9% of strikes were classified as 'political', a proportion that rose to two-thirds in the first half of 1914.[110] Much of this militancy was concentrated in the St Petersburg region. According to the statistics of the Factory Inspectorate, 40% of the nation's strikers were to be found in Petersburg province, although the province accounted for only one-tenth of workers under the Inspectorate in 1912–13. Metalworkers in Petersburg province, who comprised only 2.5% of the workforce subject to the Inspectorate, accounted for no less than 20% of the national total of strikers in 1912, for 25.5% in 1913 and for 32.6% in the first half of 1914.[111]

By 1914, Shanghai boasted a flourishing international and domestic trade, a growing manufacturing industry and the highest concentration of capital in China (it was the recipient of one-third of all foreign investment).[112] The city was one of the top half-dozen ports in the world in terms of tonnage, handling 40% of China's foreign trade by the 1920s.[113]

[108] Iu. I. Kir'ianov, *Perekhod k massovoi politicheskoi bor'be: rabochii klass nakanune pervoi rossiiskoi revoliutsii* (Moscow: Nauka, 1987), p. 119.

[109] O. S. Porshneva, *Mentalitet i sotsial'noe povedenie rabochikh, krest'ian i soldat Rossii v period mirovoi voiny (1914–1918gg.)* (Ekaterinburg: UrO RAN, 2000), p. 148.

[110] Leopold H. Haimson and Ronald Petrusha, 'Two Strike Waves in Imperial Russia (1905–07, 1912–14): A Quantitative Analysis', in Leopold Haimson and Charles Tilly (eds.), *Strikes, Wars and Revolutions in an International Perspective* (Cambridge: Cambridge University Press, 1989).

[111] Haimson and Brian, 'Changements démographiques', p. 782.

[112] Carl F. Remer, *A Study of Chinese Boycotts* (Baltimore: Johns Hopkins University Press, 1933), p. 111.

[113] *Chinese Economic Monthly*, 6 (March 1924), 2.

Although foreigners dominated the small manufacturing sector in the late-nineteenth century, Chinese entrepreneurs took advantage of the First World War to set up cotton, silk and flour factories. By the mid-1920s, textile production dominated the city's industry, although in the following decade the manufacture of machinery also made its mark. The number employed in modern industry grew rapidly into the early 1930s. In 1934 it was reckoned that the city's factory workforce stood at over 300,000, almost two-thirds of whom were women.[114] The makeup of the factory workforce was thus very different from that in St Petersburg – more female, less skilled, and less well paid. As in St Petersburg, however, a majority of migrants, at least of male migrants, found jobs not in the factory sector, but in construction and transportation – as dockers, shoulder carriers, pole carriers, flatcart-, handcart- and wheelbarrow-pushers or rickshaw pullers – or in the handicraft and retail sectors. By 1928, according to the careful estimates of Alain Roux, the regular waged workforce stood at about 600,000, of whom about half were in the modern sector.[115] The handicraft and retail sectors were much more vigorous than in St Petersburg, one index of this being the remarkable number of guilds in Shanghai, even compared with other Chinese cities: by 1936, there were 236 with a membership of 164,801.[116]

The first efforts at labour organization in Shanghai came during the 1911 revolution, when groupings, principally the Labour Party, responded to Sun Yat-sen's call to organize workers as part of the struggle to overthrow the Manchu dynasty and create a strong republic. A reformed Guomindang (GMD) revived these efforts during the May Fourth Movement of 1919, but it was only with the foundation of the CCP that modern labour unions, committed to improving the welfare of their members through industrial action, came into existence. During the early 1920s these struggled to survive in the inhospitable political and economic climate. A turning-point came with the May Thirtieth Movement of 1925 when up to 200,000 workers, backed by students, small traders and, more ambivalently, by the city's business community, displayed impressive tenacity during a general strike, targeted mainly at foreign companies, that lasted for more than three months. The Communist-controlled Shanghai General Labour Union (*Zonggonghui*) brilliantly exploited this opportunity to bring about the unionization of Shanghai's labour force. By 28 July 1925, it claimed to have 117 affiliated

---

[114] Cai Zhengya, 'Shanghai de laogong', *Shehui banyuekan*, 1, 11–12 (1934), 7.
[115] Alain Roux, 'Le mouvement ouvrier à Shanghai de 1928 à 1930.' Thèse à troisième cycle, Sorbonne (Paris, 1970), pp. 11, 45.
[116] Xin Ping, *Cong Shanghai faxian lishi*, p. 186.

unions with 218,859 members. Already, however, political tensions adumbrated the rupture of the first united front that was to come two years later. The Shanghai Federation of Syndicates (*Shanghai gongtuan lianhehui*), an anti-Communist labour organization, used its ties to the city's powerful secret societies to subvert the General Labour Union (GLU) from within. The latter nevertheless managed to maintain primacy in the labour movement, despite the effective failure of the May Thirtieth general strike. Between 1925 and 1927, the CCP in Shanghai harnessed the elemental power of workers' struggles into an organized anti-imperialist movement that embraced students, intellectuals, small traders and patriotic businessmen. In the second half of 1926, the rapid success of Chiang Kai-shek's Northern Expedition against the warlords of southern and central China led to a resurgence of the GLU in the city: by March 1927, it claimed a membership of 821,280. In that month, using the poorly armed pickets of the labour unions, the CCP succeeded in defeating the warlords who controlled the Chinese-administered areas of the city, prior to the arrival of Chiang Kai-shek's National Revolutionary Army, calculating that this would strengthen the influence of the left within the united front. By this stage, however, Chiang Kai-shek had had enough of the strikes and peasant rebellions that raged in the areas captured by the National Revolutionary Army, and on 12 April 1927 he used the city's largest secret society, the Green Gang, to crush the CCP and the GLU.

Despite the liquidation of its activists and organizational centres in summer 1927, the CCP in Shanghai, together with reformist elements of the GMD, managed to retain some influence among the city's workers until 1930. The so-called 'Nanjing decade' (1927–37), which saw Chiang Kai-shek establish an effective national government, saw the CC Clique of the GMD, backed by the Green Gang, impose tight control over labour circles. In the course of the White Terror of 1931–2, the CCP was all but wiped out, but it began to rebuild a base for itself in 1936–7 behind the façade of the national salvation movement, which clamoured for Chiang Kai-shek to end his policy of appeasing Japanese imperialism. Any limited progress the CCP made, however, was aborted in July 1937 when full-scale war with Japan broke out. Between 13 August and the end of November, nearly 200,000 people lost their lives in Shanghai, as the Japanese fought to take over the Chinese-administered areas. Over half of Chinese-owned industry in the city was destroyed in the following two years.[117] Between late 1937 and the end of

---

[117] William C. Kirby, 'The Chinese War Economy', in James Hsiung and Steven Levine (eds.), *China's Bitter Victory: War with Japan, 1937–1945* (Armonk NY: M. E. Sharpe, 1992), p. 185.

1941, Shanghai ceased to be at the forefront of national politics, becoming a 'lonely island' in a sea of occupied towns and villages. In December 1941, following the attack on Pearl Harbor, this phase came to an end, when the Japanese occupied the International Settlement. Until December 1939, labour organs loyal to the Nationalist government struggled against the Japanese but were then wiped out by the Japanese special services. With the establishment of Wang Jingwei's collaborationist government in May 1940, only pro-Japanese trade unions were tolerated in the city. The Communists, helped by patriotic secret-society bosses who were now deprived of GMD patronage, established an underground network that sought to subvert the collaborationist forces.[118] Despite very difficult conditions, workers, students and intellectuals in Shanghai made a significant contribution to transforming the New Fourth Army of the CCP from a guerrilla confederation into a modern army, some 10,000 joining it prior to 1941 and another 10,000 thereafter.[119]

In August 1945, Japan sued for peace. The GMD believed that victory gave it exclusive mandate to rule, but the Communists, in whose base areas in northern China some 95.5 million people were by this stage living, disagreed. They wished to see a coalition government and would not turn over troops and territories to a government that was little more than a revived version of Chiang Kai-shek's prewar regime. In April 1946, tensions between the CCP and the GMD came to a head, when large-scale fighting broke out in Manchuria. The ensuing civil war proved to be one of the biggest and most bitter wars of modern times. It saw the CCP expand its power through a combination of conventional and guerrilla warfare and radical social reform in the countryside. Urban support for the Communists, particularly among workers hit by unemployment and astronomical inflation, also rose significantly. In May 1949, Shanghai fell to the Communists, workers playing a relatively limited role that centred on protecting factories against retreating GMD forces. Contemporaries, however, noted a 'feeling of emancipation' (*fanshen gan*) in the ranks of labour, and during the first year of Communist rule Shanghai workers conducted a record number of strikes, slowdowns and occupations.[120]

---

[118] Elizabeth J. Perry, *Shanghai on Strike: the Politics of Chinese Labor* (Stanford: Stanford University Press, 1993), p. 109.

[119] Gregor Benton, 'Conclusion', in Feng Chongyi and Goodman (eds.), *North China at War*, p. 206.

[120] Mark W. Frazier, *The Making of the Chinese Industrial Workplace: State, Revolution and Labour Management* (Cambridge: Cambridge University Press, 2002), p. 101; Alun Falconer, *New China: Friend or Foe?* (London: Naldrett Press, 1950), p. 96.

Chapter 1 examines how migrants utilized social ties based on native place in the new urban-industrial environment and explores how native-place identities were reconfigured, as migrants looked back on their former lives with sentiments ranging from contempt to nostalgia. Chapter 2 explores how new discourses valorized the idea of the self and asks how far migrants came to see themselves as autonomous individuals through an analysis of tastes in reading, religious orientations and fashions in dress. Chapter 3 asks how far migrants developed new understandings of themselves as men and women, examining marriage and the family, the workplace and the trope of the 'new woman' as sites in which gender identities were reconfigured. Chapter 4 charts the development of national identity among migrants and explores its relationship to class identity, looking particularly at the ways in which war and revolution transformed that relationship. The first half of chapter 5 offers a more detailed comparison of the role played by workers in the two revolutions. The second half reflects on how Communist regimes came to terms with the identity transformations charted in the four central essays, indicating how the new regimes responded, positively and negatively, to those transformations, building on some, aborting others. More than the four preceding chapters, this final chapter stresses the limited nature of many of the transformations previously discussed – reasserting the atypicality of Shanghai and St Petersburg within their national contexts – by highlighting ways in which persisting 'tradition' reasserted itself as a factor shaping the evolution of Communist regimes.

1   Memories of Home: Native-place Identity in the City[1]

> It is rare for a peasant to remain a peasant and be able to move. He has no choice of locality. His place was given at the very moment of his conception. And so if he considers his village the centre of the world, it is not so much a question of parochialism as a phenomenological truth. His world has a centre (mine has not).   John Berger[2]

For the anthropologist James Clifford, the meaning of modernity is constituted by the experience of displacement and discontinuity.[3] For those peasants who migrated to St Petersburg and Shanghai the move away from the villages of their birth, hitherto the centre of their world, and arrival in the city forced them to reflect upon what it meant to be a peasant. Exposure to metropolitan modernity called into question migrants' identities as peasants, yet the experience of relocation to the city was mediated by social networks that peasants brought with them from the village. In both Russia and China, ties of kinship and native place were used by migrants to ease their interaction with strangers: they looked to fellow countrymen to help them find work and accommodation, and a paradoxical result was that, at least for first-generation immigrants, native-place identifications sharpened in the context of urban-industrial life. This chapter explores the nature of workers' identifications with the villages of their birth, the uses they made of native-place networks in negotiating the uncertainties of urban-industrial life, the discourses of town and countryside that helped make sense of the transition from

---

[1] Native-place identity is a somewhat clumsy locution, but it is preferable to 'regional' identity because, in the European context, the latter is often seen as representing a form of separation from the nation, a 'cultural expression of distinctiveness from the traditionally dominant majority in the exercise of power within the nation-state'. See 'Introduction' to Heinz-Gerhard Haupt, Michael G. Müller and Stuart Woolf (eds.), *Regional and National Identities in Europe in the XIXth and XXth Centuries* (The Hague: Kluwer Law International, 1998), p. 11.

[2] John Berger, 'The Storyteller', in Lloyd Spencer (ed. and intro.), *The Sense of Sight: Writings by John Berger* (New York: Pantheon Books, 1985), p. 18.

[3] James Clifford, *Routes: Travel and Translation in the Late Twentieth Century* (Cambridge MA: Harvard University Press, 1997).

37

one to the other, and the ways in which native-place sentiment was transfigured in the ferment of revolution.

The Chinese anthropologist Fei Xiaotong called native-place identity the 'projection of consanguinity into space'.[4] In China, native place and kinship were the most important bases on which social relations were constructed. One's *jiaxiang* was the place from whence one's ancestors came, albeit not necessarily one's actual place of birth, the place where one's family had its roots, and thus the place where one belonged and where one might hope to be buried. Numerous popular sayings capture the salience of native place to the Chinese sense of self: 'the soul returns to the native place'; 'to retire in glory to one's native place'; 'falling leaves return to their roots'; 'wine is better in one's native place, the moon is rounder in one's native place'.[5] Native place was a key basis upon which *guanxi*, the basic building block of social relations in China, could be constructed. Guanxi are ties of mutual obligation and dependency, and shared native place served as a basis upon which favours and protection could be elicited, social contacts expanded and social distance and hierarchy established.[6] A proverb states that 'one common ancestral village is worth three official seals', meaning that having a native-place connection with someone counts for far more than official authorization. In the urban-industrial context guanxi were vital in helping migrants to find jobs and accommodation and to access the resources at the disposal of regional guilds. These ties, though often instrumental in character, had an emotional component (*ganqing*) which served to deepen the psychic significance of native place for social identity.[7] Attachment to one's native place was a diffuse sentiment, strongest with regard to the village or town of one's family seat and progressively weaker the wider the geographical radius was extended beyond one's family seat; yet it was still palpable at provincial and even supra-provincial level. It represented a set of 'layered loyalties' that could extend from one's village right up to multi-provincial units, such

[4] Fei Xiaotong, *From the Soil: The Foundations of Chinese Society*. With an introduction and epilogue by Gary G. Hamilton and Wang Zheng (Berkeley: University of California Press, 1992), p. 31.

[5] Bryna Goodman, *Native Place, City and Nation: Regional Networks and Identities in Shanghai, 1853–1937* (Berkeley: University of California Press, 1995), pp. 4–46; Susan Naquin and Evelyn Rawski, *Chinese Society in the Eighteenth Century* (New Haven: Yale University Press, 1987), pp. 48–50.

[6] Susan Mann Jones and Philip Kuhn, 'Dynastic Decline and the Roots of Rebellion', in John King Fairbank (ed.), *Cambridge History of China*, vol. 10, part 1 (Cambridge: Cambridge University Press, 1978), p. 114.

[7] J. Bruce Jacobs, 'A Preliminary Model of Particularistic Ties in Chinese Political Alliances: Kan-Ch'ing and Kuan-Hsi in a Rural Taiwanese Township', *China Quarterly*, 78 (1979), 257.

as Guangdong-Guangxi, Hunan-Hubei, and Sichuan-Yunnan-Guizhou, conglomerated provinces that had once been administered under a single governor-general. The fact that native place could be defined at a number of levels made it of potentially great practical importance, allowing migrants expanding levels of affiliation as they travelled further afield.[8]

Russian peasants were also deeply attached to their *rodina*, or native place. Yet, perhaps surprisingly, given the vast expanse of the Russian Empire, cultural differentiation by region was much more limited than in China. A single, vast plain links European Russia to south-west Siberia without the high mountain ranges and great rivers that divide China into relatively defined and often isolated geographical and economic regions. Moreover, Russia's settled communities were far less ancient than China's. So although the Russian Empire contained a far bigger proportion of ethnic minorities than its Qing counterpart, there was nothing akin to the cultural and linguistic diversity among ethnic Russians that existed among the Han Chinese. That contrast registered, even between relatively proximate regions of Russia there were significant differences in dialect, farming practice, dress, music, dance, marriage, courtship and funerary customs which, combined with differences in local ecology and history, served as the basis on which native-place identities were forged. Dialects were replete with phrases that referred to the uniqueness of one's rodina, where 'birds sing differently and flowers bloom more brightly'.[9] Peasants ascribed especial value to what was *rodnoi*, i.e. native, preferring what was familiar and cherished to what was foreign and alien.[10] As in China, much value was placed on being laid to rest in one's native place, the word for 'foreign land' – *chuzhbina* – resonating with the wretchedness of dying and being buried away from one's native soil. Returning soldiers would thus bring earth from the battlefield home to bereaved families where it would eventually be mixed with the earth in the grave of the bereaved wife or mother.[11]

The act of migration sharpened awareness of native place as a dimension of social identity. Migrants to Shanghai discovered that millions of their fellow Han Chinese spoke incomprehensible dialects, ate different food, enjoyed their leisure in different ways, and practised

[8] Ambrose Yeo-chi King, 'Kuan-hsi and Network Building: A Sociological Interpretation', *Daedalus*, 120, 2 (1991), 69–70.

[9] Esther Kingston-Mann, 'Breaking the Silence: An Introduction', in Esther Kingston-Mann and T. Mixter (eds.), *Peasant Economy, Culture and Politics of European Russia, 1800–1921* (Princeton: Princeton University Press, 1992), p. 15.

[10] Kingston-Mann, 'Breaking', p. 16.

[11] Catherine Merridale, *Night of Stone: Death and Memory in Russia* (London: Granta, 2000), p. 47.

different marriage and funerary customs. And even after years of living in the city, many still tended to think of themselves as sojourners – for example, as 'Ningbo travellers to Shanghai' (*lü Hu Ningboren*) – people temporarily resident in the city until they could rejoin their ancestors.[12] One index of the pertinence of native place as a marker of social identity is the fact that most migrants to Shanghai married people from the same province: in 1927–8, among 230 cotton-worker families, 94.8% of men were married to women from the same province.[13] Heightened awareness of regional differences easily led to stereotyping of native place – or what might be considered 'sub-ethnic' – groupings. Cantonese and Ningboese immigrants enjoyed a high social standing in the hierarchy of native-place groupings, but both were perceived by others as clannish, doughty and hard to restrain.[14] Natives of Shanghai also enjoyed rather high status, being seen as urbane and flexible. By contrast, migrants from Subei were at the bottom of the pecking order. As explained in the Introduction, Subei was a large and heterogeneous region whose natives were far more attuned to differences between localities than to their common characteristics as inhabitants of the region north of the Yangtze river. Nevertheless, once in Shanghai, Subei migrants were seen as a relatively homogeneous group unified by their putative ignorance, rudeness and lack of sophistication.[15]

Native-place distinctions were never so sharply drawn in St Petersburg, although stereotyping of migrants by region of origin was not uncommon. Migrants from Pskov, for example, were heavily concentrated in unskilled jobs and had a reputation for violence, so tended to be seen similarly to those from Subei.[16] In the early 1890s, fights broke out regularly

[12] Frederic Wakeman and Wen-Hsin Yeh, 'Introduction', in Wakeman and Yeh (eds.), *Shanghai Sojourners* (Berkeley: Institute of East Asian Studies, 1992), p. 5; Goodman, *Native Place*, p. 5.

[13] Simon Yang and L. K. Tao, *A Study of the Standard of Living of Working Families in Shanghai* (Peiping: Institute of Social Research, 1931), p. 26.

[14] Wang Jingyu (ed.), *Zhongguo jindai jingji shi cankao ziliao congkan: Zhongguo jindai gongye shi ziliao* [Series of reference materials on the history of the modern Chinese economy: materials on the history of modern Chinese industry], vol. 2, part 2, (Beijing: Kexue chubanshe, 1957) p. 1267. See the remarks by Zhang Zhidong in 1895 in Sun Yutang (ed.), *Zhongguo jindai jingji shi cankao ziliao congkan: Zhongguo jindai gongye shi ziliao* [Series of reference materials on the history of the modern Chinese economy: materials on the history of modern Chinese industry], vol. 1 (Beijing: Kexue chubanshe, 1957), p. 1217; Wang Hongjiao, 'Shanghai minzhong xinli zhi tubian' [Sudden changes in the psychology of Shanghai people], *Xin Shanghai*, 5 (1925), 11–13.

[15] Emily Honig, 'Migrant Culture in Shanghai: In Search of Subei Identity', in Frederic E. Wakeman Jr and Wen-hsin Yeh (eds.), *Shanghai Sojourners* (Berkeley: Institute of East Asian Studies, 1992), pp. 239–65.

[16] Reginald E. Zelnik, *A Radical Worker in Tsarist Russia: The Autobiography of Semën Ivanovich Kanatchikov* (Stanford: Stanford University Press, 1986), p. 95. Compare the

at the Baltic Works between workers from Pskov and those from Riazan'; yet both shared a common dislike of workers from Novgorod.[17] However, the exiguous data on marriage patterns do not suggest the same social pressure as to marry fellow provincials in Shanghai. A study of marriage in the Vyborg district, the district of St Petersburg with the highest concentration of factory workers, suggests that there was only a moderately strong propensity for people to marry spouses from the same region, with 11.3% of men and 9.6% of women from Tver' marrying a spouse from the same township (volost'), and 17.9% of men and 17.1% of women from Pskov doing likewise. These percentages would be considerably higher if province rather than township were taken as the unit of aggregation. Nevertheless, the significance of this would be offset somewhat by the fact that within-group marriage correlates more with large than small groups, and workers from Tver' and Pskov constituted the largest native-place groupings among factory workers in St Petersburg.[18]

Native-place ties were of prime importance in organizing migration to Russia's cities. Peasants from the same village or township would often set off to find work in a group of a dozen or so men, headed by an elder (*starosta*) who would act on behalf of the group in negotiation with employers or those renting out lodgings. Such a work group was known as an artel, and such groups were common in industries that employed workers on a short-term basis, such as mining, construction, dock work or sugar manufacture.[19] By the twentieth century, however, they were not particularly common in St Petersburg's factories, since employers preferred to hire workers on an individual and permanent basis.[20] These artels were a simple form of *zemliachestvo*, or network based on native place, the root of the term deriving from the word *zemliak*, or a fellow countryman. Such networks supplied fellow countrymen with information about and introductions to jobs, help with accommodation,

---

'white-eyed fools' from Perm' or the 'big ears' from Iaroslavl'. Kingston-Mann and Mixter, *Peasant Economy*, pp. 15, 313.

[17] Memoirs of V. V. Fomin in E. A. Korol'chuk (ed.), *V nachale puti: vospominaniia peterburgskikh rabochikh, 1872–1897gg* (Leningrad: Lenizdat, 1975), p. 200.

[18] Evel Economakis and Robert J. Brym, 'Marriage and Militance in a Working-Class District of St Petersburg, 1896–1913', *Journal of Family History*, 20, 1 (1995), 23–43; Evel G. Economakis, *From Peasant to Petersburger* (Basingstoke: Macmillan, 1998), p. 186.

[19] Olga Crisp, 'Labour and Industrialization', in Peter Mathias and M. M. Postan (eds.), *The Cambridge Economic History of Europe*, vol. 7, part 2 (Cambridge: Cambridge University Press, 1978), pp. 377–8.

[20] Crisp, 'Labour and Industrialization', p. 377; U. A. Shuster, *Peterburgskie rabochie v 1905–07gg.* (Leningrad: Nauka, 1976), p. 41. For examples of subcontracting in St Petersburg factories, see S. A. Smith, 'Workers against Foremen in St Petersburg, 1905–1917', in Lewis H. Siegelbaum and Ronald Grigor Suny (eds.), *Making Workers Soviet: Power, Class and Identity* (Ithaca NY: Cornell University Press, 1994), p. 116.

social and possibly financial support. The worker Semyon Kanatchikov recalled: 'There were, of course, no labour exchanges in those days, but in spite of this we were very well informed about where workers were needed.'[21] Native-place networks also kept the village informed about the progress of individual migrants. 'I have seen all my friends and neighbours', wrote one peasant-worker to his wife, 'and all seemed in good health. Everyone greets you. The only one I did not see was Petr Petrov, but I hear that he has returned to the village for the winter.'[22]

Much migration in Russia was short-term or seasonal in nature, but sojourns away from the village could be the prelude to permanent emigration. Ivan Sergeevich Kruglov, later a Bolshevik activist in the Baltic Fleet, was born in 1886 in the village of Novozastolb'e in Tver' province. At the age of fourteen, he began a number of short-term migrations in search of earnings to support his widowed mother. First, he went to Moscow where he worked as a peddler, selling everything from soaked peas and tripe to wooden toys, but he was regularly beaten by rogues who stole his wares, and when this happened he would be flogged by the wholesaler for whom he worked. Subsequently, he found a job in the paint shop of the Tula arms works, but he was sacked with eleven others after one of their number daubed 'For Land and Freedom' in green paint on one of the carriages. At the age of seventeen, he bade farewell to his mother in order to start a new life in the capital:

Looking at me, my mother said: 'Take care of yourself. You children are my only joy.' I looked at her hands, dry and hardened through unremitting work, and thought of how I would help her, make her happy with the kopecks I would earn ... But what if I should not find work in Piter? What would I do then? It would be bitter and shameful to return to the village ... With these thoughts I left my native village. As was our custom, we sat down for a while before I set off. As I got up, my mother wiped her tears and blessed me.[23]

One may note that although Kruglov represents the separation from his mother as a highly charged moment, his decision to leave the village is a voluntary one and is constructed in the autobiography as a new beginning, the transition to a new social identity. It is typical of Russian worker autobiographies, most of which were composed after 1917 according to a narrative that constructs the early life as a transition from

---

[21] Zelnik, *Radical Worker*, p. 64.
[22] Cited in Jeffrey Burds, 'The Social Control of Peasant Labor in Russia: The Responses of Village Communities to Labor Migration in the Central Industrial Region, 1861–1905', in Esther Kingston-Mann and Timothy R. Mixter (eds.), *Peasant Economy, Culture and Politics in European Russia, 1800–1921* (Princeton: Princeton University Press, 1991), p. 94.
[23] I. Kruglov, *Nezabyvaemye gody* (Moscow: Moskovskii rabochii, 1970), p. 15.

peasant to proletarian. By contrast, according to Mary-Jo Haynes, in the autobiographies of German and French workers the moment of leaving home is constructed as one that was forced on the reluctant memoirist by poverty and this serves to convey a sense of continuity of social identity.[24]

We know little about the use that women made of native-place ties or about the significance of native place for their identities, since in neither Russia nor China did many female workers write autobiographies. In Russia a woman could not leave her village without her husband's permission, and she could only get a passport if he had fulfilled his obligations to the commune. Even when the passport laws were liberalized in 1906, a married woman still needed the consent of her husband to leave the village and an unmarried woman the consent of her relatives.[25] These legal obstacles were a key reason why women tended to migrate as individuals rather than as members of an artel. Some single women did form arteli, but they were seldom involved in more elaborate native-place networks.[26] Barbara Engel has hypothesized that in migrating as individuals, women may have been more exposed than men to cultural modernization.[27] But this may be to accept too uncritically the claim in the existing historiography that zemliachestva tended to shield male migrants from cultural change. In Shanghai, if a male migrant succeeded in settling in the city, his wife and children were likely to follow him, but it was much harder for single women to leave their villages by themselves than it was in Russia.

In China for a single woman even to be seen in public was to invite scandalous speculation about her moral character. This was one reason why putting one's daughter in the hands of a labour contractor was so appealing. At the same time, parents sometimes placed their daughters in the hands of labour contractors, knowing that they would be set to work as prostitutes.[28] By the 1930s, women also set off for Shanghai by themselves to work as silk reelers when the new cocoons arrived in

[24] Mary-Jo Haynes, 'Leaving Home in Metaphor and Practice: The Roads to Social Mobility and Political Militancy', in Frans van Poppel, Michel Oris and James Lee (eds.), *The Road to Independence: Leaving Home in Western and Eastern Societies, 16th to 20th Centuries* (Bern: Peter Lang, 2004), pp. 315–38.

[25] Mandakina Arora, 'Boundaries, Transgressions, Limits: Peasant Women and Gender Roles in Tver' Province, 1861–1914', Duke University PhD, 1995, p. 99.

[26] Rose Glickman, *Russian Factory Women: Workplace and Society, 1880–1914* (Berkeley: University of California Press, 1984), p. 5.

[27] Barbara Alpern Engel, *Between the Fields and the City: Women, Work and Family in Russia, 1861–1914* (Cambridge: Cambridge University Press, 1994), p. 99.

[28] Gail Hershatter, 'The Hierarchy of Shanghai Prostitution, 1870–1949', *Modern China*, 15, 4 (1989), 477.

spring. An investigation of the Hengtong cotton mill in 1952 showed that nearly half of 357 married women had husbands and children living outside Shanghai.[29] We can only speculate as to the impact of permanent or seasonal migration for women's identifications with native place. Chinese women were used to leaving their natal home upon marriage and to moving to another village to live under the roof of their in-laws. Reflecting on this in her essay 'A Night of Insomnia' (1937), the writer Xiao Hong contended that women were in permanent exile: 'It always comes down to the same thing: either riding a donkey and journeying to an alien place, or staying put in other people's homes. I am not keen on the idea of homeland.'[30] How far this reflected the attitudes of ordinary women, of course, is impossible to say.

The mounting wave of migrants to the Russian capital led to severe overcrowding, unsanitary living conditions and sky-high rents. On average 3.2 persons lived in a single-room apartment and 3.4 in a cellar, twice the average for Berlin, Vienna or Paris.[31] In the decade up to 1914, rents rose by 30%, and then doubled or trebled during the First World War.[32] Fellow countrymen thus shared accommodation often in conditions of hideous congestion. In 1879, aged nine, A. G. Boldyreva began work in a St Petersburg cotton mill, having been brought by her parents, along with her elder brother, from the village of Kinoviia in Tver' province. The family lived with seven other textile-worker families, a total of thirty people in all, in one large room. Each family had a bed, a small cupboard on which they ate their meals, and a bench. All came from two counties of Tver' province and on holidays they would dress in their local costume and dance to the concertina.[33] Similarly, P. Timofeev lived with seventeen fellow countrymen in a room infested with cockroaches and bedbugs. Eleven members of the artel were married but had left their wives in the village: one had not seen his wife for five years. Nevertheless, according to Timofeev, 'native-place ties linked

[29] Shiling Zhao McQuaid, 'Shanghai Labour: Gender, Politics and Traditions in the Making of the Chinese Working Class, 1911–49', Queen's University, Kingston, Ontario, PhD, 1995, p. 117.

[30] Quoted in Lydia Liu, 'The Female Body and Nationalist Discourse: *The Field of Life and Death* Revisited', in Inderpal Grewal and Caren Kaplan (eds.), *Scattered Hegemonies: Postmodernity and Transnational Feminist Practices* (Minneapolis: University of Minnesota Press, 1994), p. 47.

[31] S. N. Semanov, *Peterburgskie rabochie nakanune pervoi russkoi revoliutsii* (Moscow: Nauka, 1966), p. 152.

[32] S. A. Smith, *Red Petrograd: Revolution in the Factories, 1917–18* (Cambridge University Press, Cambridge 1983), p. 14.

[33] Memoirs of V. V. Fomin, *V nachale puti*, pp. 249–51; P. F. Kudelli (ed.), 1905, *Vospominaniia chlenov Sankt-Peterburgskogo Soveta Rabochikh Deputatov* (Leningrad: Priboi, 1926).

them into one family, and they put up with a lot for its sake. One member had to rise each day at 3am in order to get to work.'[34]

Shanghai was even more densely populated than St Petersburg. The eastern and western districts of the International Settlement, where most of the city's factories were situated, had population densities of up to 40,000 people per square kilometre, but this paled in comparison with that of the central district, where levels of 60,000 to 70,000 people per square kilometre were quite common.[35] As a result of the fearsome pressure on land, Shanghai also had the highest rent levels of any city in China. In 1921 it was said that rents had doubled during the preceding five years.[36] As in St Petersburg, native-place networks came to structure residential patterns. Of the two high-status native-place groupings, Ningbo sojourners tended to live in the north of the city and in the French Concession, while Cantonese lived in the south or in Hongkou.[37] Better-off migrants lived in 'alleyway houses', known as *lilong*, built in rows separated by alleys, with several rows surrounded by a wall to form a compound. A house usually consisted of two or three storeys each with a couple of rooms. A couple of reasonably well-off families might share a house, but it was common to sublet rooms to lodgers and indeed to other families, with the result that whole families might be huddled into a room eight to ten feet wide.[38] Single men were less likely to live collectively than in Russia, many lodging with families or in privately run hostels and dormitories.[39] About 60,000 cotton workers lived in company barracks, mainly belonging to foreign cotton mills, and these were relatively fortunate. But again – and quite against company regulations – it was common for those lucky enough to qualify for company accommodation to sublet it to fellow provincials, leading to appalling congestion.[40]

---

[34] P. Timofeev, *Chem zhivet zavodskii rabochii* (St Petersburg: Russkoe bogatstvo 1906), p. 16.

[35] Zou Yiren, *Jiu Shanghai renkou bianqian de yanjiu* [Research on Population Change in Old Shanghai] (Shanghai: Shanghai renmin chubanshe 1980), p. 23.

[36] *North China Herald*, 26 November 1921, p. 551.

[37] Goodman, *Native Place*, p. 16; *Zhonggong zhongyang wenjian xuanji* [Selected Materials of the Central Committee of the CCP], vol. 1 (Beijing: Zhonggong zhongyang dangxiao chubanshe, 1989), p. 260.

[38] *North China Herald*, 17 March 1923, p. 748; *North China Herald*, 12 December 1925, p. 482; Hanchao Lu, *Beyond the Neon Lights: Everyday Shanghai in the Early Twentieth Century* (Berkeley: University of California Press, 1999), pp. 110–16.

[39] *North China Herald*, 17 March 1923, p. 749.

[40] *Shanghai fangzhi gongren yundong shi* [The History of the Labour Movement among Shanghai Textileworkers] (Beijing: Zhonggong dangshi chubanshe, 1991), p. 52; The Japanese Gongda mill owned 110 houses intended to house eight persons each, but fifteen lived in each house on average. The Shanghai Cotton Company had ten two-storey blocks with a total of 107 rooms, each intended for eight people, but there were fifteen persons per room on average. *Di yici Zhongguo laodong nianjian* [The First

St Petersburg had its noisome slums, but there was nothing quite comparable to the shanty towns that sprang up along the boundary of the foreign settlements in Shanghai. Shanghai's shantytowns were a prototype for the favelas, barrios and bidonvilles that were to become such a feature of twentieth-century urban life in the underdeveloped world. By 1926, it was estimated that 200,000 to 300,000 coolies and factory workers lived in the city's shanty towns.[41] The best of these were the 'villages' along the canal banks close to where many of the factories and wharves were situated. Dwellings here had bamboo or reed walls and tiled roofs, and some even had wooden floors. In addition, the villages boasted teahouses, food shops, barbers, fortune-tellers, beggars and dogs. In one such village in Yangshupu district, each family consisted of 5.8 persons on average, with 2.4 to a room.[42] Worse were the shanty towns along the banks of Suzhou creek and in Pudong, where houses consisted of simple mud huts, with straw thatch and mud floors. One of the largest was at Yaoshui Lane where, by the 1930s, 5,000 straw huts provided shelter to around 10,000 rickshaw pullers, coolies, peddlers and workers from the Nagai Wata Kaisha (NWK) mills, most of them migrants from Subei and Hubei.[43] Yet even they were better off than those who lived on derelict boats covered by a reed mat.

Native-place ties were critical in structuring the job market, albeit less so in Russia than China. Migrants to St Petersburg from Iaroslavl' province worked mainly as traders, restaurant- and inn-workers, tailors, market gardeners, stove-setters and plasterers, those from Rostovskii county (*uezd*), for instance, monopolizing the transportation of vegetables and herbs to the capital. By contrast, those from Tver' province were concentrated in much less lucrative sectors of the job market. In the words of a zemstvo correspondent in 1894, 'Peasants from Tver' work as yardmen, coachmen, floorwashers, servants, ragpickers, garbagemen etc . . . They drive cockroaches from kitchens.'[44] 'In the business

Chinese Labour Year Book], part 3 (Beijing: Beiping shehui diaochabu, 1928), p. 3; *Shanghai fangzhi*, p. 52. In Petrograd in 1918 only 7% of workers lived in barracks or on factory premises. Z. V. Stepanov, *Rabochie Petrograda v period podgotovki I provedeniia oktiabr'skogo vooruzhennogo vosstaniia* (Moscow: Nauka, 1965), p. 59.

[41] *North China Herald*, 7 July 1926, p. 256; Hanchao Lu, *Beyond the Neon Lights*, pp. 16–31.

[42] H. D. Lamson, 'The Problem of Housing for Workers in China', *Chinese Economic Journal*, 11, 2 (1932), 144–5.

[43] *Shanghai penghu qu de bianqian* [Changes in the Shanty Districts of Shanghai] (Shanghai: Shanghai renmin chubanshe, 1965), pp. 9–16; Zhu Bangxing, Hu Linge and Xu Sheng, *Shanghai chanye yu Shanghai zhigong* [Shanghai Industry and Shanghai Labour] (Shanghai: Shanghai renmin chubanshe, 1984; orig.1939), p. 82; Lamson, 'The Problem of Housing', p. 148.

[44] Evel G. Economakis, 'Patterns of Migration and Settlement in Pre-revolutionary St Petersburg: Peasants from Iaroslavl and Tver Provinces', *Russian Review*, 56 (1997), 14–15; Engel, *Between the Fields*, p. 69.

of finding a job', K. Norinskii recalled, 'many of my countrymen were very useful. Although I did not know them personally, they had been acquainted with my grandfather or grandmother or were related in some way. They tried to help me in every way.'[45] One consequence was that it was fairly common to find workers from the same area working in the same section of a factory. In 1903, 28% of workers at the Baltic Works hailed from Tver′, and almost everyone in the boat-building shop came from Staritskii county in that province, the same county as the shop foreman. In 1917, some 70 to 80 workers in the carpentry shop were said to be relatives or zemliaki of the foreman. At the Triangle Works the largest group of workers came from Vasil′evskii county in Tver′.[46] Following the February Revolution, factory committees expelled foremen who had discriminated against those who were not their cronies or fellow countrymen. In Shanghai, by contrast hiring on the basis of personal ties was entirely taken for granted and never become a political issue.

In Shanghai segmentation of the job market by native place was much more entrenched than in St Petersburg, particular native-place groupings, known as *bang*, monopolizing particular trades and jobs. Migrants from Canton and Ningbo, the earliest to arrive in Shanghai, controlled entry into some of the most prestigious trades. Cantonese workers commandeered jobs as carpenters, mechanics and ironsmiths in the foreign-owned shipbuilding and ship-repair yards.[47] From the last quarter of the century, however, their monopoly was challenged by workers from Ningbo.[48] At the other end of the job market, women from Subei found themselves consigned to the least skilled and most arduous jobs in the silk filatures and cotton mills, particularly those owned by Japanese, or to jobs as washerwomen, menders of clothes, peddlers and scavengers.[49] Men from Subei found jobs as rickshaw pullers – a survey of 304 rickshaw pullers in 1934 showed that 96% came from Subei – dockworkers, barbers, bathhouse attendants, cobblers, night-soil collectors and garbage collectors.[50] Emily Honig suggests that fleeing from

[45] K. Norinskii, 'Moi vospominaniia', in *Ot gruppy Blagoeva k 'Soiuzu Bor'by'*, *1886–1894* (Rostov-na-Donu: Gos. izd-vo, Donskoe otdelenie, 1921), p. 24.

[46] Tsentral′nyi gosudarstvennyi istoricheskii arkhiv Sankt-Peterburga, f. 416, op. 5, d. 27, ll. 709.

[47] *Jiangnan zaochuanchang changshi, 1865–1949*, *5-yue* [The Long History of the Jiangnan Arsenal, 1865 to May 1949] (Nanjing: Jiangsu renmin chubanshe, 1983), p. 86.

[48] Elizabeth J. Perry, *Shanghai on Strike: The Politics of Chinese Labour* (Stanford: Stanford University Press, 1993), pp. 19–24; *Shanghai minzu jiqi gongye* [Shanghai's National Machine Industry], vol. 1 (Beijing: Zhongguo shehui kexueyuan, 1966), p. 15.

[49] Emily Honig, 'The Politics of Prejudice: Subei People in Republican-Era Shanghai', *Modern China*, 15, 3 (1989), 252; *Chinese Economic Journal*, 3, 5 (1928), 907.

[50] 'Shanghai shi renli chefu shenghuo zhuangkuang diaocha baogao shu' [Report on the living conditions of rickshaw pullers in Shanghai], *Shehui banyuekan*, 1, 1 (1934), 105.

destitution, and lacking powerful patrons in the business elite, Subei migrants had little choice but to accept the worst jobs on offer. Thereafter they became associated with lowly jobs and found entry into more prestigious sectors of the job market blocked to them.[51] Factory jobs were particularly coveted in Shanghai and were less in the gift of the native-place bangs, but they still depended on personal ties. Of fourteen who found jobs in the Rong company factories between 1916 and 1922, seven got their jobs via relatives, two via fellow countrymen and four via friends or mediators.[52] Zhuo Xi came to Shanghai in search of work after he lost his job in a hardware store in Nanjing following the 'Second Revolution' of 1913. Initially, he had no luck and soon spent his savings of $30. He then fell ill, but was fortunate while in hospital to meet a fellow countryman, a mill foreman, who fixed him up with a job.[53] A woman worker in east Shanghai turned to a fellow provincial in a glass factory after she lost her job. 'I'll take you to a family that will give you board and lodging', he promised. 'If you lodge with them, they will be able to recommend you for a job. If you can find some way to raise some money give four dollars to the head of the family and he will take a present to the foreman or interpreter on your behalf ... If you can't raise four dollars, two will do, though it won't be as effective.'[54]

Chinese employers, in contrast to their foreign counterparts in Shanghai, liked to hire workers according to place of origin, at least when setting up their businesses. Bao Xiamen, a founder of the Commercial Press, recruited workers from his home district of Ningbo, while his co-founder, Xia Ruifeng, recruited from Qingpu near Shanghai.[55] Mu Ouchu, founder of the Deda cotton mill in 1914, recruited peasants and fishermen from his native Pudong district, and when Rong Zongjing took over the mill in 1925 he recruited from his Wuxi fellow countrymen.[56] Hiring on the

---

[51] Emily Honig, 'Native-Place Hierarchy and Labour Market Segmentation: The Case of Subei People in Shanghai', in Thomas G. Rawski and Lillian M. Li (eds.), *Chinese History in Economic Perspective* (Berkeley: University of California Press, 1992), pp. 274–5; 291.

[52] *Rongjia qiye shiliao* [Historical Materials on the Rong Family Enterprises] vol. 1, 1896–1937 (Shanghai: Shanghai renmin chubanshe, 1980), pp. 119–21.

[53] Shanghai shehui kexueyuan lishi yanjiusuo (ed.), *Wusa yundong shiliao* [Historical Materials on the May Thirtieth Movement], vol. 1 (Shanghai: Shanghai renmin chubanshe, 1981), p. 231.

[54] Deng Tai, *Shenghuo sumiao* [Sketches of Life] (Shanghai: Daxia shudian, 1937), p. 49.

[55] *Shanghai shangwu yinshuguan zhigong yundongshi* [The History of the Labour Movement at the Shanghai Commercial Press] (Beijing: Zhonggongdang shi chubanshe, 1991), p. 15.

[56] *Shanghai di sanshiyi mianfangzhi chang gongren yundong shi* [A History of the Labour Movement in the Shanghai No. 31 Textile Mill] (Beijing: Zhonggongdang shi, 1991), pp. 19–20.

basis of native place tended to strengthen workers' identification with their employers, and encouraged a form of industrial relations that emphasized the protective role of the employer and the loyalty of the worker. Not surprisingly, some employers did not scruple to exploit rivalry between native-place groupings. In September 1911, Cantonese ship carpenters went on strike to raise their daily rate from $0.75 to $0.9, but the men from Ningbo, normally employed to do less skilled carpentry at a rate of $0.6 per day, agreed to do the strikers' jobs at the existing rate.[57]

Dreams of the City, Dreams of the Village

Native-place identities are sometimes dubbed 'primordial', insofar as they are presumed to have an ineffable quality that springs from the givens of kinship and contiguity.[58] In reality, they are as socially and culturally constructed as any other form of identity. In both St Petersburg and Shanghai the meaning of native place, together with the hopes and expectations that motivated the decision to leave one's native place, were powerfully shaped by old and new discourses of town and countryside. In Russia, compared with China and western Europe, cities remained underdeveloped at least until the eighteenth century and, arguably, until the 1860s when rapid urbanization took off, and when the cultural gulf between village and city grew perceptibly. Discourses of city and countryside were broadly consonant with those in Europe, rooted in a grid of mutually dependent dichotomies, which depicted the village as dark, quiet, slow, close to nature, traditional, backward and communal, and the city as bright, noisy, fast, a site of culture, progress, individual advancement but also individual alienation. A rapidly burgeoning commercial press did much to foster an image of the city in late-nineteenth-century Russia, one characterized, above all, by ambivalence. In the vivid words of Mark Steinberg:

Journalists and others ... portrayed the physical and social landscapes of cities as at once desirable sites of opportunity and vitality and disturbing places marked by cold indifference, greed, exploitation, immorality and suffering. The press was filled with stories about a range of troubling (but also alluring) phenomena of modern life in Russia: nightclubs and cabarets, prostitution, and suicide, the defiant anti-morality of 'hooligans', bizarre murders, vitriol-throwing women, clever swindles, car races, fires, accidents and scandals of all sorts.[59]

---

[57] Wang Jingyu (ed.), *Zhongguo jindai jingji shi*, p. 1267.

[58] Clifford Geertz, 'The Integrative Revolution', in C. Geertz, *Old Societies and New States* (New York: Free Press of Glencoe, 1963).

[59] Mark D. Steinberg, *Voices of Revolution, 1917*. Documents translated by Marian Schwartz (New Haven: Yale University Press, 2001), p. 45.

The secular and ecclesiastical authorities in Russia took a dim view of the moral consequences of migration. A village priest from Vladimir complained: 'Migration to the factory exerts a corrupting influence on the workers and their families. A departing youth, lacking supervision by family elders and having a steady flow of money and free time, does not concern himself with the household, and gets into habits of undesirable vice, debauchery and loss of morality, and indifference to religion.'[60] More alarmingly, the authorities were convinced that the decline in morality induced by city life was spreading to the countryside. In a discourse that counterposed the degenerate city to the once-healthy village, they claimed that returning migrants were bringing with them criminality, sexual immorality, fecklessness and a lack of respect for authority.[61] Peasants themselves often saw the factory and the city (not, of course, synonymous) in the same way, i.e. as a source of moral contamination. In July 1906 the denizens of Turei village in Luzhskii county in Petersburg province declared: 'Our children have to work for wages in Piter (i.e. St Petersburg), and since they are untrained for any craft they earn but a little, just sufficient to keep themselves fed but not to help their families. But Piter ruins them. They return home ill and corrupt and unfitted for farming.'[62] Concern about moral decline focused especially on the growing minority of young women who left the village to work as domestic servants and factory workers in the capital. According to a peasant from Novgorod: 'Going into the wide world (*v liudiakh*) a girl often falls, in spite of herself ... A man finds a way to seduce her. He uses money or presents or other things.'[63] In the city, it was felt, women lost the characteristics most prized in a rural spouse: modesty, sobriety, industriousness and compliance. According to a witness in a divorce case, a marriage had failed because the wife had developed a 'free and lively character' while working in a factory and had thus been unable to settle down once she returned to the village to live with her in-laws.[64]

---

[60] Cited in Burds, 'Social Control', p. 61. Even Lenin could write in 1923: 'Under capitalism the town introduced political, economic, moral, physical etc. corruption into the countryside.' V. I. Lenin, 'Pages from a Diary', *Selected Works* (London: Lawrence and Wishart, 1969), p. 688.

[61] Stephen Frank, 'Confronting the Domestic Other: Rural Popular Culture and its Enemies in Fin-de-Siecle Russia', in Stephen Frank and Mark D. Steinberg (eds.), *Cultures in Flux: Lower-Class Values, Practices and Resistance in Late-Imperial Russia* (Princeton: Princeton University Press, 1994), p. 76.

[62] L. T. Senchakova, *Prigorovy i nakazy rossiiskogo kres'tianstva, 1905–1907gg.* (Moscow: RAN, 1994), p. 126.

[63] Barbara Alpern Engel, 'Russian Peasant Views of City Life, 1861–1914', *Slavic Review*, 52, 3 (1993), 450.

[64] Engel, 'Russian Peasant Views', p. 450.

In China, the gulf between town and countryside was much narrower than in Russia, villages, marketing centres, towns and cities of different sizes being integrated into common marketing and administrative hierarchies.[65] One consequence was that the assumption that life in the city was self-evidently superior to life in the village or small rural town was historically absent. Yet by the second half of the nineteenth century, Shanghai was increasingly represented in conservative discourse as a city different from traditional cities, one that had turned its back on Confucian values in favour of the pursuit of money, a place where there was an unhealthy cult of novelty, with predictable consequences for morality and public order.[66] For conservatives, Shanghai challenged what it meant to be Chinese, threatening the dissolution of social bonds and responsibilities. Rural folk talked of the city in the same register, as a 'big dye jar' (*da ran gang*) where, if a young person became tainted by the dye, they would never be able to wash it off.[67] By the twentieth century, this negative image of the city was frequently paired with a revitalized quasi-daoist image of the countryside as the repository of eternal values. Yi Jiayue, for example, a progressive advocate of the modern family, claimed that it was in the national character (*minxing*) to shun the cities. 'Almost all the beautiful virtues of the human race can be found in the countryside: honesty, trustworthiness, affability, modesty, frugality, contentment.'[68]

By the 1920s, positive images of Shanghai were in the ascendant, the city coming to symbolize self-advancement, freedom and enlightenment. Women in Suzhou were said to dream of standing on a hotel balcony in Shanghai, watching the busy street life below them, while men were said to dream of riding around the city in a motor car.[69] A folksong declared:

> A country girl wants to imitate the manners of Shanghai/
> Desperately trying with all her strength, she still cannot do it/
> Ah! Now she is a little bit closer/
> But fashions in Shanghai have already changed.[70]

---

[65] William G. Skinner, 'Introduction', in William G. Skinner (ed.), *The Chinese City in Late Imperial China* (Stanford: Stanford University Press, 1977), pp. 253–73. Rozman offers a different view of China as having a 'bottom-heavy' urban hierarchy in which middle-ranking urban centres were missing. Gilbert Rozman, *Urban Networks in Ch'ing China and Tokugawa Japan* (Princeton: Princeton University Press, 1976).

[66] Shen Bojing (ed.), *Shanghai shi zhinan* [Guidebook to Shanghai] (Shanghai: Zhonghua shudian, 1933), pp. 140–1.

[67] Perry Link, *Mandarin Ducks and Butterflies: Popular Fiction in Early Twentieth-Century China* (Berkeley: University of California Press, 1981), p. 227.

[68] Yi Jiayue, 'Zhongguo dushi wenti' [The Question of China's Cities], *Minduo zazhi*, 4:1, 1923. Cited in Susan Mann, 'Urbanization and Historical Change in China', *Modern China*, 10, 1 (1984), 97.

[69] *Xin Shanghai*, 1, 6 (1925), 77–82.

[70] Hanchao Lu, *Beyond the Neon Lights*, pp. 7–8. Translation slightly altered.

Returning migrants and labour contractors regaled countryfolk with stories of skyscrapers, double-decker buses, good food and stylish clothes. In a moving story, written in 1936 to denounce the contract labour system, the novelist Xia Yan – later a vice-minister of culture in the PRC – described how a contractor used words that 'would turn rice straw into gold' to persuade rural parents to let their daughters go to work in Shanghai, promising that they would be given well-paying jobs, the chance to learn a skill, meat and fish to eat, a western-style house to live in, and a day off each week to see the foreign wonders of the city.[71] Women contract workers would later claim to have been duped by such enticing words. 'I'm from Subei. I lived in a village as a child ... We were very poor. When I was thirteen, a labour contractor from Shanghai came to our village to recruit children as contract workers. He said: "Shanghai is a wonderful place. You can eat good rice as well as fish and meat. You can live in a western-style house and make money." '[72] Another recalled: 'At this time, Froggy Zhou, who was a [secret-society] boss in Shanghai, came back to the village. He had been a small-time hustler for a long time and his persuasive style had enabled him to swindle many people. Seeing that my family was in difficult circumstances, he spoke to my parents about taking me to a textile mill in Shanghai. Once I got to Shanghai, he said, everything would work out fine. I would be happy, living in a foreign-style house along the Wusong river, eating good food and wearing stylish clothes.'[73] Even if women contract workers found the reality of life in Shanghai a shattering of illusions, such illusions nevertheless served to shape the meaning of migration for them.

If we should not ascribe too much importance to the 'sales pitch' delivered by a labour contractor to credulous and poverty-stricken parents, it reminds us that even among those reluctant to leave the village, the move to the city was coloured by hopes of a better life. Even allowing for the fact that he was writing as a class-conscious Bolshevik in the Soviet era, Kanatchikov's recollection of himself as a fifteen-year-old desperate to leave his village strikes an authentic note: 'My life was becoming unbearable. I wanted to rid myself of the monotony of village life as quickly as possible, to free myself from my father's despotism and tutelage and begin to live a self-reliant, independent life.'[74] He recalled the day he arrived in the city:

---

[71] Xia Yan, *Baoshengong* [Contract Labour] (Beijing: Gongren chubanshe, 1959).

[72] Cited in Perry, *Shanghai on Strike*, p. 56.

[73] Cited in Ono Kazuko, *Chinese Women in a Century of Revolution, 1850–1950* (Stanford: Stanford University Press, 1989), p. 115.

[74] Zelnik, *Radical Worker*, p. 6.

I remember what a stunning impression Moscow made on me. My father and I, sitting in our cart, walked our grey horse along the brightly lit streets. Huge multi-storied houses – most of them with lighted windows – stores, shops, taverns, beer halls, horse-drawn carriages going by, a horse-drawn tram – and all around us crowds of bustling people, rushing to unknown destinations for unknown reasons. I was not even able to read the signboards. What struck me most was the abundance of stores and shops.[75]

Migrants themselves had an investment in promoting a positive vision of the city among the folk back home. Letters to relatives were designed to reassure them that one had landed on one's feet and also perhaps to reassure oneself that the move to the city had been worthwhile. Visits home to the village were designed to reinforce that impression. One could not go back to see relatives and fellow countrymen without taking gifts and without dressing well, and Timofeev recalls that this deterred many from returning to their village:

You had to have decent clothes to go back to the village, otherwise people would say, 'Look! They live in the city and dress worse than beggars'. Here we get by somehow, they said, but in the village you have to show off. Then you have to take everyone a present: a dress for your mother, a jacket for your sister-in-law, a shawl for your mother-in-law and shoes for the kids. On top of that, as soon as you arrive, everyone tries to get drinks out of you. They know that no one comes to the village broke.[76]

Those for whom migration was a painful failure were, of course, unlikely to return home: they simply dropped out of sight.

Arriving in the city with unrealistic expectations of making good could easily engender bitter disillusionment. A. M. Buiko, who arrived in St Petersburg in 1897 to join his father, recalled. 'For a long time the city crushed me with its size, noise, traffic and mass of people. In my native village I knew everyone by sight, but in a city crowd there was nothing to say to people who were unknown and indifferent. Each person went about his business, always hurrying somewhere. In this human mass I, a village youth, often felt dreadful. I have not forgotten that feeling.'[77] The family of Fedor Samoilov moved back to their Tver' village, even though they had sold off their land and house with the intention of relocating to St Petersburg for good:

Life in the city became ever more onerous for us: a semi-starvation diet and arduous conditions of factory labour sapped our strength; the stuffy, dusty, stinking

[75] Zelnik, *Radical Worker*, p. 7.
[76] P. Timofeev, 'What the Factory Worker Lives By', in Victoria E. Bonnell, *The Russian Worker: Life and Labour under the Tsarist Regime* (Berkeley: University of California Press, 1983), pp. 83–4.
[77] A. M. Buiko, *Put' rabochego: zapiski starogo bol'shevika* (Moscow: Staryi Bol'shevik, 1934), pp. 9–10.

streets of the working-class quarter in which we lived caused melancholy. More and more often, our family began to reminisce about the village. The worst was forgotten, only the good things stayed sharp in our memory. ... When they had had their fill of proletarian life, my father, mother and two younger brothers set off back to the countryside. I remained alone in the city. With what joy I would have gone back with them to the village about which I so often reminisced. But I well knew that it was impossible for the family to survive on that little plot of land without outside earnings, so I had no alternative but to stay. On holidays and every Sunday, however, I went back to the village. This wasn't easy, since it was over forty kilometres there and back. Yet I still felt alone and half-strange in the town and factory.[78]

One frequent cause of disillusion was that those who had appeared adventurous in the village discovered that in the city they were perceived as slow-witted bumpkins. Kanatchikov recalls: 'Awkward, sluggish, with long hair that had been cut under a round bowl, wearing heavy boots with horseshoes, I was a typical village youth. The skilled workers looked down upon me with scorn, pinched me by the ear, pulled my hair, called me "green country bumpkin" and other insulting names.'[79] In Shanghai countryfolk were treated with similar condescension, often called names that suggested they were thickheads, such as electric pole (*dianxian mutou*), roof tile (*wa laoweng*), block of wood (*A mulin*), or clod of earth (*A tusheng*) or rural hicks, such as 'Pig Head Three' (*zhutou san*) or 'Old Redneck' (*chilao*).[80] Wang Xueyang, arriving in the city from a remote corner of Shandong province and speaking a thick patois, joked that even Subei folk were city-slickers compared with himself. Whenever he boarded a bus, he was instantly aware how unfashionable he looked in his thick camel-hair clothes. At the same time, he was repelled by the desire of city folk to impress, by their need to show off.[81] In China the 'hick from the sticks' spawned a whole entertainment genre in the form of a two-man comic routine, known as *xiangsheng*.[82] In his analysis of the genre, Perry Link shows that although laughter is always at the expense of the bumpkin, thereby allowing the listener or reader to feel superior, the portrayal is not without sympathy in that it highlights the purity and

---

[78] F. N. Samoilov, *Po sledam minuvshego* (Moscow: Gospolitizdat, 1954), pp. 36–7.

[79] Zelnik, *Radical Worker*, p. 8. See also A. Frolov, *Probuzhdenie: vospominaniia riadego rabochego* (Kiev: Gosizdat Ukrainy, 1923), p. 47.

[80] Shen Bojing (ed.), *Shanghai shi zhinan*, p. 143. On 'chawbacons, clods, hobnails and swains' in England, see A. Howkins, 'From Hodge to Lob: Reconstructing the English Farm Labourer, 1870–1914', in M. Chase and I. Dyck (eds.), *Living and Learning: Essays in Honour of J.F.C. Harrison* (Aldershot: Scolar, 1996), pp. 218–35.

[81] Wang Xueying, 'Wo zhi Shanghai tan', *Xin Shanghai*, 7 (1925), 95, 97–8.

[82] Perry Link, 'The Genie and the Lamp: Revolutionary *Xiangsheng*', in Bonnie S. McDougall (ed.), *Popular Chinese Literature and Performing Arts in the People's Republic of China, 1949–79* (Berkeley: University of California Press, 1984), pp. 83–111.

simplicity of country people. Peasants are seen as frank and honest (*laoshi*), in contrast to dissembling and dishonest townsfolk.[83]

Migrants could feel nostalgia for the village long after they had settled in the city. A. Buzinov remembers how his father would reminisce about the countryside when he was drunk:

My father was a hammer-man in the forge of the Semiannikovskii works. He was a man of enormous strength but he was gloomy and reticent by nature. Only on payday, when he came home tipsy, would he break his usual silence, vodka loosening his tongue. All evening until late at night he would joke with my mother, say things to her that were not clear to me, sing songs or tell me something about his native village, which was somewhere in El'ninskii county in Smolensk province. According to him it was quite different there from Nevskaia Zastava district of St Petersburg, but quite how, he himself did not seem to know too well. He couldn't even say with certainty whether he had relatives or acquaintances there. But this did not stop him solemnly promising us that he would take us there for the whole summer. That was his dream, cherished but unrealizable. And in his sober state he never mentioned it. Only when he was tipsy did he believe in the possibility of tearing through the stone walls of the city for a brief time and living the freedom of the fields and forests. But he had left the village as a youth and his long sojourn in the city meant that he had cut all ties with those who remained there. But somewhere in the depth of his soul he preserved the memory of the open spaces of the countryside and felt a vague urge towards them.[84]

The sentiments are conventional, but no less sincere for that. They touch a chord in the Russian psyche: a yearning for freedom (*volia*) that can be found only in Russia's vast plains and forests.

Within Russian marxist discourse the countryside was portrayed in an overwhelmingly negative light, and migrants who acquired an identity as 'conscious' workers (see next chapter) tended to subscribe to the view of the village as a sink of backwardness, measuring their level of 'consciousness' by the cultural and emotional distance they managed to put between themselves and their rural origins. Ivan Babushkin, the son of poor peasants in Vologda province who was destined to become a protégé of Lenin, came to the city when he was fifteen. Writing at the ripe age of 29, he boasted that he had completely forgotten his former life as a 'peasant ploughman'.[85] N. I. Shevliakov, born in 1892 in Verkhnii

[83] Link, *Mandarin Ducks*, p. 228.
[84] A. Buzinov, *Za Nevskoi Zastavoi* (Moscow: 1930), p. 11.
[85] Reginald E. Zelnik, 'On the Eve: Histories and Identities of Some Revolutionary Workers, 1870–1905', in Lewis H.Siegelbaum and Ronald Grigor Suny (eds.), *Making Workers Soviet: Power, Class and Identity* (Ithaca NY: Cornell University Press, 1994), p. 63. At the same age of twenty-nine, having been in the city for twelve years, the poet Sergei Esenin wrote in a poem about his return in 1924 to his native village – 'Vozvrashchenie na rodinu': 'How unfamiliar this place was to me'.

Momon in Bogucharskii county in Voronezh, became a platoon commander in the Soviet border police, and in summer 1924 went back to his native village 'to defend the ruling class from the attacks of unconscious muzhiki': 'I have not had any contact with the countryside for about five years and I had forgotten much. The chief thing to say is that our village lags so much behind life that anyone who lives for any time in the town finds it impossibly hard to reconcile himself to the old habits of rural life that are still fully preserved.'[86] Even a drink-sodden labourer, very far from the ideal-typical 'conscious' worker, could tell a female social investigator in the 1920s that the countryside was all 'mewing and howling' (*tol'ko miaun da revun*).[87] Though, occasionally, proletarian writers might conjure up an rural arcadia as a topos through which to explore the alienation of city life, migrants who became class-conscious, socialist workers generally were proud to claim that they had shaken the village dust from their feet.[88]

Chinese Communist discourse was much less antipathetic to the countryside than its Russian counterpart. In 1919, Li Dazhao, a professor at Beijing University who was to become a founder member of the CCP a year later, wrote an essay entitled 'Youth and the Countryside'. In his opening gambit, he dismissed the countryside as 'extremely dark' and country folk as 'foolish and ignorant of any means of protecting themselves', but then switched tack:

Listen to me, young friends adrift in the cities! You should know that there is much crime in the cities, whereas there is great contentment in the villages. You should know that life in the city is more or less the life of a ghost, whereas the work going on in the villages is the work of people. You should know that the air of the city is foul whereas the air of the village is pure. Why don't you just pack up your things, settle your expenses and go back to your native soil?[89]

Yet when leftist intellectuals did move in significant numbers to the villages in the 1930s, they were appalled by the grinding poverty, backwardness, and ignorance of rural life.[90] In the course of the 1930s, however, the CCP began to embrace the countryside as the 'cradle of the revolution' and to represent it as a site of authentic Chinese values, a foil

---

[86] Tsetral'nyi gosudarstvennyi arkhiv istoriko-politicheskikh dokumentov Sankt-Peterburga, f. 16, op. 9, d. 9800, l. 18.

[87] E. O. Kabo, *Ocherki rabochego byta* (Moscow: Knigoizd-vo VTsSPS, 1928), p. 30.

[88] Mark D. Steinberg, *Proletarian Imagination: Self, Modernity and the Sacred in Russia, 1910–1925* (Ithaca NY: Cornell University Press, 2002), pp. 153–8.

[89] Li Dazhao 'Qingnian yu nongcun' , *Li Dazhao xuanji* [Selected Works of Li Dazhao] (Beijing: Renmin chubanshe, 1959).

[90] Chang-tai Hung, *War and Popular Culture* (Berkeley: University of California Press, 1994), p. 280.

to the degeneracy and political inconstancy of the semi-westernized coastal cities. The shift was never completely shorn of ambivalence, for even as the countryside became the 'cradle of the revolution', it remained a bastion of 'feudalism' which it was the task of the revolution to overturn. Conversely, Communist representations of Shanghai became steadily more negative over time, though they, too, remained ambivalent. Shanghai continued to symbolize the proletariat and modern industry and commerce. Yet when the Communists seized the city in May 1949, a Communist newspaper declared: 'Shanghai is a non-productive city. It is a parasitic city. It is a criminal city. It is a refugee city. It is the paradise of adventurers.'[91]

The policies practised by the Bolsheviks towards the peasantry may well have sprung from the generally more negative attitudes expressed by Russian marxists towards the village. By contrast, attitudes towards the peasantry within the CCP were softer, even before the exodus into the countryside, and this may reflect the cultural tradition in which town and countryside had never been sharply counterposed. It is hard to find in the memoirs of workers in Shanghai the same unequivocal condemnation of the narrowness and backwardness of village life that became a staple of Russian workers' memoirs in the Soviet era.

In different ways, then, the discourses of city and countryside that circulated in Russia and China served to shape migrants' responses to the experience of displacement and their attitudes towards their native place. That said, in neither country were migrant responses monolithic. Attitudes ranged from enthusiastic embrace of urban life to profound alienation from it; from bitter antipathy towards rural life to an aching nostalgia for their place of birth. The firmest generalization one can make is that the decision to settle in the city shattered what John Berger called the 'phenomenological truth' that the village formed the core of the migrant's sense of identity.

The Politics of Native Place

In Russia and China most marxist leaders looked on native-place identity with suspicion, seeing it as a narrow and parochial form of consciousness that threatened to sow division in the ranks of labour. Yet it is clear that in the context of revolutionary mobilization, workers saw the special bonds of intimacy derived from 'spatial consanguinity' as ones around which it made eminent sense to organize. Native-place

---

[91] Cited in Jonathan Spence, *The Search for Modern China* (New York: Norton, 1990), p. 518.

organization was not generally an expression of desire to separate from the wider imagined communities of class or nation, but rather of a desire to work with one's fellow countrymen in the city and in the village to ensure that they played their rightful part in the larger struggles for socialism and national liberation.

James White first drew the attention of historians to the significance of *zemliachestva* in the Russian labour movement, but concluded that they 'were highly conservative bodies which insulated their members from the industrial environment and so prevented their entering it completely as urban workers, conscious of workers' interests and their common cause with all other workers outside as well as inside the *zemliachestvo*'.[92] In a similar way, but in a different register, Robert Kaiser, reflecting on the underdevelopment of Russian national identity, echoed the view that native-place sentiment was intrinsically parochial and therefore at odds with the larger imagined community of the nation: 'zemliachestva impeded the process of national consolidation'.[93] At first sight, these judgments have a certain plausibility, inasmuch as zemliak ties were indeed parochial in character and served to perpetuate forms of peasant culture in the urban-industrial environment. Yet despite a tendency for native-place groupings to dominate certain niches within the labour market, in Russia there is little evidence that native place served to divide workers in the same way that it did in China. The evidence of the strike movement, for example – which is too lengthy to review here – does not suggest that loyalty to one's fellow countrymen prevented workers from participating in collective action with workers from other provinces against employers and the tsarist autocracy.

In late-imperial Russia, zemliak ties, though an expression of deep-rooted attachment to native place, were generally used in a highly instrumental fashion, to ease the entry of migrants into the urban-industrial environment or as a means of coping with a political situation in which the government suppressed the efforts to create independent civic and political organizations. Zemliachestva had first emerged among university students in the late nineteenth century since, as relatively apolitical social and welfare organizations, they were one of the few forms of civic association tolerated by the authorities.[94] From early on, revolutionaries made

---

[92] James D. White, 'The Sormovo-Nikolaev Zemlyachestvo in the February Revolution', *Soviet Studies*, 31, 4 (1979), 482.

[93] Robert J. Kaiser, *The Geography of Nationalism in Russia and the USSR* (Princeton: Princeton University Press, 1994), p. 61.

[94] From the 1850s, zemliachestva were created in virtually all institutions of higher education, and students joined them despite their being formally banned. Most pursued the goals of mutual economic aid and 'moral education', but their major purpose was

use of zemliachestva since, as informal networks that operated through personal contact and on the basis of mutual trust, they were barely visible to the police who otherwise relentlessly monitored the activities of labour movement and socialist organizers. In 1875, Aleksandr Osipov, a twenty-four-year-old weaver at the Kozhevnikov mill in St Petersburg, was convicted of sending 'books of seditious content' to an artel of fellow countrymen at the mill in Kreenholm.[95] During the First World War, workers who came to work in the capital from the Sormovo works in Nizhnii Novgorod and from the Naval' shipyard in Nikolaev in Ukraine used their zemliak ties to keep intact the underground networks of the Social Democrats in the city, which was now renamed Petrograd.[96]

Following the February Revolution, civic organizations could be organized freely for the first time, and among the organizations that workers and soldiers in Petrograd chose to set up were ones based on native place. These were often set up with assistance from Socialist Revolutionaries (SRs), the party with the closest links to the peasantry. Judged against soviets, factory committees, trade unions and soldiers' committees, the zemliachestva were never more than a minor element in the revolutionary movement. Nevertheless by September 1917, there were twenty zemliachestva in Petrograd based on individual provinces, thirty-three based on individual counties, and nineteen based on individual volosts, and they were reckoned to have a total membership of at least 30,000. The main function of these organizations was to send agitators and propaganda to the village in order to raise the political consciousness of fellow countrymen back home. Commonly, a zemliachestvo would ask its members to donate a day's pay so that leaflets could be produced – to explain the significance of the Constituent Assembly, for example – or a subscription be taken out to the Bolshevik newspaper, *Derevenskaia Pravda*, which was targeted at rural readers, for one's fellow countrymen back in the village.[97] The presence of large

companionship rather than material help. By the 1890s there were about fifty in St Petersburg, each having about thirty members on average, though some having more than one hundred. In 1907–8, there were 134 in St Petersburg University alone, and they enjoyed a strong revival in 1906–14. Most assiduously avoided any hint of political involvement. Samuel D. Kassow, *Students, Professors and the State in Tsarist Russia* (Berkeley: University of California Press, 1989), pp. 77–87, 134.

[95] Reginald E. Zelnik, *Law and Disorder on the Narova River: the Kreenholm Strike of 1872* (Berkeley: University of California Press, 1995), p. 202. In 1883–4, the Perm' student zemliachestvo was used as a front by the nascent marxist Liberation of Labour group. *Ocherki istorii Leningradskoi organizatsii KPSS*, tom 1, 1883–1917 (Leningrad: Leninizdat, 1980), pp. 29, 34.

[96] White, 'Sormovo-Nikolaev'.

[97] T. Trenogova, *Bor'ba petrogradskikh bol'shevikov za krest'ianstvo v 1917g.* (Leningrad: Leningradskoe gazetno-zhurnal'noe i knizhnoe izd-vo 1946), p. 91.

numbers of soldiers in the capital, along with tens of thousands of migrants who had only arrived there since the outbreak of the war, meant that identities were fluid and a reflection of this was that zemliachestva defined their constituents in different ways. That of Bel'skii county in Smolensk, for example, addressed its members at the Putilov shipyard as 'comrade peasants' and summoned them to 'discuss peasant needs', whereas the zemliachestvo of Sychevksii county in the same province addressed its members at the Rozenkrants engineering works as 'workers' and referred to their zemliaki in the countryside as 'workers and the peasant poor'.[98] Such softening of divisions between workers and peasants may have been encouraged by the SRs, since it fitted their belief that workers and peasants were destined to play an equal role in building socialism, but all socialist parties were active to some degree within the zemliachestva. The Bolshevik fraction in the Smolensk zemliachestvo, for example, called on workers from Smolensk to denote a day's pay to finance the rural activities of the Bolshevik organization in Smolensk province.[99]

Despite party conflict and despite lack of consensus concerning the nature of the target audience, the existence of dozens of small zemliachestva, each representing zemliaki in a fairly narrowly defined locality, did not inhibit identification with the broader aspirations of the working class and the popular masses. A Central Bureau of Zemliachestva was formed, in which the SRs enjoyed substantial but not overwhelming influence, in order to 'unite the proletariat and the semi-proletarian peasant masses in joint defence of their political rights and to satisfy the economic and educational needs of the countryside'.[100] In October 1917, it organized a conference to unify the zemliachestva in Petrograd into a single organization. This agreed that the tasks were to raise the political awareness of the 'dark and ignorant' people and to organize the supply of industrial manufactures to the peasants in exchange for grain.[101] Nothing came of this: for in the course of the winter, the soldiers of the Petrograd garrison dispersed as war came to an end and workers began to flee the capital to escape unemployment and food shortages. As a consequence, the zemliachestva disappeared. Their

---

[98] Michael C. Hickey, 'Urban *Zemliachestva* and Rural Revolution: Petrograd and the Smolensk Countryside in 1917', *The Soviet and Post-Soviet Review*, 23, 2 (1996), 148.
[99] *Derevenskaia Bednota*, 19 October 1917, p. 4.
[100] A. S. Smirnov, 'Zemliacheskie organizatsii rabochikh i soldat v 1917g.', *Istoricheskie zapiski*, 60 (1957), 105; Trenogova, *Bor'ba*, p. 78; Michael Melancon, 'Soldiers, Peasant-Soldiers, and Peasant-Workers and their Organizations in Petrograd: Ground-Level Revolution during the Early Months of 1917', *The Soviet and Post-Soviet Review*, 23, 2 (1996), 188.
[101] *Derevenskaia bednota*, 12 October 1917, p. 4; 13 October 1917, p. 3.

significance in the Russian Revolution, therefore, should not be exaggerated: they were short-lived organizations that did not compare in strength with such organizations as soviets or factory committees. Nevertheless, they testify to the desire of workers and soldiers to bond with those from the same province or county not as an expression of separatism, but rather as a way of ensuring that one's fellow countrymen played their part in the larger struggles against war, the Provisional Government and for socialism. This was the nearest that Russia ever came to realizing Lenin's vision of a union of the proletariat and poor peasantry: after October 1917, a chasm would open up between the two classes.

In China, native-place identities were far stronger than in Russia and proved to be a far more substantial impediment to working-class unity. Moreover, native-place divisions ran deeper in Shanghai than in other Chinese cities. As we have seen, these derived, in part, from competition for jobs between regionally based groups of workers and, in part, from language barriers among Shanghai immigrants. Subei migrants, for example, spoke variants of the Yangzhou dialect which had no connection to Shanghai dialect, which itself was a cognate of the Wu dialect spoken throughout Jiangnan. Interestingly, although Shanghai dialect did slowly establish itself as a lingua franca, it was a variant of Subei dialect that was used in the Shanghai docks in the 1930s, reflecting the preponderance of Subei migrants in this low-paid and casual sector of the job market.[102] The CCP was forced from the first to confront the problems posed by language barriers. When Li Qihan pleaded with Shanghai seamen not to act as strikebreakers during the Hong Kong strike of 1922, he spoke to his audience in his native Hunan dialect and his words were translated into Ningbo dialect, the most common dialect among Shanghai seamen.[103] Later, Li Lisan, another Communist from Hunan, would try to address worker meetings in Shanghai dialect but apparently his accent and poor command of the dialect meant that his words were largely incomprehensible to his audience.[104] At times, the early CCP despaired of ever building a labour movement in Shanghai. 'The bangs are each dissimilar; there is no common feeling; they often jostle one another and forget their common enemy, the capitalist class.'[105]

---

[102] Zhang Zhongli (ed.), *Jindai Shanghai chengshi yanjiu* [Research on the City of Shanghai in the Modern Period] (Shanghai: Shanghai renmin chubanshe, 1990), p. 731.
[103] National Archive (UK): FO 228/3527/111, Consul-General, Sir E. Fraser, to Minister, Sir Beilby Alston, 10 February 1922.
[104] Liu Guanzhi, 'Guanyu 1924–1925 nian Shanghai gongren yundong de huiyu', *Zhongguo yundong shiliao*, 1 (1960), 61.
[105] *Gongchandang*, 7 July 1921, p. 58.

Even when workers from different regions were not in direct competition for jobs, they tended to mistrust one another. Workers, for example, were keen to ensure that workplace supervisors came from the same region as themselves. In June 1926, in the carding room of the NWK No. 4 cotton mill, women from Subei went on strike when a woman from Anhui province was appointed assistant forewoman. Together with men from the region, they set fire to the cotton on the machines and, when police arrived, turned fire hoses on them and showered them with missiles. Fourteen arrests were made. The Subei workers, who appear to have been in the majority, claimed that the workers from other regions had 'entered into some sort of alliance against them'.[106] In March 1927, at the Chinese-owned Shenxin No. 5 mill Hang Weizhi, a twenty-five-year-old activist from Wuxi, beat up the foreman of the fly-frame room after he prevented the workers in his shop from joining a strike. The foreman, who was Hunanese, appealed for support to his fellow provincials among the workers, claiming that the strikers' slogan was 'Beat those from Hunan, but not those from your own province.'[107] Yet if such divisions constituted a serious obstacle to working-class unity, the strength of parochial solidarities could fuel powerful industrial militancy on a sectional basis, i.e. among particular native-place groupings.[108] Occasionally, moreover, when the advantages of cooperation against a third party outweighed differences of interest, alliances could be forged across native-place boundaries.[109] Significantly, in the general strikes of 1919, 1925 and spring 1927 native-place divisions did not prevent class-based collective action. This tends to bear out Gregor Benton's observation – in the very different context of the Chinese diaspora – that associating with clanspeople is not an instinctive reflex but a strategic choice made or not made on the basis of calculation of interest.[110]

---

[106] *North China Herald*, 26 June 1926, p. 584.

[107] *Shanghai di sanshiyi mianfangzhi*, p. 58.

[108] Perry, *Shanghai on Strike*, p. 29. One notes that ties to native place could sometimes help workers to sustain strikes. During the May Thirtieth general strike of 1925 the association of Anhui workers in Shanghai reported that 20,000 unemployed workers, two-thirds from Hefei, had asked for help in buying a boat ticket home. The association appealed to the Beijing government for financial assistance, saying that they 'loved their province and their country' and were ready to fight to regain national honour. *Wusa yundong he Xianggang bagong* [The May Thirtieth Movement and the Hong Kong Strike] (Nanjing: Jiangsu guji chubanshe, 1985), pp. 142–3; Liu Mingkui, *Zhongguo gongren jieji lishi zhuangkuang, 1840–1949*, vol. 1 (Beijing: 1985), pp. 169–70.

[109] For a discussion of strikes and native-place divisions in Shanghai, see S. A. Smith, *Like Cattle and Horses: Nationalism and Labor in Shanghai, 1895–1927* (Durham NC: Duke University Press, 2002), pp. 80–91.

[110] Gregor Benton, *Chinese Migrants and Internationalism: Forgotten Histories, 1917–1945* (London: Routledge, 2007), pp. 117–18.

From the beginning of the twentieth century, students returning from study in Japan, supported by a small number of workers, reacted against the conservative and socially exclusive merchant-dominated regional guilds (*huiguan*) by forming more inclusive and more publicly involved native-place organizations, known as *tongxianghui*.[111] The first of these was formed during the anti-US boycott of 1905, as an offshoot of the Ningbo regional guild; it was renamed the Ningbo tongxianghui in February 1911. By 1925, there were 31 such organizations in Shanghai, not counting three that were open only to merchants.[112] The tong-xianghui were broader in their membership than the huiguan (although they often relied on the latter for funding and for meeting rooms), and their members elected the directors of the organization. Whereas a key concern of the huiguan was to ensure that the coffins of deceased fellow provincials were consigned for burial to their native place, the tong-xianghui took on a wider range of welfare, educational and business functions, leading one 1925 book to observe: 'Huiguan exist for the dead, tongxianghui exist for the living.'[113] Importantly, the tongxianghui were more involved in political affairs, committed to strengthening native-place sentiment (*lianluo xiangyi*) as part of the process of building the nation. Though socially less exclusive than the regional guilds, the tongxianghui nevertheless tended to discriminate against lower-class fellow countrymen by requiring letters of introduction and annual membership fees, something few workers could afford.[114] In 1923, there were only 234 workers (28 of them cooks) among the members of the Wuxi tongxianghui, compared with 5,325 who were engaged in commerce. In 1933, only 19% of the 6,362 members of the Pudong tong-xianghui were workers. And the following year, only 41 members of the Chaozhou tongxianghui were workers, compared with 1,631 engaged in commerce, 100 students and professionals, and 7 employed in govern-ment or the army.[115]

Working people nevertheless viewed these native-place organizations as ones to which they could turn for support and material assistance. Chen, a worker at the Tongmeng mill who had scabbed during the general strike of February 1927, was arrested by Chiang Kai-shek's

---

[111] In his classic study Ping-ti Ho argued that the growth of regional guilds was evidence of increased inter-regional social and economic integration rather than of local particularism. He Bingdi, *Zhongguo huiguan shi lun* [An Historical Survey of Landsmannschaften in China] (Taibei: Taiwan xuesheng shuju, 1966).

[112] Goodman, *Native Place*, pp. 91, 102; *Shanghai zhinan* [Guide to Shanghai] (Shanghai: Shangwu yinshuguan, 1925), pp. 19–26.

[113] Xiong Yuzhi (ed.), *Shanghai tongshi: Minguo shehui* (General History of Shanghai: Republican Society), vol. 9 (Shanghai: Shanghai renmin chubanshe, 1999), p. 208.

[114] Goodman, *Native Place*, p. 83.   [115] *Shanghai tongshi*, vol. 9, p. 211.

special services bureau after his workmates circulated a mendacious rumour to the effect that he was a Communist. His wife sent a letter to the Shaoxing seven-county tongxianghui (*Shaoxing qixian lü Hu tongxianghui*) asking it to intercede on her husband's behalf, which it agreed to do.[116] Similarly, the Ning-Shao tongxianghui interceded on behalf of shop-owner Luan Lianfang in 1929, when he was seized by the Changzhou bang, led by Xu Efang, following his refusal to hand over one of his employees to the bang. In a letter to the Shaoxing seven-county tongxianghui, the Ning-Shao tongxianghui explained that although Xu claimed to be acting on behalf of the labour union, he was in fact a bad person who had once blocked an increase in workers' wages and that he was considered an opportunist by the GMD. The Shaoxing tongxianghui agreed to write to the magistrate of Wuxi county, stating that the accusations against Luan were false.[117] In 1937, following the outbreak of war with Japan, employees of the Taigu shipping company asked the Shaoxing tongxianghui to intervene with their employer to prevent job cuts.[118] At this time, the tongxianghui was active organizing relief for refugees, arranging for destitute fellow countrymen to return to their villages, and expanding primary and secondary education for the children of fellow countrymen.[119] These examples suggest that workers expected the tongxianghui, dominated though they were by the wealthier members of their native-place community, to act in support of fellow countrymen, regardless of their social status.

In the early 1920s, there were sporadic efforts by groups of workers to establish native-place organizations specifically to represent working people. In October 1921, the Anhui Workers Autonomy Society (*zizhihui*, a name that resonates with the contemporary federalist demand for provincial autonomy) was set up after an Anhui worker at the NWK company was killed by another worker.[120] Similar organizations were formed by workers from Zhejiang, Hunan, Hubei, Jiangxi, Wentai, Subei and Guangdong.[121] Only a tiny minority of workers – even within a given native-place constituency – joined these organizations, so they remained very much on the fringes of the labour movement. In 1924, the Guangdong workers' union, said to be the best organized in the

[116] Shanghai Municipal Archive, Q117–5–32.
[117] Shanghai Municipal Archive, Q117–5–33 (1).
[118] Shanghai Municipal Archive, Q117–5–84.
[119] Shanghai Municipal Archive, Q117–5–14.
[120] *Laodong Zhoukan*, 5 November 1921.
[121] Ma Chaojun, *Zhongguo laogong yundong shi* [A History of the Chinese Labour Movement] (Taibei: Zhongguo laogong fuli chubanshe, 1958), pp. 223, 356.

city, had only 800 members.[122] Many of these native-place labour unions affiliated to the fiercely anti-Communist Shanghai Federation of Syndicates, which was connected politically to the right wing of the GMD. As affiliates, they formally deprecated any notion of class struggle, yet this did not prevent them occasionally clashing fiercely with the elites who controlled the regional guilds. The Shaoxing workers' association, for instance, denounced the Shaoxing huiguan after it stopped paying a subsidy to its women's normal school.[123] Not all the native-place labour unions in Shanghai were supporters of the GMD right. When Liu Hua, an influential Communist labour leader, was executed by warlord Sun Chuanfang in 1925, the Sichuan labourers' union demanded vengeance for one of its most illustrious sons and called for the overthrow of imperialism and its 'vile running dogs', the warlords.[124] In general, however, the attempt to organize workers on the basis of native place was a dismal failure, and a key reason was that the Communists, who spearheaded labour organizing between 1925 and 1927, opposed labour organization on the basis of native place rather than occupation.

After coming to power in 1927, the GMD proved no more sympathetic to concessions to native-place sentiment. Unlike the Communists, its concern was not to promote class unity but national unity. Its founder, Sun Yat-sen, had argued that a key reason why China faced 'national extinction' was that historically sentiments of solidarity stopped short at the level of the clan, never rising to the level of the nation and thereby producing a deficiency of national spirit (*minzu jingshen*).[125] This set the tone for subsequent nationalist discourse, with many nationalists in the 1920s – the federalists being a notable exception – arguing that native-place loyalties were at odds with the creation of a strong nation. In this spirit, the government of Chiang Kai-shek waged war in the 1930s on dialects (*tuhua*) and localism (*difang guandian*).[126] In point of fact, Sun Yat-sen had been rather more appreciative of the malleability of native-place sentiment than his later followers,

[122] *Zhongguo gongren yundong shiliao*, 3 (1980), 8.
[123] R. Keith Schoppa, *Chinese Elites and Political Change: Zhejiang Province in the Early Twentieth Century* (Cambridge MA: Harvard University Press, 1982), p. 29.
[124] *Gongren zhi lu*, 12 February 1926, p. 3.
[125] Sun Zhongshan, 'San min zhuyi', *Sun Zhongshan xuanji* [Selected Works of Sun Yat-sen], vol. 2 (Beijing: Zhonghua shuji, 1956), pp. 594, 615.
[126] John Fitzgerald, *Awakening China: Politics, Culture and Class in the Nationalist Revolution* (Stanford: Stanford University Press, 1996), pp. 14, 85. Though the GMD government claimed to be national, in practice it was dominated by men of Zhejiang and Jiangsu, who worked as much in the interests of their region as of the nation.

arguing that once the people were mobilized around the Three People's Principles, national sentiment could be built upon the narrower solidarities of lineage and native place.[127] Events were to prove him right. Beginning with the May Fourth Movement of 1919, and peaking with the 'national revolution' of 1925–7, the tongxianghui and native-place bangs utilized native-place sentiment in ways that were conducive to combating warlordism and foreign imperialism. As the Suzhou tongxianghui explained: 'for the wealth and strength of the nation, it is imperative to unite in groups'; and native-place groups came to be seen as primordial building blocks of a strong nation.[128]

Conclusion

Native-place ties proved far stronger among migrants to Shanghai than among those to St Petersburg. In Shanghai a combination of language barriers among immigrants plus the dense reticulation of the labour market by native-place bangs, which denied access to particular trades to 'outsiders', created powerful obstacles to unified collective action by workers. In general, native-place sentiment and organization created narrow, particularistic solidarities and forms of vertical division within the working class that placed impediments to the construction of more inclusive class or national identities. Yet when caught up in broader social and political movements, native-place sentiment was capable of endowing workers with organizational coherence and a sense of purpose that could feed into movements that spoke more universal languages of nation and class. Against a background of generalized revolutionary crisis in 1917, zemliachestva successfully constituted themselves as agencies of class politics and socialism; and during the 1920s and 1930s, tongxianghui and bangs struggled to mobilize workers in support of national salvation. Both examples demonstrate that the significance of native-place identity is not fixed, being determined more by ambient

---

[127] Sun Zhongshan, 'San min zhuyi', p. 644.
[128] Bryna Goodman, 'New Culture, Old Habits: Native-Place Organization and the May Fourth Movement', in Frederic E. Wakeman, Jr and Wen-hsin Yeh (eds.), *Shanghai Sojourners* (Berkeley, Institute of East Asian Studies 1992), pp. 76–107, 101. Keith Schoppa's study of Zhejiang shows that provincial and national consciousness could exist separately, or merge in many variant combinations. R. Keith Schoppa, *Chinese Elites, passim*. Even so, GMD and CCP discourse in China rarely imagined the nation through its local landscapes of place and time as happened, for example, in Germany. Celia Applegate, *A Nation of Provincials: The German Idea of Heimat* (Berkeley: University of California Press, 1990); and Alon Confino, *The Nation as a Local Metaphor: Württemberg, Imperial Germany, and National Memory, 1871–1918* (Chapel Hill: University of North Carolina Press, 1997).

circumstances than intrinsically parochial attributes. Because native-place loyalties – as the projection of consanguinity into space – create powerful bonds of solidarity, their political valency is high, and they are capable of fusing with diverse political ideologies and aspirations, according to the larger balance of social and political forces.

The strengthening and utilization of native-place identities by migrants to Shanghai and St Peterburg implicitly challenges the once rather influential notion that revolution stems from the deracination of rural populations under the impact of modernization. Neil Smelser best articulated this when he claimed: 'Social movements appeal most to those who have been dislodged from old social ties by differentiation but who have not been integrated into the new social order.'[129] This suggested that those most prone to revolutionary mobilization were precisely the subjects of this book, migrants cut adrift from their traditional rural moorings but not yet fully at home in urban-industrial society. The evidence adduced in this chapter, however, raises a large question mark against this thesis. The idea of 'deracination' fails to capture the diversity of migrant experience. As we have seen, some left their villages out of desperation, others left in a spirit of adventure; some made good in the city, others went to the dogs; some never felt a shred of regret for the life they had left behind, others looked back on the village with aching nostalgia.

More generally, if the act of migration to the city signalled radical discontinuity of experience and called into question the peasant's sense of his or her identity as one centred on the village, this did not necessarily amount to anomie. Relocation to the city generally sharpened native-place identity, at least for the first generation of migrants, and it served to provide orientation to the migrant's new life in the city. Moreover, native-place identity in the city was not the same as in the village: it comprised new as well as old orientations, values and dispositions. Native-place organizations did partially insulate migrants from the disruptive pressures of urban and industrial life, perpetuating ties to the countryside and thereby helping to maintain peasant identities. Yet at the same time, these organizations were put to novel uses and served to familiarize migrants with the opportunities and perils of city and factory.

So as far the connection between deracination and revolution is concerned, the most one can say is that migration eroded older patterns

---

[129] Neil J. Smelser, 'Towards a Theory of Modernization'. Cited in Victoria Bonnell, *Roots of Rebellion: Workers' Politics and Organizations in St Petersburg and Moscow, 1900–1914* (Berkeley: University of California Press, 1983), p. 12.

of social identity and made migrants susceptible to new ones. As living embodiments of two worlds that were both intimately connected yet radically separate, migrants may have been particularly sensitive to the realities of social change and thus – possibly – more receptive to political messages that sought to make sense of that change in terms that appeared to be empowering. But the evidence remains ambiguous.

2   The Awakening Self: Individuality and Class Consciousness

To address the theme of individuality in the context of working-class formation and Communist revolution may seem perverse. Class identity, after all, is usually seen as a form of collectivism, and individualism and collectivism tend to be positioned at opposite ends of a cultural spectrum. And to suggest, as I shall, that a growing sense of individuality was one of the elements that comprised the dynamic compound of changing social identities that made peasants-turned-workers susceptible to revolutionary mobilization – especially in Russia – may seem wide of the mark to those who know that a phobic antipathy to 'petty-bourgeois individualism' became a hallmark of Russian and Chinese Communism. Moreover, the apparent incongruity of the theme is heightened when one considers the cultures under investigation: Russian culture appears historically to incarnate a form of collectivism that is extreme by the standards of peasant societies in Europe; while Chinese culture appears to represent a Confucian collectivism that is the antithesis of western individualism.[1] I wish to argue, however, that while it is heuristically useful to situate individualism and collectivism at two ends of a spectrum, the relationship between collectivism and individualism was historically more complex, contingent and mutable than social scientists and philosophers often allow.

Clifford Geertz famously observed that: 'The Western conception of the person as a bounded, unique, more or less integrated motivational and cognitive universe ... is, however incorrigible it seems to us, a rather peculiar idea within the context of the world's cultures.'[2] I do not wish to get embroiled in the somewhat otiose debate between so-called

---

[1] Discourses of the self are implicitly masculine and are appropriated by men and women differentially. I try briefly to indicate the ways in which men and women were positioned differently in relation to the self, but gender and the self is the subject of the next chapter.

[2] Clifford Geertz, 'From the Native's Point of View', in Paul Rabinow and W. M. Sullivan (eds.), *Interpretive Social Science* (Berkeley: University of California Press, 1979), p. 229.

'universalists' and 'relativists', i.e. between those who believe that there has never been a culture unconcerned with human individuality and those who believe, on the contrary, that there are many cultures that have no conception of the individual separate from his or her social role.[3] I tend to agree with Charles Taylor that there are resources for self-reflexive thought, action and attitude in all societies, but that the making of the self into a noun has been a relatively recent historical development associated with the West.[4] Taylor sees the modern western self as defined, first, by powers of reason, which are in turn associated with ideals of autonomy and dignity; second, by self-exploration; and third, by personal commitment.[5] He shows how central to the development of western moral and political thinking has been the belief that each person is endowed with natural autonomy and dignity by virtue of being a human being rather than as a consequence of his or her social status. This is very much the view of a philosopher, but it is valuable to the historian as an ideal-type.

The chapter begins by examining discourses of selfhood in Russian and Chinese peasant society. It stresses the highly collectivist nature of peasant culture in both societies but argues that this did not preclude there being resources for self-reflection prior to the onset of capitalist modernity. It argues, however, that the onset of the latter served to make the category of the self a particular focus of reflection and contestation and to increase the cognitive and moral weight that attached to the individual.[6] The chapter goes on to examine that minority of workers who, having come into contact with western-influenced ideas of the self via the intelligentsia, strove to educate themselves and to acquire 'consciousness', a term that carries the idea of reworking oneself morally and intellectually in order to assert oneself against the world.[7] It was this small but articulate minority that struggled to link their aspirations for individual autonomy to the struggles of the working class for

---

[3] Richard A. Shweder and Edmund J. Bourne, 'Does the Concept of the Person Vary Cross-Culturally?', in Richard A. Shweder, *Thinking through Cultures: Expeditions in Cultural Psychology* (Cambridge MA: Harvard University Press, 1991), pp. 133–155.

[4] Charles Taylor, *Sources of the Self: The Making of Modern Identity* (Cambridge: Cambridge University Press, 1989), p. 113.

[5] Taylor, *Sources of the Self*, p. 211.

[6] Peter Burke's comment is apposite. 'It is better to think in terms of a variety of categories of the person or conceptions of the self (more or less unified, bounded and so on) in different cultures, categories and conceptions which underlie a variety of styles of self-presentation or self-fashioning.' Peter Burke, 'Representations of the Self from Petrarch to Descartes', in Roy Porter (ed.), *Rewriting the Self: Histories from the Renaissance to the Present* (London: Routledge, 1997), p. 28.

[7] Oleg Kharkhordin, *The Collective and the Individual in Russia* (Berkeley: University of California Press, 1999), p. 58.

emancipation. Among the great majority of workers, understandings of the self were rarely articulated so explicitly, and to get some sense of these the chapter examines religion as one arena in which people expressed their individual needs and aspirations, notwithstanding the fact that religion in both Russia and China was overwhelmingly communal in character. The third section examines two very different sites on which more modern understandings of the self were articulated, namely, the marketplace and mass consumption. It looks, specifically, at fashions in clothing and at commercial fiction designed for the consumption of the newly literate. Finally, the chapter asks what implications the increasing purchase of new ideas of the self among working people had for the emergence of class identity and revolutionary politics.

Selfhood in Peasant Culture

Educated observers of the Russian peasantry harped on the intense collectivism of peasant life.[8] For the Slavophiles, this was a wholly positive phenomenon, its roots lying in the Orthodox Christian ideal of *sobornost'*, a form of fellowship between believers at odds with the 'self-willed individualism and its restraint by coercion' that was deemed to be characteristic of western Christianity.[9] Certainly, when compared with Protestantism, Orthodox Christianity placed far less emphasis on individual conscience; and when compared with Roman Catholicism, it placed less emphasis on the humanity of Christ. Nevertheless sobornost' precludes neither the idea of a personal relationship to God nor the individual's responsibility for his or her salvation. For the Slavophiles, sobornost' was more than a theological ideal, it was a social fact, manifest, above all, in the peasant commune (*mir*). According to Konstantin Aksakov, 'the commune represents a moral choir, and just as in a choir one voice is not lost but is heard in the harmony of all voices, so in the commune the individual is not lost but renounces his exclusivity in favour of the common accord'.[10] Although very much a construct of intellectuals, sobornost' represented a powerful cultural ideal, one which in a secularized form would influence the Populists later in the nineteenth century in their aspiration to create a socialist society upon the collectivist values of the peasantry.

[8] Note that the term 'kollektivizm' acquired popularity only in the later part of the nineteenth century. Kharkhordin, *Collective*, p. 76.

[9] Andrzej Walicki, *A History of Russian Thought from the Enlightenment to Marxism* (Oxford: Clarendon Press, 1980), p. 95.

[10] Cited in Geoffrey Hosking, *Russia: People and Empire, 1552–1917* (London: Harper/Collins, 1997), p. 274.

If we must be sceptical of sobornost' as sociological description, it remains true that Russian peasant society was strongly characterized by collective values and norms. First, as in all peasant societies, the status of the individual was primarily defined in terms of the gender and age hierarchies of the patriarchal family. Second, and in contrast to China, collectivism was represented at the level of the local community via the peasant commune, which consisted of the male heads of household. This was responsible for ensuring that households fulfilled their obligations to the landlord and the state and for periodically redistributing the village arable land between households, in accordance with changes in family size, the land being the patrimony of the community rather than the property of individual families.[11] Third, the peasantry was constituted by law as a social estate (soslovie) with distinct rights and duties. Down to 1917, peasants were subject to laws particular to their estate, and most judicial matters affecting the peasantry were handled by special township courts. In the last analysis, it was the state that defined individual rights and obligations through the officially prescribed system of estates and through the fiscal and other demands placed on the commune.

The tight constraints of family, community and social estate did not mean that individual peasants had no resources for articulating ideas of individuality. As the ethnographer N. A. Minenko comments: 'The mir never suppressed individual peasant identity, and left considerable latitude for [expressions of] individual will.'[12] Indeed, following the abolition of serfdom in 1861, more and more commentators deplored what they perceived to be new spirit of individualism springing up in the countryside.[13] In Iaroslavl' province the zemstvo (rural local government) survey of 1896 remarked: 'Liberation from serf dependence and the long-standing association of the more active section of the rural population with town life have long since aroused a desire in the Iaroslavl' peasant to uphold his 'ego', to get away from the state of poverty and dependency ... to a state of sufficiency, independence and respect.'[14] Developments such as the growing commercialization of

---

[11] David Moon, *The Russian Peasantry, 1600–1930* (London: Longman, 1999), pp. 199, 207.

[12] N. A. Minenko, *Zhivaia Starina* (Novosibirsk, 1989), p. 11; cited in Ben Eklof, 'Worlds in Conflict: Patriarchal Authority, Discipline and the Russian School, 1861–1914', in Ben Eklof (ed.), *School and Society in Tsarist and Soviet Russia* (London: Macmillan, 1993), pp. 95–120.

[13] A. N. Engelgardt, *Letters from the Country, 1872–1887*, trans. and ed. Cathy A. Frierson (New York: Oxford University Press, 1993), pp. 86–7; pp. 115–22.

[14] V. I. Lenin, 'The Development of Capitalism in Russia', *Collected Works*, vol. 3 (Moscow: Progress Publishers, 1972), p. 577.

agriculture, increased mobility of the rural population, increased exposure to urban consumer culture, and rising levels of education and literacy seem to have brought about changes in behaviour among what this zemstvo commentator called the 'more active section of the rural population'. And one can point to a number of trends that suggest there may have been a greater willingness to assert individual rights. First, the rapid growth of schooling in the last decades of the nineteenth century appears to have produced a generation that jibbed at the constraints of the old village world.[15] Second, sons – often at the instigation of their wives – were increasingly demanding the right to break away from the multiple family household and set up their own households.[16] Household partitions occurred primarily in poor households, and were particularly widespread in provinces with high levels of outmigration such as Tver' and Pskov.[17] Partition generally led to a reduction in income, but it meant less crowded living conditions and greater freedom for the wife who was no longer subject to her parents-in-law.[18] Third, there was a growing trend for peasants to take disputes for resolution to the township courts. In her illuminating study, Jane Burbank notes that such disputes were almost always between individuals rather than 'between insiders and outsiders, between people of two distinct generations, or between people of different genders'.[19]

China was a patriarchal, family-based society par excellence, in which the self was defined in terms of ascribed social roles. According to Confucian ideology, the family was a microcosm of the social order, the father analogous to the wise ruler and his children analogous to dutiful subjects. Ancestor worship served as the link between past and present, reminding family members of the overriding importance of maintaining the patriline and subordinating individual interests to those of the family. It also provided a powerful cement that reinforced the values of hierarchy and social harmony that were at the heart of Confucian ideology. Confucianism was never the sole ideology in China, but it was the ideology of state and never yielded paramountcy to other bodies of thought, such as Daoism and Buddhism. It viewed the natural, human

[15] Orlando Figes, *A People's Tragedy: A History of the Russian Revolution, 1891–1924* (London: Jonathan Cape, 1996), p. 92.
[16] Christine D. Worobec, *Family and Community in the Period of Post-Emancipation Period* (Princeton: Princeton University Press, 1991), p. 12; Engelgardt, *Letters from the Country*, pp. 165, 166.
[17] Evel G. Economakis, *From Peasant to Petersburger* (Basingstoke: Macmillan, 1998), p. 82.
[18] *Naselenie Rossii v XX veke: istoricheskie ocherki*, tom 1, 1900–1939 (Moscow: ROSSPEN, 2000), p. 66.
[19] Jane Burbank, *Russian Peasants Go to Court: Legal Culture in the Countryside, 1905–1917* (Bloomington: Indiana University Press, 2004), p. 250.

and supernatural worlds as a single organism, consisting of an orderly hierarchy of inter-related parts and forces which, though unequal in their status, were equally essential to the harmonious working of the system as a whole.[20] An individual acted in accordance with the Confucian *li*, according to the adage 'subdue the self and follow the rites (*ke ji fu li*)'. In the narrowest sense the *li* denoted the correct observance of religious ritual and ceremonial behaviour; in a broader sense they denoted all the social relationships that made for harmonious living, in particular the five relationships of obedience – of subject to emperor, son to father, wife to husband, younger brother to elder brother and friend to friend. The individual was thus defined by his or her position within the rigid generational, gender and age hierarchy of the family; and, by extension, in terms of the extent to which he or she lived up to the obligations entailed by these roles. The underdevelopment of the idea of the individual (*gexing*) within Chinese culture was reflected in the fact that it was not uncommon for children not to have a given name, but to be referred to by a number indicating their birth order. This underdevelopment of the individual was particularly glaring in the case of women. The genealogical records of the lineage, for example, named all members of the patriline, but women were recorded only as wives and mothers, usually without personal names.[21]

It would be misleading to take the above as a literal description of a monolithic social reality. There were resources within Chinese culture through which individuality could be expressed. Mark Elvin, reflecting on the impact of Daoism on Chinese culture, suggests that there were 'compelling ways of thinking about the self in China'.[22] And proverbs suggest that within popular culture the strong emphasis on the collective was tempered by a respect for self-reliance.[23] Even the goal of moral

[20] A. F. Wright, 'Values, Roles and Personalities', in A. F. Wright and D. Twitchett (eds.), *Confucian Personalities* (Stanford: Stanford University Press, 1962), p. 6; Robert E. Hegel, 'An Exploration of the Chinese Literary Self', in Robert E. Hegel and Richard C. Hessney (eds.), *Expressions of Self in Chinese Literature* (New York: Columbia University Press, 1985), pp. 5, 7, 21.

[21] Francesca Bray, *Technology and Gender: Fabrics of Power in Late Imperial China* (Berkeley: University of California Press, 1997), pp. 240–1.

[22] Mark Elvin, 'Between the Earth and Heaven: Conceptions of the Self in China', in M. Carrithers, S. Collins and S. Lukes (eds.), *The Category of the Person: Anthropology, Philosophy, History* (Cambridge: Cambridge University Press, 1985), p. 157. See also Pei-yi Wu, 'Varieties of the Chinese Self', in Vytantas Kavolis (ed.), *Designs of Selfhood* (Rutherford NJ: Fairleigh Dickinson, 1984), pp. 107–31.

[23] David Yau-Fai Ho and Che-Yue Chiu, 'Component Ideas of Individualism and Collectivism and Social Organization: An Application to the Study of Chinese Culture', in Uichol Kim et al. (eds.), *Individualism and Collectivism: Theory, Method and Applications* (Thousand Oaks CA: Sage, 1994), p. 145; R. David Arkush, 'Orthodoxy and Heterodoxy in Twentieth-Century Chinese Peasant Proverbs', in Kwang-Ching

advancement (*xiushen*) that is central to Confucianism authorized a certain striving for self-realization, even if such realization was seen as functional to moral order. Yet for ordinary folk, the interests of family and lineage invariably took precedence over those of the self. If Russia was a highly collectivist and statist society, institutions like the commune and the Church mediated between family and state. In China, by contrast, mediating institutions, such as temples or native-place associations, were weaker and had far less salience in defining arenas for the expression of selfhood.[24] Similarly, China's religious culture, embedded as it was in local social structures, allowed less space for the ideal of individual salvation that was central to Russian Orthodoxy.

Selfhood and the 'Conscious' Worker

In Russia, beginning in the late-eighteenth century but intensifying from the 1840s, new ideologies of selfhood, heavily influenced by western philosophies, gained a foothold in the emergent intelligentsia. In China, by contrast, western discourses of individuality only arrived at the very end of the nineteenth century, and it was not until the May Fourth Movement of 1919 – often dubbed China's Enlightenment – that they took root among the nascent intelligentsia. In both societies, western-inspired discourses of the self functioned as a vehicle of social critique, serving to indict the existing social and political order for denying individual rights and suppressing personal autonomy. In both countries a small minority of workers – tiny in the case of China – responded positively to these discourses as they were propagated by radical intellectuals. In Russia such workers were known as 'conscious' (*soznatel'nye*) workers; in China as 'conscious' (*juewu*) or 'enlightened' (*qiming*) or 'awoken' (*juexing*) workers.

In Russia the central concept around which new understandings of the self coalesced was that of *lichnost'*, usually translated as 'personality', but a term that draws attention to the moral and intellectual qualities of the individual.[25] For educated Russians of whatever political stripe,

Liu (ed.), *Orthodoxy in Late Imperial China* (Berkeley: University of California Press, 1990), pp. 311–31.

24 Lucian W. Pye, 'The State and the Individual: An Overview Interpretation', in Brian Hook (ed.), *The Individual and the State in China* (Oxford: Clarendon Press, 1996), pp. 16–42; Gilbert Rozman, 'The Individual, Family and Community' in Brian Hook (ed.), *Cambridge Encyclopedia of China* (Cambridge: Cambridge University Press, 1991), pp. 112–13.

25 Derek Offord, ' "Lichnost": Notions of Individual Identity', in Catriona Kelly and David Shepherd (eds.), *Constructing Russian Culture in the Age of Revolution, 1881–1940* (Oxford: Oxford University Press, 1998), p. 15; Mark D. Steinberg, *Proletarian*

self-realization was to be achieved through the collective, through a historical process of overcoming the division between the individual and society. For Slavophiles, the development of personality consisted in developing a distinctively Russian form of individuality that was consonant with sobornost'. For westernizers, social, political and cultural progress depended on the formation of rational, responsible individuals, capable of exercising civil and political rights.[26] Yet if westernizers believed that Russia's progress depended on creating western-style institutions, they never appropriated western discourses of personhood uncritically, expressing reservations about the egoism, competitiveness, acquisitiveness and worship of private property that they believed were intrinsic to western civilization. Their hope was to combine a liberal model of personhood with the social solidarity characteristic of Russian culture. Compared with nineteenth-century British liberals, all shades of opinion within the Russian intelligentsia placed greater emphasis on the relationship of the individual to the collective: as Lavrov opined, 'individual dignity is maintained only by upholding the dignity of all'.[27]

The 'conscious' workers who emerged in the last quarter of the nineteenth century were hardly typical of the majority of migrants who came to St Petersburg. They identified with the working class, at least in an idealized sense, yet often expressed a 'burning, pungent loathing of the utter self-devouring ignorance and incomprehension' of the ordinary worker.[28] 'Conscious' workers sought to distance themselves from the latter, seeking to reconstruct their lives around the ideal of 'personality', struggling to develop as knowledgeable, autonomous individuals. The worker memoirist Shapovalov recalled that as an apprentice fitter, he 'felt like a bird in a cage. Life seemed like a prison, vague desires stirred in my soul – desires for space and air.'[29] For such workers, 'spiritual and intellectual development' was the means to achieve 'personality' and they responded warmly to the efforts of the intelligentsia to raise their

Imagination: Self, Modernity and the Sacred in Russia, 1910–1925 (Ithaca NY: Cornell University Press, 2002), pp. 63–9; Kharkhordin, *Collective*, pp. 187–90.

[26] For a discussion of the range of philosophical influences on Russian thinking about the individual in the nineteenth and early twentieth centuries thinking, see George L. Kline, 'Changing Attitudes Toward the Individual', in Cyril E. Black (ed.), *The Transformation of Russian Society* (Cambridge MA: Harvard University Press, 1960), pp. 606–25.

[27] Quoted in Mark D. Steinberg, 'Predstavlenie o "lichnosti" v srede rabochikh intelligentov', in *Rabochie i intelligentsiia Rossii v epokhu reform i revoliutsii, 1861-fevral' 1917g.* (St Petersburg: RAN, 1997), p. 99.

[28] A. S. Serafimovich, 'Sredi nochi' (1906), *Izbrannye proizvedeniia* (Moscow: Molodaia gvardii, 1953).

[29] A. S. Shapovalov, *Po doroge k marksizmu* (Moscow: Gosizdat, 1924), p. 6.

level of 'culturedness' (*kul'turnost'*) by teaching them the rudiments of high literary and scientific culture. Although most had had a basic education in the village, such workers grabbed the opportunities on offer in the Sunday schools and evening classes of the capital. 'Why', asked a young fitter in a factory in the Nevskaia Zastava district, 'are our teachers such good people? They are paid nothing and they lose their own time ... These are people who do not boast about their learning ... but seek to share it with those who have no knowledge.'[30]

Reading was the key means whereby 'conscious' workers strove to raise their level of 'culturedness' and political consciousness (both qualities that were measured according to a hierarchy of levels). Having left his village aged fifteen, Fedor Samoilov took to city life as soon as he discovered the public library. 'At first, I read such authors as Jules Verne, Mayne Reid and J. Fenimore Cooper, fascinated by their journeys and adventures. Later I went on to the Russian classics – Pushkin, Lermontov, Gogol. I also read various novels published as supplements to *Niva*, *Rodina* and other journals. Now and then, I would get hold of popular science books.'[31] Books were hugely valued and passed around avidly among workers. Some of the most passionate arguments – in the factory and at evening classes – arose as workers swapped opinions about their favourite authors and the books they had read.[32] Writing of the worker who used the people's libraries, one liberal commentator observed: 'He seeks one thing only: an answer to the questions that arise in his head; he seeks it passionately, tormentedly and in his search for a good and intelligent book will sometimes sacrifice his paltry wage.'[33] N. A. Rubakin (1862–1946), self-taught writer, educationalist and 'propagandist of the book', was hugely influential in directing the reading of aspiring autodidacts through works such as *Letters to Readers on Self-Education* and booklets on topics such as evolution and air flight.[34] Significant numbers of workers felt impelled to try their hand at writing, exploring 'questions about existential meaning and purpose; the uncertain nature and place of the self; the promise and pain of modernity; and qualities of the sacred in both their lives and imaginations'.[35]

[30] *Avangard: Vospominaniia i dokumenty piterskikh rabochikh 1890-kh godov* (Leningrad: Lenizdat, 1990), p. 326.

[31] F. N. Samoilov, *Po sledam minuvshego*, 3rd edn (Moscow: Gospolitizdat, 1954), p. 40.

[32] *Avangard: Vospominaniia*, p. 163.

[33] T. V. Boiko, *Rabochie Rossii i kul'tura: polemika na stranitsakh konservativnoi i liberal'noi periodiki nachala XX veka* (Moscow: RAN Institut rossiiskoi istorii, 1997), p. 91.

[34] N. A. Rubakin, *Pis'ma k chitateliam o samoobrazovanii* (St Petersburg, 1911); *Kak, kogda i pochemu poiavilis' liudi na zemle* (1909); *Kak liudi nauchilis' letat' i letaiut po vozdukhu* (1913).

[35] Steinberg, *Proletarian Imagination*, p. 282.

Discussing the poems, stories and essays published by workers in trade-union, party and popular journals, Maxim Gorky wrote of hundreds 'cultivating their self (*ia*) under a cloak of silence'.[36] Themes of injury to the self and of personal suffering loomed large in their oeuvre and some worker writers would later be castigated for lacking the positive, confident, militant spirit appropriate to 'proletarian' literature.[37]

Becoming conscious entailed not only sloughing off the corrupt habits of the 'dark masses' – drinking, fighting, gambling and so forth – but also the religious 'superstition' and political conservatism that befogged their minds. In their struggle to forge a 'personality', conscious workers typically embraced the platonic ideal of self-mastery through reason, convinced that reason could liberate the people from the shackles of religion and monarchism.[38] Science magazines and brochures for the mass reader, dealing with topics such as astronomy, evolutionary theory and geography and new technologies, such as radio and powered aviation, were immensely popular.[39] For Kanatchikov, discovery of evolutionary theory came like a lightning bolt: 'I struck terror in the imaginations of the superstitious inhabitants of our apartment when ... I contrasted my giants – the ichthyosaurs and plesiosaurs – with their divine or evil spirits.' His discovery of Darwin was soon complemented by his discovery of Marx: by 1902, aged 23, he had painfully mastered the first volume of *Capital*. This furnished him with a scientific understanding of society and the determination to dedicate himself to the cause of overthrowing capitalism.[40]

The acquisition of 'consciousness' frequently, but not invariably, entailed the rejection of religion. Christianity, however, continued subliminally to influence understandings of the self.[41] Ivan Babushkin, executed for his revolutionary activities in January 1906, worked at the Semiannikov metal works from 1893, where he became friends with Kostia, a young socialist like himself. 'We demanded that a socialist be

---

[36] L. M. Kleinbort, 'Rukopisnye zhurnaly rabochikh', *Vestnik Evropy*, 53, 3 (1917), 275–98; 278, 282.

[37] Steinberg, *Proletarian Imagination*, p. 135.

[38] As Susan Morrissey observes, the 'critically thinking individual formed the basis of historical progress because this individual would be able to uncover and ultimately control laws of human society'. Susan K. Morrissey, *Heralds of Revolution: Russian Students and the Mythologies of Radicalism* (New York: Oxford University Press, 1998), p. 23.

[39] James T. Andrews, *Science for the Masses: The Bolshevik State, Public Science, and the Popular Imagination in Soviet Russia, 1917–1934* (College Station: Texas A & M University Press, 2003), ch. 1.

[40] Reginald E. Zelnik, *A Radical Worker in Tsarist Russia: The Autobiography of Semën Ivanovich Kanatchikov* (Stanford: Stanford University Press, 1986), p. 111.

[41] Mark D. Steinberg, 'Workers on the Cross: Religious Imagination in the Writings of Russian Workers, 1910–1924', *Russian Review*, 53, 2 (1994), 213–39.

the most exemplary of people in all his relations and we ourselves tried to be exemplary.' If someone 'sinned even a little ... we did not consider him a proper comrade'.[42] For conscious workers who became revolutionaries the Christian ideal of renunciation of the self was transfigured into a belief that authentic self-realization required subordination of the self to the needs of revolution. After reading the book *Underground Russia* (1882) by Sergei Stepniak, who in 1878 stabbed to death the head of police in St Petersburg, Kanatchikov recalled: 'We wanted to suffer for the common cause, to sacrifice ourselves in the same way as the heroes described in the book.' In reading such literature, he went on, 'workers learned the meaning of selflessness, the capacity to sacrifice oneself in the name of the common good'.[43] Many revolutionaries, including Lenin, modelled themselves on Rakhmetev, a highly self-disciplined, puritanical character in Chernyshevsky's novel *What Is To Be Done?* (1863), determined to sublimate personal interest and emotion to the pursuit of revolution.[44] The worker Frolov fell in love, but rejected the possibility of marriage because for him the struggle was everything: 'We lived like ascetics; we passed women by; if we met one in our circle, we stifled feelings of love, regarding the woman as a comrade in ideas, a fighter for whom there could be no personal love. All of our love was invested in the struggle.'[45] The theme of self-realization through subordination to the collective good is not by any means confined to Christian cultures – it was relentlessly promoted by the CCP in China, for example – but in Russia-Christian ideas of self-denial and suffering as inherently redemptive continued to resonate in the discourse of revolution.

Calls to emancipate the individual from the fetters of Confucianism first surfaced during the Hundred Days Reform of 1898. One of the leaders of that movement, Tan Sitong, who was executed for demanding that the ailing Qing dynasty take urgent steps to reform itself, confessed in his *Study of Sensitive Concern for Others*: 'From the time I was young ... I everywhere encountered the afflictions of the bonds and relationships [of Confucianism]. I swam deep in their bitterness.'[46] Only with the New Culture Movement in 1915, however, did this theme come to the forefront of public debate. This movement was brought into

[42] *Avangard: Vospominaniia*, pp. 90, 102.   [43] Zelnik, *Radical Worker*, p. 91.

[44] A. Kelly, 'Self-Censorship and the Russian Intelligentsia, 1905–1914', *Slavic Review*, 46, 2 (1987), 194.

[45] A. Frolov, *Probuzhdenie: vospominaniia riadego rabochego* (Kiev: Gosizdat Ukrainy, 1923), pp. 62–63.

[46] Cited in Elvin, 'Between the Earth and Heaven', p. 175. Tan's reference is to the three bonds of obedience – of subject to emperor, son to father, wife to husband – and the five relationships of authority.

being with the foundation of the journal *Youth*, by Chen Duxiu, who later became the first general secretary of the CCP. Its *idée fixe* was that patriarchalism (*jiazhang zhuyi*) stifled 'free will' (*ziyou zhi yizhi*) and the personality/dignity (*renge*) of the individual.[47] Mao Zedong, an avid reader of Chen's journal, proclaimed in 1917–18: 'The goal of the human race lies in the realisation of self *(ziwo)* and that is all. What I mean by the realisation of self consists in the development of our physical and mental capacities to the highest degree ... Wherever there is repression of the individual ... there can be no greater crime. That is why our country's "three bonds" must go and why they constitute with religion, capitalism and autocracy the four evil demons of the realm.'[48] In Mao's thinking, typical of that of young radicals of the time, satisfaction of the needs of the individual was not perceived as antithetical to the needs of society. Rather individual personhood was championed precisely in order to attack and transform the status quo. As the anarchist tribune Shifu explained: 'Everybody should improve his own dignity (*renge*) in order to assist the progress of society and mankind; if we develop our own dignity ... everything we do will accord with the truth.'[49]

The burgeoning concern with freedom of the individual (*geren*) blossomed with the May Fourth Movement of 1919, which saw students, merchants and workers take to the streets in protest at the terms of the Treaty of Versailles, which transferred privileges enjoyed by Germany in China to Japan. This essentially nationalist movement gave radical intellectuals the opportunity to propagate the ideas of the New Culture Movement to a wider audience. According to the romantic writer Yu Dafu, 'the greatest success of the May Fourth Movement lay, first of all, in the discovery of individual personality'.[50] The concern to emancipate the individual from the bonds of patriarchalism, however, was never perceived to be in tension with the struggle to save the nation. Already in the 1890s, Yan Fu, translator of John Stuart Mill into Chinese, had construed Mill's individualism in social terms, as a 'means to advance the people's virtue and intellectual development, and beyond this the purposes of the state'.[51] Now New Culture intellectuals yoked

---

[47] Chen Duxiu, 'Jiefang', in *Duxiu wencun*, vol. 2 (Hong Kong: Yuandong tushu gongsi, 1965), pp. 89–91.

[48] Stuart Schram, *Mao Zedong: A Preliminary Assessment* (Hong Kong: Chinese University Press, 1983), p. 5.

[49] Edward S. Krebs, *Shifu: Soul of Chinese Anarchism* (Lanham MD: Rowman and Littlefield, 1998), p. 103.

[50] John Fitzgerald, *Awakening China: Politics, Culture and Class in the Nationalist Revolution* (Stanford: Stanford University Press, 1996), p. 92.

[51] Benjamin Schwartz, *In Search of Wealth and Power: Yan Fu and the West* (New York: Harper and Rowe, 1969), p. 141.

the emancipation of the individual to the salvation of the nation through metaphors of 'awakening' (*juewu*), 'self-consciousness' (*zijue*) and 'enlightenment' (*qimeng*). Analysing the pervasiveness of the image of 'awakening' during the May Fourth Movement, John Fitzgerald notes how the freedom and autonomy of the awakened self became a trope through which people could think about saving the nation.[52] The number of workers touched by this discourse was small. Nevertheless the labour press, which was born out of the May Fourth Movement, championed notions of individuality, dignity and awakening. In June 1919 a shop clerk declared: 'Every person has individual dignity, a right to freedom and a love of country. Yet they should never place their selfish interest above those of their fellows, or their own actions above those of others. We must submit to the dictates of our consciences.'[53] And the following year a worker from Hunan wrote to the first labour journal published by the Shanghai Communists to say that workers must become 'conscious of their dignity, conscious of their treatment, conscious of education and conscious of organization'.[54] In the course of the 1920s, however, the tensions between fostering the dignity of the individual and bringing about the salvation of the nation would become increasingly apparent.

For centuries, the written word in China had represented cosmic order, and mastery of the Confucian classics had differentiated the elite from the popular classes. Nevertheless, written materials circulated in many spheres of economic, social and religious life and the popular classes had benefited from limited, practical education. Popular schooling was cheap and widely available, even to poor males (although not to poor females), and the benefits of literacy were widely recognized, even if its value was seen primarily in utilitarian terms. If literacy is loosely defined to include limited competencies, such as the ability to write a simple letter or keep accounts, or the ability to read anything from a few score to a few thousand characters, then it was spread quite widely. In her pioneering study, Evelyn Rawski estimated that 30% to 45% of men and 2% to 10% of women in late-Qing China could read and write to some extent.[55] The 'awakened' Chinese worker, like his

---

[52] Fitzgerald, *Awakening*, p. 94.

[53] Zhongguo shehui kexueyuan jindaishi yanjiusuo (ed.), *Wusi aiguo yundong* [The May Fourth Patriotic Movement], vol. 2, (Beijing: Zhongguo shehui kexue chubanshe, 1979), p. 10.

[54] *Laodongjie*, 28 November 1920.

[55] Evelyn S. Rawski, *Education and Popular Literacy in Ch'ing China* (Ann Arbor: University of Michigan Press, 1979), p. 23. Wilt Idema reckons 30% male literacy was an absolute maximum and then only according to a minimal definition of literacy. See his review of Rawski's book, *T'oung Pao*, 46, 4–5 (1980), 322.

'conscious' counterpart in Russia, strove to expand his reading as part of a struggle for autonomy. Tan Zhenlin, who rose to become a member of the Central Committee of the CCP after 1949, was born in 1902 in the town of Yuxian in south-eastern Hunan. The family of eight children lived off the wages of his father, who was a low-grade employee in a mine. After he lost his job in 1913, the eleven-year-old Tan went to work in a bookstore:

I had spent only three years in a private school and naturally I was dissatisfied with the cultural knowledge I possessed. So after finishing a day of work, I read under the kerosene lamp at night all kinds of books in the shop ... I read *Water Margin*, *The Romance of the Three Kingdoms*, *Seven Heroes and Five Gallants*, *Journey to the West*, the *Biography of Hong Xiuquan*. They made me understand China's society and history and the unequal social life of the rich and poor. I liked most the heroic characters who resisted tyranny and opposed the exploiting class. It hit upon me that there was a need to reform society.[56]

The Confucian association of education with self-cultivation (*xiushen*) did not fade entirely following the downfall of the Qing dynasty. In 1920, for example, the night school established by the electricians' union in Shanghai taught principles of electricity, English and Chinese, arithmetic and book-keeping, calligraphy and *xiushen*. By this date, the latter signi-fied less the cultivation of the morally superior literatus (*junzi*) and something more akin to civic education.[57] Still, the curriculum testified to the desire of skilled workers to better themselves through education.

In China popular education was justified far more in terms of the needs of the state than the needs of the individual. In 1902, the Qing government belatedly established a modern school system, stating that military and economic success in the modern world necessitated edu-cating the masses.[58] After 1911, debate about common people's edu-cation was almost entirely linked to saving the nation. True, the New Culture Movement, especially after the arrival of the American phil-osopher John Dewey in China in May 1919, justified education in wider terms, praising its importance in creating modern individuals; but such a rationale existed in uneasy tension with the nationalist one.[59] Moreover, the emphasis on the individual faded rather quickly: as early as 1924, at

---

[56] *Gongren ribao*, 31 August 1961, *Survey of the China Mainland Press*, 2362, 21 October 1961.
[57] *Laodongjie*, 4 (1920), 10.
[58] Glen Peterson and Ruth Hayhoe, 'Introduction', in Glen Peterson, Ruth Hayhoe and Yongling Yu (eds.), *Education, Culture and Identity in Twentieth-Century China* (Ann Arbor: University of Michigan Press, 2001), p. 4.
[59] Cited in Nina Y. Borevskaya, 'Searching for Individuality: Educational Pursuits in China and Russia', in Peterson, Hayhoe and Yu (eds.), *Education, Culture and Identity*, p. 37.

its First Congress, the GMD called for the 'partyfication of education' (*jiaoyu danghua*), while from 1921 the CCP used common people's schools mainly to create labour unions and to instil class consciousness.[60] It is true that liberal educators such as Tao Xingzhi, founder of a 'work-study' scheme among factory workers in a suburb of Shanghai in 1932, remained committed to the Deweyite ideal of the development of the individual, but he was an exception. In general, justification for education as a means to forge individual autonomy was quickly supplanted by justification of education in terms of party- and state-building.

Selfhood and Religious Change

Historically, religion has proved to be one of the most fertile arenas in which individuals work out the meaning of their existence and their relationship to society and the cosmos. Whether in comparing 'religion' in Russia and China, however, we are comparing like with like is not clear. Wilfred Cantwell Smith argued that the modern conception of religion as a system of belief embodied in a bounded community was a relatively late invention of seventeenth- and eighteenth-century western Europe; building on this insight, Talal Asad has argued that religion cannot function as an analytical category, since it abstracts a set of practices from their historical context and subsumes them into a speciously universal concept.[61] By the late-nineteenth century, Russian Orthodoxy was certainly a religion in the modern sense, i.e. a clearly bounded system of belief and practice structured through an ecclesiastical organization. Arguably, the three 'high' religions of China – Confucianism, Daoism and Buddhism – were not religions in this modern sense; nevertheless they shared certain family resemblances with it, insofar as they had canonical scriptures, a liturgy and clerical specialists. The problem arises with the religion practised by the majority of the population, which corresponded to none of these traditions yet was influenced by all three.

Chinese popular religion fits the modern conception of religion poorly since it is diffuse in nature and its rituals are deeply embedded in local

---

[60] Zheng Yuan, 'The Status of Confucianism in Modern Chinese Education, 1901–49', in Peterson, Hayhoe and Yu (eds.), *Education, Culture and Identity*, p. 207. And see the statement of the tasks of the CCP of the First Congress of the CCP in 1921. *Zhongguo gongchandang diyici daibiao dahui dang'an ziliao* [Archival Materials on the First Congress of the CCP] (Beijing: Zhongyang wenxian chubanshe, 1997), p. 9.

[61] Wilfred Cantwell Smith, *The Meaning and End of Religion* (London: Macmillan, 1962); Talal Asad, *Genealogies of Religion: Discipline and Reasons of Power in Christianity and Islam* (Baltimore: Johns Hopkins University Press, 1993).

structures of power and in the social institutions of family, lineage and occupational and regional guilds. Given this social embeddedness, it may seem perverse to suggest that popular religion could nevertheless serve as an arena in which individuality could be expressed. Certainly, in comparison with Russian Orthodoxy, it lacked elements crucial to the forging of self such as doctrines of a transcendental God, a world fashioned by a creator God, an immortal soul, and a world perceived to be inherently sinful. Only in the redemptive sects (*huidaomen*), which flourished during the republican era, does one find a form of religion focused on the salvation of the individual soul. Yet even if popular religion lacked the critical idea of the individual responsible to God, it did not altogether lack a conception of the soul (or, more correctly, 'souls') or a notion that the soul would be punished in the afterlife for actions taken in this life. To this extent, there were resources within popular religion that could sustain a relationship between the worshipper and a god of a rather personal kind and even promote critical reflection on the existing social order. Therefore, so long as the different valency of 'religion' in the Russian and Chinese contexts is borne in mind, it is legitimate to compare it as an arena in which notions of the self were transacted.

Religious belief and practice were extensively woven into the fabric of rural society in Russia. Earlier writers suggested that the peasantry subscribed to a 'dual faith' that combined formal adherence to Orthodoxy with an enduring sub-stratum of pagan belief, but recent scholars challenge the idea of 'dual faith' with its implicit premise that the religion of the peasantry was substantially at variance with that of the official Church. Instead they present religious culture as multi-layered and mutable, with peasants actively engaging in the economy of salvation, appropriating official belief and ritual for their own, often quintessentially local purposes.[62] It is true that peasants were not ardent church-goers and that they took confession and communion only rarely (usually once a year), but local feast days marked key points in the agricultural and liturgical cycle and were major occasions for rural communities; local identities, moreover, were tightly bound up with devotion to particular saints or icons. So localized indeed was much of the peasant religion that it may have been difficult to transplant it to the town.

---

[62] Eve Levin, '*Dvoeverie* and Popular Religion', in Stephen K. Batalden (ed.), *Seeking God: The Recovery of Religious Identity in Orthodox Russia, Ukraine and Georgia* (DeKalb: University of Northern Illinois Press, 1993), pp. 29–52; Vera Shevzov, *Russian Orthodoxy on the Eve of the Revolution* (Oxford: Oxford University Press, 2003), pp. 259–61; Chris Chulos, *Converging Worlds: Religion and Community in Peasant Russia, 1861–1917* (DeKalb: Northern Illinois University Press, 2003).

Certainly, religion became an issue of contention for migrants to St Petersburg in a way that had not been true in the village. Memoirists often remark that religion was *the* issue that caused most heated debate among workers.[63] There is little doubt that the influence of the Church in the capital was in decline. Until 1900, there were no clearly defined parishes and churches were few on the ground. Many immigrants failed to register with a parish and ceased to go to services, and where male immigrants did so, they often claimed that it was only under pressure from their wives.[64] In 1908, workers in the city spent only 10 kopecks a month on religious items, compared with 30.7 kopecks in the small town of Sereda in Kostroma province.[65] Ecclesiastical commentators bemoaned the irreligion they perceived to be rampant. In the 1907 report on Kostroma diocese, the dean opined: 'Our present-day "Pitershchiki" (i.e. short-term migrants to St Petersburg, SAS) ... are bearers and disseminators of abuse towards the Orthodox Church, its institutions and servants and even of total religious unbelief.' The report on the same diocese the following year expanded: 'The majority of young people who live from wage work in Petersburg do not observe fasts and, coming back to the village, serve as a source of temptation to their fellows living in the village.'[66] We should not take such reports at face value: in some respects, they tell us more about the mind-set of a Church that perceived itself to be besieged by a rising tide of sectarianism, socialism and alcoholism than they do about the religious attitudes of migrant workers.[67] The Church was not idle in the face of evidence that it was losing touch with the urban proletariat. It launched a programme of building new churches, schools and religious libraries and a relatively successful temperance movement, yet this was not sufficient to prevent it losing ground in the city. In addition, despite the reformist initiatives of Father Gapon and some other progressive priests, during the 1905 Revolution, the influence of the Church was further undermined as Church leaders

---

[63] See the testimonies of Karelina and Boldyreva in E. A. Korol'chuk (ed.), *V nachale puti: vospominaniia peterburgskikh rabochikh, 1872–1897gg* (Leningrad: Lenizdat, 1975), pp. 225, 275.

[64] Simon Dixon, 'The Orthodox Church and the Workers of St Petersburg, 1880–1914', in Hugh McLeod, *European Religion in the Age of Great Cities, 1830–1930* (London: Routledge, 1995), p. 121; Kimberly Page Herrlinger, 'Class, Piety, and Politics: Workers, Orthodoxy, and the Problem of Religious Identity in Russia, 1881–1914', University of California, Berkeley, PhD, 1996, p. 212.

[65] E. O. Kabo, *Ocherki rabochego byta* (Moscow: Knigoizd-vo VTsSPS, 1928), p. 132

[66] L.I. Emeliakh, *Antiklerikal'noe dvizhenie krest'ian v period pervoi russkoi revoliutsii* (Leningrad: Nauka, 1965), p. 160.

[67] Herrlinger, 'Class, Piety and Politics', p. 3.

lined up behind the autocracy.[68] Religion in the city was thus severed from its roots in the rural community, no longer as integral to social life, and this meant that it became a matter of individual choice in a way that it had not been in the village.

In view of the pessimism of contemporary clerics about the declining religiosity of migrants to St Petersburg, it is important to recognize that the great majority continued to be believers. In 1910, when asked their religious affiliation in the census, 1,659,581 of the city's residents declared themselves Orthodox; 104,696 said they were Protestant; 94,460 Roman Catholic and 43,344 were non-Christians of various types; 1,462 were classified as miscellaneous or unknown.[69] The great majority of workers continued to get married in church, to have their children baptized and to have a Christian burial.[70] Moreover, the key festivals of Christmas and Easter, both preceded by stints of fasting, saw people take confession and communion and engage in self-reflection (*samouglublenie*).[71] Worker memoirists comment on the strength of religious feeling among workers at least prior to 1905. The young Buiko, on becoming an apprentice at the Putilov works at the turn of the century, found himself surrounded by people who said 'Everything comes from God' or 'You'll never reach the threshold without God' (*Bez boga, ne do poroga*).[72] Some of the bigger factories had their own churches, and services were held in most workplaces on major feast days.[73] Within workshops there were icons, the most popular being those dedicated to the Kazan' Mother of God and to St Nicholas, a popular saint in Russia, who happened also to be the patron saint of factory workers.[74] Lamp-icon funds were established in the 1880s and 1890s to support eternal votive lights, and trusted older men were permitted to collect money for these. Such funds were still widespread in Petersburg in 1906–9, and sometimes assisted members with funeral or sickness expenses.[75]

---

[68] Dixon, 'Orthodox Church', p. 123; Sergei L. Firsov, 'Workers and the Orthodox Church in Early Twentieth Century Russia', in Michael Melancon and Alice Pate (eds.), *New Labor History: Worker Identity and Experience in Russia, 1840–1918* (Bloomington: Slavica Publishers, 2002), pp. 65–76.

[69] *Statisticheskie dannye Petrograda 1916*, (Petrograd, 1916), p. 8.

[70] Herrlinger, 'Class, Piety and Politics', p. 212.

[71] L. A. Anokhina and M. N. Smeleva, *Byt gorodskogo naseleniia srednei polosy RSFSR v proshlom i nastoiashchem: na primere gorodov Kaluga, Elets, Efremov* (Moscow: Nauka, 1977), p. 283.

[72] A. M. Buiko, *Put' rabochego: zapiski starogo bol'shevika* (Moscow: Staryi Bol'shevik, 1934), p. 15.

[73] *Putilovtsy v 1905 godu* (Leningrad, 1931), p. 12.

[74] P. Timofeev, *Chem zhivet zavodskii rabochii* (St Petersburg: Russkoe bogatstvo 1906), p. 80; Shapovalov, *Po doroge*, p. 12.

[75] F. A. Bulkin, *Na zare profdvizheniia: istoriia Peterburgskogo soiuza metallistov, 1906–1914* (Leningrad: 1924), p. 93; *Materialy po istorii professional'nogo dvizheniia*, 2 (1925), 44.

Just as many 'conscious' workers asserted their 'personality' through a rejection of religion, so others strove to assert their individual autonomy through a consciously chosen form of Christian faith. A minority – possibly quite sizeable – struggled to establish a more vital, sacramentally based relationship with Christ through the Orthodox city missions. The Society for Religious and Moral Enlightenment in the Spirit of the Orthodox Church, founded in 1881, sought to bring 'moral and spiritual enlightenment' to the inhabitants of working-class areas and one of its successful initiatives was to establish dozens of temperance tearooms.[76] These temperance societies appealed to 'conscious' workers struggling to rise above the 'backwardness' of their fellow workers. By 1905, 72,315 people were said to have taken the temperance pledge.[77] For such workers, religious commitment became central to their sense of self in a way that it had not been in the village where religion was a taken-for-granted element in community life.[78] Others were drawn to Protestantism, represented by sects such as the Pashkovites and Shtundists (Baptists), who promised an unmediated relationship with God based on faith not works. Interestingly, the Orthodox Church – bewildered by a growth of evangelical Christianity that continued into the 1920s – condemned such forms of biblically based Christianity as the 'dogma of individualism'.[79] In the urban-industrial environment, therefore, where challenges to faith were common and where rival forms of Christianity flourished, religion became an issue of contention in a way that it had not been in the village, a matter upon which migrants were required to reflect and one that demanded a higher level of commitment than in the village.[80]

Popular religion in China lacked central institutions to regulate religious practice, and a clearly defined corpus of scriptures and theological doctrine. Popular religion was syncretic, combining a large dose of Confucian orthodoxy with elements of Daoism such as occult magic and the practice of deifying prominent personalities, and of Buddhism such as doctrines of the transmigration of souls and the law of causal retribution (karma). Its essential ingredients were ancestor worship; worship of an array of gods and spirits that could influence the fate of mortals; belief in the efficacy of sacrifice and divination as means of influencing these gods and spirits; and belief in forms of spirit mediumship and exorcism.[81] It was intensely local and, in consequence, remarkably flexible, capable

---

[76] Herrlinger, 'Class, Piety and Politics', p. 133.
[77] Herrlinger, 'Class, Piety and Politics', p. 132.
[78] Herrlinger, 'Class, Piety and Politics', p. 16.
[79] Quoted in Herrlinger, 'Class, Piety and Politics', p. 322.
[80] Herrlinger, 'Class, Piety and Politics', p. 226.
[81] Stephan Feuchtwang, *Popular Religion in China* (Richmond: Curzon, 2001).

of generating a wide range of practices. At its heart was sacrifice, the practice of making offerings of special food, incense and 'spirit money' to the gods in expectation of favours.[82] In a tough and uncertain world worshippers' concerns were heavily practical. The bond between them and a particular god was a transaction rather than a covenant: an exchange of sacrifice and devotion in return for protection and aid. In the words of Richard von Glahn, 'the conception of the divine realm was very much a product of active effort by ordinary people to make sense of and gain control over their lives'.[83] If a god did not reciprocate, it could be abandoned for another. In that sense, religion operated rather like a commodity with 'consumers' choosing which services to buy.[84]

From the last decade of the Qings, precisely because of its embeddedness in local social and political structures, popular religion came under attack as an obstacle to the building of a new vertically integrated society, condemned as 'feudal superstition'. Following the establishment of a republic in 1911, the new government took aim at the entire field of popular religion, deeming it to be backward and irrational and failing to meet the (implicitly western) canons of authentic, modern religion.[85] It strove to replace traditional festivals of the lunar calendar with modern national holidays, such as National Day and Sun Yat-sen's birthday, and after 1928, Chiang Kai-shek's government aggressively promoted the solar calendar.[86] In that year, too, the government launched a mass 'movement to eradicate superstition', arguing that the building of a strong nation state required that 'science' be substituted for 'superstition'. Nationalist ideologues inveighed against the 'useless gods' of popular religion, castigated wasteful expenditure on incense and spirit-money and called for many of China's innumerable temples to be 'razed to the ground so that nothing remains'.[87] In Shanghai the new municipal

---

[82] Meir Shahar and Robert P. Weller, 'Introduction: Gods and Society in China', in Meir Shahar and Robert P. Weller (eds.), *Unruly Gods: Divinity and Society in China* (Honolulu: University of Hawaii Press, 1996), p. 30; Richard von Glahn, *The Sinister Way: The Divine and the Demonic in Chinese Religious Culture* (Berkeley: University of California Press, 2004), p. 8.

[83] von Glahn, *Sinister Way*, p. 265.

[84] Robert Hymes, *Way and Byway: Taoism, Local Religion, and Models of Divinity in Sung and Modern China* (Berkeley: University of California Press, 2002), p. 198.

[85] Vincent Goossaert, '1898: The Beginning of the End for Chinese Religion?' *Journal of Asian Studies*, 65, 2 (May 2006), 307–336.

[86] Henrietta Harrison, *The Making of the Republican Citizen: Political Ceremonies and Symbols in China, 1911–1929* (Oxford: Oxford University Press, 2000), pp. 66–69.

[87] Rebecca Nedostup, 'Religion, Superstition and Governing Society in Nationalist China', Columbia University, PhD, 2001, ch. 3; Prasenjit Duara, 'Knowledge and Power in the Discourse of Modernity: The Campaigns Against Popular Religion in Early Twentieth-century China', *Journal of Asian Studies*, 50, 1 (1991), 67–83.

government, which controlled areas of the city outside the International Settlement and the French Concession, introduced regulations to eliminate 'feudal' elements in funeral rituals – such as the wearing of the uniforms of Qing officials or the carrying of banners announcing the arrival of an official, parasols and paper lanterns – and to limit expenditure on funerals and birthday celebrations. Regulations also banned the ritual use of paper money and ceremonial utensils. How far these were enforced is difficult to say: the campaign did not last long, peaking in the years 1928–30 and continuing fitfully until 1937.[88] Its impact on the practice of popular religion is also hard to gauge. Nevertheless by 1937, one half of the million plus temples that had existed in 1900 were no longer functioning.[89]

A tiny minority of radicalized workers – mainly among skilled groups such as postal workers – responded positively to notions of science and secularism.[90] There is even evidence that seeds of scepticism were sown among some female factory workers. One woman worker confided: 'I do not believe in any religion. All religions are just asking people to be better human beings. So long as I am good, there is no need to worship.' Another said: 'It is not true that there are certain buddhas who write down accounts of good and bad deeds of humans. Act right is my religion.'[91] But these were doubtless voices of a minority. Generally, the anti-superstition campaign encountered resistance, and the capacity of the government to enforce it proved limited.[92]

Migrants to Shanghai largely maintained the customary practices of making sacrifices to venerate ancestors, seek favours from gods, and propitiate ghosts. A survey of 230 cotton worker families in 1927–8 revealed that while on average only $2.76 a year was spent on religious items, this was more than expenditure on toiletries, amusements and, crucially, on education.[93] Aside from worship of the Buddha, the most

[88] Shen Bojing (ed.), *Shanghai shi zhinan* [Guidebook to Shanghai] (Shanghai: Zhonghua shudian, 1933), pp. 141–2.

[89] Vincent Goossaert, 'Le destin de la religion chinoise au 20ème siècle', *Social Compass*, 50, 4 (2003), 436.

[90] Zhu Bangxing, Hu Linge and Xu Sheng, *Shanghai chanye yu Shanghai zhigong* [Shanghai Industry and Shanghai Labour] (Shanghai: Shanghai renmin chubanshe, 1984; orig. 1939), pp. 471–3.

[91] H. D. Lamson, 'The Effect of Industrialization upon Village Livelihood: A Study of Fifty Families in Four Villages Near the University of Shanghai', *Chinese Economic Journal*, 9, 4 (1932), 1025–1082; 1072.

[92] Poon Shuk Wah, 'Refashioning Festivals in Republic Guangzhou', *Modern China*, 30, 2 (2004), 199–277.

[93] Simon Yang and L. K. Tao, *A Study of the Standard of Living of Working Families in Shanghai* (Peiping: Institute of Social Research, 1931), p. 76. This sum, moreover, may have represented an increase in the proportion spent on religion compared with the

popular cult in Shanghai was that of Guanyin, goddess of mercy, who saves people from suffering and helps women conceive. On her three main festivals folk would flock to neighbourhood temples and to her main temple on the corner of Nanjing and Fujian roads.[94] The second most popular cult was that of Guandi (Guangong), a military hero of the third century, whose loyalty and trustworthiness made him the patron of businessmen. His biggest temple was situated in what had been until the revolution of 1911 the old walled city. Like Guanyin, Guandi was venerated across the country, and during 1920s and 1930s, the Nationalist government even promoted his cult in order to encourage patriotism.[95] Also popular in Shanghai were Dizangwang who, like Guanyin, could visit purgatory on errands of mercy and free souls from torment, and Dongyue, Lord of Mount Tai, the presiding deity of the underworld, who had been awarded the rank of 'divine sovereign' by the fervently daoist emperor Zhenzong (997–1022 CE).[96] Gods, such as Dongyue, or the gods of purgatory, conform to the model of the supernatural world as a metaphor for the imperial social order, since they were perceived as heavenly officials who governed the fate of worshippers, but female deities, such as Guanyin – and the buddhist pantheon in general – did not fit this bureaucratic model. Their devotees addressed them in a personal language rather than in administrative jargon and viewed them as protectors, patrons or parents, rather than as powerful officials.[97] This offered scope to worshippers to communicate with gods in ways that met their individual needs.

Shanghai was a city where lineages were very weak, but domestic ancestor worship remained entrenched among the city's population. The worship of ancestors was based on the idea of reciprocity between the living and the dead. Family members would burn incense and present food in front of the ancestral tablets within the home and kowtow to them in order of seniority on the birthday or anniversary of the death of an ancestor. At the Winter Solstice people would also go to the temple to burn incense and recite scriptures, and at the Qingming festival, which took place on the fifteenth day of the third lunar month, people would

---

proportion spent by peasants, at least those of Ding county in Hebei. Nedostup, 'Religion, Superstition', p. 478.

[94] Cai Fengming, *Shanghai dushi minsu* [Urban Folkways of Shanghai] (Shanghai: Xuelin chubanshe, 2001), pp. 242, 251.

[95] Alvin P. Cohen, 'Popular Religion', in Mircea Eliade (ed.), *Encyclopedia of Religion* (New York: Macmillan, 1987), pp. 289–296; 292.

[96] Henry Doré S. J., *Researches into Chinese Superstitions*, vol. 7. Trans. M. Kennelly, S. J. (Taipei: Ch'eng-Wen Publishing Company, Taipei, 1966; orig. Shanghai 1922), p. 252; Cai Fengming, *Shanghai dushi minsu*, p. 243.

[97] von Glahn, *Sinister Way*, pp. 7–8; Hymes, *Way and Byway*, p. 264.

hope to return to their native places to sweep the family graves. Ancestor worship was in slow but by no means terminal decline. When the Shanghai municipal committee of the CCP launched a brief campaign in 1964 to kill off the practice, it still aroused considerable anxiety. At the Qingming festival one factory worker reportedly prayed: 'Old ancestors, please hurry up and finish your food. The inspectors are coming. Please do not all come next year. Just mother and father will do.' One old lady informed her ancestral tablets: 'Old ancestors, I should let you know in advance that this year we do things according to tradition, but next year we have to do things according to the new regulations. The cadres from the street committee have already come over and warned us.' Another retired worker complained to his neighbourhood committee: 'In the word "fatherland" (*zuguo*) [the word often used to denote the nation by the CCP], the character for "ancestor" comes before that for "country". How, then, can we not worship our ancestors?'[98]

It was above all in the guilds of the handicraft, retail and transportation sectors that religion was most clearly woven into the fabric of working life in Shanghai. Guilds held annual celebrations to honour the mythical founders of their trade and many guilds had their own temples. The most influential of the patron deities of the guilds was Lu Ban, who presided over the woodworking trades. Each craft or bang had its own Lu Ban hall, where it transacted business, the biggest belonging to the Ningbo carpenters in the Chinese City in Shanghai. On Lu's birthday on the thirteenth day of the sixth lunar month all the woodworking trades would gather at this temple for a huge celebration.[99] The patron of the dye-workers' guild was Ge Xianweng (164–244? CE), an influential daoist priest during the Three Kingdoms era, much venerated in Jiangnan. His temple, built in the Song dynasty and taken over by the dyers' guild only at the end of the Qing, hosted a big festival to celebrate his birthday on the ninth day of the ninth month. The watchmakers' guild worshipped no less a figure than Matteo Ricci, the Jesuit priest who was reputed to have brought the first watches into China.[100] Religious ritual was a vital source of guild solidarity, but it seems to have been waning in the republican era. The last guild to open a temple was the Japanese sea-food guild in 1907, and from early in the twentieth century, there were regular complaints that religion no longer carried the weight in guild life that it had once had: that 'public morality is not

[98] Propaganda Department of the CCP Shanghai Municipal Committee, 'The situation and problems regarding customs and habits during the Spring Festival', Shanghai Municipal Archive: A22-2-1190.
[99] Cai Fengming, *Shanghai dushi minsu*, p. 264.
[100] Cai Fengming, *Shanghai dushi minsu*, p. 265.

what it used to be' (*ren xin bu gu*).[101] The guilds appear to have been undergoing that same 'impoverishment or secularization of rituals' that Lucien Bianco has identified as a feature of peasant rebellions in the republican era.[102]

It is the continuities rather than changes in popular religion that are most striking in Shanghai in the republican era. Nevertheless, it is important not to lose sight of the fact that popular religion was inevitably influenced by the shattering political changes that took place in the years prior to the Communist accession to power. The abolition of the traditional civil service examinations in 1905 and the creation of modern schools dealt a devastating blow to the prestige of Confucianism, one compounded in 1911 by the removal of the emperor, who for centuries had been the guarantor of harmony between the heavenly and the secular worlds. Precisely because popular religion had always represented the supernatural world in terms that closely mirrored the secular political order, the drastic changes in the nature of the Chinese polity in the republican period were bound to influence the way in which worshippers understood and represented their relationship to the gods.

Yet if the supernatural world mirrored the worldly political order to a remarkable extent, popular religion never simply served to promote obedience to the status quo: it 'shaped it, compensated for it and changed it'; and gods 'participated in the dynamics of power and struggles over identity that characterized China as much as any other society.'[103] Emily Martin has suggested that religious ritual, far from mystifying the nature of power, provided the lower classes with a means to access divine power for their own purposes. Ritual processes, she writes, 'teach people how to obtain power, how to obtain access to those in power and how to limit those with power.'[104] If she is correct, then the abandonment of popular religion as a resource for rule on the part of the new nationalist elite may have strengthened these potentialities, increasing the capacity of the popular classes to deploy religious idioms to articulate their needs and desires. Direct evidence is hard to come by, but it is reasonable to suppose that the severance of popular religion from its traditional social contexts, combined with the abandonment of popular religion by the ruling elites, made it a sphere where ordinary people had greater capacity to work through the meanings of existence

[101] Negishi Tadashi, *Shanhai no girudo* (Tokyo: Nihon Hyoronsha, 1951), p. 8.
[102] Lucien Bianco, *Jacqueries et révolution dans la China du XXe siècle* (Paris: Éditions de La Martinière, 2005), p. 217.
[103] Shahar and Weller, 'Introduction', p. 3.
[104] Emily Martin Ahern, *Chinese Ritual and Politics* (Cambridge: Cambridge University Press, 1981), p. 108.

and their own relationships to society. Religion in Shanghai remained less important as a field in which new subjectivities were forged than in St Petersburg. Yet in both cities religious practice was no longer tied to maintenance of the status quo and if popular religion nevertheless served, to a considerable degree, to reproduce traditional mentalities and relationships, it was neither static nor immune to change and it provided individuals with resources for reflecting on their social identities amid wrenching worldly transformations.

Selfhood in the Marketplace

If the majority of migrants came to St Petersburg and Shanghai with survival uppermost in mind, they quickly became aware that the two cities embodied a consumer culture that proclaimed that the path to individual and collective happiness lay through the acquisition of desirable goods. Doubtless, the consumption patterns of the majority of migrants were dictated primarily by need, yet we know that poverty is no bar to increased desire for consumer goods. And in both cities even very poor people, especially the young, fell under the influence of discourses that suggested that what you consume defines who you are. As older, all-encompassing identity schemes based on kinship and locality started to erode, consumer culture became a site on which migrants groped towards a new sense of individuality. In this section fashions in dress and pulp fiction are examined as arenas in which migrants exercised choice and asserted their autonomy and serve as proxies for changing conceptions of individuality among migrants who were more typical than those 'conscious' workers examined above.

Individuality and Fashions in Dress

In 1897, the historian V. O. Kliuchevskii, son of a poor parish priest, commented scathingly on the obsession of contemporary society with fashion, condemning it as a rejection of religious and community values in favour of an exaltation of the individual and a shallow effort to impress.[105] His comment reflects the fact that the move to the city tended to liberate clothing from the hold of local custom and to subject it to the forces of the market. Dress began to be influenced by the dictates of fashion, with style beginning to triumph over utility. Dress was probably the sphere where the new interest in urban consumer

---

[105] Cited in Gary Thurston, *The Popular Theatre Movement in Russia, 1862–1919* (Evanston IL: Northwestern University Press, 1998), p. 111.

culture manifested itself most dramatically in both St Petersburg and Shanghai, for there is plentiful evidence that migrants quickly became attuned to the fact that clothes carry powerful messages about individuality, respectability, social status and aspiration. Even among very poor migrants one of the first changes in patterns of expenditure was an increase in the proportion of earnings spent on clothing. A study of mainly skilled metalworkers in St Petersburg in 1908 showed that, despite substantial variation according to income, they spent on average 15.6% of their income on clothing and footwear.[106] Significantly, women workers spent more than men, and single workers spent more than married workers. It is reckoned that in 1912 single skilled women textile workers spent as much as 20% of their income on clothes and unskilled singletons 14.6%.[107]

Few working women were ever likely to enter the august portals of the capital's department stores, yet working women's taste in clothes was influenced by the fashions on display in their shop windows.[108] In 1908, P. T. Galkina, an eighteen-year-old weaver, paid a seamstress three roubles to copy from a fashion magazine a rose-coloured cashmere dress, trimmed with white machine-made lace and rose-coloured satin ribbons.[109] Mikhail Isakovskii, whose sister migrated to Moscow from Smolensk to work in a textile mill, recalls how proud she was of the fashionable *sak* – a loose-fitting coat which draped from the shoulders:

Women saved because you could not live without a sak. Those who did not have a sak felt they were deprived of their full rights, not fully valued, on the slide. There were endless conversations among the women workers about buying a sak. And if they bought one, they wrote to the village at once, to tell everyone that the long-desired sak had been purchased.[110]

Such sensitivity to fashion disclosed a new concern with how one presented oneself to the world, a concern with the message one conveyed about oneself as a modern person. Isakovskii's suggestion, however ironic, that women unable to participate in fashion felt lacking in rights gestures to a new relationship between changing consumer aspirations and a sense of individuality.

[106] S. N. Prokopovich, *Biudzhety peterburgskikh rabochikh* (St Petersburg, 1909).
[107] M. Davidovich, *Peterburgskii tekstil'nyi rabochii v ego biudzhetakh* (St Petersburg, 1912), p. 11.
[108] Christine Ruane, 'Clothes Shopping in Imperial Russia: The Development of a Consumer Culture', *Journal of Social History*, 28, 4 (1995), 765–782.
[109] Barbara Alpern Engel, *Between the Fields and the City: Women, Work and Family in Russia, 1861–1914* (Cambridge: Cambridge University Press, 1994), p. 155. Magazines such as *Niva* included dress patterns in their supplements. Ruane, 'Clothes Shopping', p. 770.
[110] M. Isakovskii, *Na El'ninskoi zemle* (Moscow: Sovetskii pisatel', 1975), p. 198.

It was not only young women who were concerned about their appearance. Z. T. Trifonov struggled to find work in St Petersburg. Having found a job, he decided one Sunday morning to fulfil his cherished ambition of going to the Summer Garden to see the monument to the writer Krylov. He polished his boots, put on his leather jacket, wide trousers and peaked cap, only to be refused entry because of his peasant attire by two constables who told him the garden was open only to the 'clean' public. Smarting from the insult, he resolved to use part of his new wage to buy clothes in what he called the 'German' style.[111] Dressing well in public was an assertion of self-respect and was designed to command the respect of others. The young Kanatchikov bought himself a watch and a holiday outfit, consisting of grey trousers, a wide belt, a straw hat, and some fancy shoes. 'In a word, I dressed in the manner of those young urban metalworkers who earned an independent living and didn't ruin themselves with vodka.'[112] High, glossy boots were much in vogue and those that had a lot of creases when pulled down were ultra-chic.[113] Such fashionable young men disdained to be seen wearing their working clothes in their leisure time. Through clothes, young workers of both sexes defined themselves, asserted themselves visually, and sought to raise their social status. Ivan Shcheglov, a promoter of popular theatre, observed:

It would be a mistake to assume that the ladies with palm fronds on their heads and men in stylish bowlers comprise in any way the cream of the intelligentsia, for in the event of any unpleasant misunderstanding that leads to a confrontation, the dandy who looks like a man-about-town on Nevskii Prospekt turns out to be an ordinary metalworker from a neighbouring factory, while the lady in a cloak with a Spanish collar and an ostrich plume in her hat turns out to be a laundress from the nearby textile mill.[114]

As Tony Swift notes, Shcheglov's comment is 'tinged with a sense that the *narod* (people) is transgressing social boundaries, adopting roles inappropriate to their status, and rewriting cultural scripts that set the expectations of comportment'.[115] But revolutionaries could be just as disapproving of the messages about social aspiration, sexuality and pleasure conveyed by fashionable dress. Shapovalov was full of scorn for those whose sole ambition was to save up enough money to buy an accordion, a suit, a pair of lacquered shoes with embroidered tops, and a crimson shirt with a belt.[116]

---

[111] *Avangard: Vospominaniia*, pp. 304–5.
[112] Zelnik, *Radical Worker*, p. 71.
[113] Manya Gordon, *Workers Before and After Lenin* (New York: Dutton, 1941), p. 217.
[114] Quoted in E. Anthony Swift, *Popular Theater and Society in Tsarist Russia* (Berkeley: University of California Press, 2002), p. 145.
[115] Swift, *Popular Theater*, p. 145.   [116] Shapovalov, *Po doroge*, p. 15.

In China dress was a far more politicized issue than in Russia, the meanings of dress being heavily shaped by a discourse of foreign versus national. After 1911, one of the most telling ways of expressing identification with the new republic was for men to cut off the queues (pigtails) that had been imposed by the Qing after their seizure of Beijing in 1644. Queues were now seen as symbols of backwardness and of subjugation to a foreign power. The military government in Shanghai ordered soldiers in the revolutionary army to remove their queues and decreed that civilians be persuaded to do likewise.[117] The newspaper *Shenbao* claimed that 80% to 90% of men in Shanghai dispensed with their queues.[118] There were, however, reports of groups of soldiers and 'citizen volunteers' meeting resistance from country folk coming into Shanghai, which suggests that for the more traditional layers of the populace, the queue, originally a symbol of alien domination, had become a symbol of being Han Chinese.[119] In his brief tenure as president of the new republic, Sun Yat-sen called for the introduction of new styles of dress 'good for health, easy to move in, economical and elegant to look at', although he did not advocate the wholesale adoption of Western dress for the common people.[120] Among the middle classes of Shanghai, the revolution gave a boost to the popularity of western dress, and this caused consternation on the part of the Silk Guild and the Society to Promote National Products (*Guohuo weichi hui*) since western clothes were made from imported cloth. The government bowed to pressure and agreed that clothes should be made from Chinese cloth and that traditional styles could be worn alongside western styles.[121]

In the early years of the republic the national products movement was a key force politicizing consumption issues. From the last quarter of the nineteenth century, citizens of Shanghai had started to buy imported goods or goods made in China by foreign companies, such as lace, towels, handkerchiefs, socks, cosmetics, perfumes and confectionery. After 1911, the flow of these goods increased, as consumers began to buy hats, shoes, toothbrushes and soap.[122] By the 1920s, many working people wore straw hats, foreign-made trousers and rubber galoshes and

---

[117] Liu Huiwu (ed.), *Shanghai jindai shi* [Modern History of Shanghai] vol. 1 (Shanghai: Huadong shifan daxue chubanshe, 1985), p. 362.

[118] Cited in Harrison, *Making*, p. 30.

[119] *Municipal Gazette*, 15 February 1913, pp. 38–9; 16 May 1912, p. 144.

[120] Quoted in Sidney Chang and Leonard H. D. Gordon, *All Under Heaven. Sun Yat-sen and his Revolutionary Thought* (Stanford: Hoover Institution Press, 1991), p. 46.

[121] Liu Huiwu (ed.) *Shanghai jindai shi*, p. 363; Karl Gerth, *China Made: Consumer Culture and the Creation of the Nation* (Cambridge MA: Harvard University Press, 2003), pp. 113, 110.

[122] Gerth, *China Made*, p. 30. As a result of the 1911 Revolution, 'the people came to respect and liked to use foreign goods'. Peng Zeyi (ed.), *Zhongguo jindai shougongye shi*

a few could even afford leather shoes. Lower-class Shanghainese used foreign goods in a pragmatic, selective fashion. Asked what she thought of foreign goods, one woman worker, replied: 'If a thing is good and cheap we buy it whether it is Chinese or foreign.'[123] The national products movement feared that such attitudes were undermining the domestic economy and urged consumers to 'buy Chinese'. During the May Fourth Movement of 1919, according to the International Settlement police, 'students and loafers began to snatch and mutilate Japan-made straw hats from the heads of otherwise unoffending citizens'.[124] And at the height of the May Thirtieth Movement of 1925, wearing foreign apparel led to accusations that one was a 'foreign slave'.[125] Indeed one of the initial demands of the strikers was that Chinese should not wear foreign clothes, though this was quickly dropped.[126] In reality, the force of nationalist opinion was rarely strong enough to induce poor people not to buy foreign manufactures if these were cheaper and of better quality than their Chinese-made counterparts.

Running counter to the influence of the national products movement was the pride of Shanghainese in being up-to-date and in their reputation for having a sense of style. By the 1920s, the word for fashion (*shimao*) had ceased to be pejorative and become a term of approbation in the city.[127] Yet to be fashionable usually meant to consume foreign brands and this gave Shanghai folk an unsavoury reputation in nationalist circles of 'fawning on foreign things' (*mei wai*).[128] Compared with St Petersburg, only a small proportion of working people in Shanghai could afford to dress with a determined eye to fashion. Among 230 cotton-worker families in Shanghai, 9.4% of monthly income was spent on clothing. This represented an annual sum of $36.7 per family – a sum barely adequate to buy one fine woollen suit. Nevertheless it is noteworthy that this sum was higher than the amount spent on clothes by worker families in Beijing, where annual expenditure totalled only $14.[129] Yet if a worker's fortunes improved, the betterment of attire was an immediate priority. As income rose, the proportion spent on clothing

ziliao, 1840–1949 [Source materials on the history of the handicraft industry in modern China, 1840–1949], vol. 2 (Beijing: Zhonghua shuju, 1957), p. 718.

[123] Lamson, 'The Effect of Industrialization', p. 1063.

[124] *Municipal Gazette*, 26 July 1919, p. 256.

[125] *North China Herald*, 13 June 1925, p. 445.

[126] *North China Herald*, 6 June 1925, p. 414. The last demand was subsequently dropped. Richard W. Rigby, *The May 30th Movement: Events and Themes* (Canberra: Australian National University Press, 1980), p. 39.

[127] Ye Xiaoqing, 'Shanghai before Nationalism', *East Asian History*, 3 (1992), 42–3.

[128] Ye Xiaoqing, 'Shanghai before Nationalism', pp. 42–3.

[129] Yang and Tao, *Study*, p. 55.

increased while the proportion spent on food decreased.[130] Shanghai workers thus dressed better than their counterparts in other cities, and their garments were generally better tailored, more stylish and occasionally made of silk or wool.[131] In 1931, the social investigator H. D. Lamson noted the 'great change in appearance' of people who lived in the villages on the outskirts of Shanghai, 'especially ones who work in factories ... (they) now look better and dress better. Some of the women even bob their hair.'[132]

As in St Petersburg, dress served as a measure of the extent to which migrants had embraced social change. Among the young girls in the Japanese mills there was a division between women from Subei, who dressed scruffily and traditionally and whose indifference to fashion reflected a lesser concern to differentiate themselves individually, and the better-educated women from Jiangnan, who were far more fastidious about their attire. The latter longed for the day when they might afford lavender trousers, light-blue stockings and purple slippers. A few even affected a 'student' look by wearing a long *qipao*, a woollen coat in winter, leather shoes and – de rigueur by the 1930s – a fountain pen in their top pocket.[133] As early as the mid-1920s, the qipao became a much-talked-about type of woman's dress in Shanghai. Initially, as an all-in-one garment, it aped men's gowns; but by the 1930s, it had become more and more revealing of the contours of the female body, in a way that no previous Chinese garment had ever been.[134] In 1930, Lamson's investigators remarked that young women increasingly bought pretty clothes, silk handkerchiefs, wristwatches, face powder and cream, and even gold earrings.[135] Conservatives sometimes referred to Shanghai's women silkworkers as makers of 'Fool's Silk', seeing their desire to look pretty as a transgression of traditional norms of modesty and frugality.[136] In early 1927, a Soviet visitor described the scene outside a Shanghai tobacco factory mill: 'the entire width of the asphalt thoroughfare was thronged with young girls, hundreds of them, all dressed in bright colours, like butterflies, or birds-of-paradise, everyone

[130] H. D. Lamson, 'The Standard of Living of Factory Workers', *Chinese Economic Journal*, 7, 5 (1930), 1240–56.

[131] Olga Lang, *Chinese Family and Society* (New Haven: Yale University Press, 1946), p. 89.

[132] Lamson, 'The Effect of Industrialization', p. 1053.

[133] Zhu Bangxing et al., *Shanghai chanye*, pp. 87, 85.

[134] Antonia Finnane, 'What Should Chinese Women Wear?', *Modern China*, 22, 2 (1996), pp. 111–12, 118.

[135] Lamson, 'The Effect of Industrialization', p. 1075.

[136] Wang Simine, *Le travail industriel des femmes and des enfants en Chine* (Paris: Pedone, 1933), p. 156.

of them attractive, fragile, saucy'.[137] When 400 women workers from Shanghai arrived in Tianjin in 1936, 'looking like young ladies of the leisure class', local people expressed outrage at their 'luxurious clothes, curled hair, high heels, and coats with leather collars'.[138] Similarly, in Chongqing, Chiang Kai-shek's wartime capital between 1938 and 1945, public opinion 'disapproved of the lipstick on downriver girls; it disliked their frizzled hair; it was shocked by girls and boys eating together in public restaurants'.[139]

Among silk weavers, younger and better-educated workers from eastern Zhejiang adopted western suits and leather shoes, whereas those pushed out of Hangzhou, Huzhou and Suzhou by the decline of rural handicrafts continued to wear country clothes.[140] But the wearing of a western suit risked being seen as evidence of 'fawning on foreign things' or of a petty-bourgeois psychology. In Chongqing in 1945, a Communist arsenal worker, Xie Wanquan, filed a criticism of Tang Yun, Communist leader at the No. 20 Arsenal: 'One Sunday in October, while I was waiting at the station to take the bus to Chongqing, I saw Tang Yun also waiting for the bus. When Zhang introduced me to Tang he had been wearing workers' clothes. When I saw him this time, Tang was wearing a western-style suit. The style was something a worker should never wear.'[141] The Sun Yat-sen suit, forerunner to the Mao suit, represented an acceptably nationalist adaptation of the western suit, since it combined elements of the latter with elements of the student uniform of Meiji Japan and German military dress. In 1931, the Shaoxing tongxianghui called on men to wear the Sun Yat-sen suit, made from Chinese cloth, since it was more suited to fighting than the traditional long gown.[142] Prior to 1949, however, it remained largely confined to middle-class men, although it was taken up by some better-off workers.[143] Nevertheless, a minority of younger, more educated, better-paid workers, like their confrères in St Petersburg, did embrace the (western) modernity that Shanghai had to offer. Far more

---

[137] Marc Kasanin, *China in the Twenties* (Moscow: Nauka, 1973), p. 157.

[138] Gail Hershatter, *Workers of Tianjin, 1900–1949* (Stanford: Stanford University Press, 1986), p. 147.

[139] Theodore H. White and Annalee Jacoby, *Thunder Out of China* (New York: William Sloane Associates, 1946), p. 9. Cited in Joshua H. Howard, *Workers at War: Labor in China's Arsenals, 1937–53* (Stanford: Stanford University Press, 2004), p. 85.

[140] Elizabeth J. Perry, *Shanghai on Strike: The Politics of Chinese Labour* (Stanford: Stanford University Press, 1993), pp. 185–88; Zhu Bangxing et al., *Shanghai chanye*, pp. 128–30.

[141] Joshua Howard, *Workers at War*, p. 272.

[142] 'Yu Futian's proposal to boycott Japanese products in the event of a Japanese invasion of China' (1931), Shanghai Municipal Archive: Q117-5-44.

[143] Claire Roberts (ed.), *Evolution and Revolution: Chinese Dress, 1700s–1990s* (Sydney: Powerhouse Publishing, Museum of Applied Arts and Sciences, 1997), pp. 18, 22.

than in Russia, however, consumption proved to be a site in which aspirations to fashion, respectability and pleasure clashed with aspirations to yoke consumption to patriotism and, later, with Communist aspirations to forge a collectivist ethos.

Individuality and the Mass Reader

We have seen that for 'conscious' workers in Russia and, to a lesser extent, in China reading was an activity that was central to self-fashioning, constitutive of what it meant to be a cultured and autonomous individual. By contrast, the relation of the newly literate and semi-literate readers of the lower urban classes to new forms of commercially produced mass literature, produced with an eye to entertainment rather than education, was far less earnest. Nevertheless literature for the mass reader, whether in the form of cheap popular newspapers or pulp fiction, reported and commented on urban-industrial society in ways that helped the less educated negotiate the promises and perils of modernity and thus constituted an arena in which migrant workers could imaginatively engage with new identities and new forms of self-expression.[144] Commercially produced literature had a much greater impact on migrants to St Petersburg than Shanghai for the simple reason that literacy was much greater among the former than the latter. In 1897, 74.8% of male workers in the Russian capital and 40.8% of female workers were literate; by 1918, this had risen to 88.9% of male workers and 64.9% of female workers, respectively.[145] There are no global statistics on the literacy of the Shanghai workforce, but one study of a Japanese cotton mill showed that no fewer than 60% of male workers and 85% of female workers were illiterate.[146] Yet programmes to teach workers basic literacy had some impact and by the time the Communists came to power, 54% of those employed in the city were literate.[147]

In Russia the appearance of commercialized forms of culture aimed at the urban masses alarmed both the tsarist government and many of the intelligentsia. The government looked with disquiet on the emergence of literature aimed at a mass readership, fearing that inexperienced readers would be exposed to politically subversive or immoral ideas. It thus

---

[144] James von Geldern and Louise McReynolds (eds.), *Entertaining Tsarist Russia* (Bloomington: Indiana University Press, 1998).

[145] Z. V. Stepanov, 'Voprosy chislennosti i struktury rabochikh Petrograda v 1917g.', in *Rabochii klass i rabochee dvizhenie v Rossii v 1917g.* (Moscow: Nauka, 1964), p. 86.

[146] *Di yici Zhongguo laodong nianjian* [The First Chinese Labour Year Book], part 3 (Beijing: Beiping shehui diaochabu, 1928), p. 385.

[147] Rawski, *Education and Popular Literacy*, p. 20.

restricted the books that could be held in people's libraries or be read at public readings, only the second chapter of Lermontov's *Hero of our Time*, for example, being permitted.[148] The appearance of literature designed to entertain rather than edify affronted the sensibilities of the intelligentsia, since it posed a threat to its aspiration to raise the cultural level of the masses and to its ability to determine the value of ideas and images in circulation.[149] In 1908, the children's writer and literary critic Kornei Chukovskii, despite making a successful career as a commercial journalist, described the prospect of a 'culture market' as 'horrifying', since 'only those [products] that are most adapted to the tastes and whims of the consumer' would survive.[150] *The Copeck Newspaper* (*Gazeta Kopeika*), founded in 1908, epitomized what many intellectuals most loathed and feared. The most popular newspaper among St Petersburg workers, it had a circulation of 250,000 daily by 1910, and as its title indicates, cost one kopeck. With a motto of 'Everything that interests the world', it was rather liberal in its politics. Squeezed within its four or five pages were advertisements, domestic and foreign news, photographs, crime reports, accounts of low life and high life in the capital, and stories of success and hard luck.[151] Crucially, it published serialized fiction, much of it sensational in character, which allowed its readers vicariously to experience worlds of adventure, luxury, sexuality, crime and depravity.

One of the most popular subjects of serialized fiction was the tale of the bandit at war with society, a tale that allowed readers to explore the tensions between law and disorder, convention and freedom. The most celebrated story in this genre was 'Bandit Churkin', written by N. I. Pastukhov (1822–1911) and serialized in the early 1880s: 'From earliest childhood, Churkin exhibited his stubborn and evil character, so much so that his father truly did not know what measures to take to discipline his son. The future bandit did not fear the birch rod, the leather strap or the lash; he was afraid of nothing.'[152] Bandit Churkin proved immensely popular: so much so that the government intervened to have the serial killed off. Bandit stories, although presenting rebellious and self-assertive individuals, ultimately sent a rather conservative message about the perils of disorder, even as they allowed newly literate

---

[148] Boiko, *Rabochie Rossii*, p. 83.

[149] Jeffrey Brooks, *When Russia Learned to Read: Literacy and Popular Literature, 1861–1917* (Princeton: Princeton University Press, 1988), pp. 321–2.

[150] Solomon Volkov, *St Petersburg: A Cultural History* (London: Sinclair-Stevenson, 1996), p. 152.

[151] Bulkin, *Na zare*, p. 346.

[152] Cited in Steve Smith and Catriona Kelly, 'Commercial Culture and Consumerism', C. Kelly and D. Shepherd (eds.), *Constructing Russian Culture in the Age of Revolution, 1881–1940* (Oxford: Oxford University Press, 1998), p. 120.

readers to explore strange, enticing scenarios in which conventional notions of law and freedom were tested.[153]

Another highly popular but more modern genre was that of the detective story. Between 1907 and 1915, 6.2 million copies of detective stories about Nat Pinkerton, 3.1 million about Nick Carter and 3.9 million about Sherlock Holmes were published in Russia.[154] Adapted from or inspired by foreign originals, many were set in Europe and America and revelled in modernity, with heroes rushing from trains to automobiles, from steamships to airplanes. Their novelty lay in their celebration of the rational individual who stood apart from the enforcers of community values, but they offered thrills in the form of the excitement of the chase, the hero threatened by dastardly villains and the satisfaction of seeing wrongdoers punished.[155]

Leo Ou-fan Lee has shown how the commercialization of print culture in Shanghai yoked the project of intellectual enlightenment to modern urban life so that the act of defining a new reading public became synonymous with the creation of a new Chinese nation.[156] The republican era saw the rapid displacement of classical Chinese by the written vernacular, a trend that took off after the May Fourth Movement.[157] The first newspaper written in the vernacular, the *China Vernacular Newspaper* (*Zhongguo baihua bao*), appeared in Shanghai as early as December 1903. It was published every ten days, cost around twenty coppers and ran to eight pages per issue.[158] By the late teens, dozens of 'mosquito' newspapers (*xiaobao*) were being published, the best known being *Jing Bao*; these drew their nickname from the fact that they were said to 'sting' with gossip about politics and the entertainment world.[159] The number of workers reading such newspapers was tiny, but the growth of common people's schools and workers' night schools following the May Fourth Movement gradually boosted the number of working-class readers. Zhang Weizhen, who had had four-and-a-half years' education

[153] Brooks, *When Russia*, pp. 166–213.
[154] Brooks, *When Russia*, p. 142. During his life Dostoevsky's *Crime and Punishment* (1865–6) had sold 400 copies a year.
[155] Brooks, *When Russia*, pp. 142–6, 257.
[156] Leo Ou-fan Lee, *Shanghai Modern: The Flowering of New Urban Culture in China, 1930–1945* (Cambridge MA: Harvard University Press, 1999).
[157] Rana Mitter, *A Bitter Revolution: China's Struggle with the Modern World* (Oxford: Oxford University Press, 2004), p. 77.
[158] Perry Link, *Mandarin Ducks and Butterflies: Popular Fiction in Early Twentieth-Century China* (Berkeley: University of California Press, 1981), p. 101.
[159] Leo Ou-fan Lee and Andrew J. Nathan, 'The Beginnings of Mass Culture: Journalism and Fiction in Late Ch'ing and Beyond', in David Johnson, Andrew J. Nathan and Evelyn S. Rawski (eds.), *Popular Culture in Late Imperial China* (Berkeley: University of California Press, 1985), p. 374; Link, *Mandarin Ducks*, p. 118.

in a private academy (*shuyuan*), was one of a minority at his cotton mill who used to go to the mailing office to read the daily newspapers, although he had difficulty reading all the characters. 'I felt that what I read in the papers and what I had been told in the past were not the same thing.'[160] In 1925, the *Chinese Recorder* observed that: 'the sight of a rickshaw coolie poring over a scrap of newspaper while awaiting his passenger is becoming more and more common'.[161]

Some women workers strove to acquire basic literacy. Wang Genying, the daughter of a daoist priest and a cotton worker, entered the Hengfeng mill, aged eight, unable to read. After moving to the Ewo mill, she enrolled in a literacy class, run by local Communists, and in 1925 joined the party.[162] A thirteen-year-old girl in the spinning room of a Yangshupu mill, who had escaped from her family in Yixing county in Jiangnan, described her experience of night school: 'I am most grateful to the sister who introduced me to the reading class five months ago. The teachers are nice and the students get on well. I now know when I am being cheated, and I know about many things ... Before I often used to cry, but I don't think of crying any more.'[163]

By the 1930s, reading newspapers and magazines had become more widespread among Shanghai workers, although it was still a minority phenomenon. In 1936–7, Olga Lang discovered that in 67 out of a sample of 97 families of industrial workers in Shanghai, at least one individual in each family read a newspaper. She suggests that reading a newspaper had became associated with the idea of being a worker, one former factory employee telling her that in the factory he had read a newspaper, since in that environment he had been interested in politics, whereas he had ceased to do so after becoming a barber.[164]

The entertainment novels which flooded the market after 1911, often referred to as the 'Mandarin Duck and Butterfly' genre (*yuanyang hudie pai*) because of the liberal use they made of this traditional symbol of a pair of lovers, were still rather traditional in context. Most characters were clearly good or bad, and plots followed well-worn formulae such as 'talent meets beauty', righteous officials standing up for justice, generals

---

[160] 'Zhang Weizhen tan Hunan zaoqi gongyun' [Zhang Weizhen Discusses the Early Labour Movement in Hunan], *Dangshi yanjiu ziliao*, 1 (1980), 236.

[161] Cited in Xiaoqun Xu, *Chinese Professionals and the Republican State* (Cambridge: Cambridge University Press, 2001), p. 47.

[162] Zhonggongdang shi renwu yanjiu hui (ed.), *Zhonggongdang shi renwu zhuan* [Biographies of Past Members of the Communist Party], vol. 15 (Xi'an: Shaanxi renmin chubanshe, 1984), p. 261.

[163] Deng Tai, *Shenghuo sumiao* [Sketches of Life] (Shanghai: Daxia shudian, 1937), p. 67.

[164] Olga Lang, *Chinese Family*, p. 91. See also how workers by the 1930s relied on newspapers to find jobs. Deng Tai, *Shenghuo sumiao*, p. 112.

defeating China's foes or the fantastic feats of martial arts adepts.[165]
These novels differed from more elite fiction principally in having
action-packed plots, often with unexpected turns of event.[166] Although
their subject matter increasingly explored modern themes – e.g. the
freedom to marry a partner of one's choice – their popularity derived in
part from a capacity to keep westernization at arm's length: while
western-style love affairs were a staple of such fiction, they often ended
in tears; new-style school graduates were criticized for their callowness;
those who flaunted western gadgets were held up to mockery.[167] Butterfly fiction was a genre targeted at petty urbanites, but by the 1930s, it
had acquired a small working-class readership. The most popular of the
tales reached a much larger readership by being published in picture-
story format (*lianhuan hua*) – a staple of the travelling libraries in
working-class districts – and even as scripts for traditional drum singing.[168] Butterfly fiction offered a way of talking about new things, a way
of helping readers come to terms with rapid social and cultural change.
In Perry Link's words, 'a young person could read them as a way of
trying out new ideas without risking his or her own destiny in the
experiment'.[169]

If only a minority of workers may be said to have engaged in 'self-
fashioning', in quieter, less deliberate ways broader layers of migrants
freed themselves from some of the traditionally prescribed ways in which
lower-class people were expected to behave. Shifting tastes in dress and
reading suggest that they were groping towards a new sense of individuality, as older identity schemes based on kinship, locality or social
estate started to erode. Talk of a consumer culture in St Petersburg or
Shanghai must be qualified. Firstly, it catered mainly for the middle
classes and, secondly, its development was soon cut short by the onset of
war and revolution. In the case of China, Karl Gerth's pioneering work
has demonstrated the myriad ways in which nationalism insinuated itself
into burgeoning consumer culture in China, and Lydia Liu has argued
that by the 1930s the valorization of the individual in consumer culture
was increasingly dubbed petty-bourgeois, at variance with the interests
of a nation fighting for its survival.[170] Ordinary folk did not endorse

---

[165] Link, *Mandarin Ducks*, p. 7; Leo Ou-fan Lee, *The Romantic Generation of Chinese Writers* (Cambridge MA: Harvard University Press, 1973), p. 7.
[166] Link, *Mandarin Ducks*, p. 332.
[167] Link, *Mandarin Ducks*, pp. 341, 343.
[168] Link, *Mandarin Ducks*, p. 24.   [169] Link, *Mandarin*, p. 333.
[170] Gerth, *China Made*; Lydia Liu, *Translingual Practice: Literature, National Culture, and Translated Modernity – China, 1900–1937* (Stanford: Stanford University Press, 1995), p. 98.

capitalist modernity uncritically. They continued to be influenced by ideas of modesty, self-effacement and thrift. In Shanghai, especially, many who were intrigued and tempted by consumer culture were also suspicious of it as foreign, spendthrift and self-indulgent. Yet ideas of individual choice and freedom, and the importance of being seen to be modern, though mainly taken up by middle-class consumers, were not without influence on poorer layers of the populace. In Russia attitudes to consumption were influenced by entrenched discourses that saw culture as having a high artistic and social purpose, its role being to raise the spiritual condition of the common people, and that deprecated culture produced for profit. Consumer culture, in other words, proved to be a site across which conflicts of power and value played – conflicts between self-indulgence and self-sacrifice, liberal and collective values, between westernization and nationalism – conflicts that would be resolved after the revolution by political fiat.

Workers Defend Their Dignity[171]

That Russian workers had developed a heightened sensitivity to the innate value of the human person became massively apparent during the 1905 Revolution, when demands for polite treatment became universal.[172] Peasants, of course, had their own ideas of dignity, dishonour and shame, but there was something new about the way in which workers now demanded respect as individual human beings.

Memoirists recall their surprise and delight when 'backward' workers began to demand an end to their condition of 'rightlessness' (*bespravie*) and to protest acts of arbitrariness (*proizvol*) by the workplace administration and the civic authorities.[173] In workers' letters to *Rabochaia mysl'* (1897–1902), there are many complaints about wages, working hours and conditions, but particular odium is reserved for supervisors, whose power to fine, insult and oppress workers was bitterly resented.[174] Traditionally, for example, supervisors used the familiar 'thou' (*ty*) form when addressing workers, the form used to address serfs, children and animals. Now

---

[171] In Russian the words for 'personality' and 'dignity' are differentiated in a way they are not in Chinese, where *renge* means both. Yet the Russian word *lichnost'*, although strictly meaning 'personality', clearly meant something close to 'human dignity' in the historical context discussed.

[172] S. Gvozdev, *Zapiski fabrichnogo inspektora* (Moscow: Izd. S. Dorovatskago, 1911), p. 117.

[173] Timofeev, *Chem zhivet* pp. 96–7; Shapovalov, *Po doroge*, p. 19.

[174] *Avangard: Vospominaniia*, pp. 344–88; S. A. Smith, 'Workers, the Intelligentsia, and Social Democracy in St Petersburg, 1895–1917', in Reginald E. Zelnik (ed.), *Workers and Intelligentsia in Late Imperial Russia: Realities, Representations, Reflections* (Berkeley: Institute for International Studies, 1999), pp. 186–205.

workers insisted this cease. In January 1905, workers at the Baltic works raised demands for the use of polite language; the abolition of searches of workers since this 'profaned human dignity'; and for management to treat workers 'as people and not as things'.[175] After the revolution was put down, many of the economic gains made by workers in the strikes of 1905 were revoked, but the insistence on polite treatment was upheld. Between 1901 and 1913, the annual number of complaints to the Factory Inspectorate about 'bad treatment' rose from 2,136 to 21,873.[176] With the February Revolution, demands for polite treatment resurfaced. Except among clerical and service workers, such demands did not lead to strikes, since managements were now ready to concede this without a fight.[177] Between February and October 1917, the concern with lichnost' resonated through politics, although references to the 'creative role of personality' were more likely to emanate from SR than from Social Democratic circles.[178] No conflict was felt to exist between valuing the individual and promoting the interests of the working class. Labour and Light (*Trud i Svet*), the socialist youth organization in Petrograd, for example, announced its goals as being: 'to develop the feelings of personal dignity and class consciousness which are precious to the working class'.[179]

A similar but less pronounced development can be seen in the Shanghai labour movement. The New Culture Movement sensitized workers to their dignity (*renge*), causing them to demand the respect and treatment they felt they deserved as human beings and as workers. One Shanghai labour journal asked: 'Are not shop clerks and apprentices individuals too? Do they not have five organs and four limbs, are they not ten months in gestation regardless of their social rank? So why is it that clerks are only there to be bossed about and apprentices to be treated like slaves?'[180] From 1925, such ideas found a wider audience. In the February 1925 strikes in the Japanese Nagai Wata Kaisha mills, the strike committee announced: 'If we win, then the Japanese will not dare to hit or curse us, and everyone will maintain face. If we lose, then

[175] Bulkin, *Na zare*, p. 61; M. Balabanov, *Ocherki po istorii rabochego klassa v Rossii*, part 2 (Moscow, 1925), p. 5.

[176] K. A. Pazhitnov, *Polozhenie rabochego klassa v Rossii*, vol. 3 (Leningrad: Put' k znaniiu, 1924), p. 130; Olga Crisp, 'Labour and Industrialization', in Peter Mathias and M. M. Postan (eds.), *The Cambridge Economic History of Europe*, vol. 7, part 2 (Cambridge: Cambridge University Press, 1978), p. 382.

[177] Diane P. Koenker and William G. Rosenberg, *Strikes and Revolution in Russia, 1917* (Princeton: Princeton University Press, 1989), pp. 172–4.

[178] Donald J. Raleigh, *Experiencing Russia's Civil War: Politics, Society, and Revolutionary Culture in Saratov, 1917–1922* (Princeton: Princeton University Press, 2002), p. 149.

[179] Isabel A. Tirado *Young Guard!: The Communist Youth League, Petrograd, 1917–1920* (New York: Greenwood Press, 1988), p. 211.

[180] *Shanghai huoyou*, 24 October 1920, p. 15.

the Japanese will treat us even less like human beings and even more like cattle and horses, and we shall completely lose face.'[181] Strikers at the Chinese-owned Commercial Press in August 1925 declared:

It is maddening to see a notice posted about our dismissal as if the execution of a brigand were being publicised. How they disdain the dignity of the worker ... Our rights and liberties have been despised and stolen from us. We are in danger of losing our jobs at any minute, and our condition is so bad that our bosses treat us as beasts of burden and slaves.[182]

Workers were no longer prepared to tolerate abuse, arbitrariness and humiliation, especially at the hands of foreign employers, this despite the fact that wages and conditions in Japanese mills were generally reckoned to be better than in Chinese mills.[183] 'Treatment' was now the issue, and the demand for humane treatment touched directly on issues of justice, dignity and equality that were relevant not only to the working class, but to the Chinese as a nation. A curse or a cuff directed at a Chinese worker by a Japanese supervisor could stand metonymically for the violence inflicted on the Chinese people by foreign imperialists, and generate a passion and anger out of all proportion to the provocation. The issue of humane treatment could, without intellectual strain, be elaborated within the discourses of nationalism, of class or of both.[184]

Conclusion

We have suggested that concerns to define and heighten individual personality were a key axis along which the social identities of migrants were transformed during the last years of the *ancien régime*. In both late-imperial Russia and republican China ascriptive identity schemes based on the patriarchal family, the state-defined system of social estates or the Confucian moral order began to break down. Capitalist modernity, in turn, opened up new arenas in which workers could begin to think – in Charles Taylor's words – of the 'self' as a noun. A small layer of 'conscious' workers actively engaged in self-fashioning, taking the values and ideals of the intelligentsia as their model. Their passionate desire for education and self-improvement, their yearning to rise above the bovine

[181] *Wusa yundong shiliao* [Historical Materials on the May Thirtieth Movement], vol. 1 (Shanghai: Shanghai renmin chubanshe, 1981), p. 331.

[182] *North China Herald*, 29 August 1925, p. 252.

[183] *Shenbao*, 26 February 1925.

[184] This issue and its relation to 'face' in Chinese culture is discussed in S. A. Smith, *Like Cattle and Horses: Nationalism and Labor in Shanghai, 1895–1927* (Durham NC: Duke University Press, 2002), pp. 200–9.

mass, could lead to an elitist distancing from the working class; but by and large, their assertion of their worth as individuals was indissociable from a broader critique of the status quo, a critique couched in terms of a collective struggle of the people, the nation or the working class for radical change. Mark Steinberg has argued that for this type of worker, the critique of society was essentially a moral one, and that at its core lay the category of the self.[185] For wider groups of workers, the articulation of new notions of autonomy and dignity was less self-conscious, less linked to a project of conscious personal and social transformation.

For many, religious practice, now severed from a function of social reproduction, provided new resources for self-exploration (although for a minority it was precisely the ability to throw off the 'mind-forged manacles' of religion that marked the breakthrough into true autonomy as an individual). For many more, it was the marketplace and consumer choice that offered the most alluring terrain for self-expression. Workers, male and female, quickly learned that fashion in dress was a potent means of expressing individual aspirations and claims to respectability, dignity and social status. Others discovered in the cultural products aimed at the mass market means of exploring at the level of fantasy new social scenarios and social identities. This, I have argued, sharpened the sense of the innate worth of the human person and generated a passionate concern to uphold individual dignity, a concern that fed directly into the revolutionary ferment, especially in Russia.

The political implications of the forms of individuality promoted by the market, however, remained fraught and contentious. The emergence of a consumer society was inextricably linked to the conflicting discourses that surrounded consumption. Intellectuals tended to despise the vulgarity, lack of seriousness, escapism or outright conservatism that they perceived to inhere in cultural products designed to entertain and to make a profit. Revolutionaries, whether socialist or nationalist, worried that the aspirations to individuality, respectability, upward social mobility and simple pleasure that were promoted by the market threatened the collective projects of socialist or anti-imperialist revolution. In China, particularly, the tensions between individual pleasure and moral seriousness, between individual freedom and the pressures of state building, between westernization and nationalism were especially acute.

There was always greater space for the articulation of selfhood in Russian than in Chinese culture, and the trend towards individual self-expression associated with the decline of the *anciens régimes* and the

---

[185] Steinberg, *Proletarian Imagination*, ch. 2.

onset of capitalist modernity was considerably more advanced in Russia by 1917 than in China by 1949. Nevertheless, in both cultures traditions of hierarchical collectivism were still resilient and the social and cultural processes that undergirded the growth of modern forms of individual autonomy had not advanced very far before war and revolution intervened to nip them in the bud. Having just begun to free themselves from tight dependence on hierarchical roles sanctified by the patriarchal family, the community, the state or the Confucian moral order, migrants came under pressure – as urban life was torn apart – to find security in new collective structures promoted by state and party, structures created variously to defeat external enemies, build a strong state or develop the national economy.

Given, as we shall see in chapter 5, that collectivism ultimately trumped individuality in both societies, does not this confirm the philosophical postulate, expounded at the start of the chapter, that construes principles of individual autonomy and class-based collectivism as fundamentally antithetical? In an insightful essay, Mark Steinberg makes just this case apropos of the writings of 'conscious' workers in Russia: 'At the level of ethics', he writes, 'the moral primacy given to workers' identity as human beings ultimately acted to undermine class solidarity.'[186] I am not so sure: at least, it does not seem that working people at the time – 'conscious' or not – saw things that way. This suggests that we may need to switch the philosophical angle of vision. A different way of approaching the problem would be to think of class identity not simply as a collective response to capitalist exploitation but as a response to what some writers have called 'misrecognition'. Building on insights from Hegel and Weber, these writers criticize theories of oppression and emancipation that focus narrowly on economic inequality. Nancy Fraser, for instance, distinguishes between injustices of distribution and injustices of recognition. 'To be misrecognized ... is not simply to be thought ill of, looked down upon, or devalued in others' conscious attitudes or mental beliefs. It is rather to be ... prevented from participating as a peer in social life, not as a consequence of a distributive inequity ... but as a consequence of institutionalized patterns of interpretation and evaluation that constitute one as comparatively unworthy of respect or esteem.'[187] Craig Calhoun elaborates: 'It is not just that others fail to see us for who we are, or repress us because of who they think we are. We face problems of recognition

---

[186] Steinberg, 'Predstavlenie o "lichnosti"', p. 109.
[187] Nancy Fraser, *Justice Interruptus: Critical Reflections on the 'Postsocialist' Condition* (New York: Routledge, 1997).

because socially sustained discourses about who it is possible or appropriate or valuable to be inevitably shape the way we look at and constitute ourselves, with varying degrees of agonism and tension.'[188]

From this angle, class identity may be seen not only as a response to capitalist exploitation but also as a response to the devaluation that working people feel more generally in society, a response to systematic disrespect that is experienced both as social fact and as individual affront. What the experience of migrants in late-imperial Russia and republican China suggests is that under the impact of capitalist modernity workers came to respond to the misrecognition built into the fabric of the existing political, social and economic order not least by affirming their intrinsic worth as persons, regardless of their social status, by insisting that they be treated with the dignity that is the inalienable right of all human beings. Indeed, the belief in the natural and equal worth of individuals has been an inspiration of labour movements committed to building a more equal and just society everywhere.[189] But in *ancien régime* societies such as Russia and China the assertion of the intrinsic worth of the individual became a potent means of political critique that empowered people to come together to fight for social and political change. On this discursive terrain, the distance between the claims of the individual and the claims of the collective was not very great – far less, at any rate, than philosophers and social theorists who place individualism and collectivism at opposite ends of an ethical spectrum assume. Indeed, without denying the real potential for tension between individual autonomy and class-based collectivism, we may conclude that genuine forms of collectivism and cooperative action are possible only where class solidarity is grounded in autonomous individuals capable of demanding the recognition due to them as thinking, feeling persons. Without that, new forms of group coercion based on weak individuality are likely to be the result – a theme that is taken up in chapter 5.

---

[188] Craig Calhoun, 'Social Theory and the Politics of Identity', in Craig Calhoun (ed.), *Social Theory and the Politics of Identity* (Oxford: Blackwell, 1994), p. 21.

[189] S. A. Smith, 'Workers and Civil Rights in Tsarist Russia, 1899–1917', in O. Crisp and L. Edmondson (eds.), *Civil Rights in Tsarist Russia* (Oxford: Oxford University Press, 1989), pp. 145–69.

3   After Patriarchy: Gender Identities in the City

This chapter posits that a crisis of the patriarchal gender order was a central component of the crisis that beset the *anciens régimes* in Russia and China, one that became implicated materially and symbolically in the processes of social and political transformation that led to revolution. This crisis had little to do directly with capitalism but was inextricably bound up with the impact of capitalist modernity on a traditional dynastic polity and a patriarchal rural society. The attack on the traditional familial order – and, in particular, advocacy of the so-called 'woman question' – served as tropes though which contemporaries (usually men) could reflect on the backwardness of their societies and make demands for radical political change and, in addition, articulate their own social and gender anxieties and aspirations. There is little consensus as to how far actual gender roles and identities of migrants from the countryside to the cities underwent transformation as a consequence of the onset of capitalist modernity. An earlier literature tended to assume that the transition from Gemeinschaft to Gesellschaft was accompanied by a 'modernization' of gender roles.[1] Among historians, Edward Shorter offers the most cogent exposition of this view, arguing that traditional communities were characterized by strong interpersonal ties, by 'surveillance' of personal and interpersonal behaviour, by 'instrumental' rather than 'affective' values in marriage and family, and by 'massive stability'; whereas with the onset of modernity, the family became separate from the community, and familial and sexual relationships became based on 'sentiment' and 'individual self-realization'.[2] Feminist historians have tended to reject this view, expressing various degrees of scepticism that industrialization and urbanization changed very much

---

[1] For China, this approach is represented by Marion Levy, *The Family Revolution in Modern China* (Cambridge MA : Harvard University Press, 1949) and, to a lesser extent, by Olga Lang, *Chinese Family and Society* (New Haven: Yale University Press, 1946).

[2] Edward Shorter, *The Making of the Modern Family* (New York: Basic Books, 1975).

for women.[3] This chapter sets out to investigate how far migrants maintained customary gender relations and identities in the city, how far they developed new family patterns and gender identities, and how far they were exposed to the anti-patriarchal and feminist discourses that were a key element in the crises of the *anciens régimes*.

Following defeat in the Crimean War (1854–6), critics of the autocracy in Russia began to raise the 'woman question' in a context where the emancipation of the serfs dominated the political agenda. Critics, mainly men drawn from the gentry class, drew scathing parallels between the subjection of peasants to serf owners and the subjection of women to men.[4] Both liberals and radicals agreed that women must develop autonomy and 'self-directed activity' (*samodeiatel'nost'*) and improve their social status and employment opportunities, but some argued that the way forward lay in equal civil and political rights for women, while others argued that the moral redemption of society depended on activating the cooperative and eirenic qualities inherent in the female sex.[5] In the climate of political reaction that followed the assassination of Alexander II in 1881, the 'woman question' became more marginal to the 'society-wide' struggle against autocracy, subsumed within a larger political debate about reform versus revolution.[6] By the *fin de siècle*, there was a certain reaction against 'rights-based' approaches to the 'woman question', in favour of a cult of the 'eternal feminine' and a fascination with sexual desire.[7] Looking at the half century prior to 1917, one can say that although feminists, liberals and socialists all championed some version of the 'new woman', received norms of femininity and masculinity never became a focus of sustained political concern, since even intransigent critics of the status quo assumed that men and women had different, albeit complementary, natures.

In China the arrival of liberal and radical ideologies from the West encouraged reformers and revolutionaries to link national survival to the emancipation of women from the trammels of the Confucian order. As

---

[3] For China, see Kay Ann Johnson, *Women, the Family and Peasant Revolution in China* (Chicago: University of Chicago Press, 1983); Judith Stacey, *Patriarchy and Socialist Revolution in China* (Berkeley: University of California Press, 1983); Margery Wolf, *Revolution Postponed: Women in Contemporary China* (Stanford: Stanford University Press, 1985).

[4] Richard Stites, *The Women's Liberation Movement in Russia: Feminism, Nihilism and Bolshevism, 1860–1930* (Princeton: Princeton University Press, 1978), p. 48.

[5] Linda Edmondson, *Feminism in Russia, 1900–1917* (London: Heinemann, 1984), pp. 9, 3.

[6] Stites, *Women's Liberation*, pp. 152–54.

[7] Rosamund Bartlett and Linda Edmondson, 'Collapse and Creation: Issues of Identity and the Russian Fin-de-Siècle', in C. Kelly and D. Shepherd (eds.), *Constructing Russian Culture in the Age of Revolution, 1881–1940* (Oxford: Oxford University Press, 1998), p. 201.

early as 1897, in his essay 'On Women's Education', Liang Qichao established this connection. Condemning the reduction of women to 'slaves' ('fattened up like dogs and pigs') and 'playthings' ('decorated like flowers and birds'), he argued that the subordination of women deprived the nation of one half of its members' energies and talents.[8] For these reformers, the figure of the woman with bound feet came to symbolize the nation's weakness and backwardness. According to Kang Youwei, the driving force behind the abortive effort to drive through the 1898 reforms and a supporter of the Anti-Footbinding Society founded in Shanghai in 1897, 'the bound feet of women transmit weakness to their children ... weakening the bodies of healthy generations'.[9] The Society's campaign reaped its reward in 1907 when the Qing government banned foot binding as part of its belated programme of reform. Even conservative reformers, such as those who drafted the 1907 regulations establishing schools for women, made the link between strengthening the nation and raising the status of women. Inspired by the Meiji Japanese ideal of the 'good wife and wise mother' (*liangqi xianmu*), they argued that education would improve the quality of women as reproducers and homemakers and thereby contribute to increasing the strength of the nation. Constitutionalists, perhaps the most influential political current in the last years of the Qing, cast women as 'mothers of citizens' (*guomin zhi mu*), while revolutionaries called for the creation of 'female citizens' who would put their talents to the service of the nation. In contrast to Russia, raising the status of women was perceived to entail a radical rethinking of the hegemonic model of femininity, reformists and radicals both calling for women to be valued no longer for their 'delicacy, weakness and refined adornment, but for their robust healthiness, rosy cheeks and dignified bearing'.[10]

In China the hegemonic model of masculinity also came under scrutiny following the revolution of 1911. Among the Qing elite the most influential construction of masculine identity centred on the ideal of

---

[8] Mary Backus Rankin, 'The Emergence of Women at the End of the Ch'ing: The Case of Ch'iu Chin', in Margery Wolf and Roxane Witke (eds.), *Women in Chinese Society* (Stanford: Stanford University Press, 1975), pp. 39–66; Paul Bailey, 'Active Citizen or Efficient Housewife? The Debate over Women's Education in Early-Twentieth Century China', in Glen Peterson, Ruth Hayhoe and Yongling Yu (eds.), *Education, Culture and Identity in Twentieth-Century China* (Ann Arbor: University of Michigan Press, 2001), pp. 318–47.

[9] Cited in Fan Hong, *Footbinding, Feminism and Freedom: The Liberation of Women's Bodies in Modern China* (London: Frank Cass, 1997), p. 63.

[10] Joan Judge, 'Citizens or Mothers of Citizens? Gender and the Meaning of Modern Chinese Citizenship', in Merle Goldman and Elizabeth J. Perry (eds.), *Changing Meanings of Citizenship in Modern China* (Cambridge MA: Harvard University Press, 2002), p. 32.

wen, which signified cultured behaviour, aesthetic refinement, elegant sensibility and learning. As the crisis of the imperial order mounted, this model, in part under the influence of Social Darwinism, came to be viewed as effete, synonymous with the feminized man incapable of defending his nation.[11] Nationalists argued that the physical strengthening of the bodies of China's people was vital if 'national extinction' were to be averted: 'Without a martial spirit, citizens are effeminate, unsoldierly and useless', a textbook for young boys explained.[12] A relatively late instance of this discourse can be seen in an early essay by Mao Zedong, entitled 'On Physical Education and Exercise', published on 1 April 1917, where he urged vigorous exercise as the antidote to the traditional preference for languid motion. 'Perhaps the greatest value in exercise lies in strengthening the will. The main practical purpose of exercise is military heroism. Fearlessness, daring, tenacity and courage cannot be achieved without control over the will.'[13] The new republican rulers, clad in military uniform with their shoulders back, sought to popularize the idea of the citizen-soldier and the necessity of universal physical education.[14] A decree banning male prostitution by boy actors of 1 April 1912 reveals how the concern with a more robust model of masculinity was linked to sensitivity to foreign slights on Chinese manhood:

The youngsters are dressed for their looks and trained to be expert in singing ... They are a disgrace to our country and a cause of scandal vis-à-vis the foreign nations. Such boys are named 'false women' and act in ways contrary to human decency. With the founding of the republic old habits and immoral customs must be abolished ... the concerned parties should pursue suitable careers and in full conformity with their human dignity join the ranks of the noble citizenry.[15]

The new discourse of citizenship, in addition to evoking a more military model of masculinity, also played on ideas of fraternity, above all in the context of the citizen army. But egalitarian *fraternité* never entailed the outright rejection of paternal authority: indeed the new nationalism construed the nation as the *zuguo*, the fatherland, as a lineage rather than as a body of citizens, symbolized in Sun Yat-sen as the father of the nation (*guofu*). Don C. Price suggests that within this variant of nationalism, the

[11] Susan Brownell and Jeffrey Wasserstrom, 'Introduction: Theorizing Femininities and Masculinities', S. Brownell and J. Wasserstrom (eds.), *Chinese Femininities, Chinese Masculinities* (Berkeley: University of California Press, 2002), p. 19.

[12] Judge, 'Citizens and Mothers', p. 40.

[13] The essay is reprinted in Fan Hong, *Footbinding*, pp. 313–17.

[14] Henrietta Harrison, *The Making of the Republican Citizen: Political Ceremonies and Symbols in China, 1911–1929* (Oxford: Oxford University Press, 2000), pp. 79–83.

[15] Cited in Zou Yu, 'After Patriarchy: Masculinity and Representation in Modern Chinese Drama, 1919–1945', University of California Berkeley, PhD, 2000, pp. 236–7.

1911 Revolution was seen as having occurred for the sake of China's ancestors rather than her sons, thus giving impetus to a republican political culture that rested on the idea of the nation as a family, headed by a father.[16]

With the revolution, feminist activists demanded the franchise, educational opportunities, employment rights, inheritance rights and marriage and divorce rights equal to those of men. A few sought to align women with the masculinist discourse of the republican leadership. On 5 August 1911, a Chinese Women's Citizens Association was formed 'to reform the corrupt practices of family life and inspire women with the martial spirit' and women formed military detachments to take part in the expedition against Beijing.[17] As Ono Kazuko remarks, the middle-class women involved in these initiatives were bent on erasing gender difference, seeing themselves first as citizens, and second as women.[18] With little conviction, republican leaders toyed with notions of women's rights, but reaction quickly set in under Yuan Shikai, whose presidency (1912–16) saw a repudiation of radical feminism and an effort to reconfigure gender roles along more traditional lines. In 1915, the Ministry of Education urged women to learn modern knowledge in order to bring up the next generation of citizens in a spirit of service to the nation. School readers defined a woman's principal role as being to maintain a frugal, hygienic and well-organized household and emphasized the importance of obedience to parents, husbands and in-laws.[19] Girls were excluded from national sports competitions and their physical education restricted to hand gymnastics.[20] It was in 1915 that the New Culture Movement commenced, and it was this movement that proved most influential in creating a unified category, 'woman', out of the dispersed relational categories of 'daughter' (*nü*), 'wife' (*fu*) and 'mother' (*mu*) that had existed in imperial China. Two neologisms – *funü* and *nüxing* – were put into circulation, the latter a western-inspired category used to designate transcendental 'woman'.[21] The New Culture Movement, which enthusiastically embraced western science and democracy, took up the

[16] D. C. Price, 'The Ancestral Nation and China's Political Culture', Centennial Symposium on Sun Yat-Sen's Founding of the Kuomintang for Revolution (Taipei, November 1994). Cited in Peter Zarrow, 'Introduction: Citizenship in China and the West', in J. A Fogel and P. G. Zarrow (eds.), *Imagining the People: Chinese Intellectuals and the Concept of Citizenship* (Armonk NY: M. E. Sharpe, 1997), p. 14.

[17] Shanghai shehui kexueyuan yanjiusuo (ed.), *Xinhai geming zai Shanghai shiliao xuanji* [Selected Historical Materials on the 1911 Revolution in Shanghai] (Shanghai: Shanghai renmin chubanshe, 1966), pp. 1232, 1248–9.

[18] Ono Kazuko, *Chinese Women in a Century of Revolution, 1850–1950* (Stanford: Stanford University Press, 1989) p. 74.

[19] Bailey, 'Active Citizen', p. 333.   [20] Fan Hong, *Footbinding*, pp. 117, 102.

[21] Tani Barlow, 'Theorizing Women: *Funü, Guojia, Jiating*', *Genders*, 10 (1991), 132–60.

cause of women's emancipation in the context of a wholesale assault on the Confucian order. It called for the liberation (*jiefang*) of women and youth, whom it saw as the two most oppressed groups in traditional patriarchal society. Hu Shi, doyen of liberal thought in China, called for the awakening of women's consciousness, women's economic independence, and women's freedom to choose their spouse.[22] Significantly, it was mainly men who most energetically debated such issues as women's chastity, arranged marriage, concubinage, freedom to divorce, education and property rights, constituting these as an arena in which they could articulate their struggle as junior males against the patriarchal order.

Patriarchy and Gender Roles in the Village

Peasant society in Russia and China was patriarchal in that men held power over women and the elder generation held power over the younger generation. Only men had rights of property in the household and its land, and the assets of the household were divided equally between sons on the death of the head of the household. Even as the patriarchal order privileged males by granting them access to land and the labour of women, it subordinated sons to fathers almost as thoroughly as it subordinated women to men.[23] In both societies daughters were much less valued than sons, since they married out of their natal families, thus offering their parents no prospects of enhancing the status or wealth of the family or of care in old age.[24] Daughters were said in Russian to marry 'to the other side' (*na chuzhuiu storonu*); in Chinese to 'some other family name' (*nüsheng waixing*). The position of daughters, however, was far worse in China than in Russia, with female infanticide and the buying and selling of daughters as concubines, maidservants or adopted daughters-in-law widespread.[25] In Subei in the early 1930s, a

---

[22] Hue-Ping Chin, 'Refiguring Women: Discourse of Gender in China, 1880–1919', University of Iowa, PhD, 1995, pp. 272, 263.

[23] Barbara Alpern Engel, *Between the Fields and the City: Women, Work and Family in Russia, 1861–1914* (Cambridge: Cambridge University Press, 1994); E. Kingston-Mann and T. Mixter, 'Introduction', in Esther Kingston-Mann and Timothy R. Mixter (eds.), *Peasant Economy, Culture and Politics in European Russia, 1800–1921* (Princeton: Princeton University Press, 1991), pp. 14–15.

[24] Wolf, *Revolution Postponed*, p. 2.

[25] Hsiao-Tung Fei, *Peasant Life in China: A Field Study of Country Life in the Yangtze Valley* (London: Kegan Paul, 1939), pp. 33–4. Estimates of female infanticide in the population as a whole in late-imperial China are very high, possibly approaching 300 per 1,000 female births. Cited in David Ownby, 'Approximations of Chinese Bandits: Perverse Rebels, Romantic Heroes, or Frustrated Bachelors?', in S. Brownell and J. Wasserstrom (eds.), *Chinese Femininities, Chinese Masculinities* (Berkeley: University of California Press, 2002), p. 242.

three- or four-year-old girl sold for ten yuan as a servant, and might be sold on, aged seventeen, as a wife or concubine for fifty to sixty yuan (twice the annual wage of a male agricultural labourer).[26] Broadly speaking, both Russia and China were dowry societies, though this was not true of all regions in either country, and in China the amount of property endowed in the bride by the husband's family usually exceeded the dowry paid by her parents.[27] In China the legal position of wives in respect of dowry, property rights, marriage and divorce appears to have weakened during the Ming and Qing dynasties, as they became more tightly incorporated into their marital families and as ties with their natal families loosened.[28] Legal reforms of 1906 and 1931, however, limited the power of the husband's family over the wife.[29] In Russia, customary law protected the inalienability of a woman's personal property, which included, in addition to her dowry, revenues she might earn from selling vegetables, chickens, woven and knitted items. Moreover, if her husband left her, a woman could expect some backing from the township court.[30]

In Russia, the law dictated that a woman owed complete obedience to her husband, and compelled her to live with him, to take his name and to assume his social estate. Through the nineteenth century, as the Orthodox Church increased its control of divorce 'a marital order of a rigidity unknown elsewhere in Europe' emerged.[31] It was the duty of a wife to take care of the household and to help her husband on the farm; in return, her husband was required 'to live with her in harmony, to respect and protect her, forgive her insufficiencies and ease her infirmities.' A wife was unable to take a job, get an education, receive a passport for work or residence, or execute a bill of exchange without her

---

[26] Kathy Le Mons Walker, *Chinese Modernity and the Peasant Path: Semicolonialism in the Northern Yangtze Delta* (Stanford: Stanford University Press, 1999), p. 193.

[27] Patricia Buckley Ebrey 'Introduction', in Rubie S. Watson and Patricia Buckley Ebrey (eds.), *Marriage and Inequality in Chinese Society* (Berkeley: University of California Press, 1991), p. 4; Rubie S. Watson, 'Marriage and Gender Inequality', in Watson and Ebrey (eds.), *Marriage and Inequality*, p. 353.

[28] Kathryn Bernhardt, 'A Ming-Qing Transition in Chinese Women's History?', in Gail Hershatter et al. (eds.), *Remapping China: Fissures in Historical Terrain* (Stanford: Stanford University Press, 1996), pp. 42–58.

[29] Ebrey, 'Introduction', p. 2; Jonathan K. Ocko, 'Women, Property and the Law in the People's Republic of China', in Watson and Ebrey (eds.), *Marriage and Inequality*, p. 319.

[30] Christine D. Worobec, *Peasant Russia: Family and Community in the Post-Emancipation Period* (Princeton: Princeton University Press, 1991), p. 64; B. M. Firsov, I. G. Kiseleva (eds.), *Byt velikorusskikh krest' ian-zemlepashtsev: opisanie materialov Etnograficheskogo biuro Kniazia V.N. Tenisheva: na primere Vladimirskoi gubernii* (St Petersburg: Izd-vo Evropeiskogo doma, 1993) p. 262.

[31] Gregory Freeze, 'Bringing Order to the Russian Family: Marriage and Divorce in Imperial Russia, 1760–1860', *Journal of Modern History*, 62, 4 (1990), 711.

husband's consent. In 1914, limited reforms permitted her to separate from her husband and obtain her own passport.[32] As a young wife, she was subordinate to her mother-in-law, but her status would rise once she bore children; and after her husband became a head of household, she would wield considerable power over her own daughters-in-law.[33] Within the household women enjoyed considerable latitude in running domestic affairs. In addition to childcare, cooking, cleaning, washing clothes, making and repairing clothes, they spun yarn and wove cloth, looked after livestock, cultivated flax, assisted with the harvest and, in regions of heavy outmigration, took on heavy farming tasks that had once been considered men's work, such as ploughing, sowing, hay-making carting fuel and feeding cattle.[34] In the village, by dint of their involvement in arranging marriages, presiding at childbirth and chris-tenings and generally upholding community standards and norms, women enjoyed a certain informal authority.[35]

In China, the Qing law code dealt with women according to 'three obediences' – her subordination to her father before marriage, to her husband after marriage, and to her son as a widow – and the 'four virtues' – womanly speech, womanly conduct, modest demeanour and womanly work. Family relations were constituted along the dual axis of the subordination of sons to fathers and of daughters-in-law to mothers-in-law.[36] By comparison, the husband–wife relationship was less impor-tant: parent–child loyalties took precedence over those between husband and wife and sexual relations were valued primarily for the children produced.[37] Husband and wife would not sit near one another and would seldom talk to one another, although after the birth of a child, the husband would refer to his wife as the 'mother of my child' and behave more affectionately towards her.[38] Older men considered lack of com-munication with their wives to be entirely natural, and older women opined that it was embarrassing to display conjugal affection and intimacy.[39] Once a wife had children, however, she established a base for

[32] Wendy Z. Goldman, *Women, the State and Revolution: Soviet Family Policy and Social Life, 1917–1936* (Cambridge: Cambridge University Press, 1993) p. 49; *Naselenie Rossii v XX veke: istoricheskie ocherki*, vol. 1, 1900–1939 (Moscow: ROSSPEN, 2000), p. 57.
[33] *Naselenie Rossii*, p. 55.
[34] Mandakina Arora, 'Boundaries, Transgressions, Limits: Peasant Women and Gender Roles in Tver' Province, 1861–1914', Duke University, PhD, 1995, pp. 44–50; *Naselenie Rossii*, p. 48.
[35] Worobec, *Family and Community* p. 177.   [36] Fei, *Peasant Life*, p. 47.
[37] Deborah Davis-Friedmann, *Long Lives: Chinese Elderly and the Communist Revolution* (Cambridge MA: Harvard University Press, 1983), p. 10.
[38] Fei, *Peasant Life*, p. 47.
[39] Yunxiang Yan, *Private Life Under Socialism: Love, Intimacy and Family Change in a Chinese Village, 1949–99* (Stanford: Stanford University Press, 2003), p. 91.

herself within her husband's family; and if she was the mother of a son, she could begin to speak up for the interests of the son if her husband would not speak up for her; and once her sons were able, she could speak through them.[40]

One of the most striking contrasts with Russia was the confinement of Chinese women to the household. In theory, women were 'people of the inside' (*neiren*) with few opportunities to socialize outside the home. Since the only place where men and women traditionally consorted was the marriage bed, public interaction between men and women called into question the woman's moral reputation. In Penglai in Shandong province Ning Lao Taitai recalled: 'We were not allowed, my sister and I, on the street after we were thirteen … When a family wanted to know more about a girl who had been suggested for a daughter-in-law, neighbours would answer: "We do not know. We have never seen her." And that was praise.'[41] The confinement of women was mirrored in the sexual division of labour. According to the Confucian ideal, men farmed and women wove (*nan geng, nü zhi*), both activities being seen as vital to the wellbeing of society and to promotion of individual virtue. Learning textile skills 'inculcated the fundamental female values of diligence, frugality, order and self-discipline.'[42] A survey of industry in Ningbo in 1907 revealed that women working at home in fact performed a large variety of income-generating tasks, including cotton spinning and weaving, making mats, umbrellas and hats, curing tea, brewing soy sauce and painting fans.[43] The proscriptions against women working in agriculture, i.e. in public, remained strong, but among the very poorest families of Subei, cotton cultivation by the 1930s had come to be predominantly women's work.[44] Yet as late as the 1940s, a popular saying claimed: 'Good men don't become soldiers and good women don't go out to work.'[45]

In Russia, gender identities were seen as rooted in a natural order created by God and buttressed by the institution of marriage. Within this order, it was taken for granted that men should exercise authority over women by virtue of their moral as well as physical superiority. The male

---

[40] Wolf, *Revolution Postponed*, pp. 9–10.
[41] Ida Pruitt, *A Daughter of Han: The Autobiography of a Chinese Working Woman* (Stanford: Stanford University Press, 1967), p. 29.
[42] Francesca Bray, *Technology and Gender: Fabrics of Power in Late Imperial China* (Berkeley: University of California Press, 1997), p. 189.
[43] Susan Mann, 'Household Handicrafts and State Policy in Qing Times', in Jane Kate Leonard and John R. Watt (eds.), *To Achieve Security and Wealth: The Qing Imperial State and the Economy, 1644–1911* (Ithaca NY: Cornell University Press, 1992), p. 89.
[44] Walker, *Chinese Modernity*, p. 192.
[45] Gail Hershatter, *Workers of Tianjin, 1900–1949* (Stanford: Stanford University Press, 1986), pp. 62–3.

claim to authority seems to have derived from the fact that it was mainly men who made the earth productive, bolstered by the Christian prescription that wives owed obedience to their husbands.[46] Peasant ideals of masculinity and femininity can be inferred from the qualities prized in a marriage partner. In the villages of Vladimir a young man of bold aspect, proud bearing, tall stature and with curly hair was considered to epitomize male beauty. Village girls looked for strength and dexterity in a man, the ability to speak well, and a good dress sense, and competence on the accordion was a distinct advantage. Village lads saw female beauty in a smooth gait, modest aspect, relatively tall stature, thick hair and 'a full round rosy face'. According to one contemporary, 'beauty in a girl is not the most important thing. The most important is height, solidity, portliness.' And in order to appear taller and fuller of figure, girls would put straw in their shoes and wear thick clothes.[47] Boys often lost their virginity to older women but female chastity was much valued, though compared with China and certain parts of Catholic and Protestant Europe, relations between unmarried girls and boys were somewhat relaxed, it being not uncommon for them to hold round dances and all-night social gatherings (*posidelki*).[48] Full masculine status was achieved only with marriage – 'Without a wife and family a peasant is not a peasant' – and it was marriage that entitled a man to a share in the land held by the commune.[49] At the same time, motherhood was greatly venerated in Russian culture: the strong, self-sacrificing, long-suffering mother being a powerful cultural archetype. Russian peasants considered a mother's love gentler and purer than a father's – 'There is no other friend like your mother' – and her love was likened to that of the Mother of God.[50] In popular culture deep connections existed between biological mothers, Mother Earth, 'which feeds and nourishes us', and the Mother of God.[51] Giving birth thus gave women a measure of authority.[52]

---

[46] George Fedotov surmises that women's inferiority was rooted in notions of pollution rather than in a Christian idea of women's moral weakness. G. P. Fedotov, *The Russian Religious Mind*, vol. 1, *Kievan Christianity: The Tenth to the Thirteenth Centuries* (Cambridge MA: Harvard University Press, 1966; orig. 1946), p. 189.

[47] Firsov and Kiseleva (eds.), *Byt velikorusskikh krest'ian*, pp. 239–40.

[48] Worobec, *Family and Community* p. 128; Firsov and Kiseleva (eds.), *Byt velikorusskikh krest'ian*, pp. 241, 236.

[49] Worobec, *Family and Community*, p. 119.   [50] Worobec, *Family and Community*, p. 211.

[51] Joanna Hubbs, *Mother Russia: The Feminine Myth in Russian Culture* (Bloomington: Indiana University Press, 1988); Boris Uspenskii, 'Mifologicheskii aspekt russkoi ekspessivnoi frazeologii', part I, *Studia Slavica Hungarica*, 29 (1983), 46.

[52] For this argument see Vera S. Dunham, 'The Strong-Woman Motif', in Cyril E. Black, *The Transformation of Russian Society* (Cambridge MA: Harvard University Press, 1960), p. 470.

In China it was difficult to conceive of 'man' and 'woman' as categories outside the social relationships sanctified by Confucianism.[53] Gender concepts were anchored in beliefs about family structure and social roles more than in beliefs about biological sex.[54] For men, filiality was the central ideal; for women, chastity, since chastity was critical to ensuring the purity of the patriline.[55] In theory, gender roles were complementary, according to the model of yin and yang, the active yang principle representing the male and the passive yin principle the female, each interacting with the other to produce creation, reproduction, transformation and efficacy. Nevertheless, although theoretically complementary, the neo-Confucian construal of yin and yang concealed an implicit hierarchy, with action and initiative valued over endurance and completion. The normative male was a married, adult householder, whose wife, family and property gave him a stake in the social and moral order. A boy entered into full manhood only upon getting married, arguably only when he fathered a son.[56] Masculine identity was linked to social reputation and achievement, one critical measure of which was the capacity of the male to guarantee the chastity and obedience of his womenfolk.[57] Kam Louie suggests that masculinity was structured around the ideals of *wen* (culture) and *wu* (martial prowess, strength, mastery of physical arts).[58] It is doubtful, however, whether the refined wen model of masculinity, with its emphasis on the display of culture and mental development, had much purchase on lower-class men. The latter were more likely influenced by the wu ideal, as is suggested by the popularity of the cult of Guandi, god of war, famed for his military exploits during the Three Kingdoms (AD 220–280).[59] Women were perceived to be potentially polluting, as in Russian culture, the power of

[53] Fei Xiaotong, *From the Soil: The Foundations of Chinese Society* (Xiangtu Zhongguo – orig. 1947), intro. and epilogue by Gary G. Hamilton and Wang Zheng (Berkeley: University of California Press, 1992), p. 27.

[54] Brownell and Wasserstrom, 'Introduction', p. 25.

[55] Patricia Buckley Ebrey, 'Women, Marriage, and the Family in Chinese History', in Paul Ropp (ed.), *The Heritage of China* (Berkeley: University of California Press, 1990), p. 213.

[56] Matthew H. Sommer, 'Dangerous Males, Vulnerable Males and Polluted Males: The Regulation of Masculinity in Qing Dynasty Law', in S. Brownell and J. Wasserstrom (eds.), *Chinese Femininities, Chinese Masculinities* (Berkeley: University of California Press, 2002), p. 83.

[57] Janet M. Theiss, 'Femininity in Flux: Gendered Virtue and Social Conflict in the Mid-Qing Courtroom', in S. Brownell and J. Wasserstrom (eds.), *Chinese Femininities, Chinese Masculinities* (Berkeley: University of California Press, 2002), p. 64.

[58] Kam Louie, *Theorising Chinese Masculinity: Society and Gender in China* (Cambridge: Cambridge University Press, 2002).

[59] Cai Fengming, *Shanghai dushi minsu* [Urban Folkways of Shanghai] (Shanghai: Xuelin chubanshe, 2001), p. 243.

fertility being associated with blood and danger. Charlotte Furth notes that within medical discourse women were seen as the 'sickly sex' because they were prone to depletions of blood, whereas men were seen as capable of storing up their vital energies through abstinence and self-control. Since to be ruled by one's blood was to be controlled by one's emotions, women were depicted in moralistic literature as emotional, wilful, quarrelsome and in need of a firm male hand.[60]

Though peasant women in Russia and China were subjugated by a patriarchal order, there seems little doubt that women in China were more oppressed. There was nothing akin in Russia to the widespread sale of young daughters, infanticide or foot binding. This does not mean that Chinese women were helpless victims, bereft of agency, unable to exercise any influence or carve out authority within the inner sphere. Some popular ballads and songs depict women in assertive roles, such as Hua Mulan, the woman warrior of the Six Dynasties Period, who went to war to spare her aged father military service; but generally, women were idealized as exemplars of female chastity, virtuous widows, or martyrs who sacrifice themselves for their menfolk.[61] The material discussed below on the activities of women workers in Shanghai, however, should caution us against assuming that real women conformed demurely to Confucian stereotype. As already mentioned, it served the political ends of nationalists to portray women as downtrodden victims of an unjust social order – as physically weak, ignorant, secluded in the home – the better to promote the idea that the existing political system squandered the talents and energies of one half of the nation. As we shall see, women who migrated to St Petersburg and Shanghai demonstrated impressive agency as well as vulnerability.

Marriage and Family in the City

The growing minority of women who set off to find work in St Petersburg were the subject of censure by the guardians of public morality. In Sol'vychegodskii county in Vologda, girls who worked in St Petersburg were known as *piterianki*.

---

[60] Charlotte Furth, 'Concepts of Pregnancy, Childbirth and Infancy in Ch'ing China', *Journal of Asian Studies*, 46, 1 (1987), 28; Charlotte Furth, 'Blood, Body, and Gender: Medical Images of the Female Condition in China, 1600–1850', in S. Brownell and J. Wasserstrom (eds.), *Chinese Femininities, Chinese Masculinities* (Berkeley: University of California Press, 2002), pp. 291–314.

[61] Elizabeth Croll, *Feminism and Socialism in China* (London: Routledge, 1978), p. 15; Roxane H. Witke, 'Transformation of Attitudes Towards Women during the May Fourth Era of Modern China', University of California, Berkeley, PhD, 1970, p. 45.

As soon as they are on the road the piterianki, even young girls, forget all decencies. At home they behaved properly, avoiding familiarity and restraining their desire to find a husband; but once on the road they display themselves wantonly, especially on steamships and railways. They enjoy a reputation as loose women and have no difficulty attracting all and sundry – clerks, young students, other passengers.[62]

The female migrant was seen as entering an unregulated zone where the strict moral standards of the community no longer appertained. Although one should take such moralizing with a pinch of salt, it is clear that the proportion of women in St Petersburg who lived apart from their families or alone was strikingly high: no fewer than 86% of working women in 1897.[63] That women were more vulnerable than in the village is suggested by the high proportion of illegitimate births in the capital. Slightly over one-quarter of live births in St Petersburg were illegitimate, roughly the same as in Paris, though lower than in Vienna, Prague or Rome, and far higher than in London.[64] In addition, women had a far higher chance of coming before the courts than in the village.[65]

In Shanghai women were less likely to live alone, coming to the city to join husbands, live with kinsfolk, be lodged with labour contractors or in brothels. Some, however, sought refuge in the city to escape unhappy marriages. Zhu Xingzhen, who became an adopted daughter-in-law (*tongyangxi*) at the age of fourteen following the death of her father, fled to Shanghai after seven years of misery at the hands of her mother-in-law. There she found a job as a domestic servant, but her in-laws found her and dragged her back to the village.[66] Xu Yueming claimed her husband used to tie her to the bedstead and bite her, and that he had twice tried to have her killed. As a result, she had twice tried to commit suicide, once by jumping into a river, once by jumping into a well. Finally, she had left her husband and son and fled to Shanghai to join her father who practised as a fortune-teller there. In 1929, her husband

---

[62] Correspondence in the Tenishev archive. Cited in T. B. Shchepanskaia, 'Strannye lidery: o nekotorykh traditsiiakh sotsial'nogo upravleniia u russkikh', *Etnicheskie aspekty vlasti* (St Petesburg: LS, 1995), p. 230.

[63] Engel, *Between the Fields*, p. 135.   [64] Engel, *Between the Fields*, pp. 126–7.

[65] Stephen P. Frank, *Crime, Cultural Conflict, and Justice in Rural Russia, 1856–1914* (Berkeley: University of California Press, 1999).

[66] 'Letter to the Shaoxing Seven-County Tongxianghui in Shanghai' (Shaoxing qixian lü Hu tongxianghui) (1938), Shanghai Municipal Archive: Q117-5–58. Samita Sen suggests that in India women also came to the city to escape the shackles of family and village. Samita Sen, *Women and Labour in Late Colonial India* (Cambridge: Cambridge University Press, 1999).

arrived to fetch her home to Shangyu in Zhejiang province, but her father would not release her.[67]

In China female employment was part of a family-based economic strategy and most of a woman's earnings were handed over to her family. Nevertheless it appears that wage earning gave single women, if not their married counterparts, a modicum of economic independence.[68] One mother, asked if she thought her daughter was better off doing factory work, replied. 'She is all right. She gives me all the money that she earns. When I tried to arrange an engagement for her, she refused, saying that she doesn't want the man, that it is too early for her.' Asked what she thought of this, she replied: 'If she likes to do so, I have no authority to force her since nowadays everyone acts in this way.'[69] Another mother opined: 'Yes, mothers are always proud to have their daughters working in the factories, but really they do not save much money because they want to dress better than the rest of us.' Yet another, interviewed while she was cooking meat, said: 'I myself do not eat this meat because it costs too much, thirty coppers for about two days' worth. It is for my daughter who is working in the factory and earning the money, so I have to treat her better.'[70] If the prime responsibility, then, of a wage-earning daughter was to her family, employment nevertheless raised her status.[71] Contemporaries probably exaggerated the 'individualism' encouraged by wage earning, but we should not underestimate the sense of independence that it inspired. As one daughter said: 'To stay at home and depend on one's parents is not good. I am an independent woman now. The family has more respect for me. Life in the factory is more interesting than life at home.'[72] For single women under the contract labour system it is hard to imagine that wage work brought much independence, since they retained barely any of the money they earned. Nevertheless for all its abuses, the system provided female migrants with some security. And it is noteworthy that some chose to stay on in the contractor's house after their three-year contract had expired under what

[67] 'Nan nü Xu Yueming bei Ding Caizhang nüedai zhi jingguo' [Xue Yueming Tells of her Experience of Being Ill-treated by Ding Caizhang] (1933), Shanghai Municipal Archive: Q117–5–58.
[68] Fei, *Peasant Life*, p. 234.
[69] H. D. Lamson, 'The Effect of Industrialization upon Village Livelihood: A Study of Fifty Families in Four Villages Near the University of Shanghai', *Chinese Economic Journal*, 9, 4 (1932), 1073.
[70] Lamson, 'The Effect of Industrialization', p. 1075.
[71] Zhu Bangxing, Hu Linge and Xu Sheng, *Shanghai chanye yu Shanghai zhigong* [Shanghai Industry and Shanghai Labour] (Shanghai: Shanghai renmin chubanshe, 1984; orig. 1939), p. 105.
[72] Lang, *Chinese Family*, p. 267.

was known as the 'taking rice' (*daifan*) system, whereby they kept their wages, but paid the contractor $7 to $8 a month for food and lodging.[73]

By the late-nineteenth century, the ideal of marrying for love was admired in the Russian village – at least to judge by the number of songs that told of romance and heartbreak – even if it was more honoured in the breach than the observance.[74] Children certainly had some latitude in choosing a mate, but parents would be involved in their marriage decisions.[75] The bulk of migrants to St Petersburg were single, and those who were married tended initially to leave their families in the village. In 1897, nearly one-third of female workers and 43.7% of male workers were married, but the great majority were living apart from their families.[76] The Stolypin reforms, however, made it easier for peasants to separate from the commune and this, together with increased employment opportunities for women, intensified the trend for married migrants in the capital to live with their families.[77] In 1897, only 13.3% of workers in St Petersburg lived with their families, but by 1918 this had risen to 71%, though the latter figure should be treated with caution, since workers with close ties to the countryside had already abandoned the capital by that stage because of unemployment and food shortages.[78] At the same time, the proportion of the capital's population who stayed single remained high. European Russia had one of the lowest proportions of single people of any country in Europe. In 1897, only 4% of men and 5% of women aged forty-five to forty-nine were unmarried, compared with 12% of men and 11% of women in France and 15% and 12% in Britain.[79] In St Petersburg, however, the situation was very different: in 1897, the proportion of workers aged forty to fifty-nine who were single stood as high as 20%; and the proportion tended to rise in later years, despite the overall increase in the marriage rate.[80] This reflected the difficulties many men had in finding the financial means to marry, but it may also reflect the fact that some men chose to take advantage of the increased opportunities in the capital for extra-marital or same-sex relations.[81]

[73] Deng Tai, *Shenghuo sumiao* [Sketches of Life] (Shanghai: Daxia shudian, 1937), p. 254; Emily Honig, 'The Contract Labour System and Women Workers: Pre-Liberation Cotton Mills in Shanghai', *Modern China*, 9, 4 (1983), 435.

[74] *Naselenie Rossii*, p. 169.

[75] Firsov and Kiseleva (eds.), *Byt velikorusskikh krest'ian*, p. 245.

[76] U. A. Shuster, *Peterburgskie rabochie v 1905–07gg.* (Leningrad: Nauka, 1976), p. 26.

[77] Leopold Haimson and Eric Brian, 'Changements démographiques et grèves ouvrières à Saint-Petersbourg, 1905–14', *Annales ESC*, 40, 4 (1985), 797.

[78] Shuster, *Peterburgskie rabochie*, p. 26; S. G. Strumilin, 'Problemy ekonomiki truda', *Izbrannye proizvedeniia*, vol. 3 (Moscow: Nauka, 1965), pp. 69–71.

[79] *Naselenie Rossii*, p. 35.   [80] Engel, *Between the Fields*, p. 136.

[81] Dan Healey, *Homosexual Desire in Revolutionary Russia* (Chicago: Chicago University Press, 2001), pp. 29–48.

Shanghai had a very high and a relatively early marriage rate. Of 192 working-class men aged fifteen or over in the Yangshupu district of the city in 1929, 89.6% were married; of 138 women of the same age, 83.6% were married.[82] However, as in St Petersburg, there was a trend towards later marriage, with Shanghai men marrying around five years later than in the village, and most women workers marrying between the age of eighteen and twenty-four.[83] The May Fourth Movement popularized the idea of freedom to love (*lian'ai ziyou*) – i.e. free choice of marriage partner – and when quizzed by college students, most factory women approved the idea that a woman should choose her own husband and many were intrigued by western customs such as couples kissing and holding hands in public. They did not, however, consider such behaviour appropriate for themselves.[84] Arranged marriages, governed by conventional considerations of property and family status, remained the norm. At the same time, the forms of female seclusion that were still strong in many villages proved much weaker in Shanghai and there were more social spaces where men and women could meet. In general, the idea that a decent girl should accept the mate chosen for her by her parents remained entrenched, but many opted for a compromise whereby a couple were allowed to meet before the engagement was finalized by the matchmaker who negotiated with the two sets of parents. Typically, a wage-earning bride might cost 50 yuan plus two leather suitcases and a set of silk quilt covers, but the bride's parents would contribute goods and money almost equal to those provided by the husband's parents.[85]

In her study of 95 families of industrial workers in Shanghai in 1936–7, Olga Lang found that there was deviation from the norm of arranged marriage in about a quarter of cases.[86] To judge from cases that came to court – where judgments generally upheld traditional marriage arrangements – the course of true love rarely ran smooth for the minority that bucked tradition. Zhang Lanying, a cotton worker, had been betrothed as a child to Zhang Jisheng. In 1919, aged sixteen, she

---

[82] Fang Fu-an, 'Shanghai Labour', part 1, *Chinese Economic Journal*, 7, 2 (1930), 879. In 1929–31, 85% of Chinese women aged fifteen to forty-four were married, compared with only 67% of women of child-bearing age in Japan. J. L. Buck, *Land Utilization in China* (Nanjing: University of Nanking, 1937), p. 379.

[83] Honig, *Sisters*, p. 183. The Yangshupu survey showed that the modal age of marriage for men was twenty-six and for women twenty-two. Fang Fu-an, 'Shanghai Labour', p. 879.

[84] Lamson, 'The Effect of Industrialization', p. 1075.

[85] Shiling Zhao McQuaid, 'Shanghai Labour: Gender, Politics and Traditions in the Making of the Chinese Working Class, 1911–49', Queen's University, Kingston, Ontario, PhD, 1995, pp. 155–6.

[86] Lang, *Chinese Family*, pp. 266, 124.

fell in love with a fellow worker and they began to live together in the French Concession. However, the father of Zhang Jisheng took her lover to court and he was jailed for three months.[87] Jin Zhaodu, an employee of the Japan-China cotton mill, had also been betrothed as a child, but she fell in love with Gu Deming, who worked as an oiler at mill. They paid a lawyer to announce in the newspaper that they had married. However, her mother, under pressure from the family of the betrothed, reported her daughter to the police and a judge ruled her marriage with Gu invalid.[88] In other ways, too, a minority of women began to reject aspects traditional marriage and family norms. In 1934, after their house burned down, Yuan Juhua moved with her husband and four-year-old daughter to Shanghai. Not long afterwards, her husband died, whereupon Yuan took a job as a servant and placed her daughter in the care of her mother-in-law back in Shangyu. During the first six months, Yuan sent her 25 yuan, but she stopped all payment after she set up home with a carpenter from Hangzhou, by whom she had a son. When her mother-in-law came to Shanghai to ask for money for the upkeep of the daughter, her daughter-in-law's new partner, whom she referred to as Yuan's 'illicit husband' (*pinfu*), insulted her and offered her a derisory two yuan to cover her fare home. She appealed to the tongxianghui, and it drew up an agreement, according to which Yuan gave up her daughter permanently to her mother-in-law in return for a one-off payment of fifty yuan. The agreement stipulated that 'hereafter the relationship between the daughter-in-law and the mother-in-law shall be dissolved.'[89]

Some wives were no long prepared to accept their husbands taking concubines. Chen Zhushi, a widow, moved to Shanghai with her six-year-old daughter where she found a job as a domestic servant. At the age of thirteen, her daughter found employment in a textile mill. Mother and daughter managed to save 1,000 yuan over the next few years. When the daughter was twenty she married Wang Jinbing, and her mother invested the savings in setting up a shop for the young couple. Things went smoothly until Wang had an affair. He begged his wife to accept his lover as a concubine and to live with her in peace, but she rejected this proposal with contempt.[90]

---

[87] Shiling Zhao, 'Shanghai Labour', p. 144.
[88] Shiling Zhao, 'Shanghai Labour', p. 144.
[89] 'Letter from Liu Xie to the Shaoxing Seven-County Tongxianghui in Shanghai' (1936); 'Agreement between Yuan Shuangxi and Liu Xie Shi' (1936), Shanghai Municipal Archive: Q117–5–58.
[90] Letters from Chen Zhu and Wang Chen to the Shaoxing Seven-County Tongxianghui in Shanghai (1935), Shanghai Municipal Archive: Q117–5–58.

In St Petersburg and Shanghai migrants tended to have smaller families than was the norm in the countryside, and over time family size in the city fell. In Russia, the average size of the working-class family dropped from 4.4 members in 1897 to only 3.5 in 1923 (although it is not clear whether these figures include children resident in the countryside).[91] This compared with a reduction in the average size of the peasant household from 6.6 in 1897 to 5.74 in 1916 (although some allowance for wartime conditions must be made regarding the latter figure).[92] In the Chinese-administered areas of Shanghai, the average number of people per household was 4.83 in 1929.[93] In 1932, a survey of 800 families in eight predominantly rural districts of Shanghai county showed that the average size of family was 5.58 persons.[94] In both cities later marriage was a key cause of the decline in family size, although we cannot rule out the possibility that some of the decline is to be accounted for by the fact that urban families continued to send children to be brought up in the village by grandparents or other relatives who were thus not counted in the statistics. But there is little doubt that migrants to the city tended to have smaller families. In Shanghai the attractiveness of the Confucian ideal of the large joint family in which parents, children and grandchildren lived under one roof was waning. In 1936–7, only 5 out of 143 worker families in the city were joint families, compared with 71 that were nuclear and 24 that were 'stem' (i.e. parents, unmarried children and one married son plus wife and children living under the same roof).[95] When 100 Beijing rickshaw pullers were asked in 1929 if they liked the big family set-up, 80 said no and a further 7 added that they detested it.[96] Olga Lang nevertheless concluded that 'new

[91] E. O. Kabo, *Ocherki rabochego byta* (Moscow: Knigoizd-vo VTsSPS, 1928), p. 23. Whereas families with six or more members comprised 21.4% of the total in 1897, by 1923 they comprised only 13.5%.

[92] *Naselenie Rossii*, pp. 71–2.

[93] Luo Zhiru (ed.), *Tongjibiao zhong zhi Shanghai* [Shanghai through statistical tables] (Nanjing: 1932), table 30. The survey of 230 cotton-worker families in 1927–8 found the average family comprised 4.77 people (including 0.15 resident non-relatives). Seventy-one per cent of families had between three and six members. Simon Yang, and L. K. Tao, *A Study of the Standard of Living of Working Families in Shanghai* (Peiping: Institute of Social Research, 1931), pp. 23–4. The survey of 100 worker families in Yangshupu district in 1929 showed that the average size was still smaller at 4.11. Fang Fu-an, 'Shanghai Labour', p. 872.

[94] *Shanghai shi tongji* [Statistics on Shanghai] (Shanghai: Shanghai shi difang xiehui, 1933), part 10, p. 39.

[95] Lang, *Chinese Family* p. 140.

[96] Huang Gongdu. 'Guanyu wuchanjieji shehui taidu de yige xiaoxia ceyan' [A Short Test of Proletarian Social Attitudes], *Shehuixue jie*, 4 (1930), 167.

trends have not altered the traditional longing of the Chinese for numerous progeny'.[97]

There may have been some trend towards a family form in which the husband was principal breadwinner and the wife a full-time housewife. In St Petersburg, a social investigator noted, the 'working class family tries to keep the mother of a family at home'.[98] Barbara Engel notes that 'in the city, the extraordinary difficulty of combining full-time wage-earning with motherhood and running even a tiny household led (female) migrants to make a different choice than in the village, and to give precedence to childcare and housework'.[99] However, the ability to make this choice depended heavily on family income, and by no means all working-class families were in a position to make it. A survey of 1914 found that women in just under half of worker families worked outside the home, a proportion that rose to almost 60% in the poorest families.[100] In Shanghai, evidence points more clearly to the fact that the propensity of the wife to be a full-time housewife was linked both to family income and to stage in the family life cycle: it tended to be associated either with the families of high-earning males, such as public-utility workers, or with working-class families where grown-up children were contributing to the family budget, thus making it rational for the older mother to tend the home.[101] As in St Petersburg, the ideal of the wife as homemaker had a certain appeal, but only better-off sections of the working class were able to realize it.[102]

Barbara Evans Clements has suggested that in Russia the weakening power of fathers over adult sons was accompanied by a strengthening in the power of the husband over the wife.[103] There seems little doubt that for many married women gruelling hours of waged work simply added to the burdens of being a mother and housewife. In 1917, the journal of the

---

[97] Lang, *Chinese Family*, pp. 154, 162.

[98] M. Davidovich, 'Khozaistvennoe znachenie zhenshchiny v rabochei sem'e', *Poznanie Rossii*, 3 (1909), 122. Cited in Engel, *Between the Fields*, p. 222.

[99] Engel, *Between the Fields*, p. 222.

[100] In Vigdorchik's survey when the husband earned over 50 roubles a month, a mere 6.6% of the wives went out to work; when the man earned 31–50 roubles, 30% of wives went out to work; when men earned under 20 roubles a month, nearly 60% of wives went out to work. Engel, *Between the Fields*, pp. 218–19. A somewhat similar situation was evident in Shanghai, where wives' earnings were inversely proportional to the size of family income. In the very poorest households husbands contributed 65.4% of family income and wives as much as 23.1%. Cai Zhengya, 'Shanghai de laogong', *Shehui Banyuekan*, 1, 11–12 (February 1935), p. 99.

[101] Cai Zhengya, 'Shanghai de laogong', p. 99.

[102] Lang, *Chinese Family*, p. 157.

[103] Barbara Evans Clements, 'Women and the Gender Question', in Edward Acton, Vladimir Iu. Cherniaev and William G. Rosenberg (eds.), *Critical Companion to the Russian Revolution* (London: Arnold, 1997), p. 596.

textile workers' union bemoaned the reluctance of husbands to help their wives with domestic chores:

Having finished work at the factory, the woman worker is still not free. While the male worker goes off to a meeting, or just takes a walk or plays billiards with his mates, she has to cope with the housework – to cook, to wash and so on ... Unfortunately, one has to admit that male workers are still very prejudiced. They think that it is humiliating for a man to 'woman's work'. They would sooner their sick worn-out wife did the servile labour (*barshchinu*) by herself.[104]

That this perception corresponded to reality is borne out by a time-budget survey, carried out in 1922 among 76 worker families in Petrograd, Moscow and Ivanovo-Voznesensk, which showed that whereas men got eight hours of sleep, women only managed six hours and forty-four minutes; and whereas men did two hours eight minutes unpaid labour per day, women did five hours twelve minutes, whilst doing almost the same amount of paid work as men.[105] Yet we should not dismiss out of hand contemporary claims that in some working-class families relations between husbands and wives were – in the jargon of the time – more 'comradely' than in the peasant household.[106] In 1909, M. Davidovich, surveyor of St Petersburg textile workers, observed that the husbands of millworkers tended to lend a hand with the household chores: 'While the woman hurries straight home from the factory to the children, the husband goes off to market and to the shops to buy provisions for supper and next day's dinner ... in his spare time the husband must always look after the children.'[107] This hardly amounted to an equal division of domestic labour, and it was confined to a minority of working-class families, but it suggests that there was some recognition that women's waged work necessitated some attenuation of the notion that domestic labour and childcare were the exclusive responsibility of women.

The impact of urban-industrial life on the domestic division of labour among workers in Shanghai seems to have been similar. In addition to an arduous shift in the factory, married women continued to do the lion's share of cooking, housework and childcare. A song sung by women in the silk filatures captures the despair of a mother who is too

[104] *Tkach*, 2 (1917), p. 7.
[105] S. G. Strumilin, 'Problemy ekonomiki truda', *Izbrannye Proizvedeniia*, vol. 3 (five vols.) (Moscow: Nauka, 1963), p. 192.
[106] P. Timofeev, *Chem zhivet zavodskii rabochii* (St Petersburg: Russkoe bogatstvo 1906), p. 87; Kleinbort, 'Ocherki rabochei demokratii', part 2, *Sovremennyi Mir*, 5 (1913), p. 154.
[107] V. Ia. Krupianskaia, 'Evoliutsiia semeino-bytovogo uklada rabochikh', in *Rossiiskii proletariat: oblik, bor'ba, gegemoniia* (Moscow: Nauka, 1970), p. 277.

exhausted to care for her baby:

> I pull on my clothes and jump out of bed
> I gaze intently at the face of my child
> Your mother goes off and you look so pale
> I drop my gaze and rush out of the door
> By the time work is done, six hours have passed
> Outside the factory the streets are pitch black
> Please don't ask your mother to hold you, my son
> My body aches and I can't bear the pain.[108]

Again, there is some evidence that the status of the wife was higher in the working-class than the peasant family. Lamson noted that women did 'most of the actual family spending, planning of the meals, clothing and running of the household'.[109] And Olga Lang opined of the working-class housewife: 'She may be well-informed about income, the property of her family, the current price of land, rice and wheat, rates of interest, taxes. And she is more likely to be consulted by her husband.'[110] Crucially, in the prevailing nuclear family young wives enjoyed considerably more independence than they had done when they were under the thumb of their mothers-in-law.

Gender Identities at Work

In the Russian village the ideal of patriarchal masculinity was rooted in marriage and fatherhood, work on the land and membership of the mir. For the male migrant to St Petersburg, family, work and leisure became more clearly differentiated sites upon which masculine identity was constructed, with work on the land and membership of the village community obviously ceasing to be of importance. In the urban-industrial environment, the family remained a key site on which masculinity was transacted, and although the subordination of women may have continued to constitute a dimension of masculine identity, the subordination of junior to senior males ceased. In the workplace and consumer culture, by contrast, understandings of masculinity were promoted that were no longer based on kinship or securely attached to the procreative role of the father. That said, young men brought with them traditional understandings of masculinity, not least the idealization of physical strength and stamina, although these, too, were subtly reconfigured as they became attached to mainly homosocial sites, such as the artel, the tavern and the workplace.

---

[108] Quoted in Ono Kazuko, *Chinese Women*, p. 121.

[109] H. D. Lamson, 'The Standard of Living of Factory Workers: A Study of Incomes and Expenditures of 21 Families in Shanghai', *Chinese Economic Journal*, 7, 5 (1930), 1241.

[110] Lang, *Chinese Family*, p. 157.

The possession and display of physical strength was vital to the traditional model of Russian masculinity and it retained and possibly increased its importance in the urban-industrial environment. For unskilled workers, especially, masculinity continued to be associated with toughness, with a capacity to sustain heavy labour over long periods and with the exertion of sudden force in lifting and shifting. Outside work, it continued to be expressed through pastimes that demonstrated bodily strength, such as fighting or the capacity to drink to excess. The city tavern acquired a new significance as centre of a 'modern' drinking culture that was regular, recreational and individualistic, in contrast to rural drinking culture, which was communal, intermittent and connected to festive occasions.[111] By the 1890s, heavy drinking had assumed epidemic proportions in the lower-class districts of St Petersburg. On pay day one could stand on Malyi Prospekt in Vasilevskii Ostrov district and watch 'the taverns, inns and ale-houses filled to bursting, prostitutes strolling nearby and anxious wives waiting for their husbands to come out before they had spent all their wages'.[112] As this suggests, male sociability based on drinking was largely secured at the expense of women. Organized fights, which had always taken place in the village, continued in the city.[113] At the same time, young males became increasingly interested in sports that prized facility over brute strength. Commercialized forms of entertainment associated with the circus, such as wrestling, boxing and weight-lifting, promoted more refined, narcissistic forms of sporting prowess, and wrestlers such as the Estonian Sergei Lurikh became icons of the perfect male body, matching muscular perfection with physical skill and grace.[114] This connected to an emergent cult of *zakal*, the conscious forging of physical and mental fitness, endurance, stamina and resolve, that was to become a hallmark of the Soviet ideal of manliness in the 1920s and 1930s.[115]

---

[111] David Christian, *Living Water: Vodka and Russian Society on the Eve of Emancipation* (Oxford: Oxford University Press, 1990), ch. 3.

[112] I. Eremeev (ed.), *Gorod S-Peterburg s tochki zreniia meditsinskoi pomoshchi* (St Petersburg: Sankt-Peterburgskaia politsiia, 1987), p. 632.

[113] A. M. Buiko, *Put' rabochego: zapiski starogo bol'shevika* (Moscow: 1934), p. 15. Reginald E. Zelnik, *Radical Worker in Tsarist Russia: The Autobiography of Semën Ivanovich Kanatchikov* (Stanford: Stanford University Press, 1986), p. 60.

[114] James Riordan, *Sport in Soviet Society* (Cambridge: Cambridge University Press, 1977), p. 17; Louise McReynolds and Cathy Popkin, 'The Objective Eye and the Common Good', in Kelly and Shepherd (eds.), *Constructing Russian Culture*, pp. 76–77.

[115] Catriona Kelly, 'The Education of the Will: Advice Literature, *Zakal*, and Manliness in Early Twentieth-Century Russia', in Barbara Evans Clements, Rebecca Friedman and Dan Healey (eds.), *Russian Masculinities in History and Culture* (London: Palgrave, 2002), pp. 131–51.

Within the workplace, drink also served as a way to suffuse work culture with masculine significance. At the Skorokhod shoe factory 'treats (*prival'nye*) were considered obligatory, and if a new worker didn't treat his fellows to a round of drinks they would not let him have the tools he needed'.[116] But workplace culture was masculinized in other ways too. For the majority of 'unconscious' workers, swearing, dirty jokes, sexual boasting were ways of letting off steam, of demonstrating that you were one of the lads, and a way of gaining the respect of one's peers.[117] More crucially, they were a means by which men sustained their manliness in a capitalist workplace that conspired to make them feel powerless in a way they had not felt when working on the land. Again, this sense of masculine power was often secured at the expense of women. After 1905, employers took on women as cheap labour, a policy that threatened not only to undercut men's wages but also to undermine their belief in the manly character of the work they performed.[118] Men responded by reminding female 'interlopers' that they were trespassing on 'male' territory. At the New Aivaz engineering works a group of self-styled 'conscious workers' complained about the behaviour of their workmates. If a new woman asked for advice it would provoke 'immodest innuendos'. 'They say things that directly diminish women's dignity or insult women's honour. Sometimes they go as far as directly criminal actions, making filthy suggestions and attempting to carry them out.'[119] As this suggests, for those who had no families or were living apart from their families, the workplace took on a sharpened significance as an arena in which the meanings of masculinity were transacted and enforced.

Crucial to the formation of a more modern style of masculinity was the acquisition of work-related skill. If for the majority of unskilled migrants, physical strength and stamina continued to be the chief ways in which work bolstered their masculine identity, for a growing minority of skilled workers, masculine status became associated with the acquisition of visual, tactile and auditory skills, rapidity of reflexes, knowledge of materials and machines, and the ability to take decisions and to control the work process. The normal entry into a skilled trade was through an apprenticeship that started at the age of thirteen or fourteen. Apprentices, often known as 'boys', spent the first years of their working

[116] *Pravda*, 28 August 1912.
[117] S. A. Smith, 'The Social Meanings of Swearing: Workers and Bad Language in Late-Imperial and Early-Soviet Russia', *Past and Present*, 160 (1998), pp. 182–9.
[118] Rose L. Glickman, *Russian Factory Women: Workplace and Society, 1880–1914* (Berkeley: University of California Press, 1984), pp. 204–8.
[119] *Rabochaia Pravda*, 9 July 1913.

lives doing little more than fetching and carrying for adults. Constantly reminded of their juvenile status, they were patronized at best, brutalized at worst.[120] Completion of apprenticeship marked the entry into manhood, just as marriage had done in the village. I. V. Babushkin, who began work at the age of fifteen in the torpedo workshop of Kronstadt port, recalled: 'At the age of eighteen, according to the local rules, I was recognized as an adult and transferred from the apprentices into the ranks of the skilled craftsmen.'[121] Skilled craftsmen, such as pattern-makers, instrument-makers, fitters and turners, styled themselves *masterovye*, masters of their craft, a term that resonated with male authority. Theirs was an exclusive fraternity that distinguished itself from the world of unskilled workers, and the craftsman's sense of honour would not allow him to do the job of an unskilled worker, even if his pay was guaranteed.[122]

Male workers frequently invoked an ideal of 'fraternity' that unconsciously contrasted to the traditional patriarchal ideal. Workers' songs, for example, were stocked with references to 'brothers' and 'lads' (*rebiata*).[123] It is perhaps not surprising that migrants, who lived and worked in environments where women were largely absent, should find the idiom of brotherhood appealing. In a more explicitly ideological fashion, 'conscious' workers played upon this idiom of fraternity for political ends, seeing in it a metaphor for class solidarity and human community, apparently unaware that it silently excluded the female half of humankind. In a curious twist, however – one that raises a question mark against Carole Pateman's counterposition of a patriarchal model to a fraternal model of political authority – their discourse still invoked the ideal of the family.[124] Indeed it is striking how often 'conscious' workers articulated an identification with the working class in familial terms,

---

[120] Kabo, *Ocherki*, p. 125; *Vyborgskaia storona: iz istorii bor'by rabochego klassa za pobedu velikoi oktiabr'skoi revoliutsii* (Leningrad: 1957), p. 5.

[121] E. A. Korol'chuk (ed.), *V nachale puti: vospominaniia peterburgskikh rabochikh, 1872–1897gg.* (Leningrad: Lenizdat, 1975), p. 305.

[122] P. Timofeev, *Chem zhivet*, p. 10.

[123] A. I. Nutrikhin (ed.), *Pesni russkikh rabochikh XVIII-nachalo XX veka* (Leningrad: Sovetskii pisatel', 1962).

[124] Carole Pateman's path-breaking work contrasted classic patriarchalism of the seventeenth century, where masculine political creativity is rooted in the procreative power of the father, to contract theory where men act as brothers in order to transform themselves into a civic fraternity. She argued that in so doing, the 'brothers' split apart the two dimensions of political right that were formerly united in the figure of the father: patriarchal right was extended to all men, but the civil sphere acquired its universal meaning only in opposition to a private sphere which subordinated nature and women. Carole Pateman, *The Sexual Contract* (Cambridge: Polity, 1988), pp. 77–133.

usually in terms of leaving behind their natural family and entering the new family of workers. Buzinov recalls: 'I noticed that as my strength grew, my mother gradually acquired the aspect of a "weak creation". I no longer saw things her way and desired to follow my independent path. I thus cut myself off from my mother and headed for the family of workers.'[125] This was, of course, a strange sort of family, insofar as it consisted entirely of brothers, yet it suggests that even as they rebelled against the father and struggled to separate themselves from their mothers, these men saw in a family purged of relations of hierarchy and subordination, a model of mutual cooperation and solidarity that the working class could emulate.

Finally, we may recall the rather dandified style of masculinity discussed in chapter 2, in which young working men, usually skilled and relatively well-paid, went in for stylish dress, self-display, and a veneer of urban sophistication. This was a style of masculinity heavily influenced by consumer culture that valorized physical attractiveness, sexual choice, and aspirations for self-betterment. Through clothes, in particular, young men shaped their appearance, asserted themselves in public, and sought to raise their social standing. Not least, stylish dress helped to attract potential sexual partners. In Soligalich and Chukhlomskii counties in Kostroma local women preferred men who had lived in St Petersburg. They were 'much more sophisticated than local men; their conversation was often indistinguishable from that of an urban-dweller, though adorned with fanciful expressions; their manner was copied from that of the metropolitan petty-bourgeois; they could dance, they wore dandified suits'.[126]

In Shanghai, too, work was a prime site on which masculine identity was constructed. Ideas of masculinity rooted in Confucian patriarchy were challenged in the workplace, as much as in society at large, yet the influence of traditional notions was more noticeable than in Russia. Although the wen ideal of masculinity had never had much influence on lower-class males, the challenge posed to it by the 1911 revolution served to enhance the legitimacy of the wu ideal and thus to endorse qualities of physical strength and martial prowess that were particularly associated with lower-class masculinity. Apprentices and junior workers at the Commercial Press, for example, formed a national skills team (*guoshudui*) in 1922 to practise physical fitness each day.[127] Yet much of the emphasis on wu-style masculinity was traditional in character.

---

[125] A. Buzinov, *Za Nevskoi Zastavoi* (Moscow: 1930), p. 18.

[126] D. N. Zhbankov, *Bab'ia storona: statistiko-etnograficheskii ocherk* (Kostroma, 1891), p. 27.

[127] Shanghai Shangwu Yinshuguan zhigong yundong shi [The History of the Labour Movement at the Shanghai Commercial Press] (Beijing: Shanghai gongchang qiye dangshi gongyun shi congshu, 1991), p. 180.

From the beginning of the twentieth century, Shanghai's two main secret societies, the Green Gang and the Red Gang, extended their control of the job market, first to the transportation and construction sectors and then, by the 1930s, to the factory and public-service sectors. Though complex in its internal structure, since it was organized along the dual lines of fictive kinship and teacher–student relations, the Green Gang popularized a rather traditional ethos of brotherhood among Shanghai workers.[128] Its code of honour, like that of the bandits and *haohan*, or tough guys, of yore, was known as *yiqi*, a collocation of the characters for 'righteousness' and 'firmness of spirit'.[129] The code was immortalized in a scene in the vernacular novel *The Romance of Three Kingdoms*, where three men swear a blood oath in the peach garden. Secret-society rules enjoined members to deal fairly with one another, to keep the society's secrets, to avoid adultery and theft, and to uphold the Confucian virtues of bene-volence (*ren*), righteousness (*yi*), propriety (*li*), wisdom (*zhi*) and sincerity (*xin*).[130] This code of fraternity was different from the 'universalistic' model of civic fraternity notionally endorsed by the republic of 1912, since it was fundamentally personalistic in character. But though trad-itional, it instilled obligations of mutual aid and loyalty that transcended the social relationships sanctioned by Confucianism and it was put to new uses in the industrial context. In the strike in the Japanese cotton mills in February 1925 strikers' slogans included 'Chinese must uphold the Chinese code of honour (yiqi)' and 'Workers must uphold the workers' code of honour.'[131] And in the summer of 1926, workers at the old British American Tobacco plant in Pudong made a huge character *yi* out of cigarettes, while their counterparts at the new plant made the character *qi*, thus forming the word *yiqi*, explaining that this was an expression of support for the strikes that were then taking place.[132]

The guilds, which largely excluded women from membership, also continued to reproduce rather traditional understandings of masculinity. Entry into guild membership was largely via apprenticeship and, as in

---

[128] Jiang Hao, 'Qingbang de yuanliu ji yanbian' [The Origins and Evolution of the Green Gang], in *Jiu Shanghai de banghui*, *Jiu Shanghai de banghui* [The Secret Societies of Old Shanghai] (Shanghai: Shanghai renmin chubanshe, 1986), pp. 60–1; Atsushi Watanabe, 'Secret Societies in Modern China: Ch'ing-Pang and Hung-Pang', in *Zhonghua minguo chuqi lishi yantaohui lunwenji, 1912–27* [Symposium on the Early Years of the Republic of China] (Taibei: 1984), p. 811.

[129] W. J. F. Jenner, 'Tough Guys, Mateship and Honour: Another Chinese Tradition', *East Asian History* 12 (1996), 1–34.

[130] David Faure, 'Secret Societies, Heretic Sects, and Peasant Rebellions in Nineteenth Century China,' *Journal of the Chinese University of Hong Kong*, 5, 1 (1979), 202.

[131] *Zhongguo gongren* 4 (1925), 52.

[132] *Xiangdao* 159, 23 June 1926.

Russia, the completion of apprenticeship marked an important mile-stone on the road to manhood. Apprenticeship commenced at the age of eleven or twelve, though some boys began as young as eight or nine, and lasted two to five years.[133] Apprentices were entirely under the thumb of their master (*shifu*), and well into the 1920s, the exploitation they suf-fered was publicly justified as being character building. By learning to suffer and endure hardship, it was claimed, the apprentice stored up valuable experience, in accordance with the proverb, 'he who suffers most will become the first among men' (*ku zhong ku, ren shang ren*).[134] The May Fourth Movement encouraged apprentices to give vent to their grievances, and one can glimpse in their protests an assertion of aspirant masculinity. Yang Dixian, an apprentice in a coal depot on Xinzha Road, wrote to the *Shanghai Shopclerk* to complain about his master: 'He has two young children – one aged three and one aged five, and everyday he makes me look after them. Whenever one starts to cry he scolds me, and even hits me with a broom, saying that I'm not taking proper care of the child. I'm therefore sending you this letter to ask if an apprentice should be expected to look after babies.'[135] As in St Petersburg, com-pletion of apprenticeship signalled entry into manhood. Henceforward, as a fully qualified member of the guild, a young man was expected to uphold the 'face' of the guild through honest dealing, high-quality workmanship and by fostering fellowship (*ganqing*) among members.[136]

Working-class masculinity in Shanghai became reconfigured on the sites of home and consumer culture, albeit to a lesser extent than in St Petersburg. The challenge to the Confucian roles of father and son that followed the collapse of the imperial order, together with the New Culture Movement's assertion of the rights of the individual, weakened the idea that the paramount purpose of marriage was to reproduce the patriline. Indeed for many of the lowest-paid migrants, marriage was simply beyond their scope financially. This, together with the fact that young men in the city appear to have become sexually active earlier than in the village – at around the age of fourteen or fifteen – meant that they were major purchasers of the services of prostitutes, mainly those known as 'pheasants' (*yeji*) because of their gaudy attire and peripatetic

---

[133] H. G. W. Woodhead (ed.), *China Year Book, 1925* (Tientsin: North China Daily News, 1925), p. 551.

[134] Liao T'ai-ch'u. 'The Apprentices in Chengtu during and after the War', *Yenching Journal of Social Studies*, 4, 1 (1948), 100.

[135] *Shanghai huoyou*, 31 November 1920, p. 14.

[136] Timothy Roland Bradstock, 'Craft Guilds in Ch'ing Dynasty China', Harvard University, PhD, 1984, p. 197; John Stewart Burgess, *The Guilds of Peking* (New York: Columbia University Press, 1928), p. 184.

habits.[137] For those who could afford to marry, the trend towards nuclear families placed greater importance on the conjugal relationship between husband and wife than in the village. And if the ideal of romantic love made only slow headway, masculine identity nevertheless became more focused around heterosexual conjugality and the sexed body.[138] As we saw in chapter 2, young, better-paid and better-educated working men could afford to spend money on dressing fashionably. For these, attractiveness to the opposite sex, along with a capacity to sustain an affective relationship with a potential or actual spouse, became more salient to the production of masculine identity. However, for the majority of young male migrants, release from patriarchal authority did not lead to any radical questioning of the traditional model of masculinity, except insofar as the arena of waged work and the capacity economically to support a family acquired heightened importance.

For female migrants, home and work did not become so clearly separated sites of identity formation. In both St Petersburg and Shanghai married women's attachments to the workplace remained secondary to their attachments to home and family. This was also broadly true for single women, although, as we have seen, their wage-earning capacity raised the status of daughters in their natal families. Yet despite evidence that women often felt pride in the economic independence that work provided, the grindingly long hours, atrocious conditions and the dreary repetition of the machine do not seem to have excited among them a sense of esteem in themselves as women and workers. It seems to have been easier for men to appropriate the experience of work under capitalism in relatively empowering ways, partly because of men's greater access to skilled work and partly because of their ability to draw upon the solidarities of guild, secret society or trade union. Women, by contrast, frequently cast themselves in the role of victim, at least for the rhetorical purpose of winning public sympathy. In St Petersburg women workers likened themselves to 'little slaves' (*malenkie rabyni*) and the trope is neatly articulated in a poem by Grisha Trusova, herself a worker:

> My mother gave birth to me
> On this ill-starred earth
> From my earliest years I began to suffer
> From the early spring of childhood I went out to work
> Behind the factory wall I found much bitterness

---

[137] Tang Hai, *Zhongguo laodong wenti* [Chinese Labour Problems] (Shanghai: Guanghua shuju, 1926), pp. 10–13.
[138] Susan Brownell and Jeffrey Wasserstrom, 'Introduction: Theorizing Femininities and Masculinities', p. 33.

Even when you are ill, you run
With sorrow in your heart
You tremble in the face of the bosses
All for the sake of a crust of bread.[139]

In Shanghai, too, women cast themselves as the weaker sex, unable to defend themselves against the depredations of capital. In August 1911, women silk workers posted a notice on the factory gates: 'In recent years, the price of rice has been high and other trades have received wage increases, but our compradores have harshly put down the weaker sex (*nüliu*) and successively cut the rate so that now we only earn 3 jiao 2 fen.'[140] This example, however, pinpoints a paradox. For these women had just gone on strike and their noisy demonstrations outside the filatures and the courthouse had constituted a bold challenge to the Confucian notion of women as creatures of the inner sphere. How far, then, this trope of the woman worker as victim was purely tactical, designed to play on conventional public attitudes, and how far it was an internalized element in women's identities is hard to judge. What one can say is that the most exploited male workers would have baulked at presenting themselves as downtrodden victims in need of protection.[141]

Gender shaped the experience of the capitalist workplace in intimate ways, although contemporary champions of labour were generally reluctant to recognize this, fearing that any stress on the distinctiveness of male and female experience would foster divisions among workers that capital would turn to account. One telling instance of the distinctiveness of women workers' experience was their vulnerability to sexual harassment at the hands of employers, supervisors and fellow workers. In 1905 women at the James Beck textile mill complained of the 'vile figure of the foreman Telke, who has appeared among us girls; this filthy reptile pursues comrade women workers with the crude and obscene language of the streets and with an evil leer on his face, offering to buy favours at the price of our terrible shame'.[142] Women at a big confectionery factory in St Petersburg wrote to *Gazeta Kopeika*: 'We are tormented by the debauched lust of our director. This married man and father of three children has made a harem out of the factory... A poor girl would sooner agree to die from hunger than be compelled to give herself

[139] *Rabotnitsa*, 4 May 1914.
[140] *Shibao*, 8 August 1911.
[141] For other examples see *Shibao*, 8 August 1911; 9 October 1912; Ono Kazuko, *Chinese Women*, p. 74.
[142] *Revoliutsiia 1905–7gg v Rossii.: ianvar'-mart 1905*, vol. 1(Moscow: AN SSSR 1955), p. 160.

to this would-be sultan.'[143] The Russian Social Democrats took up the theme of sexual harassment, publishing letters of complaint from groups of women workers. Yet they defined it as a facet of capitalist exploitation, even though it was continuous with women's experience outside the workplace. Significantly, women, when complaining of sexual harassment and other gender-specific grievances, themselves generally spoke a language of class rather than of feminism. Typical was an open letter written by the women of the Thornton textile mill to its British director:

At one of your machines, Mr Thornton, a child was born and its mother took it in her arms and walked to the hospital. At a machine! Possibly his whole life will be spent behind that machine ... Mr Thornton would you describe for our newspaper the well-appointed room where your own children were born. Will you be good enough to tell us how much you paid doctors, midwives, pharmacists, nannies and nurses?[144]

Notwithstanding the ways in which the discourse of class may have slighted the gender-specific aspects of the experience of working women, it clearly spoke to their condition – and, indirectly, to what they shared with working-class men – more tellingly than did a feminist discourse that downplayed class in an effort to unite women on the basis of gender. Russia's small feminist movement did not neglect the plight of working women – indeed it enjoyed some limited success among groups such as domestic servants or telephonists – but as a heavily middle-class movement it was not easy for it to win the confidence of working women.[145]

While by no means conclusive, the evidence of the strike record suggests that women in St Petersburg were remarkably combative. The sophisticated statistical analysis of Russian Factory Inspectorate data undertaken by Leopold Haimson suggests that industries with a high proportion of female labour tended to be especially strike prone, even after multiple regressions are made to take account of factors such as level of urbanization of the industry, the size of the enterprise or the average level of pay.[146] In 1917, too, the historians of the strike movement suggest that women workers appear disproportionately active in the huge stoppages of that year.[147] Nevertheless militant working women failed to conform to the

[143] *Zhenskii vestnik*, 2 (1911).
[144] F. Barkhina and V. Efimov, *Rabotnitsa v zabastovochnom dvizhenii* (Moscow, 1931), p. 23.
[145] Edmondson, *Feminism*, pp. 77–9.
[146] Leopold H. Haimson and Ronald Petrusha, 'Two Strike Waves in Imperial Russia, 1905–07 and 1912–14', in L. H. Haimson and C. Tilly (eds.), *Strikes, Wars and Revolutions in an International Perspective* (Cambridge: Cambridge University Press, 1989), p. 112.
[147] D. P. Koenker and W. G. Rosenberg, *Strikes and Revolution in Russia, 1917* (Princeton: Princeton University Press, 1989), p. 314.

image of the 'conscious' worker, and Social Democratic and SR labour organizers alike regularly bemoaned 'the backwardness, downtrodden position and darkness of many of our sisters'.[148] This image of the 'backward' woman worker, however, served as much to construct social reality as to reflect it, constituting the 'other' against which an implicitly masculine model of the class-conscious worker could be constructed.

Working women in Shanghai experienced sharper challenges to their gender identities than their sisters in St Petersburg, at least prior to 1918. Even for women to go out to work challenged the ingrained belief that women were *neiren*, people to be kept indoors. Following the 1911 Revolution, the practice of foot binding declined quickly in Shanghai as the new republic proclaimed natural feet the hallmark of the female citizen. Female migrants to Shanghai were probably less likely to have had bound feet, or at least more likely to have been able to take off their bandages while they slept, since many came from the lower Yangtze delta where historically the relatively high participation of women in handicrafts and farming meant that footbinding was less widespread than in other regions.[149] Just as importantly, Shanghai employers preferred to hire women with unbound feet. Nevertheless, the incidence of footbinding depended on the region from which women came. In the silk mills in the early 1920s, women from Yancheng in Subei were known as the 'Little Foot Party' because of their bound feet, whereas their sisters from Taizhou, also in Subei, were known as the 'Big Foot Party' for the opposite reason.[150]

That other symbol of republican revolution, bobbed hair, dubbed the 'civilized hairstyle' (*wenmingtou*), was slower to catch on with working-class women. Not least of the reasons was that at the height of the national revolution in 1926–7, it became powerfully associated with political radicalism.[151] A woman who worked at the Naigai Wata Kaisha No. 5 mill recalled how, having cut off her pigtails for safety's sake, she was accused by the Japanese foreman of being an 'extremist'. Threatened with a knife unless she told him who had put her up to this, she grabbed his arm, only to be fired on the spot.[152] By the 1930s, bobbed

[148] Z. Lilina, *Soldaty tyla: trud vo vremia i posle voiny* (Perm': 1918), p. 8.
[149] Lamson, 'The Effect of Industrialization', p. 1067; *North China Herald*, 12 May 1905, p. 277; *North China Herald*, 6 March 1926, p. 425; Shen Bojing (ed.), *Shanghai shi zhinan* [Guidebook to Shanghai] (Shanghai: Zhonghua shudian, 1933), pp. 138–9.
[150] Robert Y. Eng, 'Luddism and labor protest among silk artisans and workers in Jiangnan and Guangdong, 1860–1930', *Late Imperial China*, 11, 2 (1990), 87.
[151] Hsieh Ping-ying, *Autobiography of a Chinese Girl*, trans. Tsui Chi (London: Pandora, 1986), p. 53.
[152] *Wusa yundong shiliao* [Historical Materials on the May Thirtieth Movement], vol. 1 (Shanghai: Shanghai renmin chubanshe, 1981), p. 215.

hair lost its associations with political radicalism and became common in Shanghai. Other considerations, however, deterred working women from cutting off their pigtails. In his survey of villages on the edge of Shanghai, Lamson noted: 'the great change in appearance ... especially ones who work in factories ... They now look better and dress better. Some of the women even bob their hair.'[153] But the female students sent to interview the village women, all of whom had bobbed hair, were told by one mother: 'Short hair is all right for girls like you (i.e. college students) and city girls, but not for country people.' Another echoed this, saying: 'We are not fit, we are country girls.' One girl who had not cut her hair said: 'Many girls in the factory have cut off their hair, but we do not want to because it is not economical; once it is cut, we must pay out several dimes a month to a hairdresser.'[154]

As in St Petersburg, sexual harassment was widespread in Shanghai factories. At the third delegate conference of the Shanghai General Labour Union on 11 July 1926, 132 activists agreed: 'In the silk filatures and cotton mills it is common for supervisors and guards to make fun of women workers, and to subject them to shameful insults. Women driven into the factories by the need to live have no option but to swallow such insults.'[155] In most factories, harassment was formally forbidden. At the Chinese-owned Sanxin mill an overlooker found guilty of 'taking liberties with women workers' (*tiaoxi nügong*) faced instant dismissal.[156] But the General Labour Union conference chose to highlight sexual harassment in Japanese-owned enterprises in order to promote its class-inflected anti-imperial nationalism: 'The abuse of women workers by Japanese is particularly terrible. They curse the ugly ones and take liberties with those who are pretty. Women are relatively weak, and the misfortunes to which they are subject are so much greater than those of men.'[157] At the Tongxing No. 1 mill strikers proclaimed on 16 February 1925: 'The Japanese are utterly licentious and take liberties with us. When they see a pretty young woman, they crane their necks and leer, whereas those who are not pretty get punched and kicked, and sometimes even dismissed.'[158] Here sexual harassment functioned as a metonymy of the condition of the nation, where the weakness of women workers stood for the 'motherland' itself, whose honour was being defiled.

---

[153] Lamson, 'The Effect of Industrialization', p. 1053.
[154] Lamson, 'The Effect of Industrialization', p. 1075.
[155] *Gongren zhi lu*, 21 July 1926, p. 3.
[156] Zhu Bangxing, Hu Linge and Xu Sheng, *Shanghai chanye* p. 71.
[157] *Wusa yundong shiliao*, vol. 1, p. 303.
[158] *Wusa yundong shiliao*, vol. 1, p. 315.

As in Russia, the evidence of the strike record in Shanghai belies the notion of women workers as simply 'backward'. In the silkworkers' strike of August 1911, some 4,000 women blatantly challenged the Confucian ideal of female self-effacement, touring the filatures in a noisy throng to bring out other workers, forming pickets to prevent scabbing, coordinating action across different factories, publicizing their grievances, and making efforts to win public support. Typical tactics included occupying the manager's office and taking him hostage as a means of pressing demands.[159] Yet Confucian understandings of womanhood were not yet superannuated. In March 1922, in an effort to prevent similar disorders, silk filature owners set up the Shanghai Women's Industrial Progress Union. Its rules forbade members to strike without cause or to kick up a fuss in the workshops or to march into the accountant's office looking for trouble, and significantly called also for the 'promotion and improvement of female virtue and customs'.[160] The Union failed to prevent a major strike occurring a few months later, and in this conflict the Confucian norms which it aspired to uphold were rudely defied by women brandishing white flags that bore the legends 'Equality of the Sexes', 'Protect Human Rights' and 'Make the World Know of our Harsh Conditions'.[161] Nevertheless the extent to which Confucian norms still had traction is revealed by the hostility encountered by some of the strikers. According to Yang Zhihua, a Communist woman organizer:

Those brave and ardent young women workers who energetically supported the strike want to extricate themselves from the bonds of the family and march forward. But in the end they have to go home. I heard that some who returned home after the strike were beaten and humiliated by parents, brothers and sisters-in-law. They were refused food. One family said: 'You haven't been back for several days. You must have a lover. For all we care, you can die.' The parents of another woman gave her a rope and knife and told her to choose. Poor women workers! They don't sleep or eat well during the strike and then they have to return to a tragic stage.[162]

---

[159] S. A. Smith 'Gender and Class: Women's Strikes in St Petersburg, 1895–1917, and Shanghai, 1895–1927', *Social History*, 19, 2 (1994), 141–68; S. A. Smith, *Like Cattle and Horses: Nationalism and Labor in Shanghai, 1895–1927* (Durham NC: Duke University Press, 2002), pp. 54–9.

[160] Jiang Peinan and Chen Weimin, 'Shanghai zhaopai gonghui de xingwang' [The Rise and Fall of Shanghai's Signboard Labour Unions], *Jindai shi yanjiu*, 6 (1984), 57.

[161] *Shenbao*, 6 August 1922; Eng, 'Luddism', p. 87.

[162] Yang Zhihua, 'Yijiu erliu nian Shanghai sichang nügong yundong zhong zhi ganxiang' [Reflections on the 1926 Shanghai Silkwomen's Movement], *Zhongguo funü*, 30 June 1926, p. 7. Cited in Christina K. Gilmartin, *Engendering the Chinese Revolution:Radical Women, Communist Politics and Mass Movements in the 1920s* (Berkeley: University of California Press, 1995), p. 144.

Yet if the ideal of the docile, sequestered woman was by no means defunct, the persistent strikes of silk women show that female migrants to Shanghai were increasingly willing to assert their legal and moral rights and to challenge male authority.

Popularizing the 'New Woman'

In both Russia and China the 'new woman' became a discursive site on which different political and commercial interests contended. The 'new woman' had emerged in the West in the late-nineteenth century as a feminist icon for educated, middle-class women. Personified in Nora, heroine of Ibsen's play, *A Doll's House* (1879), the new woman was defined by her rejection of domesticity, her quest for individual self-fulfilment and her determination to gain education and economic independence. Later, she would also become a symbol of sexual freedom.[163]

In Russia the idea of the new woman went back to the 1860s, when mainly male radicals had used the trope as a way of articulating their critique of repressive social and political institutions. After 1905, however, it was the new woman as emblem of unbridled female sexuality that, above all, caught the public imagination. Manya El'tsova, heroine of the six-volume novel by Anastasiia Verbitskaia, *Keys to Happiness*, published between 1908 and 1913, became its most notorious representative. Manya, a brilliant dancer, is torn by the passion she feels for several men. She tells her married Jewish lover, Baron Steinbach, 'I am a horrible egotist. I hate obligations and cannot stand compulsion.'[164] As leading feminist Mariia Pokrovskaia wrote of the novel, it allowed shop girls to imagine the pleasures enjoyed by their social superiors, and women to imagine themselves as having the same sexual prerogatives as men.[165] A two-part film based on the novel appeared in 1913/1917 and broke box-office records. It spurred the making of similar films, notably the 1915 film by Evgenii Bauer, called *Child of the Big City* (*Ditia bol'-shogo goroda*), in which the protagonist is a lower-class woman, Masha, a seamstress in a sweatshop. While out window-shopping, she is picked up by two wealthy young men and goes off with them to the private room of a restaurant. Her seduction, however, turns out not to be the prelude to disgrace, for Masha milks her admirer for his wealth and reduces him to penury. The final scene of the film shows her contemptuously stepping

---

[163] Bonnie G. Smith, *Changing Lives: Women in European History Since 1700* (Lexington MA: D. C. Heath, 1989), pp. 317–24.

[164] Laura Engelstein, *Keys to Happiness: Sex and the Search for Modernity* (Ithaca NY: Cornell University Press, 1992), pp. 404–414.

[165] Engelstein, *Keys*, p. 404.

over the lover who has collapsed at the door of her luxurious apartment block. As Catriona Kelly points out, such glamorous, self-serving and powerful women were completely new in Russian popular culture, although whether Masha was perceived as heroine, villain, or the woman the audience loved to hate is uncertain.[166]

Less sensational and less self-indulgent representations of the 'new woman' circulated in the Russian *fin de siècle*, including ones promoted by radicals for more serious political ends. In an essay of 1913, Alexandra Kollontai wrote a long essay in which she praised the single working woman, 'walking the streets with a businesslike, masculine tread', as the authentic exemplar of the new woman: 'self-discipline instead of emotional rapture, the capacity to value her own freedom and independence rather than impersonal submissiveness, the assertion of her own individuality instead of the naïve effort to internalize and reflect the alien image of the 'beloved'".[167] Though this representation of the working woman was largely fanciful, it acquired a degree of purchase on social reality after Kollontai and Inessa Armand came to head the Women's Department of the Bolshevik government in 1919. According to Bolshevik feminists, the socialist 'new woman' was to be 'bold, impetuous, practical, prudently intelligent', a 'strong, free citizen, not inferior to man in anything'.[168] She was to grab an education and throw herself wholeheartedly into making the revolution. Various real-life women were held up as models for emulation. Efrosiniia Marakulina from Sharanovskaia township in Viatka province, for example, formerly an uneducated and devout peasant woman, 'forgot her family, her children, the household and with enthusiasm threw herself into the new business of enlightening her dark, downtrodden sisters ... From a devout Christian, she turned into a stalwart revolutionary, ready to put her energies into the service of liberating humanity.'[169]

This new woman was a far cry from Nora; but insofar as she threw off the shackles of family responsibility she had some kinship with her Norwegian sister. Many representations of the new socialist woman circulated in the first wave of literature and drama inspired by the Bolshevik revolution, which explored the dilemmas faced by women seeking to reconcile commitment to the revolution with motherhood – a vocation

---

[166] Steve Smith and Catriona Kelly, 'Commercial Culture and Consumerism', in Kelly and Shepherd (eds.), *Constructing Russian Culture*, p. 119.

[167] Alexandra Kollontai, *Autobiography of a Sexually Emancipated Woman* (London: Orbach and Chambers, 1972), p. 94.

[168] Barbara Evans Clements, 'The Utopianism of the Zhenotdel', *Slavic Review*, 51, 3 (1992), 485–96.

[169] Liudmila Stal', 'Novye zhenshchiny', *Kommunistka*, 6 (1920).

still very much valued by the Bolsheviks – and family responsibilities.[170] Predictably, for the vast majority of women, adding the 'liberation of the whole of labouring humankind' to the tasks of wage work, family and household proved not to be appealing. This was particularly so, given that civil war was devastating the economic position of the majority of lower-class women, taking away their menfolk and destroying the fragile family economy.

In June 1918 the liberal philosopher Hu Shi published *A Doll's House* in a special issue of *New Youth* devoted to 'Ibsenism'. In China, he argued, the 'doll's house' was not so much married life as the patriarchal family, typified by the four evils of selfishness, dependence, hypocrisy and cowardice. Hu counterposed individual dignity (*renge*) and love to the traditional emphasis on a woman's chastity.[171] However, as Vera Schwarcz notes, Nora's predicament spoke most directly to the needs of young men, trapped in social duties not of their choosing.[172] Soon the New Culture Movement figure of the new woman became politicized in that her 'awoken' status led her to link her individual emancipation to the liberation of the nation. By the late 1920s, leftists had largely renounced the individualism of the Ibsenite new woman, seeing romantic love and self-expression as a distraction from the cause of saving the nation. In the film *The New Woman* (1934) China's most famous actress, Ruan Lingyu, who had risen from a working-class background, played a music teacher who sold herself for one night to pay for the medical care of her daughter, and who was driven to suicide after her client leaked the story to the press. Months later, when Ruan herself, aged twenty-five, took a fatal overdose, almost 10,000 people turned out for her funeral. Ironically, the film ends with a scene in which a group of women workers, upon hearing of the teacher's death, march under the morning sun, singing 'Don't indulge in love/We want self-respect/Don't be parasites/We want to work hard!'[173]

It was the national revolution of 1926 to 1927, in which Chiang Kai-shek's National Revolutionary Army (NRA) overcame the warlords to reunify the country that saw, in the words of Christina Gilmartin, 'the most comprehensive effort to alter gender relations and end women's

---

[170] R. Kovnator, 'Novaia zhenshchina v revoliutsionnom literature', *Kommunistka*, 5 (1920).

[171] Hue-Ping Chin, 'Refiguring Women', p. 279.

[172] Vera Schwarcz, *The Chinese Enlightenment: Intellectuals and the Legacy of the May Fourth Movement of 1919* (Berkeley: University of California Press, 1986), p. 114.

[173] Yingjin Zhang and Zhiwei Xiao, *Encyclopedia of Chinese Film* (London: Routledge, 1998), pp. 250–1; Yingjin Zhang, *The City in Modern Chinese Literature and Film: Configurations of Space, Time, and Gender* (Stanford: Stanford University Press, 1996), pp. 198, 202.

subordination of all of China's twentieth-century revolutions'.[174] In the spirit of the New Culture Movement, the united front of the GMD and the CCP committed itself to far-reaching social, political and economic rights for women and the overthrow of the patriarchal family. Women's associations encouraged women to unbind feet, cut their locks, choose marriage partners, terminate bad marriages, acquire literacy, end child brides, female indentured labour, concubinage, polygamy and prostitution.[175] The Left GMD government in Wuhan gave women the legal right to choose husbands, to divorce, to obtain alimony, to inherit property and banned the sale and maltreatment of women. Although inspired by the Soviet example, the CCP placed much greater emphasis on the oppression of women than the pre-revolutionary Bolshevik party had done. Secret societies, local elites and militarists were outraged. After the bloody rupture between the Communists and the GMD in the summer of 1927, right-wing NRA officers used horrific brutality against activist women. When the leading female Communist, Xiang Jingyu, was publicly executed in Wuhan on 1 May 1928, the official statement made a point of emphasizing her supposed sexual misconduct.[176]

Following the establishment of a national government, Chiang Kai-shek's administration repudiated radical feminism, closing down the GMD women's bureau in 1929, yet it never formally rejected the ideal of women's emancipation. The family code of 1931, premised on the idea that the modern family would constitute the bedrock of a strong nation, endorsed women's equality, free-choice marriage, easier divorce, more equitable property rights for women and the abolition of concubinage and bigamy. The government promoted the image of the responsible housewife in charge of a 'modern' nuclear family, doing her duty to the nation by raising civic-minded children.[177] By empowering women with greater rights, and by encouraging men and women to choose their mates, it hoped to free the adult population for full but gender-specific participation in nation-building. Women were summoned to take seriously their roles as mothers and housewives, to recognize the weight of responsibility they carried in bringing up the young generation in a spirit of patriotism,

---

[174] Gilmartin, *Engendering the Chinese Revolution*, p. 210.
[175] Gilmartin, *Engendering the Chinese Revolution*, p. 180.
[176] Gilmartin, *Engendering the Chinese Revolution*, p. 212.
[177] Susan L. Glosser, 'The Contest for Family and Nation in Republican China', University of California Berkeley, PhD, 1995, pp. 14, 157; Kathryn Bernhardt, 'Women and the Law: Divorce in the Republican Period', in Kathryn Bernhardt and Philip C. C. Huang (eds.), *Civil Law in Qing and Republican China* (Stanford: Stanford University Press, 1994), pp. 187–214.

and to strengthen the nation by becoming rational and thrifty consumers of native produce and by creating modern, well-run homes.[178]

Within consumer culture, the new woman appeared in a very different guise, as an alluring figure used to sell products. Images of women in advertising sometimes featured middle-class women idling away their time, dressing fashionably, putting on make-up, looking for romance. More often, however, they combined appeals to western-inspired glamour with more traditional images of modest and compliant femininity. Indeed in the more conservative moral climate of the 1930s, the 'modern girl' was increasingly castigated as spendthrift, unproductive and parasitical; and western fashions such as high heels, silk stockings, and one-piece bathing suits were deplored as un-Chinese. The New Life Movement, in particular, launched in 1934, reconfigured Confucian elements with a view to developing a specifically Chinese model of modern womanhood, urging women to cultivate virtues of chastity, domesticity and respectability for the sake of the regeneration of the nation. 'For the modern Chinese woman, let her freedom be restrained by self-control, her self-realization be coupled with self-sacrifice, and her individualism circumscribed by family duty.'[179]

The conflicting discourses of the 'new woman' served more to articulate the social aspirations and anxieties of elites than to provide models for emulation for the lower classes. These discourses, though sharing certain features in common, pointed in different directions: more or less against the family, more or less in favour of self-expression, more or less in favour of sexual freedom, more or less in favour of tying women's emancipation to the needs of national salvation. In other words, their implications for personal behaviour were by no means clear. It is probably safe to say that these discourses did little to alter the subordinate relationship of most working-class women to men in the family or the factory, yet this is not to say that their impact on social identities was negligible. We saw in chapter 2 that images of fashionable women in advertising influenced how young women workers presented themselves in public and how pulp fiction allowed them to explore new scenarios at the level of fantasy without risking the possibly fatal consequences of acting them out. A minority of women, moreover, did opt for romantic love over arranged marriage and many more came to feel that love *ought* to be the basis of marriage.

At the same time, in Russia as well as in China, images of the 'new woman' within commercial culture were never wholly positive. Manya

[178] Glosser, 'The Contest for Family', p. 205.
[179] Elisabeth Croll, *Feminism and Socialism in China* (London: Routledge, 1978), p. 161.

El'tsova, stepping over the prostrate body of her impecunious lover, was not a figure to be admired; nor indeed was she typical of the heroines of Russian silent movies, most of whom were innocents seduced, ruined and even murdered by unscrupulous men or else driven to take their own lives.[180] And in Shanghai, serialized fiction, advertisements and movies regularly underscored the dangers of Chinese people losing touch with what was of value in their own tradition in the uncritical rush to ape western values. Consumer culture, in other words, presented lower-class consumers with enticing and unsettling scenarios that allowed them vicariously to explore ideas of freedom and rebellion and to shape new identities, but the images, values, personalities there presented were never consumed uncritically: rather lower-class consumers engaged with consumer culture selectively and from within an established framework of norms and values as they struggled to become modern people in the new context of the city.

We began by asking how far the gender roles and identities of migrants to the city 'modernized' in the *fin de siècle*. At one level, the answer is not very much. Notwithstanding loud talk about the equality of the sexes, lower-class women made only limited progress towards equality with men in the family, workplace or society. Nevertheless change was underway. In both cities the patriarchal family gave way rather rapidly to the nuclear family. In St Petersburg, the trend towards romantic love and conjugality between spouses was decisive and rapid, albeit much less so in Shanghai. Among migrants to Shanghai 'familism' continued to be strong, yet the control exercised by the older generation over the younger generation was fast eroding. In both Russia and China, women's identities came under far greater political scrutiny than men's, yet for lower-class women, the extent of change in the available social opportunities was considerably less than that for lower-class men.

If real change in familial and sexual relations, then, was fairly limited, gender identities were nevertheless called into question more than one might expect. This was largely because the crisis of patriarchy served as a trope through which the bankruptcy of the *ancien régime* could be construed and imagined. In both societies the gender relations based on the traditional patriarchal family became a metonymy of the wider sociopolitical system, and women's liberation came to function as an allegory through which the transformation of that system could be imagined. For

---

[180] Neia Zorkaia, *Na rubezhe stoletii: u istokov massovogo iskusstva v Rossii, 1900–1910 godov* (Moscow: Nauka, 1976), pp. 184, 186. Richard Stites, *Russian Popular Culture: Entertainment and Society since 1900* (Cambridge: Cambridge University Press, 1992), p. 32.

many migrants, this had consequences for the way in which they invested their own sufferings within family and society with meaning, and for how they came to see themselves as modern people. The rejection of patriarchy, especially by young men, thus fed into the revolutionary crisis that overtook Russia and China. And when the Communist revolution arrived, gender issues figured surprisingly high on the political agenda, although higher on that of the CCP than that of the Bolsheviks. For neither party, of course, was gender ever the primary basis of political mobilization; indeed it was potentially in tension with the need to mobilize working people on the basis of class and of national unity. The fact that there was little pressure from working-class women themselves to mobilize on the basis of gender had the happy result – from the point of view of the Communists – of helping to ensure that gender never came to split the working class in the way that was feared, despite tension between the sexes in the workplace and in the family.

4   Saving the Nation: National and Class Identities in the City

This chapter explores the interrelationship of class and national identities in two ailing dynastic empires struggling to become modern nation states. A central element in the crisis of the *anciens régimes* in Russia and China was that imperial structures of government were steadily pressed to breaking point by external forces, i.e. economically powerful and militarily expansionist foreign states, and by internal forces, i.e. by political movements demanding that the dynastic state become representative of an ethnically defined people. These external and internal pressures combined to push both governments in the direction of emulating the institutions and practices of the nation state as exemplified by the western powers, in the belief that this path alone promised salvation in a modern world of competing nationalisms.[1]

Until the second half of the nineteenth century, the Russian Empire was held together by an autocratic regime that cooperated relatively comfortably with the non-Russian nobilities on its peripheries and tolerated non-Russian cultures and religions. Only with the rise of nationalism and the increasing systematization of administration did the privileges of regional elites, such as those of Poles, Baltic Germans and Finlanders, come under attack, at roughly the same time as the tsarist government launched its project of colonization in Central Asia and the Caucasus.[2]

The Qings, too, proved capable of accommodating local particularities, ruling their empire – of which China was notionally only one part – in what Pamela Crossley calls 'multiple frames' (*hebi*).[3] Notwithstanding

---

[1] The chapter does not address the question of how far the dissolution of multi-ethnic empires and their replacement by nation states is an ineluctable feature of modernity, although it assumes that the relationship between empire and nation in the modern world is more complex than is often allowed.

[2] Andreas Kappeler, *The Russian Empire: A Multiethnic History* (Harlow: Pearson, 2001).

[3] Pamela Kyle Crossley, *A Translucent Mirror: History and Identity in Qing Imperial Ideology* (Berkeley: University of California Press, 1999), p. 3.

substantial periods of territorial fragmentation and conquest by non-Han peoples, the Chinese empire held together largely by virtue of its enduring culture. The Qings, as essentially a conquest dynasty, were able to secure their rule through utilizing the universalist ideology of Confucianism, at least until the late nineteenth century when internal disorder, weakening administrative and military capacity, and the steady encroachment of the foreign powers, made this impossible.

It is against this background of disintegrating empire that the rise of new movements claiming to represent nations and classes needs to be set. The chapter explores the relationship between new social identities of nation and class among migrants to Shanghai and St Petersburg who went on to become workers.

In the Russian case, the relationship between class identity and national identity appears straightforward. As Petr Struve, philosopher, member of the liberal Kadet party and deputy foreign minister in the Provisional Government of 1917, observed in August 1918: 'The Russian Revolution was the first case in world history of the triumph of internationalism and the idea of class over nationalism and the idea of the nation.'[4] At first sight, the triumph of class over nation does seem to mark out Russia as exceptional among the belligerent countries in the First World War, since the war laid bare the intensity of nationalist sentiment in the civilian populations. It also seems to mark out the Russian Revolution as exceptional in the context of later Communist revolutions, such as those in China, Vietnam, Yugoslavia and Cuba, where anti-imperialist nationalism was the driving force of revolutionary mobilization. In the case of China, for example, Chalmers Johnson argued in his classic history of the CCP during the war against Japan that the class-based policies practised by the Communists in the Jiangxi soviets between 1929 and 1934 – principally the confiscation of landlords' land – were set aside, and that the key to the resurgence of the party from 1937 to 1945 lay in its abandoning radical socioeconomic reform in favour of patriotic defence.[5]

What we appear to see, therefore, is a contrast between a revolution in Russia, carried out in the name of class, and one in China, carried out in the name of the nation. The aim of the chapter is to interrogate and qualify that dichotomy by demonstrating that the interactions between class and nation among workers in both countries were more complex

---

[4] P. V. Struve, 'Istoricheskii smysl russkoi revoliutsii i national'nye zadachi', *Iz glubiny. Sbornik statei o russkoi revoliutsii* (Moscow: Izd-vo Moskovskogo univ-ta, 1990; orig. 1918), p. 235.

[5] Chalmers Johnson, *Peasant Nationalism and Communist Power: The Emergence of Revolutionary China* (Stanford: Stanford University Press, 1963).

and contradictory than this account allows. In the case of Russia, the argument is not that workers became *nationalist* in the way that their Chinese counterparts did; rather that the hostility to nationalism articulated by those who presumed to speak for Russian workers did not preclude a growing sense of national identity among the urban working population. In the case of China, the argument is not to deny that the dominant idiom of revolutionary discourse was nationalist, but to suggest that it was precisely through this discourse that certain elements of class identity were forged.

Proto-national Identities

In the scholarship on nationalism that burgeoned in the last decades of the twentieth century, a broad consensus emerged to the effect that the nation is a product of modernity. Writers such as Ernest Gellner and Benedict Anderson argued, in different ways, that it is only possible for a political community to imagine itself as a unified subject of history in conditions where modern communications, markets and bureaucratic institutions exist, where the state extends its reach deep into the population through taxation and conscription and, above all, where schooling and 'print capitalism' are developed.[6] If one defines the nation as a community that demands self-rule and sovereignty over a specific territory on the basis of a putatively shared culture, language or history, then the phenomenon was self-evidently a product of western modernity. A minority of scholars, however, argues that such a definition is too restrictive, especially if one infers from it that 'national identity' could not exist prior to the onset of modernity. Defining national identity as identification with a 'named human population sharing an historic territory, common myths and historical memories, a mass public culture, a common economy and common legal rights and duties for all members', Anthony Smith, for example,. argues that national identity long predated the world of competing nation states that emerged in the nineteenth century.[7]

This chapter, while insisting that national identity, like the nation, was a product of modernity, nevertheless argues that in long-formed dynastic empires, such as Russia and China, the nation was not 'invented' *ex nihilo*. It is sympathetic to Smith's critique of 'modernist'

---

[6] Ernest Gellner, *Nations and Nationalism* (Oxford: Blackwell, 1983); Benedict Anderson, *Imagined Communities: Reflections on the Origins and Spread of Nationalism* (London: Verso, 1983).

[7] Anthony D. Smith, *National Identity* (London: Penguin Books, 1991), p. 14; Anthony D. Smith, *Theories of Nationalism* (London: Duckworth, 1983), pp. 158–9.

views that assume that members of pre-modern societies lack the cultural resources with which to imagine themselves as members of a larger imagined political community, whether that community is defined in relation to a divinely appointed emperor, an ancestral land, a shared religion or a civilization, or simply defined as one that is ethnically different from those of neighbouring peoples. This may appear to be saying not very much: but it is to insist that people in the pre-modern world were perfectly capable of imagining communities larger than those of which they had immediate face-to-face experience, and to contend that such communities were political in the minimal sense that they connected with some notion of a wider polity. In long-established states, such identifications were deeply entrenched and provided the raw materials out of which, when fused with new conceptions of sovereignty, modern national identities were created. We do not have to insist, with Smith, that such older identifications were 'national' for, crucially, they did not seek to tie 'rights' to an ethnically defined people or territory.[8] But they may usefully be termed 'proto-national' identities, if only to challenge the tendency in so much of the literature to insist that membership of an imagined community is possible only under conditions of capitalist modernity.

The tsarist empire never fully developed a conception of itself as a nation. Down to 1917, the form of government remained a dynastic monarchy in which the population was defined not in terms of citizenship but of social estate, religion and (towards the end) ethnicity. From the late nineteenth century, however, and especially during the First World War, the tsarist government did begin to act like a nationalizing state.[9] Russification, which had originated as a policy designed to improve administrative efficiency, increasingly by the 1880s entailed

---

[8] I have avoided trying to define national identity except to affirm that it entails a claim for political sovereignty on behalf of a community defined in terms of ethnicity, language, territory or history. I believe that there is usually an ethnic dimension to national identity – i.e. that it is rare for citizenship not to be ethnically marked in some way.

[9] The following have all influenced my thinking about the relationship between imperial and national identity in Russia: Geoffrey Hosking, who argues that the imperial state impeded the formation of a nation in Russia; Eric Lohr, who argues that 'a type of Russian nationalism played a more important role in the last years of the empire than most scholarship has granted', but nevertheless contends that the exacerbation of ethnic differences within the Russian Empire during the First World War inhibited the emergence of Russian national identity; and Joshua Sanborn, who argues that wartime mobilization took place in a national framework that transcended ethnic differences. Geoffrey Hosking, *Russia: People and Empire* (London: HarperCollins, 1997); Eric Lohr, *Nationalizing the Russian Empire: The Campaign Against Enemy Aliens during World War One* (Cambridge MA: Harvard University Press, 2003), pp. 2, 8; Joshua Sanborn, *Drafting the Russian Nation: Military Conscription, Total War, and Mass Politics, 1905–25* (DeKalb: Northern Illinois University Press, 2003).

cultural assimilation. This was never pursued consistently, however, since any far-reaching programme of Russification challenged the legitimacy of the multi-ethnic elites and threatened the stability of the empire; the regime thus made periodic compromises in respect of educational, hiring, linguistic and other policies.[10] As Robert Geraci comments, 'though Russification of the empire was in one sense the fulfilment of Russian nationhood, it also threatened to obliterate the nation by making its *imperial* status obsolete.'[11] After 1905 the promulgation of civil liberties further weakened the drive to cultural assimilation. Nevertheless, by this stage the regime was well aware of the potential advantages of populist nationalism, and it made a resolute effort to firm up the national identity of the ethnic Russian population during the First World War.[12]

Many scholars argue that the Russian peasantry never developed an identification with any community beyond the most local. (I have in mind in this chapter only the ethnically Russian population of the empire.) Richard Pipes is typical: 'the muzhik (male peasant) had little sense of "Russianness". He thought of himself not as a "russkii" but as a "Viatskii" or "Tul'skii"' (i.e. from Viatka or Tula provinces, not from Russia).[13] Yet if local identities were indeed paramount, there were within Russian culture longstanding idioms through which the populace could imagine a link between itself as an ethnically defined community and the Russian state. Perhaps the most profound marker of ethnic identity among Russian peasants was adherence to Russian Orthodoxy, whose divinely appointed defender the tsar claimed to be. Pushkin, among countless others, observed in his *Remarks on Russian History in the Eighteenth Century*, that 'Greek Orthodoxy, alone of anything else, gives us our particular national character.'[14] For peasants, the terms 'Orthodox' (*pravoslavnyi*) and 'Russian' (*russkii*) were virtually synonymous.

Second, to be Russian was to be a subject of the tsar, the 'little father' (*tsar-batiushka*), who was appointed by God to embody and defend the

---

[10] Theodore R. Weeks, *Nation and State in Late Imperial Russia: Nationalism and Russification in the Western Frontier, 1863–1914* (De Kalb: Northern Illinois Press, 1996); Geoffrey Hosking, *Russia and the Russians* (London: Penguin, 2001), ch. 8.

[11] Robert P. Geraci, *Window on the East: National and Imperial Identities in Late Tsarist Russia* (Ithaca NY: Cornell University Press, 2001), p. 351.

[12] Lohr, *Nationalizing the Russian Empire*; Sanborn, *Drafting the Russian Nation*.

[13] Richard Pipes, *The Russian Revolution* (New York: Knopf, 1990), p. 203; Robert Service, *A History of Twentieth-Century Russia* (London: Allen Lane, 1997), p. 10; David Branderberger, *National Bolshevism: Stalinist Mass Culture and the Formation of Modern Russian National Identity, 1931–1956* (Cambridge MA: Harvard University Press, 2002), ch. 1.

[14] A. S. Pushkin, 'Zametki po russkoi istorii XVIII veka', in A. S. Pushkin, *Polnoe sobranie sochinenii*, vol. 11 (Moscow: Izd-vo Akademii Nauk SSSR, 1949), p. 18.

unity and strength of the Russian land. Down to 1905, millions of peasants saw him as 'defender of truth' and 'upholder of the commonweal'.[15] In theory, the figure of the autocrat was supranational – after all, the throne had been occupied from 1762 to 1796 by a German woman – but in the course of the nineteenth century it became increasingly Russified.[16] Third, the peasants' sense of what it meant to be Russian was bound up with rich understandings of the country's history, territory, culture and institutions. Folksongs were sung and ballads recited about St Vladimir, the first ruler to embrace Christianity, about Ivan IV, who triumphed over the Tatars at Kazan′, about Peter the Great, who finished off Sweden as a great power at Poltava in 1709. The 30th of August was celebrated as the feast day of St Alexander Nevskii, who had heroically defended his native land.[17] Certain places associated with the country's saints, heroes and military champions had become suffused over the centuries with 'national' significance, to a degree that leads A. V. Buganov, the only serious student of the phenomenon, to conclude that popular identifications with the history and territory of Russia suggest a 'high level of national consciousness' among Russian peasants by the nineteenth century.[18]

That Russians identified emotionally with an ethnic community defined by shared religion, history, territory and political and social institutions was most evident at times of war. Not for nothing was the war against Napoleon of 1812 called the 'fatherland war' (*otechestvennaia voina*). But it was only in the decades following the emancipation of the serfs that new cultural developments enhanced popular familiarity with symbols of nascent nationhood. Woodcuts (*lubki*), fairground attractions (*balagany*) and peepshows (*raek*) familiarized rural communities with Russia's military victories and leaders.[19] During the Russo-Turkish war of 1877–78 – the first following the introduction of universal conscription in 1874 – peddlers toured the villages, selling scarves depicting the 'leaders and heroes of the Serbian uprising in Bosnia and Herzegovina

[15] L. T. Senchakova, *Prigovory i nakazy rossiiskogo krest′ianstva, 1905–1907gg.* (Moscow: RAN, 1994), p. 208.
[16] Richard S. Wortman, *Scenarios of Power: Myth and Ceremony in Russian Monarchy*, vol. 2, *From Alexander II to the Abdication of Nicholas II* (Princeton: Princeton University Press, 2000).
[17] M. Cherniavsky, 'Russia', in O. Ranum (ed.), *National Consciousness, History and Political Culture in Early-Modern Europe* (Baltimore: Johns Hopkins University Press, 1975), pp. 118–43.
[18] A. V. Buganov, *Russkaia istoriia v pamiati krest′ian XIX veka i natsional′noe samosoznanie* (Moscow: Institut etnologii i antropologii, 1992).
[19] Catriona Kelly, *Petrushka: The Russian Carnival Puppet Theatre* (Cambridge: Cambridge University Press, 1990), pp. 27–8; A. F. Nekrylova, *Russkie narodnye gorodskie prazdniki, uveseleniia i zrelishcha* (Leningrad: Iskusstvo, 1988), pp. 116–125.

who fought for the Christian faith and liberation of the fatherland from the barbarians'. Pictures showing 'The Marvellous Dinner of General Skobelev under Hostile Fire', 'The Storming of Kars', and 'The Taking of Plevna' were widely sold. It is notable, however, that while the peasants among whom Aleksandr Engelgardt lived knew that Russia was fighting the Sultan, they could not actually recognize the Russian flag. 'No, it's the Turkish one. You see, there's an eagle drawn on it, and there'd be a cross on the Russian one.'[20]

Secondly, the growth of a commercial press from the 1870s, evident in journals such as *Rodina*, promoted new renditions of national identity that focused less on loyalty to the tsar and more on the geography of empire and Russia's cultural and historical achievement.[21] Journals such as *Golos* became standard-bearers for Russian's 'civilizing mission' in Asia, representing the conquest of exotic regions as proof of Russia's European status.[22] New renditions of national identity began to circulate that went far beyond devotion to Orthodoxy and the 'little father'. The appearance of the postcard in 1872 played its own role in popularizing visual images of the empire-nation, as did the proliferation of cultural and scientific organizations, museums and exhibitions, by no means all of whose efforts at popular enlightenment were consonant with the doctrine of Official Nationality ('Autocracy, Orthodoxy, Nationality'). Furthermore, the not insubstantial efforts of the late-imperial government itself to expand popular schooling, which began with the Education Statute of 1864, enlarged popular knowledge of the history and geography of Russia. If there was nothing akin to the assiduous efforts of the Third Republic in France to turn peasants into Frenchmen, through the written word, schooling, military service and, not least, migration to the cities, the younger generation began to imagine itself as Russian in a more genuinely 'national' way.

During the 1905 Revolution these 'proto-national' idioms began to coalesce into something like a national identity as they were mobilized to support claims for popular sovereignty. The dominant political idiom in both town and countryside was that of 'citizenship' (*grazhdanstvo*) and 'liberty' (*svoboda*). Reform-minded elements of the gentry and middle classes joined forces with the labour movement in what they characterized as an 'all-nation struggle' to end the war with Japan and achieve a

---

[20] A. N. Engelgardt, *Letters from the Country, 1872–1887*. Translated and edited by Cathy A. Frierson (New York: Oxford University Press, 1993), p. 135.

[21] Jeffrey Brooks, *When Russia Learned to Read: Literacy and Popular Literatures, 1861–1917* (Princeton: Princeton University Press, 1985), ch. 6.

[22] Alfred J. Rieber, 'Russian Imperialism: Popular, Emblematic, Ambiguous', *Russian Review*, 53, 3 (1994), 333.

constitution. At this moment, the 'nation' was defined in largely negative terms as one united by its lack of civil and political rights (*bespravie*) though also by its determination to wrest those rights from the autocracy. Even in the countryside, some began to identify themselves as 'free Russian citizens' and there were widespread expectations 'that the body politic could be thoroughly reordered'.[23] More than ever before, peasants read newspapers, composed petitions, and eagerly sought information about the proceedings of the new duma, which opened in April 1906. Senchakova's analysis of 661 petitions shows the extent to which peasants vested hopes in the duma, which they saw as the democratic representative of the wishes of the people and which they expected to meet their pressing demand for the redistribution of public and private land.[24] Yet the profound fissures within Russian society could not be papered over. Peasant concerns, though partially 'national', were dominated by the land question and the revolution gave birth to the most intense wave of agrarian disorders since the Pugachev rebellion of 1773–5.

China, a country of continental dimensions inhabited by people speaking mutually unintelligible languages and exhibiting a wide array of ethnic differences, was held together by culture and by an ideographic script that cut across different speech communities. James Watson has suggested that ritual, rather than belief, ritual shared by elites and commoners alike, bound Chinese society together, making Chinese culture far more unitary than that of the more pluralist societies of South Asia.[25] From the perspective of ordinary people, to be Chinese was to understand that there was a correct way to perform the rituals associated with birth, marriage, death and the ancestors. This is broadly consonant with the view that membership of the political community was defined by participation in the *Zhonghua*, or 'cultural efflorescence', i.e. the ritual order based on Confucian norms and values, at the centre of which stood the emperor. Insofar as this enabled identification with a political community based on the 'world-under-Heaven' (*tianxia*), the civilizational ecumene of which China was the centre, this may be considered a proto-national idiom.[26] It was participation in this

---

[23] Abraham Ascher, *The Revolution of 1905: Authority Restored* (Stanford; Stanford University Press, 1992), p. 5; Andrew Verner, 'Discursive Strategies in the 1905 Revolution: Peasant Petitions from Vladimir Province', *Russian Review*, 54, 1 (1995), 68.

[24] Senchakova, *Prigovory*, pp. 109, 111–24.

[25] J. L. Watson, 'Rites or Beliefs? The Construction of a Unified Culture in Late-Imperial China', in L. Dittmer and S. S. Kim (eds.), *China's Quest for National Identity* (Ithaca: Cornell University Press, 1993), pp. 81, 83, 87.

[26] Joseph Levenson, *Liang Ch'i-ch'ao and the Mind of Modern China* (Cambridge MA: Harvard University Press, 1953), pp. 109–22; Tsung-I Dow, 'The Confucian Concept of a Nation and Its Historical Practice', *Asian Profile*, 10, 4 (1982), 350.

ecumene that made Chinese superior to the 'barbarians' who surrounded them.[27] Nevertheless, as Prasenjit Duara has argued, the
universalism of this conception overlay a subliminal ethnic identification,
in that the *Zhonghua* was implicitly equated with a bounded community
of the ethnically Han (*Zhongguo*).[28]

In addition, Duara points to a second, more explicitly ethnic idiom
through which Chinese imagined a relationship to the imperial polity,
namely, as Han people (*Han ren*) who were descendants of the 'Yellow
Emperor' (*Huangdi zisun*). A phrase in the *Spring and Autumn Annals* –
'if they are not of the same kin (*zu*) as us, their minds will be different' –
had for centuries been used to provide a Confucian gloss for this ethnic
conception. By the late-eighteenth century, as large numbers of Han
migrants encountered non-Han peoples on the peripheries of the Middle
Kingdom, they began to apply categories such as *zhong* (seed, race), *lei*
(category, group) and *zhonglei* to designate these non-Han neighbours.[29]
Qing frontier officials, moreover, used the term *guojia* – literally 'country-
family', the term that was to come to mean 'nation state' by the twentieth
century – to distinguish those who were subjects of the emperor from
new groups that were being absorbed.[30] The term *Zhongguo ren*, 'people
of the Middle Kingdom', was thus used as a synonym for the Han, yet it
never narrowed to the point where it was used exclusively to designate
this ethnic group. It remained located in the culturalist problematic of
the 'world-under-Heaven'.[31]

If identifications with families, lineages, villages, towns, dialect groups
or provinces were paramount for most Chinese, a shared culture
nevertheless provided fertile resources through which a broader Han
identity could be transacted and transmitted. Worship of local gods and
heroes, such as Yue Fei (1103–42), an upstanding official executed on
the orders of the southern Song dynasty for opposing the cession of part
of north China to the enemy, constituted one such vehicle. Though his
cult was regulated by provincial and imperial authorities, who sanitized

---

[27] On the ideological implications of the standard translation of *yi* as 'barbarian', see Lydia
H. Liu, *The Clash of Empires: The Invention of China in Modern World History*
(Cambridge MA: Harvard University Press, 2004), ch. 2.
[28] Prasenjit Duara, *Rescuing History from the Nation: Questioning Narratives of Modern
China* (Chicago: Chicago University Press, 1995), p. 56.
[29] David Yen-ho Wu, 'The Construction of Chinese and non-Chinese Identities',
Daedalus, 120, 2 (1991), 166; Duara, *Rescuing History*, p. 57; Tsung-I Dow, 'Confucian
Concept', p. 353.
[30] Peter Perdue, 'Empire and Nation in Comparative Perspective: Frontier
Administration in Eighteenth-Century China', *Journal of Early Modern History*, 5, 4
(2001), 301.
[31] M. Kriukov, V. Maliavin and M. Sofronov, *Etnicheskaia istoriia kitaitsev na rubezhe
srednevekovogo i novogo vremeni* (Moscow: Nauka, 1987), pp. 257–9.

it to conform with Confucian values, it served as a reminder of the sacrifices that common soldiers had made for the fatherland and of the treachery of scholar-officials.[32] Operas such as those about the Yang Family Generals, which again harked back to the Song dynasty when Chinese fought to defend their homeland against northern invaders, along with vernacular novels, such as *The Romance of the Three Kingdoms* and the *Water Margin*, provided a repository of representations of China's glorious past, with gripping adventures and larger-than-life heroes. We noted in chapter 2 the popularity of Guandi, god of war, to whom far more temples were dedicated than to Confucius. This god was based on General Guan Yu (c. 162–219 CE), whose virtues of loyalty and righteousness were extolled in the *Romance of the Three Kingdoms*. The plots and characters of such vernacular novels were endlessly recycled by professional storytellers, through regional opera, popular theatre, drum singing and folk song, so that Chinese with little or no formal schooling displayed an impressive knowledge of, and concern for, the history of their country. Later, such knowledge was supplemented by book-peddlers who sold chapbooks and songbooks at temple fairs and festivals.[33]

The inexorable decline of the Qing dynasty, brought about by foreign aggression, by the massive disorders of the Taiping rebellion (1851–64) and, subsequently, by declining fiscal, military and administrative capacity, dramatically highlighted the question of whether China could survive in a world of rapacious nations and empires. Her defeat at the hands of Japan in 1895, a people Chinese had once dismissed as 'dwarf slaves', generated a new and urgent discourse of nationhood among her educated elites. Henceforth, nationalism would hegemonize the terrain of modern politics in a way that marks a critical difference from Russian politics in the twentieth century. Drawing on western ideologies of Social Darwinism and constitutionalism, nationalists forged a concept of the 'nation', borrowing the term *minzu* from Japanese. This concept, which joined the 'people' (*min*) to its 'ancestral line' (*zu*), suggested that the state should become the representative of a lineage sharing a common racial stock and territory. It thus connected an older ethnic idiom of

---

[32] Wang Gungwu 'Questions of Identity during the Ch'ing Dynasty', in Gregor Benton and Liu Hong (eds.), *Diasporic Chinese Ventures: The Life and Work of Wang Gungwu* (London: RoutledgeCurzon, 2004).

[33] Robert Ruhlmann, 'Traditional Heroes in Chinese Popular Fiction', in Arthur Wright (ed.), *Confucianism and Chinese Civilization* (Stanford: Stanford University Press, 1964), p. 144; Evelyn Rawski, 'Problems and Prospects', in David Johnson, Andrew J. Nathan and Evelyn S. Rawski (eds.), *Popular Culture in Late-Imperial China* (Berkeley: University of California Press, 1985), p. 410.

the Han people – one that played on the fiction of common descent from the Yellow Emperor – to an evolutionist and racialized concept of nationality in tune with the Social Darwinism then in vogue. This concept of the nation was in the early years of the twentieth century construed very much in terms of 'biological descent, physical appearance and congenital inheritance'.[34] The rhetoric of national extinction (*wangguo*) and of national humiliation (*guochi*) dramatized fears that China might die at the hands of fitter races, because of the corruption of her rulers and the absence of patriotism and military ardour among her people. After 1911, this racialized conception of national identity competed with various more civic construals that centred on citizenship, government as a reflection of the 'people's will' and, by the mid-1920s, on anti-imperialism. In the last years of the Qings, however, nationalist elites harped principally on the threat of national extinction in propagating their message among the common people, reworking existing proto-national idioms, using speaker teams, slogans, songs, cartoons, posters, handbills, the vernacular press, banners and flags. It was, above all, participation in new forms of collective action that did most to foster national identity among the workers and traders of Shanghai, whether taking part in a boycott, such as the anti-American boycott of 1905 or the anti-Japanese boycott of 1915, going on strike against a Japanese or British employer, or taking to the streets as in the May Fourth Movement.

Nationalism and Consumer Culture

It is only recently that historians have registered the importance of consumer culture as an arena in which national identities were fashioned in the early-twentieth century. In this respect, there is a telling contrast between Russia and China, since nationalist themes featured relatively little in the promotion of mass cultural products in Russia. Advertising flourished in Russia from the start of the twentieth century, through shop signs, brand packaging, flyers and, above all, mass-circulation newspapers. By the 1910s, newspapers devoted up to half their pages to advertisements.[35] Foreign firms promoted their goods by suggesting that they offered Russian consumers the chance to participate in western-style modernity. In general, Russian advertisers did not respond by stressing the superiority of national produce, except in the tobacco

---

[34] Frank Dikötter, *The Discourse of Race in Modern China* (London: Hurst, 1992), pp. 75, 101; Frank Dikötter (ed.), *The Construction of Racial Identities in China and Japan* (London: Hurst, 1997), p. 1.

[35] Sally West, 'The Material Promised Land: Advertising's Modern Agenda in Late Imperial Russia', *Russian Review*, 57, 3 (1998), 345–63.

industry where a few firms trumpeted the superiority of Russian cigarettes.[36] They nevertheless proved as innovative as their western competitors in advertising their wares, especially articles of mass consumption such as liquor, cigarettes, tobacco-related products, soaps and cosmetics, presenting them as the quintessence of modernity and the means of achieving personal satisfaction.[37] Russian firms, especially those producing clothing, perfumes and sometimes cigarettes, capitalized on the allure of western goods, not least by using English brand names, such as 'Adorable' or 'Sir', or visual images of western sophistication; but their range of reference was promiscuous, and producers of, for example, 'Tango' champagne were just as likely to seize on Orthodox Easter, the celebration of Pushkin's birth or the tricentennial of the Romanov dynasty to promote their goods.

With the outbreak of the First World War, consumer culture did begin to deploy patriotic motifs in a more deliberate fashion. Mass-produced prints and postcards featured sentimental scenes of parting couples, nurses caring for wounded fighters, and soldiers standing under birch trees dreaming of their families. Yet the absence of the tsar as a symbol of the nation in the semiotics of consumer culture was glaring. As Hubertus Jahn contends, mass culture 'suggests that lower-class patriotism did not provide an adequate conceptual framework for supporting the existing state or ultimately even the war itself. Once the simple vilification of the enemy gave way to the actualities of war, patriotism lost its clarity.'[38]

By contrast, consumerism and nationalism flourished symbiotically in China.[39] Beginning with the anti-American boycott of 1905 and continuing into the 1930s, a succession of boycotts made consumption an arena of struggle against imperialism, reminding Chinese consumers of the need to shield the national economy from foreign imports. Since the Chinese government was unable to defend the domestic market through tariffs, indigenous manufacturers of mass consumption goods sought to encourage citizens to buy Chinese. Typical slogans of the movement were 'Business enterprises rescue the nation', 'Establish factories for national self-preservation'.[40] The national products movement, which

---

[36] West, 'Material Promised Land', p. 355.
[37] West, 'Material Promised Land', pp. 354, 348.
[38] Hubertus F. Jahn, 'Patriots or Proletarians? Russian Workers and the First World War', in Reginald E. Zelnik (ed.), *Workers and Intelligentsia in Late Imperial Russia: Realities, Representations, Reflections* (Berkeley: International and Area Studies, University of California at Berkeley, 1999), pp. 333, p. 343.
[39] Karl Gerth, *China Made: Consumer Culture and the Creation of the Nation* (Cambridge MA: Harvard University Press, 2003), p. 3.
[40] Gerth, *China Made*, p. 10.

was supported by many traders and manufacturers, powerfully shaped consumer culture by seeking to differentiate between national and foreign commodities. National products were invested with an aura of patriotic pride and concern, as well as with more subliminal and traditional values such as 'propriety', 'righteousness', 'integrity' and 'shame'.[41] In the 1920s, the Sanyou towelling company dubbed its manufactures 'freedom cloth' and 'patriotic blue cloth'.[42]

As in Russia, newspapers were a key vehicle through which advertisers reached the public. In 1925, the leading Shanghai newspaper, *Shenbao*, devoted 54% of its columns to advertising – the three largest categories being for medical items (27.5%), entertainment (14%) and luxury goods (12.6%).[43] In its battle for market share with British American Tobacco, the Nanyang tobacco company excelled at playing the patriotic card even though its owners, the Jian brothers, held Japanese passports and had close ties with Japanese suppliers in South-east Asia.[44] In 1920 one of its advertisements proclaimed: 'If you used foreign products previously, now you should want to use China-made goods ... Awakened people never forget this.'[45] Later advertisements featured a bust of Sun Yat-sen, alongside quotations from his writings that urged consumers to buy national products and reclaim national rights.[46] Wei-pin Tsai points out that in most advertisements the written text overshadowed the visual image, with advertisers apparently feeling that consumers needed to be told not only which brand to buy but the appropriate mentality to adopt. Some cigarette advertisements, for example, urged people to think of the sorrows of China or the memory of the May Thirtieth Movement while smoking.[47] Yet Chinese advertisers, like their Russian counterparts, were not afraid to marry seductive images of western life to patriotic themes.[48]

Karl Gerth concludes that from an economic point of view the national products movement was a 'dramatic failure'.[49] Sherman Cochran has shown that most people living in the interior did not differentiate brands clearly.[50] British American Tobacco may have suffered briefly

[41] Gerth, *China Made*, p. 187.
[42] Gerth, *China Made*, p. 11.
[43] Weipin Tsai, 'Nationalism, Consumerism, and the Image of the Individual in Shenbao Newspapers, 1919–37', University of Leeds, PhD, 2004, p. 41.
[44] Sherman Cochran, *Big Business in China: Sino-foreign Rivalry in the Cigarette Industry, 1890–1930* (Cambridge MA: Harvard University Press, 1980), ch. 1.
[45] Weipin Tsai, 'Nationalism, Consumerism', p. 153.
[46] Henrietta Harrison, *China: Inventing the Nation* (London: Arnold, 2001), p. 182.
[47] Weipin Tsai, 'Nationalism, Consumerism', p. 37
[48] Weipin Tsai, 'Nationalism, Consumerism', p. 27.
[49] Gerth, *China Made*, p. 355.
[50] Cochran, *Big Business*, p. 219.

from the May Fourth boycott but its effects were not lasting. Even after the new national government established national certification standards to determine what counted as a national product in 1928, it remained difficult to determine whether a commodity was or was not national, not least because semi-processed Japanese imports were often finished off in China. Moreover, because consumers continued to associate foreign manufactures with luxury and quality, Chinese goods often sought to give themselves the appearance of foreignness, by using romanized names.[51] A Chinese light-bulb factory manufactured the 'Yapuer' brand – a word that is meaningless in Chinese but which sounds foreign – presumably because it knew that consumers considered foreign-made light bulbs to be superior to Chinese-made ones.[52] So considerations of price and quality, along with the difficulties of strictly distinguishing national from foreign products, meant that consumers continued to buy foreign goods in spite of some bitter boycotts and a vigorous national products movement. As Gerth recognizes, however, if the national products movements was an economic failure, consumer culture nevertheless succeeded in popularizing images and understandings of the nation, often far more effectively than political propaganda.

The Construction of Class Identity

Although we still tend to think of China, not Russia, as the country of peasant revolution in the twentieth century, peasants in Russia were historically more engaged in what we might term 'proto-class' conflict than their Chinese counterparts. It is true that both countries had long traditions of peasant militancy, albeit mainly small in scale and defensive in character. In China, however, open warfare between peasants and landowners was rare, most peasant rebellions targeting tax collectors or other civil and military officials.[53] In Russia, too, conflicts with officials over taxes or compulsory obligations – or even with other peasants – may well have outnumbered conflicts with landowners; but in 1905–7, it was the battle between peasants and landowners that swept the countryside. Even in the first months of 1905, it was the demand for the transfer of privately owned crown, monastic and gentry land to those who worked it that predominated in petitions to the authorities, accompanied by heart-rending descriptions of the poverty, ignorance and absence of political

---

[51] Gerth, *China Made*, p. 189.
[52] Gerth, *China Made*, p. 183.
[53] Lucien Bianco (with the collaboration of Hua Chang-Ming), *Jacqueries et révolution dans la China du XXe siècle* (Paris: Éditions de La Martinière, 2005).

rights that characterized peasant life.[54] The protests were not class conflict in a pure sense, since they were often triggered by grievances of a particularistic nature and were generally rooted in the solidarity of the local community. Nevertheless memories of serfdom were raw, and the agrarian disorders of 1905–7 pitted peasants against the gentry in a two-way struggle that had only rare parallels in China.[55]

In China patterns of social differentiation in the countryside were altogether more complex than in Russia, with groupings such as lineages, community self-defence organizations and secret societies crosscutting any horizontal division between peasants and gentry. Rural society was not dominated by large landowning families in the same way as in Russia, the extended families of the gentry rarely maintaining their position in the community more than a few generations unless their land was assigned to a lineage association. In addition, about half of peasants were owner-occupiers, especially in the North, and only about 30% rented all their land from the gentry. So the taxation and conscription by the state rather than gentry exactions were the key problem for many peasants. Moreover, collective action on the part of the peasants was frequently conducted along lineage and community lines, and often led by bandits, local militias, secret societies or redemptive religious sects.[56] During the republican era, most peasant protest in the commercially developed lower Yangtze delta continued to be directed against government hikes in taxes, but strife between tenants and landlords probably intensified. This is somewhat paradoxical, since rents do not appear to have increased in real terms, whereas taxes did; but the slow decline in the status of landlords, accompanied by their refusal to mitigate rents in times of hardship, led to sharper contention over rents, often directed against landlords' agents rather than landlords themselves, who were generally resident in towns.[57] Peasant struggle against landlords was not

---

[54] O. G. Bukhovets, *Sotsial'nye konflikty i krestian'skaia mental'nost' v rossiiskoi imperii nachala XX veka: novye materialy, metody, rezul'taty* (Moscow: Mosgorarkhiv, 1996), p. 141.

[55] David Moon, *The Russian Peasantry, 1600–1930* (London: Longman, 1999), ch. 7.

[56] Lucien Bianco, 'Peasants and Revolution in China', *Journal of Peasant Studies*, 2, 3 (1975), 313–35; Albert Feuerwerker, 'Rebellion in Nineteenth-Century China', *Michigan Papers in Chinese Studies*, No. 21 (Ann Arbor: Center for Chinese Studies, University of Michigan, 1975); Frederick Wakeman, 'Rebellion and Revolution: The Study of Popular Movements in Chinese History', *Journal of Asian Studies*, 36, 2 (1977), 201–37; Elizabeth J. Perry, *Rebels and Revolutionaries in North China, 1845–1945* (Stanford: Stanford University Press, 1980).

[57] Kathryn Bernhardt, *Rents, Taxes, and Peasant Resistance: The Lower Yangzi Region, 1840–1950* (Stanford: Stanford University Press, 1992). Lucien Bianco is sceptical that conflict between landlords and tenants increased in this region in the republican era. See Lucien Bianco, *Peasants without the Party: Grass-roots Movements in Twentieth-Century China* (Armonk NY: M. E. Sharpe, 2001), pp. 290–1.

absent in China, then, but it was by no means as common in Russia. Nevertheless, what R. David Arkash in his study of peasant proverbs calls a 'spirit of resentment towards elites, a sort of proto-class consciousness' was not uncommon, although he finds no evidence of normative opposition to the political and religious traditions of ruling elites.[58]

Running through peasant culture in Russia was a profound sense of them and us, of landlords versus peasants, of regime (*vlast'*) versus people (*narod*), of the upper classes (*verkhi*) versus the lower classes (*nizy*).[59] I want to argue that this dichotomous vision of the social order made Russian workers particularly susceptible to class politics after 1905. For if 1905 seemed to hold out the promise of a nation united in the struggle against the autocracy, it also starkly underlined the danger of society polarizing between the upper and lower classes. As early as October 1905, the nascent labour movement, dissatisfied with the constitutional reforms on offer from Nicholas II in the October Manifesto, split from its liberal allies. It launched a general strike, in which soviets appeared for the first time, that culminated in the abortive insurrection in Moscow in December. Social strife also deepened in the countryside. Between 1905 and 1907, peasants took advantage of the breakdown of authority to press their claims against the landlords. Aghast at peasant violence, the liberal gentry moderated its hostility towards the autocracy. Meanwhile the SRs and the Social Democrats seized the opportunity to promote their rival visions of socialism, reworking crude understandings of 'them' and 'us' into a more elaborate ideology of class and popularizing notions of citizenship, equality and socialism.

The new category of 'worker', still not recognized in the estate-based classification of society used by the government, came into common usage. Never a neutral social descriptor, it carried a political resonance of being opposed to the status quo. For 'conscious' workers, the language of class came to hegemonize their identities, giving political focus to those transformations of self-understanding that we have traced in the preceding chapters, situating these workers in social space as

---

[58] R. David Arkash, 'Orthodoxy and Heterodoxy in Twentieth-Century Chinese Peasant Proverbs', in Kwang-Ching Liu, *Orthodoxy in Late Imperial China* (Berkeley: University of California Press, 1990), pp. 311–331.

[59] As Herzen put it: 'On the one hand there was governmental, imperial, aristocratic Russia, rich in money, armed not only with bayonets but with all the bureaucratic and police techniques taken from Germany. On the other hand, there was Russia of the dark people, poor, agricultural, communal, democratic, helpless, conquered, as it were, without battle.' A. I. Herzen, *Sobrannye sochinenie v tridzati tomakh*, vol. 12 (30 vols.) (Moscow: AN SSSR, 1957), p. 55.

opponents of autocracy and capital. For less politically conscious workers, the language of class had less purchase on their sense of self, but gave
edge to their antipathy to employers and supervisors.[60] This growth in
class sentiment was both cause and effect of a wave of industrial battles.
In the decade prior to the First World War – a decade when strikes were
numerous throughout Europe – no other European country matched
Russia's overall level of industrial unrest. Metalworkers, the largest sector
of the workforce, were the most militant as well as the most politically
conscious group of workers. By 1914, strikes were running at a level
comparable to that of 1905, with many having a political coloration. In
contrast to the more measured tones of the labour movement in Britain
or Germany, moreover, the discourse of labour in Russia was remarkable
for its visceral antipathy to the status quo.

The socialists of populist and marxist provenance who came to shape
the culture of the Russian working class in the period between 1905 and
1917 explicitly repudiated the language of nationalism. For them the
appeal of socialism lay precisely in an ideal of international brotherhood
that promised salvation from the chauvinistic nationalisms that were
tearing Europe apart, especially in the Balkans. Nationalism as a political
ideology was, in any case, firmly associated in Russia with the political
right, citizens having few investments in a 'nation' in which they were
largely stripped of civil and political rights. Indeed the absence of a
nationalist politics usable by the people helps explain the unusual
salience of class as a modality of political action in Russia. The tenor of
many worker memoirs – not all of them written after the revolution – is
often decidedly anti-national. Shapovalov, who became an apprentice at
the age of thirteen in the workshops of the Petersburg–Warsaw railway,
contrasted the 'barbarism, Asiatic backwardness, boorishness and
dreadful lack of culture' of his Russian workmates with the education,
industriousness and politeness of his Finnish, German, Latvian and
Polish colleagues. Finns and Germans, he recalled, although consuming
large amounts of alcohol, were always punctual in attending work unlike
Russians; they held themselves with greater dignity, dressed in European
fashion, and rarely stole from the factory.[61] Many 'conscious' workers
marvelled at the good manners, orderliness and dignity of their foreign
counterparts:

Unlike us, they do not wallow in the mud in their hours of rest in torn clothes
close to taverns and bars, they do not curse their comrades or come to blows like

---

[60] Tim McDaniel, *Autocracy, Capitalism, and Revolution in Russia* (Berkeley: University of
California Press, 1988).
[61] A. S. Shapovalov, *Po doroge k marksizmu* (Moscow: Gosizdat, 1924), p. 14.

the Russian muzhik. They gather together to discuss how to improve their condition. Or if they wish to enjoy themselves, they get on their bikes and go for ride together and thus increase their muscular strength.[62]

Yet such comparisons could conceal a certain pride in being Russian. Shapovalov disliked the way that foreign workers looked down on him, saying that snobbery was alien to the Russian national character.[63] Kanatchikov was put off by the aloofness of foreign workers and their inability to express emotion in a way that came naturally to Russians.[64] Frolov contrasted the open-heartedness and sincerity of the Russian people to the affectation and duplicity of foreigners.[65] This belief in the simplicity and honesty of the Russian people was one of those 'proto-national' tropes that had long circulated in popular culture. And for a few, at least, radical political commitment seems to have arisen as much from a concern to see Russia realize her potential as a great nation as from a concern to improve the woeful condition of her workers and peasants. The worker Svirskii records: 'My homeland, my great boundless home-land, appeared to me as a heroic knight, whose eyes have been gouged out. Strong, wise, great-souled, he stands alone among the peoples of the world, and does not move from his place. He is blind and does not know where to go or to what he should apply his heroic strength.'[66]

It is doubtful that the unpopularity of the First World War among the people of Russia can be attributed to an absence of national sentiment.[67] In Russia, as in other countries, the immediate effect of the war was to unleash a brief wave of patriotism that was probably strongest in the middle classes but which also affected sections of the working class. The most striking instance of this was the precipitate collapse of the strike movement that had paralysed the capital in the first half of 1914. Prior to 1915, not a single protest strike against the war occurred across the whole of Russia.[68] V. Vinogradov, a worker at the Petrograd Metal Works, wrote: 'the mood of workers during the first year of the war was such that

---

[62] An ungrammatical workers' leaflet quoted in K. M. Takhtarev, *Ocherk Peterburgskogo rabochego dvizheniia 90-kh godov* (Petrograd: Gosizdat, 1921), pp. 39–40.

[63] Shapovalov, *Po doroge*, p. 14.

[64] Reginald E. Zelnik, *A Radical Worker in Tsarist Russia: The Autobiography of Semën Ivanovich Kanatchikov* (Stanford: Stanford University Press, 1986), p. 90.

[65] A. Frolov, *Probuzhdenie: vospominaniia riadego rabochego* (Kiev: Gosizdat Ukrainy, 1923), p. 199.

[66] A. I. Svirskii, *Zapiski rabochego* (Moscow: Zemlia i fabrika, 1925; orig. 1907), pp. 46–7.

[67] S. A. Smith, 'Citizenship and the Russian Nation during World War One: A Comment', *Slavic Review*, 59, 2 (2000), 316–29.

[68] Iu. I. Kir'ianov, 'Rabochie Rossii i voina: novye podkhody k analizu problemy', in V. L. Mal'kov (ed.), *Pervaia mirovaia voina: prolog XX veka* (Moscow: Nauka, 1998), p. 438.

even to contemplate any kind of political strike was unthinkable'.[69] Soviet historians ascribed the cessation of the strike movement to the disruption caused by conscription and the repression of the Bolshevik underground. These were certainly factors, but far more important was workers' desire not to jeopardize the war effort and to support soldiers who were suffering from a shortage of arms and supplies.[70] Enthusiastic supporters of the war, like outright opponents, were relatively few, but the majority, though unenthusiastic about the war, was broadly patriotic.[71] After carefully reviewing the contradictory evidence on popular attitudes at the outbreak of the war, Joshua Sanborn concludes that a 'significant minority' was fully mobilized within the framework of the nation, which it tended to see as a 'multi-ethnic Russian (*rossiiskii*) brotherhood' rather than as an ethnically Russian *Volk*; but that the majority 'harbored few illusions that they would gain any particular benefit from military victory'.[72] This did not indicate lack of patriotism so much as a lack of enthusiasm for war. There was a certain willingness to defend the motherland against foreign aggression but little support for the government. In this regard, the public mood in Russia did not differ radically from that in other belligerent countries where chauvinism was far less widespread than was once supposed.[73] In Britain and Germany there was a brief moment of enthusiasm in August 1914, but the public mood soon became sombre and restrained.[74] It is doubtful, therefore, whether one can read the lack of enthusiasm for war as evidence of an inability among the lower classes to identify with the nation.

The catastrophic defeats in Poland and the advance of Germany in spring and summer 1915, combined with the fall in living standards brought about by inflation, changed the mood of the working population

---

[69] V. Vinogradov, 'Organizatsiia bol'shevikov na Peterburgskom Metallicheskom zavode v 1915g.', *Krasnaia Letopis'*, 18 (1926), 34.

[70] S. V. Tiutukhin, 'Pervaia mirovaia voina i revoliutsionnyi protsess v Rossii', in V. L. Mal'kov (ed.), *Pervaia mirovaia voina: prolog XX veka* (Moscow: Nauka, 1998), p. 242.

[71] Robert McKean reviews some of the contradictory evidence about responses among St Petersburg workers though his judgment is inconclusive. Robert B. McKean, *St Petersburg Between the Revolutions: Workers and Revolutionaries, June 1907–February 1917* (New Haven: Yale University Press, 1990), pp. 355–8.

[72] Joshua Sanborn, 'The Mobilization of 1914 and the Question of the Russian Nation: A Reexamination', *Slavic Review*, 59, 2 (2000), 267–89.

[73] L. L. Farrar, 'Nationalism in Wartime: Critiquing the Conventional Wisdom', in Frans Coetzee and Marilyn Shevin-Coetzee (eds.), *Authority, Identity and the Social History of the Great War* (Providence RI: Berghahn, 1995), pp. 133–51.

[74] Jeffrey Verhey, *The Spirit of 1914: Militarism, Myth and Mobilization in Germany* (Cambridge: Cambridge University Press, 2000); A. Gregory, 'British "War Enthusiasm" in 1914: A Reassessment', in Gail Braybon (ed.), *Evidence, History and the Great War* (New York: Berghahn, 2003), pp. 67–85.

of Petrograd. During 1915, the strike movement revived, initially largely economic in character, but increasingly politicized from autumn by events such as the shooting of workers in Kostroma and Ivanovo-Voznesensk in June and August 1915 and the refusal of Nicholas II to make any concessions to the Duma. In 1915, 1.3 million workers in Russia took part in political strikes; in 1916, 2.2 million; and in first two months of 1917, 800,000 – vastly more than the numbers in France, Germany or the United Kingdom. In Petrograd the proportion of political strikes was particularly high, especially among metalworkers.[75] Workers were angered by the incompetence and corruption of the government and by the fact that the burdens of war fell disproportionately on the common people. Yet even at this stage, they had little desire to jeopardize the war effort.[76] When workers at the Naval' shipyard in Petrograd embarked on a one-and-a-half month strike in January 1916, they ordered their comrades in the shell department to continue work as normal.[77] Nevertheless in the course of 1916 national identity and class identity began to pull apart. Workers now perceived the privileged classes to be failing to bear their share of war-related suffering and to be reaping vast profits from the carnage. This played into the hands of the Bolsheviks and Left SRs, the most militant opponents of the war. The main beneficiaries of the radicalized mood, however, were probably the Mensheviks and SRs, who used legal openings, such as the workers' groups of the Central War Industries Committees, the semi-legal medical funds and the effectively illegal trade unions, to lend working-support to the Duma campaign for a government enjoying the confidence of the people.[78] During winter of 1916–17, war weariness grew apace, as civilian living standards began to collapse and as the toll of death and injury from the war climbed inexorably.

The cultural and social barriers to the development of class identity proved far stauncher in China than in Russia. The idea of class struggle was abhorrent to Confucianism, which esteemed social harmony and compromise: axiomatically, it was better to yield and meet an opponent halfway than to stand firm on principle. Social hierarchy – imagined as one of four vocations (*simin*) – was powerfully endorsed, with scholars at the top, followed by peasants, artisans, and merchants at the bottom. Even more powerfully registered was the distinction between those who worked with their hands and those who worked with their brains.

---

[75] O. S. Porshneva, *Mentalitet i sotsial'noe povedenie rabochikh, krest'ian i soldat Rossii v period mirovoi voiny (1914–1918gg.)* (Ekaterinburg: UrO RAN, 2000), pp. 183, 187.
[76] Porshneva, *Mentalitet*, p. 206.
[77] Tiutiukhin, 'Pervaia mirovaia voina', p. 245.   [78] Kir'ianov, 'Rabochie Rossii', p. 444.

In Mencius's maxim 'Some work with their minds, others with their bodies. Those who work with their minds rule, while those who work with their bodies are ruled. Those who are ruled produce food; those who rule are fed.' But if social hierarchy was taken for granted, large disparities of wealth were deprecated, since it was felt that everyone should have enough to be able to support themselves and to live in peace.[79] Righteousness (*yi*) was thus a pertinent consideration when judging social relations, so long as it was reconciled with harmony (*he*). Sun Yat-sen maintained this tradition, resisting the rhetoric of class struggle even after his alliance with the Communists in 1923.[80] According to Sun, class divisions had always been narrow in Chinese society, and since modern economic development was as yet still limited, it was possible to ensure that China developed in a way that avoided the strains and cleavages associated with capitalist development in the West. He reasoned that capital had a vital part to play in developing the productive forces of the nation, but advocated its 'restriction' in order to minimize class polarization.[81] By 'unifying the middle against the two extremes', China could avoid becoming a society of antagonistic classes.[82] Other GMD ideologues, such as Hu Hanmin, elaborated on this, arguing that class divisions were minimal in China since she was in effect a proletarian nation, a weak and poor country exploited by imperialism: 'society as a whole is revolutionary and only a few people are counter-revolutionary'.[83]

---

[79] Yuji Muramatsu, 'Some Themes in Chinese Rebel Ideologies', in A. F. Wright (ed.), *The Confucian Persuasion* (Stanford: Stanford University Press, 1960), p. 257.

[80] Following Sun's death in 1924, right-wing members of the GMD rejected the united front with the CCP that had been authorized by Sun, arguing that Communism was incompatible with the Chinese 'national temperament' (*guoqing*). For a humorous rebuttal of this view, see the short story by Guo Moruo (1892–1978), who became president of the Chinese Academy of Sciences after 1949. It tells of a visit by Marx to Confucius and three of his disciples in 1925. Confucius explains that respect for the material world has been at the core of traditional Chinese thought and that human happiness can only thrive if production is first increased and then equal distribution of wealth implemented. A rude and vainglorious Marx exclaims: 'I never imagined that two thousand years ago in the East an old comrade like yourself already existed! Our views are completely identical.' Guo Moruo, 'Makesi jin wenmiao' [Marx Enters the Confucian Temple], *Guo Moruo quanji* [Collected Works of Guo Moruo], vol. 10 (Beijing: Xinhua shudian, 1985), p. 167.

[81] Harold Schiffrin, *Sun Yat-sen: Reluctant Revolutionary* (Boston: Little, Brown, 1980), p. 103.

[82] *Yijiuerqi nian de Shanghai shangye lianhehui* [The Shanghai Commercial Association of 1927] (Shanghai: Shanghai renmin chubanshe, 1983), pp. 255–6; *Zhongguo guomindang dierci quanguo daibiao dahui geshengqu dangwu baogao mulu* [Reports and lists from each province to Second GMD National Congress] (Shanghai: Guomindang zhongyang zhixing weiyuanhui, 1926), pp. 121–2.

[83] Cited in Joseph Fewsmith, *Party, State and Local Elites in Republican China: Merchant Organizations and Politics in Shanghai, 1890–1930* (Honolulu: University of Hawaii Press, 1985), p. 92.

If we look at the issue from a sociological perspective, we would expect Chinese workers to be more resistant to the idea of class than their Russian counterparts. First, relations between workers and employers were not as harsh as in tsarist Russia, industrial relations being framed, to some extent, by the norms of the Confucian ritual order. The influential GMD labour leader Ma Chaojun argued that industrial relations were permeated by a patriarchal ethos (*jiazu jingshen*) that meant that employees judged their employers according to the norms of morality and justice.[84] How far this appertained in larger factory settings – and how far it appertained at all in foreign-owned establishments – is debatable, but it was not without relevance in inhibiting the acceptance of a dichotomous view of the social order. Second, and more pertinently, as the anthropologist Fei Xiaotong argued, social relationships in China were organized via discontinuous, overlapping networks, each link of which comprised a personalistic tie.[85] By the twentieth century, such networks were no longer based so much upon the moral obligations of the Confucian order as upon instrumental calculation, which is not to say that they could not also have a strong affective or moral dimension. This way of putting social groups together promoted vertical personalistic ties at the expense of horizontal collective ties and was thus inimical to the emergence of class-based organizations.[86] Within the world of labour, the bangs (see chapter 1) based on craft and native place, the clientelistic ties to foremen and labour contractors, the secret societies, or the very informal ties of sworn brotherhood and sisterhood exemplified such personalistic networks. Such networks, which frequently drew on the vocabulary of kinship, set up social and psychological barriers to the establishment of identifications with larger, more abstract collectivities such as those of class and nation, since both of these 'imagined communities' share an understanding of social groups as sets of equivalent persons rather than as webs of relationships among persons organized along hierarchical lines.[87]

The historical record suggests that if such networks inhibited the development of class identity, they did not pose an absolute impediment

[84] Ma Chaojun, *Zhongguo laogong yundong shi* [A History of the Chinese Labour Movement] (Taibei: Zhongguo laogong fuli chubanshe, 1958), p. 433.
[85] Fei Xiaotong, *From the Soil: The Foundations of Chinese Society* (Xiangtu Zhongguo – orig. 1947), introduction and epilogue by Gary G. Hamilton and Wang Zheng (Berkeley: University of California Press, 1992), pp. 19–21.
[86] Wang Ze, 'Chuantong wenhua de jiazhi quxiang zhuti jiazhi wenti', in Zhang Liwen (ed.), *Chuantong wenhua yu xiandaihua* [Traditional Culture and Modernization] (Beijing: Renmin chubanshe, 1987), pp. 85–94.
[87] Craig Calhoun, 'Nationalism and Ethnicity', *Annual Review of Sociology*, 19 (1993), 230.

to short-term unity of workers in struggle. In the handicraft, retail and construction sectors of the economy of Shanghai, guilds uniting employers and employees predominated. Moreover, within each trade, employees were generally divided by craft and native-place ties, it being common for specific crafts within the trade to be monopolized by a particular regional grouping. Nevertheless, in the first two decades of the twentieth century, these native-place bangs displayed an increased propensity to overcome their differences when faced by a common threat from the employers. A number of guilds formed separate sections for employers and employees, usually known as *dahang* and *xiaohang*, respectively; and the latter proved able to unite the different bangs when disputes with the guild directors broke out. In October 1914, for example, the 7,000 workers in the painters' guild, split between five native-place bangs, were brought together by the xiaohang in a strike against the rising cost of rice and the depreciation of the copper currency.[88] Significantly, they were joined by 7,000 masons, carpenters and joiners, themselves divided into three native-place bangs, who were temporarily united by the xiaohang of the construction workers' guild.[89] On 19 November, there were angry clashes between the guild directors and strikers after more than 1,000 masons, carpenters and joiners tried to gain entry into the Lu Ban temple in the Chinese City. Arrests were made and the next day strikers attacked a police station.[90] After four days on strike, the construction workers accepted a compromise settlement, but the painters, who had been on strike for several weeks by this stage, refused to settle. Relations between the employers' and employees' sections of the painters' guild deteriorated to such an extent that in 1916, with the help of the Labour Party, painters formed a trade union, the first such union in the handicraft sector.[91] This did not signal the demise of corporate guilds and their replacement by class-based trade unions: the painters' union proved to be short-lived, and guilds continued to flourish well into the 1930s. Nevertheless the abrasiveness of disputes between masters and men within the guild sector, precipitated by rapidly declining real wages and a republican experiment turned sour, left its mark.

Antagonism between employees and employers within the guilds was not a new phenomenon, even if its scale and intensity was unprecedented. What was new is that there were now political organizations in existence that aspired to constitute such conflict in a vocabulary that

---

[88] *Shibao*, 3 September 1916; 25 September 1916.
[89] *Shibao*, 23 November 1914.
[90] *Shibao*, 19 November 1914; 23 November 1914; *NCH*, 21 November 1914, p. 590.
[91] Shanghai Municipal Police File (SMPF), IO series, 561, p. 618.

stressed the common interests of workers. Leaving to one side early anarchist and socialist organizations, which spoke a more unambiguous language of class,[92] it was nationalists who championed the need for workers to organize in the early years of the republic. Sun Yat-sen and the GMD, formed in August 1912, argued that labour unions were necessary not only to improve the conditions of the workers but also to build a strong national economy. They maintained that labour organization would actually help the two sides of industry to cooperate in the interests of national development.[93] This class-collaborationist perspective did much to legitimize the 'workers' section of society' (*gongjie*) and to establish its importance in the struggle to save the nation. The GMD imagined the nation as a corporate entity consisting of distinct *jie*, or sections of society, chief of which were those of the merchants, students and workers, and it posited the interests of the nation would best be served by promoting the occupational or functional organization of its constituent jie. Under Chiang Kai-shek this served to advance a politics of corporatism, but in the 1920s it did much to legitimize and promote the creation of labour unions.

It was the May Fourth Movement of 1919 that highlighted the potential of organized labour to participate in nation-building. In the *sanba*, or 'triple strike' of merchants, students and workers, protesting the terms of the Treaty of Versailles and in the boycott of Japanese goods, workers played what contemporaries called a 'back-up' role. Initially, the Shanghai Commercial Association, the organization of nationalistically minded businessmen, and the Shanghai Student Union were not keen to involve workers. But workers made it clear that they would not be left out. On 5 June, the crews of merchant vessels proclaimed: 'We cannot sit idly by. We are going on strike for the recovery of national territory and for the release of arrested students.'[94] They were joined by stewards, cooks and cabin boys: 'The students have stopped classes, the merchants have ceased trading, the factory owners have shut down their enterprises, the seamen's mess has stopped work in order to show that the nation is of one mind. We ... too wish to see the nation rid of its traitors, so we are stopping work. We shall not give the

---

[92] See S. A. Smith, *Like Cattle and Horses: Nationalism and Labor in Shanghai, 1895–1927* (Durham NC: Duke University Press, 2002), pp. 68–75, 85–88.

[93] Li Shiyue, 'Xinhai geming qianhou de Zhongguo gongren yundong he Zhonghua minguo gongdang' [The Chinese Labour Movement and the Chinese Republic an Labour Party around the Time of the Xinhai Revolution], *Shixue jikan*, 1, 3 (1957), 73.

[94] *Wusi yundong zai Shanghai shiliao xuanji* [Selected Historical Materials on the May Fourth Movement in Shanghai] (Shanghai: Shanghai renmin chubanshe, 1960), p. 321.

foreigners chance to mock our half-hearted enthusiasm.'[95] Between 6 and 11 June, as many as 100,000 workers, including 20,000 workers in transportation (mainly dockers) and 23,000 workers in the handicraft sector – not including the 70,000 traders and workers in the retail sector – stopped work.[96] Signs of class-consciousness were evident in the way in which some workers responded to efforts to dissuade them from joining the patriotic protests. One public utility worker retorted: 'You students and merchants happen to be better educated and richer than we. Do you think we have no conscience to express our indignation against these traitors? Do you think for a moment that patriotism is confined to your classes alone?'[97]

In theory, nationalist ideology constitutes citizens as equal members of the nation. Yet in the course of the 1920s, different 'sections of society' began to appropriate nationalist discourse for their own ends. If in the May Fourth Movement many middle-class patriots had argued that the ignorance and proclivity for disorder of workers ruled them out of participation in the nation, labour leaders – by no means all of whom were influenced by the nascent CCP – increasingly presented labour as the true core of the nation. The twelve labour organizations that signed the 'Shanghai Labour Manifesto' in October 1921 denounced plans to deprive workers with less than three years' education of the right to vote in elections to a national assembly. 'We labourers may have a low level of education but we still have our consciences ... The country is sustained by us. We labourers have consistently offered the nation our service and have done it no crime. Only we, the labourers, deserve to say what the qualifications for the national assembly should be. It is we who should be ashamed of you, the intellectuals and politicians, with your shady deals.'[98] They thus projected labour as the true bearer of the nationalist interest against parasitic elites. By the mid-1920s, the consolidation of a labour movement, combined with the increasing influence of the radical left within it, shifted nationalist discourse towards registering the centrality of the common people – if not the 'working class' – to the imagined community of the nation.

It was, however, the success of the CCP in reconfiguring nationalism along the lines of radical anti-imperialism that opened up a discursive space in which the language of class could take root. Until 1923, when

[95] *Wusi yundong*, pp. 342, 344.

[96] Shen Yixing, Jiang Peinan and Zheng Qingsheng, *Shanghai gongren yundong shi* [A History of the Shanghai Labour Movement], vol. 1 (Shenyang: Liaoning renmin chubanshe, 1991), p. 49; National Archive (UK), FO 228/3526, item 116.

[97] *North China Herald*, 14 June 1919, p. 721. I assume that 'class' here is a translation of *jie*.

[98] *Laodong zhoukan*, 5 November 1921.

its programme was recast under Soviet influence, the GMD had not deployed a concept of imperialism. Sun Yat-sen had touched on the issue in 1904 and again in 1912, but he perceived imperialism merely as territorial expansion by the foreign powers, and did not consider it to be at the root of China's problems. Right up to 1922, he made regular efforts to persuade Japan or the western powers to assist his quest to reunify China.[99] However, as a result of the first united front between the CCP and the GMD, the First Congress of the GMD in January 1924 laid responsibility for China's civil chaos squarely at the door of the foreign powers (*lieqiang*), whose activities were now seen as being aimed, inter alia, at the 'seizure of economic rights'. Defining nationalism as 'freedom and independence' for the Chinese people, the congress demanded the nullification of the unequal treaties, the return of the foreign concessions, the abolition of extraterritoriality, the regaining of control over the customs and an end to reparations payments.[100] It was this reformulation of nationalism around the idea of anti-imperialism that enabled the CCP and the left wing of the GMD to promote a discourse of class following the May Thirtieth Movement of 1925.

Nation and Class in Revolution

The effect of the February Revolution of 1917 was to transform 'Holy Russia' into 'Revolutionary Russia' and to boost flagging patriotism. Over the next eight months, Russian society became a battleground in which different and shifting combinations of class and national politics competed for popular support. The new Provisional Government appealed to the 'living forces of the people' to unite to build a free and democratic nation. Yet even at this moment of unity, fault lines in the way that the nation was imagined were already visible. In their statement welcoming the Provisional Government, the Kadets proclaimed:

Citizens, have faith as one in this regime, unite your forces, allow the government created by the state duma to complete its great work of liberating Russia

---

[99] F. Gilbert Chan, 'Sun Yat-sen and the Origins of Kuomintang Reorganization', in F. Gilbert Chan and T. H. Etzold (eds.), *China in the 1920s* (New York: New Viewpoints. 1976), pp. 15–37; Chester C. Tan, *Chinese Political Thought in the Twentieth Century* (Garden City NY: Doubleday, 1971), pp. 123–5; Jürgen Domes, *Vertagte Revolution: Die Politik der Kuomintang in China, 1923–7* (Berlin: De Gruyter, 1969), pp. 110–11.

[100] *Zhongguo Guomindang diyi, erci quanguo daibiao dahui huiyi shiliao* [Historical Materials on the First and Second Guomindang Congresses], vol. 1 (Shanghai: Jiangsu guji chubanshe, 1986), pp. 82–3, 88. The extent to which the GMD adopted a full-blooded anti-imperialism may be doubted. The reference to the big powers as *lieqiang* rather than *diguo* is a small indicator of the persistence of older conceptions.

from the external enemy and of establishing internal peace in the country on the basis of the principles of equality and liberty. Let all differences of party, class, estate and nationality be forgotten. Let a united Russian people take heart from this great upsurge and create conditions for the peaceful existence of all citizens.[101]

The Kadets subscribed to a concept of statehood (*gosudarstvennost'*) that saw the state as distinct from any particular government, as located above classes (*nadklassovnost'*) and above partisanship. They saw February as a political not a social revolution, whose objectives were to win the war and to secure a parliamentary political system based on private property.[102]

By contrast, for the Menshevik and SR leaders of the Petrograd Soviet the core of the 'nation' was the so-called 'revolutionary democracy', the alliance of popular classes that had brought about the downfall of the old regime. 'Russian Democracy has cast the age-old despotism of the tsar into the dust and enters the family of democratic nations as an equal member and with terrifying strength struggles for our emancipation. Our victory is the great victory of global peace and democracy. Russia will no longer be the major foundation for world reaction and the gendarme of Europe.'[103] The moderate socialists registered the existence of social classes, but hoped to preserve the unity of revolutionary democracy in the interests of advancing the bourgeois-democratic revolution. On the crucial question of the war, the Soviet leaders were pro-peace and internationalist, yet committed to defending Russia, now construed as a revolutionary and democratic nation. This doctrine of 'revolutionary defencism' captured rather well the changed balance between class and national loyalties brought about by the February Revolution. Most workers were eager to see an end to the war and a comprehensive peace settlement that repudiated imperialist objectives, but they were also determined to protect Russia's hard-won freedoms from Austro-German assault. This made them unsympathetic to Bolshevik claims that the war had not changed its imperialist nature as a consequence of the February Revolution. Yet workers sympathetic to revolutionary defencism soon began to suspect that the Provisional Government had no serious commitment to peace. And the decision of the Kerensky government to launch a major offensive in June, followed by its bloody failure, shifted

---

[101] *Revoliutsionnoe dvizhenie v Rossii posle sverzheniia samoderzhaviia* (Moscow: AN SSSR, 1957), p. 420.
[102] William G. Rosenberg, *Liberals in the Russian Revolution* (Princeton: Princeton University Press, 1974), p. 134.
[103] *Petrogradskii Sovet rabochikh i soldatskikh deputatov v 1917 godu. Protokoly, stenogrammy i otchety* (Leningrad: Nauka, 1991), p. 323.

working-class sentiment towards the Bolsheviks.[104] The pointless bloodshed, combined with mistrust of the Provisional Government, led soldiers and workers to ever more bitter attacks on the war, and the Bolshevik linkage of the war to capitalist self-interest became increasingly persuasive.

By late summer 1917, deepening polarization of society produced a polarization of political languages, whereby the educated and propertied classes spoke the language of nation, and the 'toilers' spoke the language of class. As the principal representative of the elites, the Kadets indulged in ever more bellicose rhetoric of the nation-under-siege, peppered with terms such as betrayal, cowardice, desertion and treachery. Faced by social breakdown and popular revolt, they became obsessed by enemies within and by the need to restore order. For their part, the Bolsheviks spoke an equally intransigent language that appeared to reject any appeal to national identity, in favour of an appeal to class and proletarian internationalism. At times, Bolshevik claims stretched credibility, as when they accused the Provisional Government of deliberately sabotaging the war effort in order to crush the revolution, but workers now responded to the rhetoric of class struggle as fervently as they had responded to the rhetoric of revolutionary unity a few months previously. This rhetoric of class – at least in popular quarters – was not marxist in a doctrinally pure sense: rather than differentiate social classes carefully, it played on the deeply rooted idiom in popular culture that pitted 'those at the bottom' (*nizy*) against 'those at the top' (*verkhi*). Moreover, the distinction between workers and peasants was frequently blurred in this rhetoric by a populist preference for terms like 'toilers' (*trudiashchiesia*) who were cast in dichotomous fashion against the 'burzhui' and 'gentlemen' (*gospoda*).[105]

Yet even in Bolshevik rhetoric, the rejection of class and internationalism never entirely displaced the rhetoric of nation. Many in the party were reluctant to follow the unyielding logic of Lenin's defeatism if it meant that the party appeared to be betraying the motherland. The fall of Riga to the Germans on 21 August 1917, for example, was reported by the Bolshevik newspaper in Ivanovo-Voznesensk under the headline: 'The bourgeoisie has ceased to love the fatherland'. It went on: 'The recent breakthrough at Riga' in the prevention of which conscious proletarian (Bolshevik) regiments took an active part, many of them now lying on the field of battle, was caused by the treachery of Supreme

---

[104] *Revoliutsionnoe dvizhenie v Rossii posle sverzheniia*, p. 466.
[105] Boris Kolonitskii, 'Anti-Bourgeois Propaganda and "Anti-Burzhui" Consciousness in 1917', *Russian Review*, 53, 2 (1994), 183–96.

Commander Kornilov, who thought to heap the blame on the revolution and create a mood in the masses in his favour as "saviour of the fatherland" and thus lead the country into dictatorship.'[106] Such Bolsheviks angrily rejected the charge that it was their agitation that was the cause of the disintegration of the army. 'We have never sought to disorganize the front by means of calling for a retreat or for flight. Soldiers who consciously understand the ideas of revolutionary Social Democracy would not be party to such shame.'[107] In the same way, the party repudiated the charge that it was in favour of a separate peace with Germany.

Bolshevik soreness to accusations of being unpatriotic reflected the fact that though political discourse had become polarized between the language of nation and the language of class, popular political affiliations were still subliminally governed by the pull between class and national identities. Even as the most unwavering advocates of class politics, the Bolsheviks recognized that they could not afford to let their enemies have a monopoly on so emotionally charged a political language as that of nation. So they challenged the elites's claim to be the true patriots, and advanced an alternative rhetoric of nationhood that pivoted upon the populist category of the 'toiling people' (*trudovoi narod*). This projected the 'true' nation as the collectivity of toilers, as those who produced the wealth of the nation through the sweat of their brow; in this idiom it was workers, peasants and soldiers who represented the true national interest, whereas 'those on top' self-evidently stood for selfish class interest. As the worker L. Ryzhik wrote: 'Their patriotism consists in persecuting peasants, soldiers and workers. You will never succeed in splitting these three blood brothers, related to one another in body and soul. Remember that it is the Russian soldier, worker and peasant who are the true Russia.'[108] This conception of the nation played on the ambiguity of the term *narod*, with its double sense of 'nation' and 'common people'. As popular politics swerved sharply to the left, it was this term that was used to moderate the acute tensions felt between class and national identities. This rendition of the nation as one of toilers, the true nation as those who laboured to produce its wealth, a nation betrayed by the appropriators of that wealth, by those accustomed to lord it over the common people, provided one of the deepest wellsprings of popular support for the Bolsheviks and Left SRs in late 1917.

---

[106] *Revoliutsionnoe dvizhenie v Rossii v avguste 1917g.* (Moscow: AN SSSR, 1959), p. 103.
[107] *Zvezda*, 16 July, 1917. Cited in V. F. Shishkin, *Velikii oktiabr' i proletarskii moral'* (Moscow: Mysl', 1976), p. 57.
[108] Cited in Shishkin, *Velikii oktiabr'*, p. 48.

Struve's claim, therefore, that 1917 saw the triumph of class over nation cannot be accepted without qualification. When workers and soldiers backed the Bolsheviks in their bid to establish soviet power – and their firm support proved brief – they did so because they believed that therein lay the salvation of Russia.

The May Thirtieth Movement of 1925 saw Shanghai's workers move to the fore of the nationalist movement, a position they would maintain for the next two years but would never subsequently regain. The shooting by British police of workers and students demonstrating in the International Settlement on 30 May 1925 left twelve dead and seventeen wounded. The incident provoked a second 'triple strike' in which students embargoed classes, traders shut down stores and workers walked off the job on a scale never seen before. One reliable estimate suggests that 206 industrial stoppages took place to protest the May Thirtieth Incident, involving 201,978 workers.[109] By 28 July 1925, the Shanghai General Labour Union (GLU), created by the CCP, claimed to have 117 affiliated unions with 218,859 members, though the number of union members fell from autumn 1925, owing mainly to repression by the militarists who controlled the Chinese areas of the city.[110] The explosion of mass labour unions introduced a dynamic element into the national revolution and hugely strengthened a rendition of national identity that aligned the fate of the nation to the struggles of its workers and peasants. The GLU convinced tens of thousands of workers that through organization and militant defence of their class interests they could rid China of the imperialists and their 'running dogs'. By standing up to the British and Japanese in a punishing three-month strike, Shanghai's workers had, it averred, upheld the nation's 'face'. With the onset of the Northern Expedition by the National Revolutionary Army of Chiang Kai-shek in July 1926, peasant and worker movements swept through southern and central China. In Shanghai the first months of 1927 saw a spectacular revival of strikes and unionization. According to probably exaggerated figures of the Shanghai GLU, between January and March the number of labour unions increased from 187 to 502, and membership rose from 79,956 to 821,280.[111] When the National

---

[109] *Wusa yundong shiliao* [Historical Materials on the May Thirtieth Movement], vol. 2 (Shanghai: Shanghai renmin chubanshe, 1986), pp. 70–83. Many estimates put the figure closer to 150,000, but these ignore workers in the traditional sector.

[110] *Shenbao*, 6 August 1925, p. 13. This is probably too high, since the figures for membership in individual factories sometimes exceed the number of workers employed there.

[111] *Shanghai zonggonghui baogao* [Report on the Shanghai General Labour Union] (Shanghai, 1927), p. 13.

Revolutionary Army entered Shanghai on 22 March, armed pickets of the GLU had already defeated the Zhili-Shandong warlord troops and taken over the city.

During 1925–7, the CCP in Shanghai very effectively forged a discursive link between labour and the nation by playing on the sense that Chinese – whether workers exploited by foreign capitalists or citizens under semi-colonial rule – had been stripped of their dignity. Such 'class-inflected anti-imperialism' is well illustrated by the strike that took place in the Japanese cotton mills in February 1925. In their manifesto the strikers proclaimed:

China is being insulted by Japan in every way. We are workers in the Japanese cotton mills and our sufferings are indescribable. The opening of cotton mills in China by Japanese is a trespass on our national rights. China has not yet been annexed by Japan, but they already treat us worse than slaves. Our people employed in their mills suffer worse than the devils in hell. They work twelve hours a day, yet the Japanese foremen beat them with their fists and sticks ... Japanese capitalists treat Chinese labourers like cattle and horses ... Save us, and so save yourselves! Rise and fight for the prestige of China![112]

Labour unions justified themselves by claiming to mobilize the nation to fight imperialism as well as to defend the interests of workers. The Shanghai cotton workers' union defined its aims as being 'to concentrate our forces, to resist imperialist oppression, to struggle for the sovereignty of the nation (*minzu*) and to seek the emancipation of the working class'.[113] The bulk of labour protest in this period was targeted at foreign companies. Chinese who cooperated with foreigners were seen as no better than 'foreign slaves' (*yangnu*) or 'running dogs' (*zougou*). A 'running dog' could be anyone from a warlord, a compradore, a police spy to a factory foremen, the term implying that the behaviour of such collaborators put them on a par with beasts. Chinese who worked as lower-level supervisors in foreign enterprises were particularly likely to attract such odium. Charges of 'bullying others on the strength of one's powerful connections' (*zhang shi qi ren*) and of being 'foxes borrowing the tiger's terror' (*hu jia hu wei*) were widely levelled. Moreover, as lackeys of foreigners, such foremen were seen not only as agents of capital but also as *hanjian*, i.e. 'Han' or 'national' traitors, a particularly pejorative term that had originated in the Ming dynasty and that in the late 1930s came to be used widely to denigrate Chinese political leaders

---

[112] Ma Chaojun, *Zhongguo laogong yundong*, p. 374.
[113] *Gongren zhi lu*, 20 September 1925, p. 4.

who collaborated with the Japanese.[114] Like other such terms, these insults switched easily between the registers of nationalism and class: thus during the Hong Kong–Guangzhou strike-boycott of 1925–6, the labour press published the names of strike breakers in a column headed 'list of national traitors' (*hanjian lu*), yet referred to them interchangeably as 'labour brigands' (*gongzei*).[115]

It is a moot point how far 'class-inflected anti-imperialism' generated class consciousness if we understand this to mean a firm and fixed antagonism towards capital in general. Chinese workers may have regarded foreign employers as 'tigers' and 'devils', but it is less clear that they viewed Chinese employers in the same way for the reasons outlined above. In addition, although the GMD and the CCP supported workers in their struggle to better their condition and to liberate the nation from foreign control, they invoked very different conceptions of the wider social order. The CCP saw Chinese society in class terms: all capitalists, whether foreign or Chinese, were the workers' enemy, although 'national capitalists', i.e. Chinese entrepreneurs without links to foreign capital, constituted a partial exception in the short-term, since they were destined to play a limited progressive role in the anti-imperialist struggle. By contrast, the GMD, while conceding that capital must be restricted, vigorously reprehended class conflict in the Chinese-owned sector.[116] The influence of GMD ideology, along with the deeper cultural barriers to class antagonism outlined above, were reasons why Chinese-owned firms were less badly affected by industrial unrest than their foreign rivals during the national revolution.

Yet even if Chinese firms were relatively less strike-prone than their foreign competitors, many did succumb to bitter disputes in this period. In 1926, 165 enterprises in Shanghai were hit by strikes (some more than once), of which no fewer than 121 were owned by Chinese, as opposed to 24 by Japanese, 13 by British and 7 by other nationalities.[117] Workers showed few inhibitions in taking militant action against Chinese employers. In 1926, for example, 200 wooden-trunk makers in the Chinese city stayed out on strike for eighty days.[118] For their part, Chinese employers showed few inhibitions in crushing labour unrest.

---

[114] *Zhongguo Gongren*, November 1924, p. 55; Sherman Cochran and Andrew C. K. Hsieh with Janis Cochran, *One Day in China, May 21 1936*, (New Haven: Yale University Press, 1983), p. 204.
[115] *Gongren zhi lu*, 17 July 1925.
[116] *Zhongguo Guomindang diyi, erci quanguo daibiao dahui*, pp. 121–2.
[117] H. G. W. Woodhead (ed.), *China Year Book, 1928* (Tientsin: North China Daily News and Herald, 1928), p. 957.
[118] *North China Herald*, 17 July 1926, p. 111.

In March 1927, the Shenxin mill imposed a lockout for 45 days after workers beat up a foreman and threatened a deputy manager.[119] Occasionally, workers in Chinese-owned enterprises deployed a robust language of class when talking about their bosses. The ready-made clothing workers, having listed their sufferings, declared: 'The masters (*yezhu*) do not understand; and at a time when the cost of living is soaring, they continue to increase their profits regardless and to intensify exploitation. How can we workers endure this? Workers of all kinds are now organizing in their own interest to resist the aggressor class (*qinlüe jieji*).'[120] Generally, however, the many workers who took militant action against Chinese employers did not see them straightforwardly as the 'aggressor class'.

What we see in this period is an unstable compound of growing class antagonism tempered by still resilient Confucian norms of reciprocity. This made for deep ambivalence on the part of Chinese workers towards Chinese employers. Workers, for example, were quite willing to accept the mediation of the General Chamber of Commerce, the employers' organization, in industrial disputes, something that would have been unimaginable in St Petersburg. Yu Xiaqing, in particular, Shanghai's leading businessman, came to the rescue of strikers on several occasions, by bringing about a face-saving settlement in disputes affecting both Chinese-owned and foreign-owned companies. Workers may have felt uneasy mistrust towards business leaders but this was tempered by an acceptance that they had inherited the Confucian responsibility of elites to achieve social harmony. More significantly, ambivalence towards employers sprang from the fact that class polarization was overdetermined by the struggle for national liberation (in a way that was never true of Russia). The General Chamber of Commerce, for example, had helped to bankroll the May Thirtieth general strike, in the belief that it would force the foreign powers to negotiate restoration of Chinese sovereignty and squeeze foreign business rivals. In the event, this dramatic expression of business support for workers was a one-off occurrence, but it helped sustain the view – dinned into the ears of the populace by the GMD – that workers and employers had a common, overriding interest in ridding the country of foreign aggressors and that differences of class interest were secondary to that end. In this period, then, workers' perceptions of the social order were changing, but outbursts of anger against Chinese employers were still more likely to be

---

[119] *Zhongguo gongren yundong shiliao* [Historical Materials on the Chinese Labour Movement], 2 (1958), 123.
[120] *Shenbao*, 23 March 1927.

passing moods than expressions of an entrenched perception of the social order as indelibly riven by class division.

On 12 April 1927, Chiang struck a devastating blow at the CCP, thereby bringing the phase of 'national revolution' to an end. The party's influence in Shanghai was not snuffed out immediately. Between 1928 and 1930, against a background of strikes fuelled by soaring inflation, the GLU just managed to retain a base in sectors at the Commercial Press, in the post office and the textile mills, while reformist elements of the GMD created seven or eight unions that supported workers' efforts to maintain their living standards within the officially approved framework of corporatism.[121] Had economic conditions been more favourable, it is possible that GMD corporatism of a mildly reformist hue might have proved successful. In Shanghai a few companies experimented with welfare schemes, centred on housing and medical provision, but these did not prove sufficient to compensate for the severe downward pressure on wages. Some factory owners made half-hearted efforts to promote the ideal of the 'factory community' through slogans and songs. At the Yong'an mill, the 'Yong'an spirit' was captured in the motto: 'Be of One Mind, Unite in Cooperation. Keep Watch, Help and Defend One Another, Never Let the Small Self Forget the Big Self.' At the Kangyuan glass-jar factory the company song exhorted: 'Actively Strive for the Superiority of National Produce. Struggle to be Hardworking and Thrifty and Oppose Foreign Produce.'[122] But this failed to achieve the cooperation between labour and capital that the GMD hoped to see.

The exhortation of the Meiya silk-weaving company to its employees to 'Fulfil the Needs of Society and Follow the Will of the People' did not prevent a bruising 51-day strike by 4,500 workers in 1934. This exploded after French Concession police fired on workers, killing one and injuring dozens more.[123] The strikers put out a statement: 'General Manager Cai Shengbai doesn't understand the meaning of cooperation between labour and management; he only knows how to increase company profits. He uses every possible scheme to exploit the

---

[121] Alain Roux, *Grèves et politique à Shanghai: les désillusions, 1927–32* (Paris: Éditions de l'École des Hautes Études en Sciences Sociales, 1995), ch. 9.

[122] Xin Ping, *Cong Shanghai faxian lishi: xiandaihua, jinchengzhong de Shanghai ren ji qi shehui shenghuo, 1927–37* [Discovering History from Shanghai: Modernization, Urban Shanghainese and their Social Life, 1927–37] (Shanghai: Shanghai renmin chubanshe, 1996), pp. 122–3.

[123] For accounts of the strike, see Elizabeth J. Perry, *Shanghai on Strike: The Politics of Chinese Labor* (Stanford: Stanford University Press, 1993), pp. 188–201; Edward Roy Hammond, 'Organized Labor in Shanghai, 1927–37', University of California, Berkeley, PhD, 1978, pp. 213–231.

workers ... We will not rest until we have expelled this violent, senseless capitalist running dog.'[124] Notwithstanding the virulence of the language, it is noteworthy that the strikers invoked the notion of cooperation between labour and capital as well as the notion of class exploitation. This may have been a conscious tactic, but the fact that the strikers bore placards of Sun Yat-sen in their demonstrations suggests they believed that class cooperation in the interests of national economic development was desirable in principle. The bitterness of the dispute, however, reminds us that the elements of class identity that had emerged in 1925–7 had not gone away, and Chinese employers continued to be extremely nervous about the possible resurgence of Communist influence among their employees. At the Shenxin No. 9 mill, for example, 'manifesting dangerous thoughts or behaviour' was an offence that warranted instant dismissal.[125]

In 1931–2, the reformist labour unions of the GMD were suppressed when Chiang Kai-shek launched a 'white terror' against remnants of the CCP in the city. The CC Clique, whose base was in the security organs and organization department of the GMD, in cahoots with the Green Gang, set up state-controlled unions whose principal function was to guarantee labour quiescence. By the mid-1930s, members of the Green Gang occupied all five seats on the standing committee of the remodelled General Labour Union (*Zonggonghui*) and headed three or four departments of the Bureau of Social Affairs.[126] The labour movement was emasculated not only by political repression, but also by the dire economic situation. The onset of the Depression led to spiralling unemployment, and by late 1935 it was estimated that one-third of the city's population was without work.[127] Unsurprisingly, the number of strikes fell sharply, although they remained at a higher level than before 1925.[128]

If class-inflected anti-imperialist nationalism went into decline during the Nanjing decade, working-class concern for the nation grew exponentially. Following the Japanese invasion of Manchuria on 18 September 1931, Chiang Kai-shek opted to delay resistance in order to concentrate on eliminating Communists and regional militarists and

---

[124] Perry, *Shanghai on Strike*, p. 193.
[125] Zhu Bangxing, Hu Linge and Xu Sheng, *Shanghai chanye yu Shanghai zhigong* [Shanghai Industry and Shanghai Labour] (Shanghai: Shanghai renmin chubanshe, 1984; orig. 1939), p. 71.
[126] Brian G. Martin, *The Shanghai Green Gang: Politics and Organized Crime, 1919–1937* (Berkeley: University of California Press, 1996), p. 170.
[127] Hammond, 'Organized Labor', p. 231.   [128] Hammond, 'Organized Labor', p. 214.

on building up his armed forces. This policy of 'pacification before resistance' proved hugely unpopular with the Shanghai public. On 24 September 1931, nearly 30,000 workers in the city's Japanese factories went on strike in protest at the invasion. The following month, workers and Japanese marines became embroiled in violent clashes. The Shaoxing seven-county tongxianghui exhorted men to shave their heads and women to cut their hair above the forehead to remind the public that China was in the same trouble as their heads (*guo nan dang tou*).[129] On 28 January 1932, another bloody confrontation proved to be the prelude to the so-called 'undeclared war', which was to lead to the loss of between 10,000 and 20,000 civilian lives in Shanghai.[130] On 31 January, 40,000 workers at the Japanese mills struck 'to guarantee our subsistence and our lives and to save the independence and freedom of the Chinese nation'.[131] Amid fierce fighting, the stoppage ended in defeat, its chances not helped by calls from the CCP for workers to arm and form a soviet.[132]

It was almost four years before nationalist sentiment found vigorous organized expression again. Only in December 1935 did the national salvation movement re-emerge in the city, after students in Beijing and Tianjin took to the streets to protest Japan's extension of its control into the northern provinces of Hebei and Chahaer.[133] Through spring 1936, patriotic associations sprang up despite the imposition of emergency powers, which the CCP endeavoured to use as a base from which to rebuild its influence.[134] Following an incident on 23 September, in which four Japanese sailors came under fire, the Japanese navy demanded that the Nanjing government crush the protests. The management caved in following a violent incident at the Toyoda mill on 17 November, which led to a strike by 45,000 workers in twenty-six Japanese mills. The 'seven gentlemen' deemed to be leaders of the national salvation movement were arrested, and were awaiting trial when full-scale war broke out in July 1937.[135]

---

[129] 'Yu Futian's proposal to boycott Japanese products in the event of a Japanese invasion of China' (1931), Shanghai Municipal Archive: Q 117-5-44.

[130] Parks Coble, *Facing Japan: Chinese Politics and Japanese Imperialism, 1931–37* (Cambridge MA: Harvard University Press, 1991), pp. 35, 39.

[131] Zou Pei and Liu Zhen (eds.), *Zhongguo gongren yundong shihua* [History of the Chinese Labour Movement], vol. 3 (five volumes) (Beijing: Zhongguo gongren chubanshe 1993), pp. 239–40.

[132] Zou Pei and Liu Zhen, *Zhongguo gongren*, vol. 3, pp. 241, 335.

[133] Coble, *Facing Japan*, p. 285.

[134] Patricia Stranahan, *Underground: The Shanghai Underground and the Politics of Survival, 1927–37* (Lanham MD: Rowman and Littlefield, 1998).

[135] Coble, *Facing Japan*, p. 388; Zou Pei and Liu Zhen, *Zhongguo gongren*, vol. 3, pp. 388–9.

The outbreak of the Sino-Japanese war drastically transformed the balance of forces within the city, with labour politics now galvanized by the conflict between pro-resistance and pro-collaboration forces. Between 13 August and late November 1937, the city endured what proved to be the biggest battle of the entire war, with a loss of nearly 200,000 lives.[136] The Nationalist government retreated first into central and then into south-east China, taking much of Shanghai's heavy industry with it. By the end of 1942, the number of enterprises in the city had fallen to one-third of the 1937 level and the number of workers to one-half.[137] On 5 December 1937, the Special Service Department of the Japanese army set up the first of a series of collaborationist administrations that ran the Chinese areas of the city until 8 December 1941 when the Japanese extended their control into the two foreign settlements. During this 'lonely island' phase, unions loyal to Chiang's government – those that had been under the control of the CC Clique – went into the underground, forming clandestine units to attack collaborators; but in winter 1939 they were wiped out by the Japanese.[138] In this period, the collaborationist Workers' Common Progress Association (*Gongyun xiejinhui*) launched a series of crippling strikes against western-owned enterprises in the International Settlement and the French Concession.[139] Meanwhile, many workers assisted the Communist New Fourth Army by providing medical services – notably, the Ningbo coal traders' 500-strong ambulance brigade – aid to refugees, gifts to soldiers, and skilled labour and equipment.[140] In March 1940, Wang Jingwei, former leader of the left wing of the GMD, was appointed head of a 'national' government based in Nanjing. In December 1941, following the attack on Pearl Harbor, the Japanese took over the foreign settlements and installed a pro-Wang administration in Shanghai. Communists and secret-society bosses now cooperated in seeking to subvert pro-Japanese unions.[141] The CCP's paramount concern, however, was

---

[136] Christian Henriot and Wen-hsin Yeh (eds.), *In the Shadow of the Rising Sun: Shanghai under Japanese Occupation* (Cambridge: Cambridge University Press, 2004), p. xi.

[137] C. Henriot, 'Shanghai Industries under Japanese Occupation: Bombs, Boom, and Bust (1937–45)', in Henriot and Wen-hsin Yeh (eds.), *In the Shadow*, pp. 20, 38.

[138] Gregor Benton, *New Fourth Army: Communist Resistance along the Yangtze and the Huai* (Richmond: Curzon Press, 1999), p. 62; Alain Roux, 'From Revenge to Treason: Political Ambivalence among Wang Jingwei's Labor Union Supporters', in Henriot and Wen-hsin Yeh (eds.), *In the Shadow of the Rising Sun*, pp. 209–228.

[139] Perry, *Shanghai on Strike*, p. 114; Zou Pei and Liu Zhen (eds.), *Zhongguo gongren yundong shihua*, vol. 4 (five volumes) (Beijing: Zhongguo gongren chubanshe 1993), p. 321. Benton, *New Fourth Army*, p. 62.

[140] Zou Pei and Liu Zhen (eds.), *Zhongguo gongren*, vol. 4, pp. 305–9; Benton, *New Fourth Army*, pp. 235–8.

[141] Perry, *Shanghai on Strike*, p. 109.

to build and protect its underground organizations, and by 1945 it had re-established an organization of 2,000 in the city and claimed to have set up 300 labour union cells.[142]

In August 1945 the war came to an end. With the foreign powers finally departed, class identities came to the fore for the first time in the history of the Shanghai labour movement.[143] The CCP had been readying itself for the moment of victory by planning a series of workers' uprisings in the major cities. In Shanghai the New Fourth Army helped train a workers' underground army, although by August it still had only 260 workers with forty rifles and pistols and three machine guns. However, it claimed to have influence over 100,000 workers, mainly public-utility workers and workers laid off by the closure of the Japanese cotton mills. On 23 August 1945, the uprising began when 7,000 workers seized the Xinyi iron works in west Shanghai, which had been a key supplier of the Japanese army. Later the same day, however, the central party organs called off the uprising, along with a plan for the New Fourth Army to occupy Shanghai, after Moscow insisted that the CCP pursue negotiations with the GMD for the formation of a coalition government.[144] The onset of civil war between the GMD and the CCP in mid-1946, accompanied as it was by a rapidly worsening economic situation, fuelled a revival of labour militancy. The Nationalist government maintained a state of emergency, refusing to recognize unions, prohibiting strikes, and enforcing compulsory arbitration of labour conflict, yet weakened by factional struggles and powerless to get to grips with the terrifying economic situation, it proved unable to impose the repressive control over labour it had enjoyed in the 1930s.[145] As prices soared and unemployment rocketed, the number of disputes (*zhengyi*) in Shanghai reached 2,538 by 1947 and labour unions partially re-established themselves in spite of the GMD clampdown.[146] Foreign businesses were no longer dominant in the city, so almost all the strikes were targeted at Chinese entrepreneurs. Many had relocated to the

[142] Perry, *Shanghai on Strike*, p. 117; Zou Pei and Liu Zhen (eds.), *Zhongguo gongren yundong shihua*, vol. 5 (five volumes) (Beijing: Zhongguo gongren chubanshe 1993), p. 7.

[143] Emily Honig, *Sisters and Strangers, Women in the Shanghai Cotton Mill, 1919–49*, (Stanford: Stanford University Press, 1986), pp. 245–9. In his fine book on the Chongqing arsenals, Joshua Howard shows that even during the war, when the fate of the nation hung in the balance, workers showed little hesitation in making claims on the state officials who ran the arsenals. Joshua Howard, *Workers at War: Labour in China's Arsenals, 1937–1953* (Stanford: Stanford University Press, 2004).

[144] Zou Pei and Liu Zhen, *Zhongguo gongren*, vol. 4, pp. 342–9.

[145] Israel Epstein, *Notes on Labor Problems in Nationalist China* (New York: Institute of Pacific Relations, 1949), p. 116.

[146] Mark W. Frazier, *The Making of the Chinese Industrial Workplace: State, Revolution and Labour Management* (Cambridge: Cambridge University Press, 2002), p. 84.

International Settlement after 1937 and collaborated with the pro-Japanese administration after December 1941. Few had done so with enthusiasm, but few had acted with heroism, and many had made fat profits.[147] This increased the persuasiveness in the eyes of many workers of the CCP rhetoric of class. The party meanwhile steadily expanded its clandestine networks, continuing to exploit its ties with the secret societies; by late 1946, it claimed, perhaps exaggeratedly, to control 324 labour unions in the city with a membership of over 280,000.[148]

It is clear that more radical elements in the CCP expected that the overthrow of the GMD in Shanghai would come about through a workers' uprising backed by the People's Liberation Army. The 'new democratic' perspective of the CCP, however, ruled out any frontal clash between labour and capital. In April 1945, the Seventh Congress of the CCP pledged to work for root-and-branch improvements in workers' conditions and, at the same time, to protect the interests of entrepreneurs, including maintenance of an appropriate level of profit. In August 1948, the Sixth All-China Labour Congress re-jigged the old GMD slogan of cooperation between labour and capital (*lao zi hezuo*) into one of 'mutual benefits for labour and capital' (*lao zi liangli*). Meanwhile, party leaders in Shanghai rebuked their labour and student committees for cleaving to an insurrectionist strategy, insisting that this was impractical given the strength of the GMD military in the city. Activists were ordered to concentrate instead on protecting factories, public utilities, schools and offices against the retreating GMD army.[149] By the time the People's Liberation Army entered Shanghai in May 1949, some 60,000 people, including more than 20,000 workers, were involved in protection teams in factories, schools and offices.[150] Ironically, however, in spite of the CCP's continuing propaganda claim that the proletariat was the leading force in the new democratic bloc, its actual role in the transfer of power was minimal. Nevertheless, contemporaries noted a 'feeling of emancipation' (*fanshen gan*) in the ranks of labour, and in the year following the takeover, workers in Shanghai's private factories were involved in 3,939 disputes, the highest number ever recorded in a single year.[151]

---

[147] Parks M. Coble, 'Chinese Capitalists and the Japanese: Collaboration and Resistance in the Shanghai Area, 1937–45', in Wen-hsin Yeh (ed.), *Wartime Shanghai* (London: Routledge, 1998), pp. 62–85.

[148] Perry, *Shanghai on Strike*, p. 122.

[149] Zou Pei and Liu Zhen, *Zhongguo gongren*, vol. 5, p. 154.

[150] Yu Jin, *Shanghai 1949: da bengkui* [Shanghai 1949: The Great Collapse], vol. 2 (Beijing: Jiefang jun chubanshe, 1993), pp. 955–8.

[151] Frazier, *Making*, p. 101; Alun Falconer, *New China: Friend or Foe?* (London: Naldrett Press, 1950), p. 96.

Conclusion

Class relationships were less polarized in China than in Russia. National identity proved to be the driving force of much labour protest in a way that was never true of Russia. At the same time, I have argued that even in the Chinese-owned sector, not to speak of the foreign sector, industrial relations were more vulnerable to class-based protest than the historiography has recognized. The paradox was that through radical anti-imperialism the CCP succeeded in promoting class identity. The high point of this development came early, in the form of what I have called 'class-inflected anti-imperialism', namely, during the national revolution of 1925–7, when the brunt of worker protest was targeted at Japanese- and British-owned companies in Shanghai. For most of the 1930s, worker protest was either strictly economic in nature or more narrowly nationalist in targeting Japanese firms. Yet despite the energetic efforts of the Nationalist government to extirpate class politics from the labour movement, it is likely that more and more workers acquired a class identity in the course of the 1930s and 1940s, even if this was never the fixed, hegemonic identity of Communist myth. From the silk women's strike of August 1911, examined in chapter 3, through to 1949, Chinese employers were the target of the majority of strikes, for the simple reason that they constituted the majority of employers in Shanghai. After 1945, with foreign companies a shadow of their former selves, Chinese employers, along with the GMD government, became the target of worker antipathy as inflation ran rampant. By that stage, elements of social deference and shared moral norms that had once inflected industrial relations in the 1920s were becoming obsolete. Typical of the more abrasive mode of industrial conflict was the four-day occupation of the Shenxin No. 9 mill by 6,000 women and 1,000 men on 30 January 1948, in pursuit of coal and rice rations, maternity leave and child care facilities, which left 3 women dead and over 100 injured, 40 of them seriously.[152]

In the many discussions that have taken place about the 'Russian idea' since the collapse of Communism it is regularly suggested that national identity was always weak in Russia and that class identity compensated for this. The chapter has qualified that thesis. Certainly, national identity was only beginning to emerge in the populace by the time that war broke out in 1914 and class politics dominated the revolutionary landscape in 1917. However, I have argued that national and class identities were as often mutually reinforcing as mutually counterposed. The stark antithesis between a politics of class and a politics of nation

---

[152] Honig, *Sisters*, pp. 234–43; Zou Pei and Liu Zhen, *Zhongguo gongren*, vol. 5, pp. 91–8.

that characterized 1917 was much more a conjunctural phenomenon than an expression of the deep structure of Russian political culture. This is not to deny that class politics had deep roots in the gulf between 'them' and 'us' that was so noticeable in the post-emancipation era, but it was principally the unequal privations of the First World War that caused nascent national identity to separate from class identity. Yet even in the eight months between February and October 1917, national identity continued to be articulated with class identity in a number of combinations, class coming to 'triumph' (Struve's word), rather late in the day.

National identity is never monolithic, nor is it something that is achieved once and for all. In modern societies, different visions of the nation compete and, in part, are a stake in political struggle. In the words of Prasenjit Duara, the nation is an object of contestation as well as of loyalty.[153] Class has proved to be one of the important vectors through which national identity is contested and appropriated. Visions of the nation, moreover, are mutable, and significant shifts can take place in relatively short spaces of time, even if certain elements of national identity can prove enduring. Nowhere in the course of the twentieth century did class identity and national identity become mutually incompatible, as many socialists in the early part of the century had predicted. Russia was the country where that came closest to happening, but as we shall see in the next chapter, it did not take long for the Bolsheviks to begin to formulate new renditions of national identity that fed off idioms of class identity and working-class internationalism. From the vantage point of the twenty-first century, the hegemony of class politics in Russia looks to have been relatively short-lived – thirty years at most – whereas a 'mass sense of national identity' grew from the late 1930s to the early 1950s.[154]

---

[153] Prasenjit Duara, 'Deconstructing the Chinese Nation', in J. Unger (ed.), *Chinese Nationalism* (Armonk, NY: M. E. Sharpe, 1996), p. 44.

[154] Brandenberger, *National Bolshevism*, p. 2.

5   Workers and Communist Revolution

Revolutions in the Chinese phrase 'turn heaven and earth upside down' (*tianfan difu*). They are moments of rupture that release fresh energies and set in train all manner of new developments. Yet the course of revolutionary regimes is also powerfully constrained by the legacies of the past. In the preceding four chapters it has been argued that in the decades leading up to the Communist revolutions in Russia and China, the onset of capitalist modernity led to migrants undergoing complex transformations of social identities as they mutated into urban workers, some of which proved compatible with the Communist project, others of which did not. The purpose of this chapter is to explore some of the positive and negative relationships between these pre-revolutionary transformations of social identity and the subsequent evolution of Communist regimes (looking, chronologically, at the period up to 1941, the onset of the Second World War, in the case of the Soviet Union, and up to 1976, the end of the Mao era, in the case of the PRC). It is not intended to provide a comprehensive discussion of the fate of workers under Communism, still less a synoptic account of the development of Communist societies; nor is it intended to suggest that pre-revolutionary transformations in workers' social identities were a major factor determining the course of post-revolutionary regimes. Unquestionably, that course was shaped far more by the ideology and practices of the Communist regimes themselves and by the domestic and international circumstances in which they found themselves than by the identities and ideals of the working classes they claimed to represent. Not least of the reasons why the self-understandings and aspirations of workers had so little bearing on the evolution of Communist regimes is that labour movements were rather rapidly demobilized once the overthrow of the old regimes had been achieved: in Russia this took place from early in 1918, as a consequence of economic collapse and civil war; in China it took place no later than 1953, when experiments in 'democratic management' were supplanted by a state-controlled type of industrial corporatism. The chapter begins by comparing the role played by workers in bringing Communist regimes to power.

It is often said that the Chinese Revolution was a peasant revolution and the Russian Revolution a proletarian revolution. This can be maintained only with the most stringent qualifications. If we look at China, it is clear that the rise to power of the CCP rested more on building coalitions of diverse social constituencies than on mobilizing peasants per se. There proved to be no natural affinity between the CCP and the peasantry, much depending on the ability of local Communists to persuade peasants that they could provide the best defence against Japanese brutality, Guomindang (GMD) retaliation, local militarists or bandits. Once protected, peasants could be mobilized through party-led campaigns for tax relief, rent reduction, increased production or, in the latter stage of the civil war, for land reform.[1] The tactics of the Communists were flexible and varied a good deal according to local circumstances. In his seminal work on the New Fourth Army, Gregor Benton shows how those Communists left behind in the mountains of the south following the Long March to the north-west in March 1934 relied much less on peasant mobilization than their confrères in the new base at Yan'an. These guerrillas, who went on to form the New Fourth Army, survived by allying with 'gang leaders, baojia [the household mutual responsibility system] chiefs, daoist wizards and magic soldiers'.[2] In 1937, following the signing of the second united front, they descended from the mountains to the densely populated lower Yangtze plain where they opted to build alliances with local notables rather than to organize the peasantry. By 1945, the New Fourth Army held sway over areas of central China with a population of 34 million; but in Benton's words, class struggle 'did not well up from below, as a precondition for their triumph, but was whipped up from above, after they had achieved power by co-opting and reorganizing the groups and networks that honeycombed rural China'.[3] By 1945, the CCP nationally had established nineteen base areas, stretching in an arc across north China and south along the east coast, and the alliances and tactics applied in these bases varied according to local ecology, the relative influence of different social and cultural elites, and the particular needs and grievances of the peasantry. In general, the extent of peasant mobilization reflected not the depth of peasant grievances, acute though these were, but the extent of military and political control exercised by the CCP and the particular balance of social and political forces in the local area.

---

[1] Lucien Bianco (with the collaboration of Hua Chang-Ming), *Jacqueries et révolution dans la China du XXe siècle* (Paris: Èditions de la Martinière, 2005), ch. 17.

[2] Gregor Benton, *New Fourth Army: Communist Resistance along the Yangtze and the Huai* (Richmond: Curzon Press, 1999), p. 708.

[3] Benton, *New Fourth Army*, pp. 729–30.

If the idea of the Chinese Revolution as a peasant revolution needs substantial revision, the idea of the Russian Revolution as a workers' revolution is more credible. As we have seen, the development of industry in St Petersburg spurred a rapid flow of peasants to the capital, which meant that peasants formed a sizeable section of the population and that there was a substantial peasant element in the wage-earning population. Nevertheless, in the capital the transformation of peasants into workers was rapid; and a broad alliance of proletarianized and semi-proletarianized layers, led by skilled 'conscious' workers and discursively constituted as 'the working class', played a major role in the revolution of 1917. By world standards, this was a working class whose level of organization and degree of political radicalization was altogether remarkable. Nevertheless, if the Bolsheviks won support from a majority of workers by the eve of October, they could not have seized power without the support of a radicalized army and peasantry. In the course of summer and autumn 1917, Bolsheviks and Left SRs, by promising an immediate end to the war, won support from war-weary soldiers. Indeed in many provincial towns where a working class was lacking, the Bolshevik seizure of power amounted to little more than the local garrison declaring its support for soviet power. Similarly, during the autumn and winter of 1917, peasants expropriated the landed gentry, carrying out an agrarian revolution that stretched the capacity of the Provisional Government to breaking point. Nevertheless, in spite of the contribution made by the soldiers and peasants, the Russian Revolution was essentially made in the cities, and it was the working class above all that made the greatest contribution to overthrowing the old order.

The capacity of the working class to shape the course of a revolution, however, is always a relational matter. In both Russia and China the impact of the labour movement was primarily determined by the larger balance of social and political forces within the revolutionary process and only secondarily by the intrinsic characteristics of the working class itself. First, it is unlikely that either country would have succumbed to a Communist revolution had not state structures and social relationships been profoundly destabilized by war. The First and Second World Wars, respectively, deprived the existing regimes of a monopoly of armed force. In Russia prior to 1914 the tsarist state had proved consistently stronger than those who would overthrow it by violence. After the February Revolution, however, the army proved useless as an instrument for maintaining internal order, and by the summer of 1917 was completely beyond the control of the Kerensky government. From 1916 to 1949, China faced almost continual warfare, and following the brutal rupture of the first united front in 1927, the CCP recognized that it could only break out of a situation in which social relations were heavily militarized by creating an army of its own. Chiang Kai-shek's government, particularly at local level, was seriously weakened during the war of resistance against Japan, which saw around 20 million military and civilian deaths between 1937 and 1945. As GMD officials and regular army units withdrew from the localities, rural elites and former warlord forces were left to contend for influence with the Communists and the Japanese. This allowed the Eighth Route Army and New Fourth Army to become instruments of revolution in a way that the Bolshevik Red Army never was, enabling the CCP to establish base areas and instil its ideology, values and discipline into the local populace.

Second, in both countries capitalists proved to be a weaker political force than the working class. In Russia the class of manufacturers and financiers was politically unassertive, deeply segmented by region and branch of industry and tied to the traditional merchant estate. It showed little desire to reform the authoritarian system of industrial relations prior to 1917 and little capacity to shape the political course of events following the February Revolution. In China the capitalist class was small and not sharply differentiated from traditional merchants and urban gentry. It faced a strong challenge from foreign capital in trade, banking and industry, yet seized the opportunities to promote native business created by the weakening of foreign competition during the First World War. In the 1920s, businessmen, still organized largely through regional guilds, exerted a degree of political clout, showing themselves to be both moderately nationalist and sympathetic to western modernity. Nevertheless, although opposed to foreign imperialism, they felt uneasy at the depth of popular radicalism. After 1927, businessmen cooperated with the Chiang Kai-shek in developing and managing the national economy but their political influence was severely curtailed by the GMD bureaucracy. That influence – at least in Shanghai – was further reduced by a widespread popular perception that they had put profit before honour by working with the pro-Japanese administration in the city during the war. The balance of force between capital and labour was probably more finely balanced in Shanghai than in St Petersburg, but the relative weakness of the employers in both cities was a factor that allowed workers to play a role in the revolutions out of proportion to their numbers. Finally, if the 'alliance between the proletariat and poor peasantry' was always an ideological figment, the fact that many workers were former peasants helped to promote political exchange between town and countryside, and the simultaneity of revolution in town and countryside was a further factor that strengthened the leverage of the working class during the revolutionary process, especially in Russia where it stretched the capacity of government to maintain order to breaking point.

In both countries the labour movement was a relatively recent creation – to a large extent, the product of the revolutionary situation itself – brought into being by activists whose primary loyalties were to their respective political parties. The labour movement in Russia was more experienced, better organized and more autonomous of the political parties than its counterpart in China, partly reflecting the fact that peasants had been in the process of transformation into proletarians for longer than in China. Following the February Revolution, workers were drawn into building a dense network of soviets, factory committees, trade unions, workers' militias and Red Guards, cultural and educational clubs. The soviets, in particular, succeeded for a brief time in establishing a form of direct democracy based on factories and barracks. Within these organizations, the socialist parties assumed a leadership role, but no one party was ever completely dominant, so there was a genuine element of political pluralism in 1917. In China, by contrast, the labour organizations which flourished in 1925 and again in spring 1927 were to a substantial degree creatures of the CCP, although behind the façade of party control these bodies were frequently colonized from within by secret-society bosses, labour contractors and foremen, who brought workers into the unions, but very much as their clients. The reformist and 'loyalist' unions created in the Nanjing decade were similarly colonized by GMD factions and the secret societies, articulated by networks of personalistic ties that lay beneath their apparently bureaucratic structures.

Strikes were the principal form of collective action through which workers made their presence felt in the public arena. The overwhelming majority of these were economic in nature, but in both St Petersburg and Shanghai the number of political strikes – illegal in both countries – was extremely high by the standards of other countries. Key political strikes in Russia included 1905, the strike precipitated by the massacre of workers in the Lena goldfields in 1912, and the strike that helped bring down the tsar in February 1917. Between February and October 1917, no fewer than 2.4 million workers went on strike in Russia.[4] In China, from the May Fourth Movement on, strikes became a weapon in the arsenal of the nationalist movement as a whole, and even purely economic strikes in foreign-owned enterprises would garner support from the patriotic public, especially students. Incidentally, the close

---

[4] Diane P. Koenker and William G. Rosenberg, *Strikes and Revolution in Russia, 1917* (Princeton: Princeton University Press, 1989), pp. 68, 4–5.

relationship between student and labour organizations in Shanghai, which continued right up to 1949, had no parallels in Russia after 1905, where the student movement drifted in a more nationalist direction after 1907. Strikebreaking was less common in St Petersburg than in Shanghai, and this is reflected in the fact that strike pickets were less common in the Russian capital. That said, the workers' militias and Red Guards that appeared in 1917 in Petrograd were far more elaborate and politicized organizations than the pickets that were formed in Shanghai in 1925 and 1927, even if they were not destined to play the major role in state-building they later played in Communist China.[5]

We saw in chapter 2 that for female peasants migration to St Petersburg and Shanghai signalled greater personal freedom but also greater insecurity, greater equality with men, but also new forms of subordination to them. These contradictory experiences seem to be refracted in the record of women's participation in the labour and revolutionary movements. If the immediate precipitant of the downfall of Nicholas II was a demonstration on 23 February 1917, International Women's Day, by thousands of female textile workers and housewives, women subsequently did not mobilize qua women to any great extent – in contrast to that other non-class category, 'youth'.[6] Insofar as women were mobilized, they were mobilized as workers. During 1917 women participated in strikes and joined trade unions: in the food and textile industries of Petrograd, for example, where women comprised over two-thirds of the workforce, trade-union membership stood at 80% and 70%, respectively.[7] Nevertheless, women were poorly represented in leadership positions within both the socialist parties and working-class organizations. Paradoxically, although they were almost certainly politically more active than they had ever been, their relative quiescence vis-à-vis men served to entrench in Bolshevik political culture an image of women as

---

[5] Koenker and Rosenberg, *Strikes*, p. 209; Elizabeth J. Perry, *Patrolling the Revolution: Worker Militias, Citizenship, and the Modern Chinese State* (Lanham MD: Rowman and Littlefield, 2006).

[6] In 1917 organized feminism largely failed to overcome working women's suspicions, not least because of many feminists' support for the war. The general attitude was encapsulated by a woman worker who addressed a demonstration organized by the League of Women's Rights on 19 March 1917 to demand women's suffrage, which was attended by 3,500 women: 'We part company with the women of the bourgeois classes (stormy protests, cries of "Enough! Now is not the time for disunity!", followed by shouts of "True!" "Correct!"). We have no special women's interests. Our interests are the same as those of male workers.' *Rabochaia Gazeta*, 21 March 1917, p. 3; *Izvestiia*, 21 March 1917. Richard Stites, *Women's Liberation Movement in Russia: Feminism, Nihilism and Bolshevism* (Princeton: Princeton University Press, 1978), pp. 306–7.

[7] S. A. Smith, *Red Petrograd: Revolution in the Factories* (Cambridge: Cambridge University Press, 1983), p. 194.

politically 'backward'. In Shanghai, too, women were not reluctant to join labour unions during the national revolution (1925–7) – union membership carrying a patriotic as well as a class resonance – yet they remained poorly represented in leadership positions. In spite of the fact that up to three-quarters of the cotton workforce was female, most cotton unions were chaired by men. This was replicated in other sectors: in August 1925, out of 114 chairs of affiliated labour unions, only 14 can be positively identified as female.[8] The CCP regularly castigated the General Labour Union for paying insufficient attention to the needs of women workers. In May 1926, its labour department called on union executives to set up women's committees and to train women for positions of responsibility. It also reminded CCP members that they had an obligation to promote women's equality within the working class and to fight male chauvinism.[9] The frequency of the party's subsequent complaints on this score, however, suggests that these measures were never effectively implemented. On balance, the Chinese labour movement was more sensitive to the needs of women workers than its Russian counterpart, and the assumption was not as entrenched in the CCP as it was in the Bolshevik party that women were intrinsically 'backward'.

Notwithstanding deep party divisions, the labour movement in Russia was far more unified and more democratic than its Chinese counterpart. Apart from a brief flirtation with police unionism in 1901–3, there was never any systematic effort to establish non-socialist trade unions in Russia such as existed in Germany or the USA. The various socialist parties operated within unified labour organizations – only briefly did the Bolsheviks break this rule by setting up 'red' unions among railway workers and printers after 1918 in order to break the dominance of Mensheviks – and competition between political parties helped to foster autonomous labour activity. That said, there were always 'workerist' elements who resented the dominance of the socialist parties in the labour movement, who accused leaders of using labour organizations for their factional ends. Yet until police repression made it impossible, the trade unions that came into flickering existence after 1907 did strive to ensure that conferences and democratic election of officials took place. And in 1917, competition between political parties ensured that soviets, trade unions and factory committees forged a healthy – if short-lived – democratic culture. Nevertheless the general dependence

[8] S. A. Smith, *Like Cattle and Horses: Nationalism and Labor in Shanghai, 1895–1927* (Durham NC: Duke University Press, 2002), ch. 11; Tang Hai, *Zhongguo laodong wenti* [Chinese Labour Problems] (Shanghai: Guanghua shuju, 1926), pp. 511–20.
[9] Smith, *Like Cattle and Horses*, p. 231.

of labour organizations on party activists meant that once the Bolsheviks chose to oust their socialist opponents from leadership positions, soviets and trade unions were absorbed relatively easily into the state apparatus.

By contrast, labour unions in China were, to a large degree, extensions of political parties, factions and secret-society networks and this precluded their becoming organizations accountable to their members. At the same time, after 1927 no one party or faction succeeded in gaining control of what was a weak and fragmented labour movement. Communist activists could boast the longest record of labour organization in Shanghai by 1949, but though they were skilled in fomenting strikes and creating underground cells, they had little experience in building democratic labour organizations.

Violence was a more endemic feature of industrial relations in Shanghai than in St Petersburg, notwithstanding the Confucian exaltation of social harmony. In part, this was a function of the extreme militarization of social and political relations that beset China after 1916; in part, a function of competition between native-place and clientelist groupings for control of the labour market. It is true that the extent of violence in Russian industrial relations was underplayed by Soviet historians who glossed over the uglier sides of labour protest when compiling collections of documents.[10] Nevertheless, in 1905, as Abraham Ascher notes, what astonished contemporaries was the discipline not the disorderliness of workers.[11] This was despite the drunkenness that was rampant among St Petersburg workers, which had no counterpart among the workers of Shanghai. After the end of the nineteenth century, destruction of machinery and factory property during industrial disputes, for example, was rare in the Russian capital, whereas it continued in Shanghai into the 1930s. Indeed, it was sometimes encouraged by the Chinese Communists (something that was never true of their Bolshevik predecessors): in May 1932, for example, the CCP in Shanghai encouraged rickshaw pullers to destroy buses and trams owned by French and British companies.[12] Similarly, strike breakers and foremen in Shanghai were regularly beaten up, kidnapped and even murdered, again something that was relatively rare in Petrograd,

---

[10] The point is made by Daniel J. Brower, 'Labor Violence in Russia in the Late Nineteenth Century', *Slavic Review*, 41, 3 (1982), 417–31; Charters Wynn, *Workers, Strikes and Pogroms: The Donbass-Dnepr Bend in Late Imperial Russia* (Princeton: Princeton University Press, 1992).

[11] Abraham Ascher, *The Revolution of 1905: Russia in Disarray* (Stanford: Stanford University Press, 1988), p. 218.

[12] Zou Pei and Liu Zhen (eds.), *Zhongguo gongren yundong shihua* [History of the Chinese Labour Movement], vol. 3 (Beijing, Zhongguo gongren chubanshe, 1993), p. 244.

at least before the First World War produced a headlong collapse of civility and legality in public life.

Historians of Russia tend to accentuate political divisions within the working class – between workers who supported the SRs against the SDs, the Mensheviks against Bolsheviks. These divisions were indeed important, but they risk masking the fact that the vast majority of workers took it for granted that socialism in some form or another was the goal for which they were striving. Socialism achieved hegemony among workers in Russia to an extent that has few parallels elsewhere in the world in the twentieth century. In the November 1917 elections to the Constituent Assembly, 67.4% of the electorate of Petrograd cast their votes for a socialist party, and in the working-class district of Vyborg, 86.5% of the population voted for socialist parties (70% voting for the Bolsheviks).[13]

One might argue that this was paralleled in China by workers' strong support for the nationalist goals of eliminating warlordism, combating imperialism and, above all, resisting Japanese aggression in the 1930s. But divisions over what nationalism meant – over who could claim to speak for the nation – probably ran deeper than divisions in Russia over socialist strategy. Democratic elections never took place in China, so we shall never know the number of workers who supported the respective projects of the GMD, the CCP or of Wang Jingwei. There is evidence that by the 1930s 'conscious' workers in Shanghai had a fairly clear sense of the ideological issues at stake in the conflict between the GMD and the CCP, but it is doubtful that party-political consciousness was high among workers in general, at least prior to the civil war, when the Communists gained support from substantial numbers of workers. War and foreign occupation nevertheless proved to be a great politicizing force: 'even illiterate workers can be heard talking about Chamberlain and Hitler', a contemporary wrote.[14] One telling index of the difference in the level of politicization between workers in the two cities is that there was an almost total absence of political resolutions passed by worker gatherings in Shanghai in 1927 and 1949, whereas in Petrograd in 1917 these were a daily occurrence. Shanghai strikers, of course, drew up manifestoes, and demonstrators bore slogans, but the practice whereby workers listened to resolutions put by different political parties and then chose which one to endorse was entirely absent.

---

[13] O. N. Znamenskii, *Vserossiiskoe uchreditel'noe sobranie* (Leningrad: Nauka, 1976), appendix 1.
[14] Zhu Bangxing, Hu Linge and Xu Sheng, *Shanghai chanye yu Shanghai zhigong* [Shanghai Industry and Shanghai Labour] (Shanghai: Shanghai renmin chubanshe, 1984; orig. 1939), p. 663.

The Bolsheviks established their power in the localities through soviets, soldiers' committees, factory committees, and Red Guards. Numbering less than 350,000 in October 1917, the party initially had little option but to allow such independent organizations extensive leeway. Yet the same desperate problems of unemployment and lack of food and fuel that helped turn workers against the Provisional Government soon began to turn workers against the Bolsheviks. In the first half of 1918, some 100,000 to 150,000 workers across Russia took part in strikes, food riots and other protests, roughly on a par with labour unrest on the eve of the February Revolution.[15] In this context, the Bolsheviks struggled to concentrate authority in the hands of the party and state organs. Not all pressure to centralize power came from the top down: soviets, trades unions and factory committees in the localities quickly discovered that they lacked the wherewithal to get to grips with a shattered economy and a breakdown in social order and pressured central government to intervene. In spring 1918, worker discontent translated into a renewal of support for the Mensheviks and, to a lesser extent, the SRs, causing the Bolsheviks to cancel soviet elections and close down soviets that proved uncooperative, thus initiating the process whereby soviets and trade unions were turned into adjuncts of a one-party state. When the Whites seized leadership of the anti-Bolshevik movement in the latter months of 1918, however, most workers swung back in support of the government. During the civil war, labour unrest continued, principally in response to the government's inability to fulfil food rations. The Bolsheviks generally reacted by rushing in emergency supplies and by arresting the leaders of protest, who were often Mensheviks or Left SRs. Caught up in a life-and-death struggle for the very existence of the workers' state, however, they did not scruple when they deemed it necessary to deploy armed force to suppress strikes, to confiscate ration cards or even to dismiss strikers en masse and then rehire them selectively. The Bolsheviks expected the working class to speak with one voice – in favour of the regime – and when it didn't they, who had once excoriated the Mensheviks for their refusal to accept that a true proletariat existed in Russia, charged the working class with being no more than a mass of uprooted peasants with a thoroughly petty-bourgeois psychology.

Despite the tense standoff between Bolsheviks and workers during the civil war, the Bolsheviks never indulged in the kind of manipulation of

---

[15] D. O. Churakov, 'Dinamika rabochego protesta v SSSR i Rossiiskoi Federatsii (1917–2001 gody)', in A. V. Buzgalin, D. O. Churakov, P. Shul'tse (eds.), *Rabochii klass i rabochee dvizhenie Rossii: istoriia i sovremennost'* (Moscow: RIG-IZDAT, 2002), p. 65.

workers practised by the CCP. One admittedly extreme example occurred following the brutal suppression of the labour movement in 1927, when the party, now led by Qu Qiubai, was under the sway of what Maoists would later call the 'first left-opportunist line'. Despite the fact that the city was in the grip of GMD reaction, the CCP called on 9 November for a fourth workers' uprising in Shanghai, to be coordinated with a peasant uprising in Wuxi. The Jiangsu provincial committee seized on a stoppage at the Chinese-owned Hengfeng mill, where workers were on strike against a delay in wage payment, as the pretext for launching the uprising. The mill management, with the backing of Liu Wenxi, chief detective in the eastern district of the city, was holding firm against the strikers. The provincial committee sent a red terror squad to assassinate two of Liu's henchmen in the hope that this would trigger an uprising, but it had the unintended effect of persuading the management to negotiate with the strikers. In negotiations, Zhang Weijun, an activist at the mill and a secret Communist, achieved what amounted to a victory for the strikers, but the provincial committee was incensed that the strike had been resolved so quickly and demanded that it be resumed, even though the Hengfeng workers had been on strike for almost a month. They demanded, moreover, that it be spread to all the mills in the east of the city. At the Japanese mills marines ensured that workers continued to work normally, as they did at the British mills. At several Chinese-owned mills workers showed great reluctance to stop work and were forced out only after red terror squads infiltrated the site. The strike at the Hengfeng mill soon began to crumble, so a red terror squad planted a bomb at the mill gate to prevent a return to work. It was sheer luck that no one was hurt. On 24 November, twenty strike leaders were arrested and six factories resumed work. Later, the Communists conceded their mistake, admitting that workers had told them: 'You want us to go to meetings, to go on strike, to distribute leaflets, but we won't, because we only get our skulls smashed in.'[16]

In both countries, the weakness of state structures, compounded by the fragmentation and militarization of social relations, placed a premium on building armies and parties. It was these organizations, directed from the top by the Communist leadership, which shaped the course of the revolution far more than the grass-roots initiatives of the mass organizations. The historiography of the Russian Revolution tends to make an artificial divide between the October seizure of power, seen as the point when the Bolshevik regime was established, and the civil war, seen as the first phase of Bolshevik rule. But it is more useful to

---

[16] Zou Pei and Liu Zhen, *Zhongguo gongren*, vol. 3, pp. 93–8.

think of the three-and-a-half years between October and spring 1921, when the Kronstadt rebellion and a nation-wide wave of peasant revolts were crushed, as the period in which the Bolsheviks struggled to establish a monopoly of political and military power in order to establish a regime. From this perspective, the establishment and consolidation of Bolshevik power was due more to the Red Army than to the mass organizations. Though it numbered only 1.8 million early in 1919, of which number only 383,000 were combat troops, the army proved a more effective force in establishing Bolshevik power in the localities than the soviets. Recent historiography has tended to present Bolshevik use of coercion against independent labour organizations and rival socialist parties as an expression of their anti-democratic ideology or inherent nastiness. No doubt an authoritarian ideology, operating in a culture where democratic norms were weak, played a part in fostering the monopolization of power by a one-party state. But this cannot explain why SRs, the victors of the Constituent Assembly elections, who established anti-Bolshevik governments in the summer and autumn of 1918, resorted to similar tactics, including martial law, conscription of the male population, and the forced seizure of grain from the peasantry. The principal dynamic seems rather to have derived from a situation where power was massively fragmented and where a weak state struggled to neutralize and absorb rival power centres. In such a situation it is very doubtful whether the Bolsheviks could have consolidated their authority through the popular organizations that in 1917 had lent their support to the party even had they wished to. The civil war proved that armies and party-controlled administrations able to secure and command territory and resources were what counted. This was certainly the lesson that Stalin drew and applied to China. On 30 November 1926, when seeking to persuade the Chinese commission of the Executive Committee of the Comintern to push its Chinese policy in a more leftist direction, he stressed the 'special role of the military factor' as one of the 'advantages of the Chinese revolution'.[17] Mao Zedong took the lesson to heart, concluding that without its own army the CCP would never be in a position to secure and defend its own territories. Ultimately, when the CCP did take power in 1949, it was not primarily by mobilizing the peasantry through cooperatives, mutual aid teams or 'struggle sessions', important though these were, but by virtue of its possession of an army

---

[17] S. A. Smith, 'The Comintern, the Chinese Communist Party and the three armed uprisings in Shanghai, 1926–27', in Tim Rees and Andrew Thorpe (eds.), *International Communism and the Communist International, 1919–43* (Manchester: Manchester University Press, 1998), p. 260.

nearly five million strong (many of them GMD defectors) and a party of about 4.5 million members.

The Bolsheviks were quick to elevate their form of party organization, their strategy of insurrection and their policies of socialist construction to the status of a model that had universal applicability, especially following the Second Comintern Congress of 1920. Yet it is arguable that the October insurrection was the least typical of the Communist revolutions that occurred in the twentieth century, in some respects being much closer to nineteenth-century urban insurrections – more like the revolutions of 1848 or the Paris Commune – than the revolutions that were to come in China, Vietnam, Yugoslavia or Cuba. Firstly, even in 1905, notwithstanding extensive disaffection in the armed forces, insurgent workers proved no match for a damaged but functioning army. The anachronistic character of the Moscow uprising of that year is reflected in advice to the would-be insurrectionists from Lenin: 'The contingents ... must arm themselves as best they can (rifles, revolvers, bombs, knives, knuckle-dusters, sticks, rags soaked in kerosene for starting fires, ropes or rope ladders, shovels for building barricades, pyroxylin, cartridges, barbed-wire, nails against cavalry etc. etc.)'.[18] Nails against cavalry hardly adumbrated twentieth-century counter-insurgency, with its tanks, armoured cars, heavy artillery, automatic rifles and tear gas.

Secondly, the Bolshevik revolution was the twentieth-century revolution that was least brought about by the conscious planning and organization of a Communist party. The Bolsheviks were rather marginal players in the history of Russia between 1905 and February 1917: their ability to seize the political initiative was conjunctural, a matter of a few key months. Without minimizing the importance of Lenin and his party in bringing about the seizure of power, what is striking from a comparative perspective is just how much events flowed in the Bolsheviks' favour and, in particular, just how weak the opposition proved to be. The war-induced revolutionary crisis bankrupted a succession of political forces from monarchism and liberalism to moderate socialism and the Bolsheviks must be given credit for sheer survival. Where they came into their own as a relatively centralized, disciplined body was not so much in October as in turning the tide against anarchy and creating an effective army from 1918 on. During the civil war they displayed a remarkable ability to shape events (even though narratives of this period tend to stress how little room for manoeuvre they enjoyed, as a result of

[18] V. I. Lenin, 'Tasks of the Revolutionary Army Contingents', in V. I. Lenin, *Collected Works*, 4th edn, vol. 9 (Moscow: Progress, 1972), p. 423.

the difficulties posed by civil war and economic collapse). By contrast, the Chinese Revolution was more typical of twentieth-century revolutions in that the agency of the CCP proved to be of overriding importance: China's was a long revolution, in which only the heroic determination of the Communists to create base areas and armies remote from GMD interference allowed them eventually to seize power. Of course, 'objective' factors – Japanese invasion, civil war, economic collapse – worked in their favour, but it was the CCP's ability to exploit the opportunities it faced, – 'subjective' factors, such as policy-making, organization, strategic calculation – that proved vital, in a way that was not true in Russia. Even so, recent historians have not erred in stressing the huge role of contingency in helping the CCP to power in the years 1946 to 1949.[19]

Communist Modernity

Having consolidated their regimes, the Bolsheviks and the Chinese Communists proceeded to try to realize a form of modernity that would be superior economically, politically and ethically to the modernity promoted by the market and the nation state. In important respects, Communist modernity was intended to continue the processes of structural differentiation inaugurated by capitalist modernity – the application of scientific knowledge to nature and society, industrialization and urbanization, forms of mass production, greater penetration of society by the bureaucratic state, the rudiments of a welfare state, secularization, the celebration of reason as the source of social progress and so forth. In other respects, it was intended to signal a decisive break with the capitalist modernity that had been developing in imperial Russia and republican China, since it was designed to eliminate private ownership of the means of production, promote production at the expense of consumption, curtail the dominance of the market and commodification, resist social and cultural pluralism, and resist the full-scale regulation of social life by law and formal rationality and, supposedly, celebrate the superiority of internationalism over barren

---

[19] Cf. Joseph Esherick. 'Yet however much socio-economic structures formed the preconditions for revolution, the revolution itself was an extended historical process in which a series of contingent events interacted over time and space to constrain and ultimately determine the revolutionary outcome.' Joseph W. Esherick, 'Ten Theses on the Chinese Revolution', *Modern China*, 21, 1 (1995), 55; Odd Arne Westad, *Decisive Encounters: The Chinese Civil War, 1946–50* (Stanford: Stanford University Press, 2003); Hans J. van de Ven, *War and Nationalism in China, 1925–45* (London: RoutledgeCurzon, 2003).

nationalism. Furthermore, once the project of achieving Communist modernity got underway, it quickly became apparent that a side-effect of massive social and economic transformation was to revitalize many 'neo-traditional' practices and representations, some common to both the Soviet and Chinese cases, some not. These included the emergence of a charismatic leader, the revival of clientelism as a principle of social organization, and the reconstitution of social hierarchies more akin to status groups than to modern social classes. Because of these 'counter-modernizing' forces, some recent scholars have argued that Communist revolutions in fact aborted the development of true modernity, and that the process was resumed only with the collapse of the Soviet Union in 1991 and the abandonment of Maoism in China from the 1980s.[20] The problem with this view, however, is that if Communism was not a variant of modernity, then what was it? To dismiss it as 'counter-modernity' or as 'incomplete' modernity is implicitly to accept that only the western model counts as authentic modernity.[21] This, however, is to contradict the 'multiple modernities' paradigm set out in the introduction. In the remainder of this chapter, then, we examine the contradictoriness of Communism as a type of modernity, exploring how it maintained, rejected and reconfigured the processes that had been shaping worker identities during the last decades of the old regimes, highlighting similarities and differences between the Soviet and Chinese cases.

In no sphere was the rejection by Communist regimes of the socio-cultural trends spurred by capitalist modernity more marked than with respect to the slow and uneven development of forms of individuality in the last decades of the old regimes. In chapter 2 we saw that in neither Russia nor China was the idea of the individual as marked by civil, political or economic rights highly developed by the time the countries succumbed to war and revolution, even though as a result of the decline of the patriarchal family, the growth of education and new religious movements, and the beginnings of a consumer culture, modern conceptions of the self had begun to circulate. Once in power, the Communists, inspired by ideologies that upheld strong forms of collectivism, closed down many of the social spaces in which individuality had been increasingly transacted. The Bolsheviks, for example, exalted the idea of

[20] Pierre Clermont, *Le communisme à contre-modernité* (Paris: Presses Universitaires de Vincennes, 1993).
[21] See Yanni Kotsonis, 'Introduction', and David L. Hoffmann, 'European Modernity and Soviet Socialism', in David L. Hoffmann and Yanni Kotsonis (eds.), *Russian Modernity: Politics, Knowledge, Practices* (Basingstoke: Macmillan, 2002), pp. 1–18 and 245–60.

self-sacrifice in the service of revolution. Obituaries in the press praised exemplary individuals for denying self and family for the socialist cause. 'Comrade Frunze did not know any personal life, he strove with all his force towards the social ideals of socialism.'[22] M. N. Liadov, rector of the Sverdlov Communist University, opined: 'We imagine the society of the future as one in which everyone will feel that his interests conform with the interests of the entire collective. Every person will feel pain, will feel burdened, if his personal interests in any way contradict the interests of the collective.'[23]

Yet it would be too reductive to infer that this entailed a crushing of the self. Social relations in the Soviet Union remained fluid until the Second World War, and spaces multiplied in which individuals could achieve a degree of self-advancement in broad conformity with the goals of the revolution: for example by getting themselves an education, joining the Komsomol or the party, getting a job in a soviet institution or in the administration of an industrial enterprise or, at its most basic, by leaving the countryside to become an industrial worker.[24] Moreover, as we saw in chapter 2, the relationships between self and collective were complex, 'conscious' workers having generally understood authentic individuality as something to be realized through the collective, through alignment with the forces of history. Recently, some historians have developed this idea productively by analysing the positive, empowering dynamic that existed between subjectivity and identification with the revolution. Jochen Hellbeck, for example, has shown how, for some at least, identification with the revolutionary project encouraged an assertion of the self as a political subject with a right, indeed a duty, to speak out: something, he correctly points out, that is missed by accounts that recognize individuality only in dissent or in resistance to the demands of the regime.[25] And Oleg Kharkhordin has gone so far as to argue that the Stalin era witnessed a 'curious individualization of the populace', by virtue of the relentless emphasis on practices of self-perfection, albeit without a counterbalancing emphasis on individual autonomy.[26]

---

[22] Jeffrey Brooks, 'Revolutionary Lives: Public Identities in Pravda during the 1920s', in Stephen White (ed.), *New Directions in Soviet History* (Cambridge: Cambridge University Press, 1992), p. 33.

[23] Cited in Eric Naiman, *Sex in Public: The Incarnation of Early Soviet Ideology* (Princeton: Princeton University Press, 1997), p. 93.

[24] Sheila Fitzpatrick, *Education and Social Mobility in the Soviet Union, 1921–34* (Cambridge: Cambridge University Press, 1979).

[25] Jochen Hellbeck, 'Speaking Out: Languages of Affirmation and Dissent in Stalinist Russia', *Kritika* 1, 1 (2000), 71–96.

[26] Oleg Kharkhordin, *The Collective and the Individual in Russia* (Berkeley: University of California Press, 1999), p. 2

Soviet culture, in other words, even under Stalin, was never mono-lithic in the ways that it construed selfhood. If the call to self-sacrifice was ubiquitous, so, for example, was the call to self-improvement. Catriona Kelly astutely points out that although the 'amelioration of self' was thought of exclusively in terms of making one's 'contribution to the task of building a rational society', it nevertheless required individuals to manifest a high degree of self-reliance and even initiative.[27] Individuals were, for example, expected to improve their minds through reading and other cultural pursuits, expected to be physically and mentally strong, to be clean and tidy, industrious, punctual and well organized.[28] Furthermore, if Stalin could notoriously liken the individual to a cog in the machine of socialist society, Stalinist discourse nevertheless applauded outstanding individual performances so long as these were in harmony with state goals, encouraging ordinary folk to emulate 'hero-figures' in such spheres as sport, culture, aviation or labour productivity, and appealing variously to individuals' material self-interest, desire for prestige and altruism.[29]

In late-imperial Russia, nascent consumer culture provided an important arena in which individuality could be expressed. The Soviet Union never became a society where individuals expressed individuality and aspirations for social status through consumption choices. By the 1930s, the market had been largely displaced by the state as the principal allocator of consumer goods, at least for the urban population. The command economy, however, proved unable to meet demand for basic consumer goods, leading to chronic shortages and the ubiquitous queue. As Elena Osokina notes, customers always chased goods rather than goods customers, with the result that after the Second World War, consumption became increasingly tied to the 'second economy'.[30] In addition, the economy was plunged into crisis in 1917–22, 1928–33 and 1939–47, causing the government to resort to rationing, shutting down peasant markets and protecting urban consumers at the expense of the rural population.[31] Yet, as Julie Hassler points out, in periods of economic recovery a certain pleasure in shopping in the outdoor markets, if not in the dour state-owned department stores, can be detected. And after

[27] Catriona Kelly, *Refining Russia: Advice Literature, Polite Culture and Gender from Catherine the Great to Yeltsin* (Oxford: Oxford University Press, 2001), p. 260.

[28] Kelly, *Refining Russia*, ch. 4.

[29] Mark Sandle, *A Short History of Soviet Socialism* (London: UCL Press, 1999), p. 247.

[30] E. Osokina, *Za fasadom 'stalinskogo izobiliia': raspredelenie i rynok v snabzhenii naseleniia v gody industrializatsii, 1927–1941* (Moscow: ROSSPEN, 1998), p. 5.

[31] Julie Hessler, *A Social History of Soviet Trade* (Princeton: Princeton University Press, 2004), pp. 5–6.

Stalin made his speech to the First All-Union Congress of Stakhanovites in 1935, in which he announced that 'life has become better, comrades, life has become happier', there was some improvement in the range and supply of consumer goods. The state even began to use advertisements to 'help channel newly awakened consumer aspirations toward officially sanctioned goals'.[32] So if the Soviet Union never became a society where individuals expressed individuality and aspirations for social status through consumption choices – and if the regime was ideologically hostile to the tendency of capitalism to reduce human beings to inexhaustible consumers – working people still managed, to a limited extent, to use consumption as a site of self-expression. In her study of Soviet printers, Diane Koenker shows how 'ample food, warm and comfortable housing, clothing, books, the cinema, decorative arts on the walls' remained important for the constitution of working-class identities, even if the official representation of proletarian identity focused narrowly on production.[33] Notwithstanding the daily struggle to survive, the choice and use of commodities remained one vector, alongside labour movement traditions, socialist ideals and official propaganda through which what Koenker calls the 'complicated tangle' of worker identities was negotiated.[34]

In the PRC the subordination of the individual to the collective was far greater than in the Soviet Union. Although the early CCP shared the May Fourth Movement commitment to individual 'enlightenment' and autonomy, these goals quickly proved to be at odd with the goals of nation-building and state-building to which the GMD and the CCP both subscribed. By the 1930s, in the words of Vera Schwarcz: 'the need to defend a collective identity at all costs overshadowed the earlier commitment to individual autonomy. In this process, other May Fourth commitments were transformed as well. The right to doubt collective beliefs, a right that had been upheld through the cultivation of individual conscience during May Fourth Movement, withered from lack of use.'[35] The desperate struggle against the Japanese intensified the CCP's animus against individualism. In his 1937 essay, 'Combat Liberalism', Mao Zedong criticized eleven manifestations of selfish 'liberalism', his message being that a good Communist 'should be more concerned about the Party and the masses than about any private person, and more

---

[32] Hessler, *Social History*, p. 212.
[33] Diane P. Koenker, *Republic of Labour: Russian Printers and Soviet Socialism, 1918–1930* (Ithaca NY: Cornell University Press, 2005), p. 310.
[34] Koenker, *Republic*, p. 194.
[35] Vera Schwarcz, *The Chinese Enlightenment: Intellectuals and the Legacy of the May Fourth Movement of 1919* (Berkeley: University of California Press, 1986), p. 231.

concerned about others than about himself '.[36] What may be read as a warning against self-indulgence appropriate to a time of war was after 1949 canonized as a norm around which Communist culture should be built, an imperative for the individual to align his or her goals with those of the party. As Lei Feng, a model soldier extolled in propaganda, supposedly confided in his diary in the early 1960s: 'I eliminate my individualism as an autumn gale sweeps away fallen leaves/And to the class enemy, I am cruel and ruthless like harsh winter.'[37] By the time of the Cultural Revolution, hatred of the individual reached such a pitch that some talked of smashing and vanquishing the very word 'I' (Dadao wo zi, yasui wo zi).[38] The beneficiary of such thinking, as Ci Jiwei explains, was always the state: 'what is at stake in all of this is the maximization of the freedom of the ruler and the minimization of the freedom of the ruled'.[39] Or as the dissident journalist Liu Binyan came to realize, condemnation of the 'original sin of individualism. ... was directed at keeping the masses in check so that the leadership could pursue its interests'.[40]

As in the case of the Soviet Union, however, we should not confuse rhetoric with reality. If in practice the CCP was far more active than its Soviet 'elder brother' in seeking to extirpate individualism, it could not close off all the trends that during the republican era had made for greater self-expression. Indeed during the relatively open climate of the 1950s, there was public debate about whether it was individualistic to pursue private hobbies, to devote oneself to study in order to advance one's position, or to express one's views in study and discussion. In the journal of the Communist Youth League (as the organization became known in 1957) readers regularly sent in letters, complaining that cadres were discouraging their hopes for further study and advancement or placing obstacles to their prospects for courtship and marriage, and these received a relatively sympathetic hearing from the editors. Dress, in particular, continued to be an issue around which debate about the relative merits of identification with the collective and individual self-expression raged. If there was general agreement that extravagance in dress was a bad thing, there was no agreement that colourful dress in

[36] Selected Works of Mao Tse-tung, vol. 2 (Beijing: Foreign Languages Press, 1967), pp. 31–33.
[37] Ban Wang, The Sublime Figure of History: Aesthetics and Politics in Twentieth Century China (Stanford: Stanford University Press, 1997), p. 220.
[38] Frederic Wakeman, Jr, History and Will: Philosophical Perspectives of Mao Tse-tung's Thought (Berkeley: University of California Press, 1973), p. 43.
[39] Ci Jiwei, Dialectic of the Chinese Revolution (Stanford: Stanford University Press, 1994), pp. 125, 126.
[40] Liu Binyan, A Higher Kind of Loyalty (New York: Pantheon, 1990), p. 201.

itself was a sign of petty-bourgeois tendencies.[41] With the Great Leap Forward (1958–61), this changed. By the early 1960s, as one scholar recalled: 'One might be considered backward if any aspect of one's lifestyle was out of the ordinary, such as wearing brightly coloured clothes, applying hair oil, going to a restaurant, cultivating flowers, raising goldfish, or playing chess.' Personal hobbies and eccentricities became prime grounds for accusation that one was a 'backward element'.[42] Such attitudes would reach their frenzied peak in the Cultural Revolution.

The potency of collectivism after 1949 in part reflects the resilience of Confucian norms, values and practices. The CCP might rant against Confucian culture, denouncing its values of order, stability and hierarchy, yet in crucial respects it subtly reconfigured Confucian assumptions. It took for granted, for example, that individuals are defined in terms of their obligations to their primary social groups: but now obligations were no longer to the family or lineage, but to the work unit, one's rural collective or one's class category. Similarly, it took for granted that political rule is mediated through ritual, but now the rituals were no longer those of ancestor worship, the village lecture (*xiangyue*) or local sacrifice, but the dramas of 'speak bitterness' and self-criticism or the ritual of the political study session. This, however, was not simply a matter of the 'persistence of tradition': rather it represented a complex entanglement of modernizing and 'neo-traditional' elements in the effort to produce a form of modernity that was both Communist and Chinese.

This can be illustrated by reference to CCP policy towards the family. Broadly speaking, the party-state continued the modernizing trends of the republican era, taking radical steps to institute gender equality and to remove women out of the home into collective production. The effect of this, in part, was to strengthen the rights of the individual against the family. The Marriage Law of 1951 made marriage a matter of free choice between two individuals and seriously weakened parental control over marriage arrangements, although many rural marriages continued to be arranged.[43] Nevertheless, aware of the extent of resistance in the countryside, especially among the older generation, the CCP was careful not to push things too far. When Wang Dongan of Houying commune in

[41] James R. Townsend, 'Revolutionizing Chinese Youth: A Study of Chung-kuo Ch'ingnien', in A. Doak Barnett (ed.), *Chinese Communist Politics in Action* (Seattle: University of Washington Press, 1969), pp. 455–6.

[42] Wang Shaoguang, *Failure of Charisma: The Cultural Revolution in Wuhan* (Hong Kong: Oxford University Press, 1995), p. 54.

[43] Richard Madsen, 'The Countryside under Communism', in Roderick MacFarquhar and John K. Fairbank (eds.), *Cambridge History of China*, vol. 15 (Cambridge: Cambridge University Press, 1991), p. 651.

Shandong province wrote to the Beijing newspaper of the Communist Youth League in May 1962 to ask if a daughter-in-law was obliged to defer to her parents-in-law, she was told:

> On the basis of family relations, since you are married to your husband, that means you and your father-in-law and mother-in-law are members of the same family. If they are strong enough to work, you as their daughter-in-law may share and enjoy the fruit of their labour. If they lose their ability to labour, it is a duty for both son and daughter-in-law to support them .... Although tradition is not law, it has moral force. We should forsake some traditional practices (such as feudal marriages, arranged by parents for their children), but must inherit good traditions.[44]

It is hard to imagine that Communists in the 1920s could ever have given such a reply.[45]

After October, the Bolsheviks launched an attack on the traditional gender order that was unprecedented since the French Revolution. Their programme focused on the 'liberation of women', which as we saw in chapter 3 was a leitmotif of reformist discourse from the 1860s. The comprehensive Code on Marriage, the Family and Guardianship, ratified in October 1918, equalized women's legal status with men's, allowed both spouses to retain the right to their own property and earnings, granted children born outside wedlock the same rights as those born within, and made divorce available upon request. In contrast to liberal champions of women's rights, however, Bolshevik theory saw the key to woman's liberation as lying in the removal of women from the confines of the family and their transfer to the sphere of wage labour. There they would gain economic independence and acquire the class-consciousness that was inseparable from true emancipation. For this to happen, it was recognized that the state would need to take over the tasks of child care and household labour – described by Lenin as 'the most unproductive, the most savage and the most arduous work a woman can do' – that confined women to the home. Tentative steps were taken towards socializing these tasks during the civil war through setting up child-care centres, communal dining halls and other services. The Women's Department (Zhenotdel), established in 1919, allowed leading feminists in the Bolshevik party, such as Inessa Armand and Alexandra Kollontai, a vehicle with which to mobilize lower-class women. And though chronically underfunded, the Department did

---

[44] *Zhongguo qingnianbao*, 12 May 1962. *Survey of the China Mainland Press*, 2756, 12 June 1962.
[45] S. A. Smith, *A Road is Made: Communism in Shanghai, 1920–1927* (Richmond: Curzon, 2000), pp. 122–6.

undertake a range of campaigns during the 1920s against wage and hiring discrimination, sexual harassment, layoffs of women from industry, alcoholism and wife beating.

In the early years, a minority of Bolsheviks believed that the family, as an institution based on private property, would wither away under Communism. In the event, it was the strains of civil war and economic collapse that caused the structures of family life to buckle, with spouses separating, children being abandoned and casual sexual relationships flourishing.[46] Left to support families without the assistance of menfolk, many poor, vulnerable women yearned for the restoration of stable family life. Once the turmoil of civil war was over, the marriage rate rose so that it was over a third higher by 1926 than in 1913. At the same time, cuts in state subsidies led to the closure of the public dining halls, crèches and communal laundries that had been a feature of War Communism, leaving women once again responsible for looking after children, cooking, cleaning and sewing. The family responsibilities of women, combined with rising female unemployment, shaped the debate on the new Family Code of 1926. This simplified divorce procedure, but introduced stricter rules on alimony, making men rather than the state responsible for upkeep of children, and establishing joint ownership of property acquired during marriage. To some extent, this represented a compromise with popular assumptions about the mutual responsibilities of family members; but it was also in tune with an emerging consensus in the party that the family would have to serve as the basic institution of social welfare for the foreseeable future. It also chimed with public belief that mounting social problems such as illegitimacy, abandoned children, hooliganism and juvenile crime were linked to the breakdown of family life. [47]

The 1920s thus saw a strengthening of more conservative attitudes to the family and marriage. Yet Soviet Russia at this time proved to be a harbinger in many respects of trends in family patterns that would later be seen as characteristic of capitalist modernity. Within less than a decade, European Russia had the highest divorce rate in the world, divorce becoming widespread even in rural communities. The age of marriage rose in both town and countryside and church marriage went into steep decline. The birth rate rapidly recovered from its nadir of 1922, yet the long-term trend was towards a decline in fertility, especially in the towns, as levels of female education and employment rose

---

[46] Wendy Goldman, *Women, the State and Revolution: Soviet Family Policy and Social Life, 1917–1936* (Cambridge: Cambridge University Press, 1993), ch. 3.
[47] Barbara Alpern Engel, 'Engendering Russian History', *Slavic Review*, 51, 2 (1992), 309–21.

and as the age of marriage was delayed. Abortion, which was legalized by the Bolsheviks for the first time in history in 1920, albeit out of concern that society could not support children properly in prevailing economic conditions rather than out of a concern with women's reproductive rights, soon became commonplace. By the late 1920s, the number of abortions in cities surpassed the number of births and the typical woman having an abortion was not the unmarried or unemployed young woman envisaged in the 1920 decree, but a married woman with at least one child, with an equal chance of being a housewife or a wage earner.[48]

The Bolsheviks showed much less concern to challenge male gender roles. In line with Lenin's call to 'root out the "old master right of the man"', they repudiated traditional patriarchy, with its acceptance of men's God-given right to rule over women, but the revolutionary script exalted the public over the private, production over reproduction, and thus implicitly prioritized men, leaving women little discursive space to enter into the comradeship that existed outside the realms of family and motherhood. The subliminal primacy of the male was evident in early Soviet posters, in which workers, peasants or Red Army soldiers were generally portrayed as men and in which women were notable by their absence. The male image represented the universal – standing for the entire working class or peasantry – and thus buttressed assumptions that revolution was men's business.[49] At best, then, the Bolshevik revolution reinforced trends already underway as patriarchy entered into crisis in the last decades of the empire, supplanting the patriarchal model with one of revolutionary fraternity, summoning young men to define themselves through comradeship with other men in the struggle for socialism. The 1930s saw a shift away from the model of fraternal masculinity towards one in which masculine identity was once again linked to procreation and the family, the recriminalization of homosexuality in 1934 marking a reinscription of a combative heterosexual masculinity as a marker of Russian national identity.[50] Yet the rhetoric of gender equality was never abandoned, and the entry of women into the workforce during the 1930s on a massive scale put paid to the notion of the male as the family breadwinner.

[48] Goldman, *Women, State and Revolution*, pp. 261–80.
[49] Victoria E. Bonnell, 'The Representation of Women in Early Soviet Political Art', *Russian Review*, 50 (1991), 267–288.
[50] Karen Petrone, 'Masculinity and Heroism in Imperial and Soviet Military-Patriotic Cultures', in Barbara Evans Clements, Rebecca Friedman and Dan Healey (eds.), *Russian Masculinities in History and Culture* (Basingstoke: Palgrave, 2002), pp. 172–93; Thomas G. Schrand, 'Socialism in One Gender: Masculine Values in the Stalin Revolution', in Clements et al. (eds.), *Russian Masculinities*, pp. 194–209.

With the consolidation of the Stalin dictatorship, there was a decisive retreat away from the radicalism of early policy on the family towards a more rigidly defined gender order. The new woman who abandoned family and children for involvement in the revolution was set aside in favour of a mother figure whose contribution to Soviet society was made through having children and bringing them up in the spirit of socialism. This was signalled by the ban on abortion in 1936 and the limitation of the right of divorce. New welfare entitlements were announced for women who bore seven or more children and funding for new maternity homes and day-care facilities was increased. Accompanying this was a press campaign that condemned 'so-called "free love"' as bourgeois and anti-Soviet. The movement of 'wife-activists' (*obshchestvennitsy*), launched in 1936, promoted a public role for the wives of the new elite of industrial executives, engineers and army officers. These women, without paid employment and cast as 'mistresses of the great Soviet home', were encouraged to supervise factory amenities and to organize cultural activities.[51] Yet the identities promoted by the Stalinist state were never simply 'neo-traditional' – there was never a return to the notion that a woman's place was in the home – nor monolithic. The party continued to encourage women to enter the workforce and implemented policies to train, promote and educate them. And some of the most vigorously promoted identities for women during the Stalin era were as model factory and collective farm workers, tractor drivers and even aviators. Such images of woman as exemplars of technical skill, industrial productivity or warriors had a clear filiation with the earlier attack on conventional 'bourgeois' femininity. Identities at variance with traditional norms of femininity thus continued to be promoted, even though the discursive field in which they circulated was now overshadowed by the resurrection of maternal and family-centred notions of womanhood.[52]

The CCP, like the Bolsheviks, stressed that the route to the emancipation of women lay through participation in the public sphere of work. The republican trend to paid employment among urban women continued apace. Wages of women doing the same work as men were roughly equal, but women were more likely to be concentrated in the collective sector, such as neighbourhood workshops, where pay and

---

[51] Sheila Fitzpatrick, *The Cultural Front: Power and Culture in Revolutionary Russia* (Ithaca NY: Cornell University Press, 1992), pp. 231–5; Rebecca Neary, 'Mothering Socialist Society: The Wife-Activists' Movement and Soviet Culture of Daily Life, 1934–41', *Russian Review*, 58 (1999), 396–412.

[52] Anna Krylova, 'Identity, Agency and the "First Soviet Generation",' in Stephen Lovell (ed.), *Generations in Twentieth-Century Europe* (Basingstoke: Palgrave, 2007), pp. 100–20.

conditions were worse than in the state-owned sector.[53] The economic position of peasant women also improved, first, with land reform, when women technically gained a right to land, and then, more substantially, with collectivization (1955–6), when rural women began to work in cooperatives and, subsequently, communes, earning work points for their labour. Men, however, predominated in work deemed 'heavy' – which could mean no more than that it involved use of machinery – and earned more work points than women, who were concentrated in less skilled farming jobs.[54] During the Great Leap Forward, both rural and urban women were mobilized into production on a massive scale and the skill, strength and enthusiasm of female 'labour models' was much feted. During periods of economic downturn, however, greater emphasis was placed in official propaganda on women's domestic roles.[55]

The speed with which the hierarchical relations of gender and generation within the patriarchal family 'modernized' is hard to judge. The Marriage Law of 1951 abolished the traditional family system 'based on arbitrary and compulsory arrangements and the superiority of man over woman'. Women were taken out of the home with collectivization and given the opportunity to earn work points, affirming their economic contribution to the rural household and enlarging their social networks. This tended to undercut the economic primacy of the head of household, yet significantly did not eliminate it altogether, since work points were assigned to him rather than to individual household members.[56] Moreover, domestic labour, along with cultivation of the family's private plot, remained very much the responsibility of the women of the household. In early 1950s, there was some discussion about transforming the sexual division of labour, but little if any pressure was invoked to involve men in domestic chores. Only with the utopianism of the Great Leap Forward was there a radical effort to collectivize housework, childcare and cooking, but socialized facilities were never popular and the onset of famine brought this experiment to a savage close.[57] Despite fierce ideological attacks on 'feudal ideology', then, social pressures to preserve elements of patriarchy remained strong: even in the communes, for example, the prosperity of any single household depended mainly on the number of labourers it had at its disposal, and

---

[53] Delia Davin, *Woman-Work: Women and the Party in Revolutionary China* (Oxford: Clarendon Press, 1976), p. 177.

[54] Margery Wolf, *Revolution Postponed: Women in Contemporary China* (Stanford: Stanford University Press, 1985), pp. 83–5.

[55] Davin, *Woman-Work*, pp. 169–70.

[56] Davin, *Woman-Work*, p. 150.

[57] Davin, *Woman-Work*, p. 128.

this encouraged couples to have large numbers of children and to prefer boys over girls.[58] Longer-terms trends, however, inherited from the republican era, were towards a decline in fertility and the formation of nuclear families, and state policy tended towards strengthening the rights of the younger generation against the older generation, the rights of women against men, and the rights of the individual against the collective pressure of the family. Following the Marriage Law, for example, the divorce rate rose rapidly as people took advantage of the legislation to escape loveless marriages; later in the 1950s, divorce appears to have became more difficult, at least in the circumstances where only one partner petitioned for it. Kay Ann Johnson observes that 'divorce threatened to disrupt the exchange of women upon which patrilineal families and rural communities were based'.[59] Yet, as Neil Diamant demonstrates, there is evidence that young peasants were rather willing to take advantage of the new ease of divorce, more so than city-dwellers, who tended to be more conciliatory when handling family disputes and more timid when approaching the authorities.[60] Furthermore, by the 1960s and 1970s, even in rural areas the desire for personal freedom within the family was making steady progress, romantic love coming to occupy a crucial place in courtship and spouse selection.[61]

Compared with the attack on traditional masculinity and femininity that began in the late-Qing and culminated in the May Fourth era, the policy of the CCP towards gender stereotypes was relatively cautious. Only in the Cultural Revolution was an aggressive assault on gender stereotypes unleashed, in accordance with Mao's slogan that 'the times have changed, so men and women are the same'.[62] As in the Soviet Union – and as had been the case in the republican era – it was conventional femininity rather than masculinity that was targeted. 'Iron girls' – strong, robust, muscular women who performed physically demanding jobs – were exalted in official propaganda. This represented not the 'erasure of gender' so much as a requirement that women act like men. Some scholars interpret the violence perpetrated by some female Red Guards as a reaction to the extreme sexual repression of the

---

[58] Kay Ann Johnson, *Women, the Family and Peasant Revolution in China* (Chicago: Chicago University Press, 1983), p. 215.

[59] Johnson, *Women, the Family*, p. 214.

[60] Neil Diamant, *Revolutionizing the Family: Politics, Love, and Divorce in Urban and Rural China, 1949–1968* (Berkeley: University of California Press, 2000).

[61] Yunxiang Yan, *Private Life Under Socialism: Love, Intimacy and Family Change in a Chinese Village, 1949–99* (Stanford: Stanford University Press, 2003).

[62] Kam Louie, *Theorizing Chinese Masculinity: Society and Gender in China* (Cambridge: Cambridge University Press, 2002), p. 107.

times; others see it as resistance to the social control of women; others as excess whipped up by the hysterical propaganda of the state.[63] By contrast, conventional masculinity was subject to less radical challenge. During the 1950s, People's Liberation Army (PLA) soldiers were promoted as model men – selfless, frugal, fearless fighters for the nation – but the model was not easy to emulate since, as Kam Louie notes, 'they were portrayed like virtuous women of traditional China. That is they were good-looking, extremely loyal ... and most importantly they die young. In fact, they die with their virginity intact, ensuring that they are devoid of any pollution, and not tainted by any capitalist ideas.' This model was sidelined during the Cultural Revolution. There was a partial return to the *haohan* model of virile masculinity that had been influential among Shanghai migrants in the 1920s and 1930s, as worker rebels formed themselves into a revolutionary fraternity to topple 'capitalist roaders' and to demonstrate loyalty to the Great Helmsman.[64] All in all, gender stereotypes seem to have been more polarized in the Soviet Union than in China, and this seems to represent continuity in the gender order across the revolution.

Feminist scholars have justly criticized the CCP's vision of women's emancipation, arguing that the state remained patriarchal and that its notion of 'liberation' served to increase the burden on women by forcing them to take up wage work without substantially reducing their burden of domestic labour. However, changes in women's lives in the direction of greater personal freedom were real, if only slow and partial, and they came about not solely as the result of party directives, but also as a result of long-term social, demographic and cultural trends. Moreover we must be cautious about bringing our own anachronistic benchmarks to bear when judging the improvement in women's lives: it is surely not without significance that older women today in the PRC – like women at the time – continue to believe that the CCP brought them 'liberation'.[65]

---

[63] Diamant, *Revolutionizing the Family*, ch. 7; Emily Honig, 'Maoist Mappings of Gender: Reassessing the Red Guards', in Susan Brownell and Jeffrey Wasserstrom (eds.), *Chinese Femininities, Chinese Masculinities* (Berkeley: University of California Press, 2002), pp. 255–68.

[64] Elizabeth J. Perry and Nara Dillon, ' "Little Brothers" in the Cultural Revolution: The Worker Rebels of Shanghai', in Susan Brownell and Jeffrey Wasserstrom (eds.), *Chinese Femininities, Chinese Masculinities* (Berkeley: University of California Press, 2002), pp. 269–86.

[65] Lisa Rofel 'Liberation Nostalgia and a Yearning for Modernity', in Christina K. Gilmartin et al. (eds), *Engendering China: Women, Culture and the State* (Cambridge MA: Harvard University Press, 1994), pp. 225–49; Gail Hershatter, 'The Gender of Memory: Rural Chinese Women and the 1950s', *Signs*, 28, 1 (2002), 43–70.

Although native-place identities are 'categorical' in nature – in that people identify with others on the basis of a perceived common attribute – they tend to generate social ties of a narrow, particularistic type. For that reason, one might expect them to lose salience as Communist modernity got underway, marginalized by larger identifications with class or nation, with social networks based on native place displaced by formal organizations of a more universalistic type. It is probably true to say that in both Russia and China native-place identities weakened over the long-term, although this is a slightly reckless generalization to make in the case of China. In both states, civil war, collectivization and urbanization massively disrupted traditional networks that knit together town and countryside and rural-to-urban migration was severely curtailed by state policy and socioeconomic dislocation. Nevertheless native-place sentiment in China has revived in the reform era, even if native-place organizations no longer have the influence they once wielded; and in Russia such phenomena as the popularity of village prose writers of the 1960s who mourned the loss of rural traditions, revelled in the beauty of the Russian countryside, and celebrated the innocence and cohesion of the villages of their birth suggests that native-place sentiment is still strong in Russian culture.

If rural-to-urban migration is seen as a feature generic to modernity then the efforts by both the Soviet and PRC governments to curb migration must be counted as evidence of a counter-modernizing thrust within their developmental programme. There was, however, a significant contrast between the two societies. In the Soviet Union in late 1932, as millions flooded into the cities to escape the brutalities of collectivization, the Stalin government reintroduced the internal passport, confining it to urban residents and certain categories of rural wage earners and thereby depriving millions of peasants of the right to leave the kolkhoz. Only in 1976–81 were peasants given the right to leave their place of residence and move elsewhere.[66] Despite this, the Stalin regime never managed to close down rural-to-urban migration and it continued to be a key factor boosting the rapid growth of the urban population. In 1929, for example, 81% of the population lived in the countryside, but this had already fallen to 68% ten years later (the urban population coming to outnumber the rural population only at the beginning of the 1960s).

In the PRC the situation was very different. There the urban population grew extremely slowly, thanks to a very effective government policy of limiting migration from the countryside. As a result – and leaving to one

[66] Sheila Fitzpatrick, *Stalin's Peasants: Resistance and Survival in the Russian Village after Collectivization* (Oxford: Oxford University Press, 1994), p. 96.

side a thicket of definitional and statistical problems – the urban population grew from 12.3% to only 14.4% between 1950 and 1976. It is true that in 1958, the Great Leap Forward provoked a huge exodus of peasants into the cities, but this was decisively reversed in 1961–2, and thereafter the urban population actually fell from its 1962 peak of 16%. Over the Mao era as a whole, the contribution made by migration to urban growth was only about 18% per annum, which suggests that the government was largely if not completely successful in preventing migration. If anything, movement tended to be from the cities to the countryside, especially with the rustication of urban youth in 1968–9 (a policy reversed only ten years later).[67]

Given the ideological significance of the proletariat's leadership of the poorest layers of the peasantry, one might expect both regimes to have used native-place networks and organizations to cement relations between town and countryside. To a limited extent, this happened in the Soviet Union. During the New Economic Policy, when the idea of an alliance (*smychka*) between workers and peasants was in vogue, the government encouraged the utilization of zemliak ties. By 1926, nearly 7,000 factories and other urban institutions, involving 1.2 million people, had organized sponsorship (*shefstvo*) of particular rural areas, supplying them with agricultural tools and credit, sending experts and political literature, and supporting veterinary points and model farms in the localities.[68] The Komsomol, too, sought to build a bridgehead to rural youth by summoning its members to organize cells of zemliaki to develop contacts with their home areas.[69] Relative to the size of the rural population, however, these initiatives were a drop in the ocean, and Stalin's brutal collectivization of agriculture largely brought them to an end.

If the Soviet state made only limited use of native-place ties, it sought more energetically to tap into the complex emotions that lay at the heart of native-place identities. Fitful efforts were made to capitalize for class ends on the emotional valency of the idea of rodina, most strangely as in the idea of the 'native factory' (*rodnoi zavod*), the factory that gave birth to one as a worker.[70] More successfully, but still tentatively, the state sought to incorporate the idea of rodina into an emergent Soviet

[67] Harry Xiaoying Wu, 'Rural to Urban Migration in the People's Republic of China', *China Quarterly*, 139 (1994), 686–7, 694.
[68] I. N. Il'ina, *Obshchestvennye organizatsii Rossii v 1920-e gody* (Moscow: RAN Institut rossiiskoi istorii, 2000), p. 94.
[69] *Smena*, 7 May 1925, p. 3.
[70] Stephen Kotkin, 'Coercion and Identity: Workers' Lives in Stalin's Showcase City', in Lewis Seigelbaum and Ronald G. Suny (eds), *Making Workers Soviet: Power, Class and Identity* (Ithaca NY: Cornell University Press, 1994) p. 300.

nationalism, in the hope that the powerful emotional attachments felt to native place would be projected onto the Soviet motherland. School textbooks in the 1930s, for example, continuing a tradition of late-imperial pedagogy, emphasized the connection between love for one's 'little motherland' (*malaia rodina*) and love for the Soviet motherland.[71] By this stage, the word rodina had acquired a somewhat sentimental, even old-fashioned ring; and when in 1934, *Pravda* used the word in reference to the Soviet Union, speaking of 'love and dedication to the motherland', it provoked outrage from the Menshevik emigré organ, *Sotsialisticheskii Vestnik*, which declared the term 'discredited in revolutionary and socialist consciousness' and reflective of 'zoological patriotism'.[72] With the Nazi invasion of 1941, however, official propagandists took up the term unashamedly, playing for all they were worth on its maternal connotations, the better to connect the endangered motherland to attachments to family and native place. Ol'ga Berggol'ts, disillusioned with the Communists, mused on how much the rodina now meant to ordinary folk, when saving the life of a friend equated with defending the motherland.[73]

There was nothing akin in the PRC to the violent onslaught on the peasantry waged by Stalin, yet the CCP implemented a raft of policies that served for the first time in Chinese history to create a profound division between town and countryside, one that systematically privileged townsfolk above peasants in respect of income, housing, grain rationing, education, medical and other services, education, employment and retirement provision. The household registration (*hukou*) system, introduced by stages in the 1950s to prevent migration from the countryside, was central to the entrenchment of this divide. It made it nigh impossible to live in the city without an official registration. Without a residence permit, one had no entitlement to food, clothing or shelter, employment, education or healthcare and one could not marry or enlist in the army. The system began as a response to the appalling problems placed on urban infrastructures by the influx of wartime refugees. Shanghai's population had swollen by some three million people during the war and the city authorities began to put pressure on

---

[71] V. L. Soskin, *Obshchee obrazovanie v sovetskoi Rossii: pervoe desiatiletie*, Part 2, (1923–1927gg.) (Novosibirsk: Novosibirskii gosudarstevennyi universitet, 1998), p. 81.

[72] Cited in A .I. Vdovin, *Rossiiskaia natsiia: natsional'no-politicheskie problemy XX veka i obshchenatsional'naia rossiiskaia ideia* (Moscow: Libris, 1995), p. 101.

[73] Geoffrey Hosking, 'The Second World War and Russian Nationalist Consciousness', *Past and Present*, 175 (2002), 162–87; Lisa A. Kirschenbaum, 'Our City, Our Hearths, Our Families: Local Loyalties and Private Life in Soviet World War Two Propaganda', *Slavic Review*, 59, 4 (2000), 825–47.

refugees to return to their native places as early as 1951. Between 1949 and 1957, it is reckoned the city offloaded more than a million people, but 1,820,000 migrants came to the city in the same period, so that immigration accounted for about 34% of the city's growth. The ever-tightening hukou system largely put a stop to this. The household registration system, together with the fact that the urban population had an entitlement to grain rations whereas the rural population had a duty to give up grain to the state at fixed prices, served to fix the status of Chinese peasant as second-class citizens, just as firmly as that of their Soviet counterparts.[74] As early as 1953, the neo-Confucian philosopher Liang Shuming, founder of the Shandong Rural Reconstruction Institute, aroused the ire of Mao by apparently alleging that 'the workers are up in the ninth heaven whereas the peasants are down in the ninth hell'.[75]

Against this background, it is perhaps not surprising that the PRC government showed little enthusiasm to promote or utilize native-place ties. By the time the Communists came to power, the war had drained the regional guilds and tongxianghui of money and personnel so they were a pale shadow of their former selves. In Shanghai they survived and were reorganized into a federation by the city authorities, but during the Cultural Revolution most were shut down, their buildings turned into schools or public offices.[76] In the post-Mao era, they were quick to revive. In 2004, the Shaanxi provincial government opened a building in Shanghai for the use of Shaanxi sojourners; and in the city's universities, *laoxianghui* exist for students from different provinces, the Cantonese and Fujian communities being especially well organized.[77] With regard to the native-place bangs that controlled sectors of the labour market, the Communists took vigorous measures upon their accession to eliminate their influence. Nevertheless, in the 'neo-traditional' order that emerged in the state-owned sector of the economy (see below), native-place ties continued informally to shape patterns of recruitment and promotion.[78] In the reform era, as the central state withdrew from economic life, and as the relationship between local officials and local businessmen became critical, native place once again became significant

[74] Tiejun Chang and Mark Selden, 'The Origins and Social Consequences of China's *Hukou* System', *China Quarterly*, 139 (1994), 644–68.
[75] Mao Tse-tung, 'Criticism of Liang Shu-ming's Reactionary Ideas', *Selected Works of Mao Tse-tung*, vol. 5 (Peking: Foreign Languages Press, 1977), pp. 121–30.
[76] My warm thanks to Bryna Goodman for this information.
[77] *China Daily*, 24 September 2003.
[78] Andrew Walder, *Communist Neo-Traditionalism: Work and Authority in Chinese Industry* (Berkeley: University of California Press, 1986), pp. 181–4.

as a determinant of employment prospects and business opportunities.[79] By the same token, native-place solidarity once again came to facilitate strike mobilization by migrant workers.[80]

We saw in the previous chapter how the Romanov and Qing dynasties toyed with the idea of divesting themselves of the garments of empire and donning the garb of the nation state, convinced that only nation states could compete in the modern world. Between October 1917 and the end of 1918, some thirteen new states came into existence on what had been the territory of the Russian empire, and the borders of Soviet Russia retreated to those of the pre-Petrine state. It looked a safe bet that the empire was destined to go the way of its Austro-Hungarian and Ottoman counterparts. By 1922, however, the Bolsheviks had reconquered all of the territory of the former empire – apart from an estimated 3.7% – in a process that was governed not by the imperatives of international socialist revolution but by the same geopolitical and security considerations that had determined the growth of the tsarist state. In a similar fashion, in spite of secessionist movements emerging on its peripheries after 1911, the Chinese state had by 1945 re-emerged as more or less coterminous in territory with the Qing empire. Ironically, then, both the Soviet Union and the PRC, though champions of anti-imperialism and proletarian internationalism, found themselves facing the task of consolidating empire-nations. It was this irony of history that was to shape the interplay of class and national elements in the two states.

The establishment of the Bolshevik regime in Russia seemed to mark the triumph of the principles of class and internationalism over the principle of nationality. And the Soviet Union rapidly institutionalized the principle of class, in that exploiters and people not engaged in socially useful labour were excluded from soviet elections, and in areas as diverse as housing, education, rationing and taxation, policy discriminated in favour of proletarians and poor peasants and against rich peasants and 'alien elements'. The latter included the 'former' classes, such as the nobility, bourgeoisie, tsarist bureaucrats and former White officers, along with those simply judged to be 'not loyal to Soviet power'.

---

[79] Sally Sargeson, *Reworking China's Proletariat* (Basingstoke: Macmillan, 1999), pp. 42, 44. Her ethnographic data demonstrate the continued salience of native-place identities: 'People from the Shaoxing area claim that Hangzhou people fear their sharp tongues and shrewdness in business and politics; Hangzhou people disparage those from Jiaxing as crude country bumpkins and, in turn, are reviled by Jiaxing natives for their arrogance; Ningbo residents insist they are more skilled in commerce, banking and technology than are Hangzhou people.' Sargeson, *Reworking*, p. 47.

[80] Ching Kwan Lee, 'From the spectre of Mao to the spirit of the law: Labour insurgency in China', *Theory and Society* 31, 2002, 211.

As Sheila Fitzpatrick notes, for Bolshevik ideologists 'class was a complex attribute that could not be reduced to class origins'. Nevertheless in some contexts – albeit not to the same extent as in the PRC – it was perceived to be a heritable characteristic, so that the son of a priest might be deemed 'alien' simply because of his father's occupation.[81] In the course of the 1930s, however, the regime moved away from policies of class discrimination, and the 1936 constitution in theory accorded all Soviet citizens equal civil and political rights. Victory in the Second World War further strengthened the emphasis on the united body of the Soviet citizenry rather than on class divisions within its ranks.

Notwithstanding the initial institutionalization of class as the basis of social policy, it was nationality that was destined to become entrenched as the primary principle of sociopolitical organization. In 1922, the Soviet Union was formally constituted as a federation of ethno-territorial republics. The 1920s witnessed an extraordinary process of nation-building among the non-Russian nationalities in which ethnographers classified ethnic groups, many of them with little sense of themselves as nations, and devised programmes to promote minority languages and cultures. The state awarded territories and forms of political autonomy to the ethnic minorities it recognized and encouraged the formation of indigenous Communist elites and intelligentsias. The process was designed, in Stalin's words, to produce republics and autonomous regions that were 'national in form, but socialist in content'. In effect, nationality, once seen as an impediment to socialism, had come to be viewed positively – as the modality through which the economic, political and cultural development of the non-Russian peoples could take place. Yet even as it was creating embryonic nations, the Soviet government continued to claim that it represented the transcendence of the nation state as a form of political organization and, when it suited, it deployed a rhetoric of ultimate 'fusion' of nations into a single Soviet people. Moreover, if in the 1920s the predominant understanding tended to be, in the words of Ronald Suny, a 'contingent understanding of nationality as the product of historical development', by the 1930s there was a shift towards a 'more primordial sense that nationality was deeply rooted in the culture, experience, mentality, even biology of individuals'.[82] Nationality, therefore, now understood as something that

---

[81] Sheila Fitzpatrick, *Everyday Stalinism: Ordinary Life in Extraordinary Times: Soviet Russia in the 1930s* (Oxford: Oxford University Press, 1999), pp. 116–17.

[82] Ronald Gregor Suny, 'Constructing Primordialism: Old Histories for New Nations', *Journal of Modern History*, 73 (2001), 862–96; Terry Martin, *An Affirmative Action Empire: Nations and Nationalism in the Soviet Union, 1923–39* (Ithaca NY: Cornell University Press, 2001).

inhered in birth and heredity, became a dominant social identity in the Soviet Union. As Yuri Slezkine puts it: 'Every Soviet citizen was born into a certain nationality, took it to day care and through high school, had it officially confirmed at the age of 16, and then carried it to the grave through thousands of application forms, certificates, questionnaires and reception desks. It made a difference in school admissions and it could be crucial in employment, promotions, and draft assignments.'[83] None of this meant that the nations of the Soviet Union were perceived to be equal. The Soviet centre, dominated as it was by Russians, enjoyed a quasi-imperial relationship to the national republics, and Russians tended to enjoy higher status than ethnic minorities no matter where they lived.

Unevenly, in the course of the 1930s Russian nationalism was covertly recuperated at the level of official ideology. In February 1931, a speech by Stalin to industrial leaders marked a significant démarche towards nationalism.[84] Stalin quoted a verse from the nineteenth-century writer N. A. Nekrasov, a verse that had been used in 1918 by Lenin as an epigraph to a piece entitled 'The Chief Task of the Day', written at the time of the peace of Brest-Litovsk. Nekrasov's verse proclaims: 'Thou art poor and thou art plentiful/Thou art mighty and thou art helpless/ Mother Russia!' In his article Lenin used the quotation to call for socialism 'so that Mother Russia may cease to be poor and helpless and so that she may become in the full sense mighty and plentiful'.[85] It reminds us that the Bolsheviks were not afraid to appeal to Russian patriotism. Yet while Lenin lived, such appeals were relatively rare, with official propaganda preferring to stress proletarian internationalism. From about 1932, Stalin consciously crafted a form of state nationalism that exalted the history and culture of Russia, even as it extolled the Soviet rather than the Russian people.

---

[83] Yuri Slezkine, 'The USSR as a Communal Apartment, or How a Socialist System Promoted Ethnic Particularism', *Slavic Review*, 53, 2 (1994), 450.

[84] In this speech Stalin declared: 'One feature of the history of old Russia was the continual beatings she suffered because of her backwardness. She was beaten by the Mongol khans. She was beaten by the Turkish beys. She was beaten by the Swedish feudal lords. She was beaten by the Polish and Lithuanian gentry. She was beaten by the British and French capitalists. She was beaten by the Japanese barons. All beat her – because of her backwardness, because of her military backwardness, cultural backwardness, political backwardness, industrial backwardness, agricultural backwardness. They beat her because it was profitable and could be done with impunity.' 'Speech Delivered at the First All-Union Conference of Leading Personnel of Socialist Industry' 4 February, 1931. V. I. Stalin, *Works*, vol. 13 (Moscow: Foreign Languages Publishing House, 1955), pp. 31–44.

[85] V. I. Lenin, 'The Chief Task of Our Day', *Collected Works*, 4th edn (Moscow: Progress, 1972), pp. 159–63. Lenin was citing N. A. Nekrasov's poem, 'Who Lives Well in Russia?'.

With the accession of the CCP to power in 1949, class-inflected anti-imperialist nationalism became the official ideology of the PRC. Ironically, given the relative underdevelopment of class relations in pre-Communist China, class was far more vigorously pursued as a form of state categorization by the PRC than it had been by the Soviet state even in the 1920s. Central to land reform, for example, was a massive effort to classify the rural population into categories of landlord, rich peasant, middle peasant, poor peasant and landless labourer, that was designed to supplant traditional identities based on kinship, native place, religion or secret society. One's social entitlements and one's political fate were crucially determined by one's class classification, which was registered in official documents. Yet if class proved to be a potent social identity throughout the Mao era, national identity also increased its salience, in a process that saw class and national identities develop in tandem.

The CCP's record in restoring centralized government and national unity to an extent unseen since the mid-Qing dynasty massively strengthened its nationalist credentials. These were further boosted by the Korean war when China showed that it could defend itself against the world's most powerful imperial power. Symbolized by the charismatic figure of Mao Zedong, state nationalism proclaimed that the peoples of China under the leadership of the CCP would drag themselves out of backwardness by their own efforts and forge a shining example for the oppressed peoples of the world. In this rendition, the Chinese nation consisted of all citizens regardless of ethnicity. Like its Soviet counterpart, the PRC government rejected the idea that the socialist empire-nation could be equated with the history and culture of the Han Chinese alone. Nevertheless, it seems that millions rallied to the new government because it symbolized the resurgence of the Han people rather than the advance of international Communism. The PRC faced nothing like the challenge from minority nationalisms that confronted the early Soviet state, since approximately 93% of the population was classed as being of Han ethnicity.[86] Like its Soviet forebear, the government strove to bind non-Han ethnicities to the Communist state through an elaborate programme of nation-building, but rejected the idea of organizing the state as a federation of ethno-national republics. As in the Soviet Union, a massive effort of categorization got underway, conducted in accordance with the Stalinist criteria of nationhood, to

---

[86] James Townsend, 'Chinese Nationalism', in Jonathan Unger (ed.), *Chinese Nationalism* (Armonk NY: M. E. Sharpe, 1996), pp. 1–30; Samuel S. Kim and Lowell Dittmer, 'Whither China's Quest for National Identity?', in Samuel S. Kim and Lowell Dittmer (eds.), *China's Quest for National Identity* (Ithaca NY: Cornell University Press, 1993), pp. 237–90.

determine the variable levels of qualification for political autonomy of some 565 recognized ethnicities. As in the Soviet Union, this démarche towards nationalism existed alongside a rhetoric that talked about fusion (*ronghe*) of nationalities in the long-term in a process whereby each 'will influence and learn from one another'.[87] As in the Soviet Union, the effect of nationalizing practices was to entrench nationality as a social identity, each individual's nationality being registered in their passport and official documents and influencing social and political entitlements.[88]

Revolutions Against Backwardness

Both the Stalinist and Maoist regimes destroyed pre-revolutionary class structures and political institutions and struggled to create 'socialist' societies based on rational planning and far-reaching social equality. Yet in fundamental respects, both may be seen as revolutions against socioeconomic backwardness that pursued objectives not radically dissimilar from those of the late-tsarist and republican regimes they supplanted. The paramount necessity for both Stalin and Mao, as for Nicholas II and Chiang Kai-shek, was to industrialize, urbanize, modernize agriculture, and bring education and prosperity to the mass of the people. Ideology, obviously, defined the terms in which these tasks were construed: the First Five-Year Plans in the Soviet Union and China, for example, purported to break with the irrationalities and inequalities of capitalism and to modernize economy and society through planned action by the state.[89] Nevertheless in concrete terms, the imperatives of modernization, whether in socialist or capitalist form, had remarkably similar consequences for the working class. The urgency felt by both pre-revolutionary and Communist regimes to become leading military and economic powers as rapidly as possible entailed that popular living standards be cut in order to increase investment in industry, that levels

---

[87] Colin Mackerras, *China's Minorities: Integration and Modernization in the Twentieth Century* (Hong Kong: Oxford University Press, 1994), p. 8

[88] Dru C. Gladney, 'Representing Nationality in China: Refiguring Majority/Minority Identities', *Journal of Asian Studies*, 53, 1 (1994), 92–123.

[89] For the locus classicus of the view that the goals of the late-imperial and Soviet polities were set by the imperatives of modernization, see Theodore von Laue, *Why Lenin? Why Stalin?* (London: Weidenfeld and Nicholson, 1966). For a trenchant argument that the GMD and Communist regimes were both 'developmental states' pledged to the planned, centralized development of a reunified China, see William C. Kirby, 'The Nationalist Regime and the Chinese Party-State, 1928–1958', in Merle Goldman and Andrew Gordon (eds.), *Contemporary East Asia in Historical Perspective* (Cambridge MA: Harvard University Press, 2000), pp. 211–37.

of productivity be raised, that technical expertise and managerial authority take precedence over worker participation, that the rights of trade unions be curbed. These imperatives shaped the lives of working people under Communism just as much as aims and aspirations derived from Communist ideology. That said, the determination of Communist regimes to bring about socialist modernization as rapidly as possible led them to embark on measures that would have been ideologically unthinkable, as well as politically unachievable, for their predecessors. Such measures frequently had little to do with any rational assessment of the imperatives of modernization, being inspired by blind faith that objective constraints could be overcome by feats of human will. The consequence was to unleash violent and convulsive change on large sections of the populace. In the case of the PRC, the trauma engendered by breakneck collectivization, the Great Leap Forward with its famine of 1959–61, and by the Cultural Revolution were all directly attributable to the political utopianism of the party-state. In the case of the Soviet Union, the convulsions engendered by violent collectivization, crash industrialization and the Great Terror were also directly attributable to the party-state, but were compounded by traumas not of its making, including a sanguinary civil war (1918–21) and the Nazi invasion of 1941.

In the Soviet Union the desire to put an end to what Stalin called 'the continual beatings suffered because of backwardness' ensured that the needs of its citizens were ruthlessly subordinated to those of expanding the industrial and military might of the state. The First Five-Year Plan (1928–32) saw a massive surge in iron and steel production, mining, metallurgy and machine-building, and the establishment of prestige projects, such as the building of the steel city of Magnitogorsk in Siberia and the hydroelectric dam at Dneprostroi. The command economy, though capable of promoting rapid growth of heavy industry, engendered waste, shortages, breakdowns and low output quality and endemic corruption, as managers sought to bypass supply and repair problems and to coordinate phases of production. The best that can be said is that it succeeded in transforming the Soviet Union into a military power capable of defeating Nazi Germany. In the short-term, however, the 'socialist offensive' led to misery for its citizens: popular living standards plummeted in order to sustain massive investment, and life for urban workers remained tough well into the 1950s, though never as hopeless as life for the peasantry. The First Five-Year Plan not only saw real wages fall and working conditions slump, but also saw trade unions lose the right to defend workers against management, reduced to becoming organizers of 'socialist competition' in the workplace and dispensers of welfare benefits. Labour turnover and absenteeism ran at astonishing levels, which led to draconian legislation such as that introduced in December 1938 and June 1940 to stem the problem. In practice, industrial managers had no alternative but to tolerate lax labour discipline and to pay above the rate in order to negotiate bottlenecks in production and to retain labour.[90] During the second half of the 1930s, real wages began to rise, but housing conditions, diet and clothing remained grim. A rudimentary welfare state was put in place, but only following the ravages of the Second World War would subsidized housing and transport, free education and healthcare become the features of the system most valued by its citizens.[91]

It is not easy to generalize about workers' attitudes to the Stalin regime. Sheila Fitzpatrick suggests that popular attitudes fell mainly in the range between passive acceptance and cautious hostility.[92] There was endemic dissatisfaction, fatalism and indifference, yet many learned, in Stephen Kotkin's phrase, to 'speak Bolshevik', to appropriate the omnipresent ideology for their own ends.[93] Despite the general repression, people were not afraid to complain, present petitions or write denunciations to the authorities – a fact that implies that they ascribed some minimal legitimacy to the regime. In more subliminal ways, the bombardment of working people with slogans and images of a glorious future made some believe that they were 'building socialism', even if the reality of the present was that they were struggling to survive. Some scholars argue that citizens fundamentally subscribed to the aspirations of the regime, lacking the 'mental equipment – the sources of information as well as the categories of thought' to posit an alternative to Soviet socialism.[94] Others counter that the regime never succeeded in wiping out 'alternative frames of reference, such as memory of life under the old regime, or alternative fulcra of identity such as confession, community, and family'.[95] Jeffrey Rossman, for example, shows that in

---

[90] Donald A. Filtzer, *Soviet Workers and Stalinist Industrialization: the Formation of Modern Soviet Production Relations, 1928–41* (London: Pluto, 1986); Vladimir Andrle, *Workers in Stalin's Russia: Industrialization and Social Change in a Planned Economy* (Brighton: Wheatsheaf, 1987).

[91] Brian D. Silver, 'Political Beliefs of the Soviet Citizen: Sources of Support for Regime Norms', in James R. Millar, *Politics, Work and Daily Life in the USSR: A Survey of Former Citizens* (Cambridge: Cambridge University Press, 1987), pp. 100–41.

[92] Fitzpatrick, *Everyday Stalinism*, pp. 223–6.

[93] Stephen Kotkin, *Magnetic Mountain: Stalinism as a Civilization* (Berkeley: University of California Press, 1995).

[94] Stephen Kotkin, review of Sarah Davies, *Popular Opinion in Stalin's Russia: Terror, Propaganda, and Dissent, 1934–1941*, *Europe-Asia Studies* 50, 4 (1998), 741; Kotkin, *Magnetic Mountain*; Jochen Hellbeck, *Revolution on My Mind: Writing a Diary Under Stalin* (Cambridge MA: Harvard University Press, 2006).

[95] Jeffrey J. Rossman, *Worker Resistance under Stalin: Class and Revolution on the Shop Floor* (Cambridge MA: Harvard University Press, 2005), p. 13; Sarah Davies, *Popular*

the Ivanovo Industrial Region from 1928 to 1932 resistance to Stalin's 'revolution from above' was widespread, with men and women raising 'questions that cast in sharp relief the enormous gulf between radiant promises of official ideology and grim realities of everyday life'.[96] The fact that these protestors presented themselves as true 'defenders of soviet power' is seen by those who stress popular support for the regime as evidence that the horizon of expectation was set by official discourse. The evidence of the preceding chapters, however, suggests that workers had undergone complex identity transformations in the tsarist era and that they brought with them into the Soviet era varied resources with which to reflect on their own past, present and future.

At risk of being schematic, one might generalize by saying that there was a significant minority of workers in the 1930s, such as those who achieved heroic feats of production in the Stakhanovite movement in 1935–6, who believed they were building socialism. For such young, energetic, mainly male enthusiasts, support for the regime was very likely to translate into opportunities for rapid promotion through the ranks of the party-state or the industrial hierarchy.[97] At the other extreme was a probably larger minority who were consciously antipathetic to the regime, for reasons that might be rooted in political opposition, religious faith, or the fact that their personal behaviour – as drunkards, anti-semites or male-chauvinists – placed them beyond the pale of officially endorsed conduct. In between were the majority who were critical of the policies and behaviour of the leadership, resentful at endemic poverty, the privileges enjoyed by the 'new masters' and the general absence of equality and rights for the working class, yet who endorsed 'soviet power' and held the regime to account in terms of its own proclaimed goals of equality and social justice.

This contradictoriness of worker attitudes provides a clue as to why collective protest was less frequent than one might expect. Leaving aside the fear of reprisals, which was only too real, many workers in an inchoate way felt that the regime was 'theirs'. This attitude was under-pinned by the fact that in spite of poor living and working conditions, they enjoyed certain privileges relative to other social groups. This contrasts with countries where Communism was imposed by the Red Army, where workers saw themselves as subordinate to an alien state.[98]

Opinion in Stalin's Russia: Terror, Propaganda, and Dissent, 1934–1941 (Cambridge: Cambridge University Press, 1997).

[96] Rossman, *Worker Resistance*, p. 8.
[97] Fitzpatrick, *Education and Social Mobility*.
[98] Katherine Verdery, *What Was Socialism, And What Comes Next?* (Princeton: Princeton University Press, 1996), p. 63.

Moreover, the Soviet government constantly hammered away at the notion that the proletariat was the ruling class, and therein lay the rub. For having been appropriated by the regime itself, class became an increasingly problematic language for the articulation of worker grievances. Workers could still use it – especially to contrast rhetoric with reality – but the most powerful exponent of the language of class, with power to determine its strategic uses through the mass media, organs of censorship, schools and the like, was the state itself. And through use of categories such as 'conscious' and 'backward' workers, through the idea of disaffection as an expression of 'petty-bourgeois' consciousness or of – *horribile dictu* – 'Trotskyism', it did much to undermine the effectiveness of a language that in 1917 had served to knit together the disparate elements of the workforce into a self-conscious entity.

The PRC state, too, ensured that the consumption needs of the population – above all, of the rural population – were ruthlessly subordinated to the needs of investment. Chinese workers were very poor but relatively privileged compared both with the peasantry and with proletarians in the underdeveloped world at the time. Many workers enjoyed a stable income, guaranteed employment, housing, medical care and education and, in the words of Marc Blecher, 'a work environment that was far from draconian and that often involved considerable workers' power'.[99] Moreover, by historic standards, the range of inequality between workers and managers and officials was extraordinarily low. In the early 1950s, workers' standard of living rose rapidly, but after 1957 it was government policy to create jobs rather than raise wages. And between 1957 and 1977, adjusting for the cost of living, average real wages fell by nearly one-fifth, although living standards did not worsen since the average number of employed family members increased substantially.[100] That said, it is seriously misleading to speak of workers in the aggregate, for the working class was significantly stratified into more and less privileged sectors. Only permanent employees of state-owned enterprises enjoyed the 'iron rice bowl': by 1981, they constituted 42% of the industrial workforce (29 million in absolute terms). Those in small-scale enterprises run by municipalities, towns or counties (the so-called 'collective' sector) were not paid according to state pay scales and did not enjoy full insurance or welfare benefits, yet they were considerably better off than the serried ranks of contract and temporary workers whose benefits were minimal.[101]

[99] Marc Blecher, 'Hegemony and Workers' Politics in China', *China Quarterly*, 170 (2002), 283.
[100] Andrew G. Walder, 'The Remaking of the Chinese Working Class, 1949–1981', *Modern China*, 10, 1 (1984), 22.
[101] Walder, 'Remaking', pp. 32–6.

Andrew Walder argued that within the state-owned sector clientelism was the principal mode of labour politics. The party committee and the managerial hierarchy distributed goods, services and career opportunities preferentially to their clients. Workers pursued their interests not by collective action, but by cultivating ties with powerful individuals to whom they gave loyal support in exchange for favours.[102] Within an enterprise there would be rival networks of patronage, networks that Walder sees as lying behind many of the factional conflicts of the Cultural Revolution. His model is broadly persuasive, although access to archives since the 1990s suggests that workers were more likely to engage in collective action (albeit along stratified lines) than was once assumed. There were, for example, waves of labour unrest in Guangzhou in 1956 and in Shanghai in autumn 1956 and spring 1957, the latter involving some 30,000 workers, mainly those excluded from the emerging work-unit system.[103] Similarly, during the Cultural Revolution thousands of contract and temporary workers in Shanghai took to the streets to demand redress of grievances, creating a so-called 'wind of economism' that was quickly denounced by authorities.[104] Moreover, as state and party organs were plunged into crisis during the Cultural Revolution, 'rebel' Red Guards – notably, the Workers' General Headquarters in Shanghai – acquired a degree of political autonomy, striving to create in the Shanghai commune (January 1967) a political space outside the control of the CCP. The Cultural Revolution apart, however, labour protest ran at low levels through the Mao era.

Large numbers of workers participated enthusiastically in both the Great Leap Forward and the Cultural Revolution, but it is hard to generalize about workers' political attitudes to the regime, not least because, as in the Soviet Union, the working class was not a homogeneous political entity.[105] Archival material suggests that as in the Soviet Union there was no lack of 'alternative frames of reference' to official ideology or lack of workers prepared to criticize the regime.[106] But

---

[102] Walder, *Communist Neo-traditionalism*.

[103] Mark W. Frazier, *The Making of the Chinese Industrial Workplace: State, Revolution and Labour Management* (Cambridge: Cambridge University Press, 2002), p. 213; Elizabeth J. Perry, 'Shanghai's Strike Wave of 1957', *China Quarterly*, 137 (1994), 1–27.

[104] Elizabeth J. Perry and Li Xun, *Proletarian Power: Shanghai in the Cultural Revolution* (Boulder CO: Westview Press, 1997), pp. 97–117.

[105] For an argument that Walder exaggerates the extent to which 'neo-traditional' networks in the enterprise produced loyalty to the state, see Eddy U, 'Leninist Reforms, Workplace Cleavages, and Teachers in the Chinese Cultural Revolution', *Comparative Studies of Society and History* 47 (2005), 106–133.

[106] A small example can be seen in the fact that six out of nine women workers at No. 9 State Textile Mill in Shanghai in June 1962 asked about the causes of the famine that had arisen out of the Great Leap Forward, explained that it had been sent by the gods (*pusa*)

compared with the Soviet Union, it does seem that worker loyalty to Mao and enthusiasm for the goals of the party-state was widespread, especially among those in the state sector. During the Great Leap Forward, for example, industrial workers shoved technical experts and managers aside in a 'red-hearted' effort to double steel production, thereby demonstrating their loyalty to Chairman Mao', inspired by a belief that they could jump from 'socialism' to 'communism' in one fell swoop. We should not treat present-day nostalgia for the Mao era among older workers as evidence of how they felt at the time, yet it is striking how many look back with favour on the Maoist attempt to eliminate hierarchy and material inequality. 'Our lives would be so much better if there were still struggle meetings and political campaigns .... Back then, we the masses had a weapon against corrupt cadres.' 'I really miss the time of Chairman Mao. We all got the same wage, 50 yuan. At that time there was no pain and worry. Children got parents' jobs when they graduated from school.'[107] Both Ching Kwan Lee and Sally Sargeson note that idioms of labour and subsistence rights (what workers call *shengcunquan*) bit deeply in the Mao era and that they shape responses to conditions today, and that workers of all types use the language of exploitation to describe their present plight in the era of privatization.[108]

Conclusion

It is clear that Communist regimes deviated fundamentally from the hopes and aspirations vested in them by many workers at the time of the revolutions of 1917 and 1949, but probably more so in the Soviet than the Chinese case. Life was tough for working people, although less tough for some than for others. Crucially, it was less tough for workers than for peasants; and this, together with the fact that workers were bombarded with propaganda to the effect that they were the rulers of the new society, led some (probably many in the Chinese case) to believe that they were the beneficiaries of Communist revolution. That said, workers in both countries did not hesitate to articulate their many grievances in ways that went beyond the purely economic, at times venturing to criticize the party-state for its failure to meet – or even for its betrayal

---

because the regime was inhibiting the traditional rituals of propitiation and exorcism. S. A. Smith, 'Talking Toads and Chinless Ghosts: The Politics of "Superstitious" Rumors in the PRC, 1961–65', *American Historical Review*, 111, 2 (2006), 411.

[107] These are the views of workers interviewed in Ching Kwan Lee 'From the Spectre of Mao to the Spirit of the Law: Labour Insurgency in China', *Theory and Society* 31 (2002), 213.

[108] Sargeson, *Reworking*, p. 174; Ching Kwan Lee, 'From the Spectre', p. 207.

of – the ideals of Communism. Both regimes spoke primarily to workers in the language of class, a language dinned into the population through the press, radio, film and political study, and there is evidence that for many – female as well as male – the identity of 'worker' was empowering. The fact that this was an identity that had developed in opposition to the pre-revolutionary social and political order, however, whereas now it was an identity appropriated and defined by the state, created tensions, a space for contestation in which workers could potentially identify with the state and yet at the same time hold it to account.

More quietly, both regimes promoted national identity, however much they may have hedged the official language of state nationalism with qualifications about proletarian internationalism and the rights of ethnic minorities. To be Russian or Han Chinese became increasingly a matter of pride for workers in a way that had not been true in the last years of the empire. A few workers may have been committed to inter-nationalism, but class identity generally proved to be entirely compatible with a strong sense of national identity. Neither regime in reality evolved into a nation state, yet each strove to institutionalize national identity to an extent their imperial predecessors had not dared. Such worker enthusiasm for 'socialist construction' as there was – evident in the First and Second Five-Year Plans in the Soviet Union or the Great Leap Forward – can be explained to a considerable extent as an expression of pride that the nation was finally pulling itself out of economic backwardness.

In respect of gender identities, the record is mixed. Here, too, Communist regimes were broadly modernizing in their policies; yet in critical ways they recuperated elements of the traditional gender order (as seen in Stalinist pro-natalism or Maoist efforts to stress the obliga-tion of individuals to family). Neither regime, despite talk of 'women's emancipation, did much seriously to weaken male domination across society, yet both accelerated policies begun under capitalist modernity that enlarged opportunities for women.

In we look at the situation as a whole, and seek to compare the range of worker identities approved by the Communist regimes with the range of identities fostered by capitalist modernity among the migrants to St Petersburg and Shanghai, it is clear that overall it was narrower. Worker identities under Communism were more focused on production than consumption, on the public rather than the private, on the collective rather than the individual. Crucially, there was less space for individual self-expression – whether in the spheres of consumer culture, high culture or religion. Nevertheless, just as migrant identities were shaped by processes that went beyond the realms of wage labour and production – by capitalist modernity in general – so the identities of working people under Communism developed along axes other than those determined by central state policies, propaganda and repression or by the exigencies of state-led economic development. Social and demographic processes beyond the reach of the state, new forms of urban and industrial life, new relationships between state and society, processes of cultural change such as secularization and the cult of science, all served to shape the identities of working people under Communism. Communism, too, was a form of modernity.

Index